Hiking Missouri

SECOND EDITION

Kevin M. Lohraff

Human Kinetics

Library of Congress Cataloging-in-Publication Data

Lohraff, Kevin M., 1964-
  Hiking Missouri / Kevin M. Lohraff. -- 2nd ed.
    p. cm.
  ISBN-13: 978-0-7360-7588-6 (soft cover)
  ISBN-10: 0-7360-7588-7 (soft cover)
  1. Hiking--Missouri--Guidebooks. 2. Trails--Missouri--Guidebooks.
  3. Parks--Missouri--Guidebooks. 4. Natural history--Missouri--Guidebooks.
  5. Missouri--Guidebooks. I. Title.
  GV199.42.M8L65 2009
  917.7804'44--dc21

                    2008044985

ISBN-10: 0-7360-7588-7
ISBN-13: 978-0-7360-7588-6

The Web addresses cited in this text were current as of December 2008, unless otherwise noted.

Acquisitions Editor: Justin Klug; **Developmental Editor:** Amanda Eastin-Allen; **Assistant Editor:** Laura Podeschi; **Copyeditor:** Bob Replinger; **Proofreader:** Coree Clark; **Permission Manager:** Martha Gullo; **Graphic Designer:** Nancy Rasmus; **Graphic Artist:** Tara Welsch; **Cover Designer:** Keith Blomberg; **Photographer (cover):** Jane Epperson; **Photographer (interior):** Kevin M. Lohraff; **Photo Production Manager:** Jason Allen; **Art Manager:** Kelly Hendren; **Associate Art Manager:** Alan L. Wilborn; **Illustrator:** Tim Shedelbower; **Printer:** Versa Press

The maps on the following pages were adapted from maps from the Missouri Department of Natural Resources: 7, 11, 15, 19, 23, 29, 33, 37, 42, 47, 52, 56, 66, 70, 82, 86, 90, 94, 102, 107, 116, 119, 123, 133, 135, 139, 146, 160, 170, 181, 201, 206, 210, 215, 230, 234, 238, 248, 252, and 257. Map on page 74 of Forest Park adapted by permission of the City of St. Louis Forestry Division; maps on pages 110, 127, 137, 144, 166, 177, 179, 185, 187, 189, 193, 219, and 246 adapted from maps from the U.S. Forest Service; map on page 112 adapted from a map from the U.S. Fish and Wildlife Service; source for text and trail map on page 225 adapted from the Missouri Department of Conservation *Henning Homesteaders Trail* brochure.

Human Kinetics books are available at special discounts for bulk purchase. Special editions or book excerpts can also be created to specification. For details, contact the Special Sales Manager at Human Kinetics.

Printed in the United States of America   10 9 8 7 6 5 4 3 2 1

Human Kinetics
Web site: www.HumanKinetics.com

United States: Human Kinetics
P.O. Box 5076
Champaign, IL 61825-5076
800-747-4457
e-mail: humank@hkusa.com

Canada: Human Kinetics
475 Devonshire Road Unit 100
Windsor, ON N8Y 2L5
800-465-7301 (in Canada only)
e-mail: info@hkcanada.com

Europe: Human Kinetics
107 Bradford Road
Stanningley
Leeds LS28 6AT, United Kingdom
+44 (0) 113 255 5665
e-mail: hk@hkeurope.com

Australia: Human Kinetics
57A Price Avenue
Lower Mitcham, South Australia 5062
08 8372 0999
e-mail: info@hkaustralia.com

New Zealand: Human Kinetics
Division of Sports Distributors NZ Ltd.
P.O. Box 300 226 Albany
North Shore City
Auckland
0064 9 448 1207
e-mail: info@humankinetics.co.nz

Acknowledgments

I am grateful to many people who helped me with this project. My thanks go to all of the staff members and volunteers at the visitor centers, nature centers, and park offices at which I asked for help. I especially appreciate the support provided by Kelley Brent, State Trail Coordinator of the Missouri Department of Natural Resources. Many thanks go to Mike Leahy and Teresa Kight of the Missouri Department of Conservation for information on natural areas and hiking trails.

I appreciate Janet Price of Johnson's Shut-Ins State Park and Dana Hoisington of Bennett Spring State Park, both of whom hiked with me and expertly answered my incessant questions. David Bruns and Les Fortenberry of the Missouri Department of Conservation stopped what they were doing to help me. Colleen Scott of Columbia Bottom Conservation Area and Kathryn DiFoxfire of Rock Bridge Memorial State Park were very helpful with information as well.

Special thanks go to the leaders and members of the Runge Hiking Club and Midweek Trekkers (Runge Conservation Nature Center) of Jefferson City for sharing their love of hiking with others for nearly 10 years. Their dedication inspires me.

Thank you, Jane, for taking care of things while I was gone and for all your support. I appreciate you!

Finally, my thanks go to the people of Missouri, whose support of taxes for parks, soils, and conservation has helped to purchase and manage healthy public land that we can all enjoy.

To our son Finn. May life's trails take you to wonder, beauty, gratitude, and joy. With love, Dad.

Contents

How to Use This Book

Hiking is an antidote to the rigors of modern life. It gives the body some much-needed (and enjoyable) exercise, and it gives the mind both rest and stimulation. Hiking even lifts the spirit to reconnect with this earth, which we're a part of but seldom have time to think about. We hope to provide you with an incentive to start or continue hiking for the pleasure and the challenge of it.

The assortment of trails in this book range from short, easy hikes for occasional hikers and families with young children to longer, more rugged ones for experienced trailblazers. None of the trails take more than a day to hike, although some trails may be linked together to create a hike of several days.

The trails are divided into four main areas—North, Southeast, South Central, and Southwest. Within each area, trails are listed from east to west. Divider pages signal the beginning of each new area, and those pages include information on the local topography, major rivers and lakes, flora and fauna, weather, and the best features of the area.

The innovative format of the book makes exploring new parks and trails easy. Information on each park begins with the park's name and a small state map that shows the park's general location. Bulleted highlights point out the park's most interesting features. A description of the park's history and terrain appears next; there you can find directions to the park and the hours of operation, available facilities, permits and rules, and the address and phone number of a contact who can give you more information. The section titled Other Areas of Interest mentions nearby parks and recreational opportunities and lists phone numbers to call for more information. After the general information is a list of trails in the park. The length and difficulty of hiking each are stated along with a brief description of the terrain. The difficulty rating, shown by boot icons, ranges from 1 (easiest) to 5 (most difficult).

After the introduction are descriptions of the best trails in the park along with a trail map. (A few parks have only one hike with just one map that primarily shows the trail.) Each hike begins with information on the length and difficulty of the trail and the estimated time to walk it, plus cautions to help you avoid potential annoyances or problems. The description of the trail provides more than directions; it's a guided tour of what you will see as you hike along. The scenery, wildlife, and history of the trail are all brought to life. Points of interest along the trail are numbered in brackets within the text, and those numbers are shown on the trail map to guide you. The approximate distance from the trailhead to each point of interest is given.

If you want to quickly find a park or trail to explore, use the trail finder on pages viii to xx. It gives essential information about each highlighted trail in the book, including the trail's length, difficulty, special features, and the park's facilities.

We hope this book inspires you to get out and enjoy some outdoor experiences. We've included interesting trails from all parts of the state. Some are unexpected treasures—places you'd never dream exist in the state. Some may be favorites that you've already hiked and recommended to friends. But whether you live in a city or in the country, are away vacationing or are at home, some of these trails will be near you. Find one you like, lace up your hiking boots, and go!

Trail Finder

Park	Trails	Miles	Difficulty	Hills	Prairie/Grass	Forest	Lake	Wetlands	Overlook	River/Stream	Page #
NORTH											
1 Columbia Bottom Conservation Area	Confluence and River's Edge Trails	5.9	👣		X	X		X	X	X	5
2 Cuivre River State Park	Lone Spring Trail	6	👣👣👣	X		X				X	8
	Big Sugar Creek Trail–North Loop	3.75	👣👣👣	X		X				X	9
3 Graham Cave State Park	Graham Cave and Indian Glade Trails	2.35	👣👣👣👣	X	X	X				X	12
	Loutre River Trail	2.8	👣👣👣	X	X	X				X	13
4 Mark Twain State Park and Historic Site	Whitetail and Dogwood Trails	3	👣👣	X		X	X		X		16
	Post Oak and White Oak Trails	3	👣👣👣	X		X	X		X		17
5 Battle of Athens State Historic Site	Yellow–Red Historic Trail	1.75	👣👣👣	X		X			X	X	20
	Green–Blue River Trail	1.75	👣👣👣	X		X				X	21

 RV camping   tent camping   picnicking   fishing   swimming   canoeing   boating   biking

	Park	Trails	Miles	Difficulty	Hills	Prairie/Grass	Forest	Lake	Wetlands	Overlook	River/Stream	Page #
Landscape												
NORTH												
6	Thousand Hills State Park	Redbud-Hickory-Oak Trails	1.5	3 boots	X		X	X			X	24
		Thousand Hills Trail	5	3 boots	X	X	X	X			X	25
7	Pinnacles Youth Park	Pinnacles Trail	2	6 boots	X		X			X	X	27
8	Katy Trail State Park	Historic Rocheport and MKT Tunnel	1.5	1 boot							X	30
		McBaine to Lewis and Clark Cave	9.75	1 boot							X	31
9	Arrow Rock State Historic Site	Pierre A Fleche Trail	1.5	3 boots	X		X	X		X	X	34
		Lewis and Clark Trail of Discovery and Arrow Rock Historic River Landing Trail	1.85	2 boots			X		X		X	35
10	Van Meter State Park	Earthwork Monument Trail	2	3 boots	X		X					38
		Loess Hills Trail	2	3 boots	X		X	X			X	39
		Oumessourit Wetland Boardwalk Trail	1	1 boot					X	X		40
11	Pershing State Park	Wetland Boardwalk Trail	1.5	1 boot		X	X		X	X	X	43
		Scout Lake Trail	.5	1 boot			X	X				44
		Riparian Trail	12.8	1 boot			X				X	45

» continued

 RV camping tent camping picnicking fishing swimming canoeing boating biking

» continued

Park	Trails	Miles	Difficulty	Hills	Prairie/Grass	Forest	Lake	Wetlands	Overlook	River/Stream	Page #
NORTH											
12 Crowder State Park	River Forks Trail	2.5	🥾🥾🥾	X		X				X	48
	Tall Oaks Trail	3.6	🥾🥾🥾	X	X	X	X				49
	Thompson River Trail–North and South Loops	9.6	🥾🥾🥾	X	X	X				X	50
13 Wallace State Park	Deer Run Trail	3.5	🥾🥾	X		X				X	53
	Old Quarry Trail	1.25	🥾🥾	X	X					X	54
14 Weston Bend State Park	West Ridge and Harpst Trails	2.5	🥾🥾	X		X			X	X	57
	Hiking–Bicycling Trail	3	🥾🥾	X	X	X					58
15 Squaw Creek National Wildlife Refuge	Loess Bluff Trail	1	🥾🥾🥾	X	X	X			X		61
	Eagle Overlook Trail	1.35	🥾					X	X		62
SOUTHEAST											
16 Big Oak Tree State Park	Boardwalk Trail	1.25	🥾			X		X			67
	Bottomland Trail	1.4	🥾			X	X	X			68
17 Trail of Tears State Park	Sheppard Point Trail	2	🥾🥾🥾🥾	X		X			X	X	71
	Peewah Trail	8.75	🥾🥾🥾🥾🥾🥾	X		X			X	X	72

RV camping · tent camping · picnicking · fishing · swimming · canoeing · boating · biking

x

Park	Trails	Miles	Difficulty	Hills	Prairie/Grass	Forest	Lake	Wetlands	Overlook	River/Stream	Page #
SOUTHEAST											
18 Urban St. Louis	Arch Area	2	🥾🥾🥾						X	X	75
	Forest Park	2.5	🥾				X				76
19 Rockwoods Reservation	Trail Among the Trees	2	🥾🥾🥾	X		X			X		79
	Rock Quarry Trail	2.25	🥾🥾	X		X					80
20 Dr. Edmund A. Babler Memorial State Park	Virginia Day Memorial Nature Trail	1.5	🥾🥾	X		X				X	83
	Hawthorn Trail	1.15	🥾	X	X	X			X		84
21 Mastodon State Historic Site	Limestone Hill Trail	2.25	🥾🥾	X		X			X	X	87
	Spring Branch Trail	.75	🥾			X				X	88
22 Washington State Park	1,000 Steps Trail	1.5	🥾🥾🥾	X		X			X	X	91
	Opossum Track Trail	3	🥾🥾🥾	X	X	X			X	X	92
23 St. François State Park	Mooner's Hollow Trail	3	🥾🥾🥾	X	X	X		X	X	X	95
	Swimming Deer Trail	3	🥾🥾🥾	X	X	X			X	X	96

» continued

 RV camping tent camping picnicking fishing swimming canoeing boating biking

» continued

	Park	Trails	Miles	Difficulty	Hills	Prairie/Grass	Forest	Lake	Wetlands	Overlook	River/Stream	Page #
SOUTHEAST												
24	Hickory Canyons Natural Area	East Trail	.5	▣▣	✗		✗				✗	99
		West Trail	1	▣▣▣	✗		✗			✗	✗	100
25	Hawn State Park (RV camping, tent camping, picnicking)	Pickle Creek Trail	1.5	▣▣	✗	✗	✗			✗	✗	103
		Whispering Pine Trail	10	▣▣▣	✗		✗			✗	✗	104
		White Oaks Trail	4	▣▣	✗		✗				✗	105
26	Pickle Springs Natural Area (picnicking)	Trail Through Time	2	▣▣	✗		✗			✗	✗	108
27	Rock Pile Mountain Wilderness (tent camping)	Rock Pile Mountain Trail	7	▣▣	✗	✗	✗					110
28	Mingo National Wildlife Refuge (picnicking, fishing, canoeing, boating)	Hartz Pond and Bluff Trail	.75	▣	✗		✗		✗	✗		113
		Boardwalk Nature Trail	1	▣			✗		✗	✗		114

 RV camping   tent camping   picnicking   fishing   swimming   canoeing   boating   biking

Park	Trails	Miles	Difficulty	Hills	Prairie/ Grass	Forest	Lake	Wetlands	Overlook	River/ Stream	Page #
SOUTHEAST											
29 Morris State Park	Beech Tree Trail	2.35		X		X					117
30 Lake Wappapello State Park	Asher Creek Trail	2		X		X	X			X	120
	Allison Cemetery Trail	3.5		X	X	X	X		X		121
31 Sam A. Baker State Park	Mudlick Trail–East Loop	7.15		X	X	X			X	X	124
	Shut-Ins Trail	3		X	X	X			X	X	125
32 Silver Mines Recreation Area	Air Conditioner Trail	1.4		X		X			X	X	128
	Boulder Hike to Turkey Creek	1.65		X		X			X	X	129
33 Hughes Mountain Natural Area	Devil's Honeycomb Trail	1.75		X	X	X			X		131

» continued

 RV camping tent camping picnicking fishing swimming canoeing boating biking

» continued

	Park	Trails	Miles	Difficulty	Landscape							Page #
					Hills	Prairie/ Grass	Forest	Lake	Wetlands	Overlook	River/ Stream	
SOUTHEAST												
34	Elephant Rocks State Park	Elephant Rocks Braille Trail	1	👞			X			X		133
35	Taum Sauk Mountain State Park	Mina Sauk Falls Trail and Ozark Trail to Devil's Toll Gate	5	👞👞👞	X	X	X			X	X	135
36	Crane Lake Recreation Area	Crane Lake Trail	5	👞👞👞	X	X	X	X		X	X	137
37	Meramec State Park	Natural Wonders Trail	1.3	👞👞	X	X	X		X		X	140
		Bluff View Trail	1.5	👞👞👞	X		X			X	X	141
		Wilderness Trail	9	👞👞👞👞	X	X	X			X	X	142
38	Bell Mountain Wilderness	Bell Mountain Trail	10	👞👞👞👞	X	X	X			X	X	144
39	Johnson's Shut-Ins State Park	Shut-Ins Trail	3.1	👞👞👞	X	X	X			X	X	147
		Horseshoe Glade Trail	2.2	👞👞	X	X	X			X	X	148

 RV camping   tent camping   picnicking   fishing   swimming   canoeing   boating   biking

	Park	Trails	Miles	Difficulty	Hills	Prairie/Grass	Forest	Lake	Wetlands	Overlook	River/Stream	Page #
SOUTHEAST												
40	Blue Spring	Blue Spring Trail	3	🥾🥾			✗			✗	✗	150
41	Big Spring	Stone Ridge Trail	2.5	🥾🥾🥾	✗		✗			✗	✗	153
		Chubb Hollow Trail	4	🥾🥾🥾	✗		✗			✗		154
42	Peck Ranch Conservation Area	Ozark Trail to Stegall Mountain	4	🥾🥾🥾	✗	✗	✗			✗	✗	157
		Ozark Trail to Rocky Point Glade	6.4	🥾🥾🥾	✗	✗	✗					158
43	Onondaga Cave State Park	Blue Heron Trail	1	🥾			✗	✗	✗		✗	161
		Deer Run Trail	2.5	🥾🥾🥾	✗	✗	✗			✗	✗	162
SOUTH CENTRAL												
44	Lane Spring Recreation Area	Blossom Rock Trail	1	🥾🥾🥾	✗	✗	✗				✗	167
		Cedar Bluff Trail	1	🥾🥾🥾	✗	✗	✗			✗	✗	168

» continued

 RV camping   tent camping   picnicking   fishing   swimming   canoeing   boating   biking

» continued

#	Park	Trails	Miles	Difficulty	Hills	Prairie/ Grass	Forest	Lake	Wetlands	Overlook	River/ Stream	Page #
SOUTH CENTRAL												
45	Montauk State Park	Pine Ridge Trail	2		X		X					171
46	Alley Spring	Spring Branch Trail	.75				X				X	174
		Overlook Trail	1.5		X	X	X			X	X	175
47	McCormack Recreation Area	McCormack-Greer Trail	8.5		X	X	X	X		X	X	177
48	Greer Spring	Greer Spring Trail	2		X		X			X	X	179
49	Grand Gulf State Park	Chasm Loop Trail	.25		X		X			X	X	182
		Northwest Rim Trail	1		X		X				X	183
50	Slabtown River Access	Slabtown Bluff Trail	1.75		X	X	X			X	X	185
51	Mill Creek	Kaintuck Trail–Northern Loops	9		X	X	X				X	187

 RV camping   tent camping   picnicking   fishing   swimming   canoeing   boating   biking

Park	Trails	Miles	Difficulty	Hills	Prairie/Grass	Forest	Lake	Wetlands	Overlook	River/Stream	Page #
SOUTH CENTRAL											
52 Paddy Creek Wilderness	Big Piney Trail	4.5	👣👣👣	✗		✗			✗	✗	190
	Paddy Creek Trail	.85	👣👣👣			✗				✗	191
53 Stone Mill Spring Recreation Area	Stone Mill Spring Trail	1.9	👣👣👣	✗	✗	✗			✗	✗	193
54 Clifty Creek Natural Area	Natural Arch Trail	2.2	👣👣👣	✗		✗			✗	✗	196
55 Painted Rock Conservation Area	Osage Bluff Scenic Trail	1.6	👣👣👣	✗		✗			✗	✗	199
56 Rock Bridge Memorial State Park	Devil's Icebox Trail	.75	👣👣👣	✗		✗			✗	✗	202
	Spring Brook Trail	2.5	👣👣👣	✗		✗				✗	203
	Sinkhole Trail	1.6	👣👣	✗		✗					204

» continued

 RV camping   tent camping   picnicking   fishing   swimming   canoeing   boating   biking

» continued

	Park	Trails	Miles	Difficulty	Landscape Hills	Prairie/ Grass	Forest	Lake	Wetlands	Overlook	River/ Stream	Page #
SOUTH CENTRAL												
57	Lake of the Ozarks State Park	Rocky Top Trail	3		X	X	X	X		X	X	207
		Coakley Hollow Trail	1		X	X	X		X		X	208
58	Ha Ha Tonka State Park	Spring Trail	1.5		X		X	X		X	X	211
		Acorn Trail	1		X	X	X					212
		Turkey Pen Hollow Trail	7		X	X	X				X	213
59	Bennett Spring State Park	Natural Tunnel Trail	7.5		X		X			X	X	216
		Savanna Ridge Trail	2.35		X	X	X			X	X	217
60	Hercules Glades Wilderness	Coy Bald Trail	6.75		X	X	X			X	X	220
		Lookout Tower Trail	4.5		X	X	X			X	X	221

 RV camping tent camping picnicking fishing swimming canoeing boating biking

	Park	Trails	Miles	Difficulty	Hills	Prairie/Grass	Forest	Lake	Wetlands	Overlook	River/Stream	Page #
								Landscape				
SOUTH CENTRAL												
61	Ruth and Paul Henning Conservation Area	Glade and Streamside Trails	1.75	(3 boots)	X	X	X				X	224
		Henning Homesteaders Trail	3.7	(3 boots)	X	X	X				X	225
SOUTHWEST												
62	Knob Noster State Park	Hawk Nest and Clearfork Savanna Trails	2.5	(3 boots)	X	X	X	X			X	231
		Discovery and North Loop Trails	2.75	(3 boots)	X	X	X		X		X	232
63	Harry S Truman State Park	Western Wallflower Savanna Trail	.75	(3 boots)	X	X	X	X		X		235
		Bluff Ridge Trail	2	(3 boots)	X	X	X	X		X		236
64	Pomme de Terre State Park	Indian Point Trail	3	(3 boots)	X	X	X	X		X		239
		Cedar Bluff Trail	2	(2 boots)	X	X	X	X		X		240
65	Wilson's Creek National Battlefield	Gibson Mill Site and Ray Cornfield	1.75	(2 boots)		X	X				X	243
		Bloody Hill and Wire Road	2	(3 boots)	X	X	X				X	244
66	Piney Creek Wilderness	Pineview Lookout Tower Trail	3.75	(4 boots)	X	X	X			X	X	246

» continued

RV camping   tent camping   picnicking   fishing   swimming   canoeing   boating   biking

» continued

	Park	Trails	Miles	Difficulty	Hills	Prairie/ Grass	Forest	Lake	Wetlands	Overlook	River/ Stream	Page #
					Landscape							
SOUTHWEST												
67	Roaring River State Park	Devil's Kitchen Trail	1.75		X		X				X	249
		Pibern Trail	1.75		X		X				X	250
68	Big Sugar Creek State Park	Ozark Chinquapin Trail	3.75		X		X				X	253
69	George Washington Carver National Monument	Carver Trail	.75			X	X	X			X	255
70	Prairie State Park	Drover's Trail	2.5		X	X					X	258
		Path of the Sky People and Sandstone Trails	6.5		X	X					X	259
71	Urban Kansas City	Country Club Plaza	1									262
		Kansas City Sculpture Park	1									263

 RV camping tent camping picnicking fishing swimming canoeing boating biking

Missouri

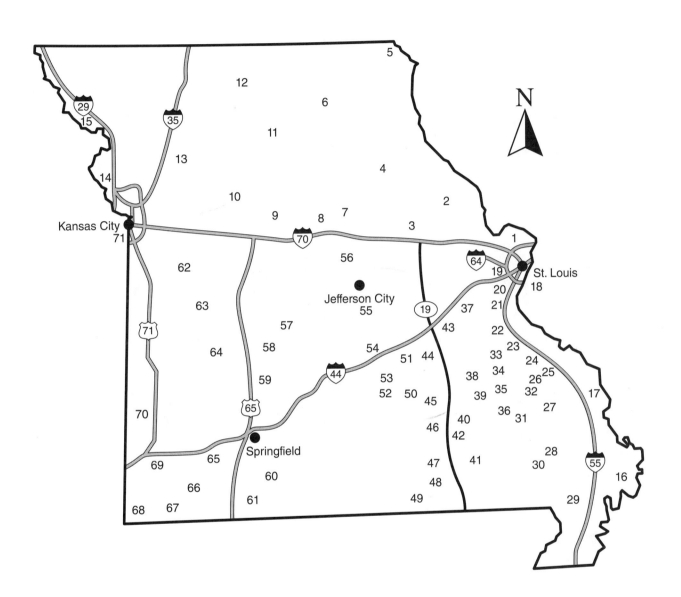

Kansas City

St. Louis

Jefferson City

Springfield

N

North

The north region of Missouri is defined as the area north of Highway 70.

Topography

The topography of the northern third of the state was greatly affected by at least two major glaciers that scraped and leveled most of the state north of the Missouri River. The last ice sheet retreated around 450,000 years ago, making this northern landscape much younger than unglaciated portions of the state. Because rivers and streams have had less time to carve and dissect the land, this area has less relief and lower elevation than southern regions.

Much of north Missouri's fertile soil is composed of loess, which is glacially deposited silt picked up by wind and deposited along the Missouri River Valley. Loess is highly cohesive, forming steep dunes and sheer, vertical walls at road cuts. Loess creates especially well-developed dunelike topography, and loess hills are an unusual geologic feature in the state's northwest corner along the east side of the Missouri River. These great drifts of glacial dust are often 70 feet deep. Good examples are in the Squaw Creek and Rock Port areas.

While rolling plains dominate the topography of north Missouri, the Lincoln Hills are an exception. A narrow band of ridges along the Mississippi River, the Lincoln Hills have steep topography, bedrock exposures, and rugged bluffs, and may have partially escaped glaciation.

Major Rivers and Lakes

North Missouri is surrounded on three sides by the two largest continent-draining rivers in the country—the Missouri and Mississippi. The Missouri, which drains about one-sixth of the nation, marks the approximate southern reach of glaciers in Missouri and, in fact, was largely formed by outwash from glacier meltwater. The Missouri River forms the northwest boundary of the state and flows to St. Louis, where it joins the Mississippi River. The Missouri makes a 553-mile trek within the state, while the Mississippi River forms Missouri's entire 486-mile eastern boundary. No other natural feature has influenced the state's culture, history, and economy as much as these two rivers.

The Grand, Platte, Chariton, and Salt Rivers form major drainages in north Missouri, and the lower Des Moines River forms the state boundary in the northeast corner. Locust Creek is one of the last sizable stream segments in north Missouri that has not been channelized. Cuivre River drains the southern Lincoln Hills area. Major reservoirs include Smithville, Thomas Hill, and Long Branch lakes. Mark Twain Lake, an impoundment of the Salt River, is north Missouri's largest reservoir.

Common Plant Life

Before north Missouri was settled, vast tallgrass prairies covered half of the region's rolling plains. The rest of the landscape was oak savanna and deciduous forest in the uplands and river valleys. The Missouri River was a braided stream, with accompanying sloughs, islands, sandbars, wet prairies, oxbows, marshes, and wetland natural communities.

But north Missouri's gentle terrain and deep soils from glacial till and alluvium made it ideal for agriculture. Today, pasture and large fields of corn and soybeans dominate the landscape. Prairies are now found only in tiny fragments in cemeteries and along railroads. The Missouri River has been deepened and channelized, eliminating its backwater habitat. Locks and dams on the Mississippi River have converted it into a series of large pools, and most of the original riverine natural communities are no longer present.

Though fragmented, several deciduous forest and plant communities persist in the region's state parks, wildlife refuges, and conservation areas. Mesic (moderately moist) forests are the most common and include northern red oak, sugar maple, white oak, basswood, and pawpaw. Drier forests include shagbark hickory, post oak, and chinquapin oak. Forests along the rivers include cottonwood, bur oak, pecan, sycamore, shellbark hickory, and silver maple. Prairie grasses dominate in the dry prairies of the northwest, and silky aster, prairie larkspur, compass plant, and purple coneflower may also be found. A system of wetland communities is preserved along Locust Creek, and its wet prairie includes cordgrass, sawtoothed sunflower, false dragonhead, swamp milkweed, and numerous sedges.

Common Birds and Animals

Wildlife refuges in north Missouri, such as Squaw Creek, Swan Lake, Fountain Grove, and Ted Shanks, attract concentrations of birds and birdwatchers alike. Various ducks, geese, swans, pelicans, herons, egrets, wading birds, and other birds associated with water congregate in these areas by the hundreds of thousands, mostly during fall and spring migrations. Bald eagles also use these areas, as well as the major rivers, during winter months. Northern harriers may be seen gliding low over grass fields. Other common birds include the mourning dove, redheaded woodpecker, kingbird, common yellowthroat, dickcissel, meadowlark, and red-winged blackbird.

Other common animals include the coyote, white-tailed deer, red fox, raccoon, ground squirrel, and box turtle. Muskrat, beaver, massasauga rattlesnake, aquatic turtles, and water snakes are characteristic inhabitants of wet prairies and marshes.

Climate

North Missouri is the first area in the state to show fall colors and the last area to warm up each spring. The mean average temperature is 54 degrees F in spring, 78 degrees F in summer, 56 degrees F in fall, and 24 degrees F in winter. The northwest corner has the driest climate in the state, with a mean annual precipitation of 35 inches. The rest of north Missouri averages between 36 and 39 inches annually.

Best Features

- Unusual dunelike loess hills
- Loess hill prairies
- The two largest rivers in the nation
- The primeval roar of 10,000 geese lifting off a refuge marsh at sunrise in December
- Brilliant colors of sugar maples in autumn
- Natural marshes along the Missouri River
- Winter congregations of bald eagles
- Rich cove ravines along steep, north-facing slopes overlooking the Des Moines River
- A system of wetland natural communities along Locust Creek
- Native American petroglyphs at Thousand Hills State Park

- See the spot where the two mightiest rivers in the nation converge.
- Hike next to your new buddy, the Big Muddy.
- Watch for waterfowl, shorebirds, raptors, songbirds, and other creatures in this wildlife mecca.

Area Information

You might assume that there is a lot going on at the confluence of the two largest rivers (measured by drainage area and length) in the United States. You would be right. Sac, Fox, and Cahokia Native Americans hunted and fished at the confluence of the Missouri and Mississippi rivers. St. Louis had already become the nation's capital of the western fur trade by the time of the Louisiana Purchase, and the journals of the Lewis and Clark expedition are full of observations about the beauty and richness of the area. Undoubtedly, the abundance of game, fish, and edible plants along the Missouri River made the expedition possible.

Beginning in 1912, however, the U.S. Army Corps of Engineers (USACE) built dikes and piers to direct the river's current into the center. Once a wide maze of braided streams with rich wetlands, the river is now straighter, narrower, and deeper, and confined to a third of its historic floodplain. USACE estimates that over 300,000 acres of floodplain forests, wetlands, and other habitats were lost because of the navigation project.

In 1997 the Missouri Department of Conservation (MDC) purchased 4,318 acres at the confluence of the Missouri and Mississippi rivers to create Columbia Bottom Conservation Area. As part of the ongoing effort to restore critically needed wildlife habitat lost along the Missouri River, MDC recently completed a habitat restoration project with USACE at Columbia Bottom, which included planting 275 acres of native prairie grasses and developing a pumping station that regulates water levels in seven managed wetland pools. Recreational opportunities abound in the area, and visitors can view wildlife, hunt, fish, hike, bike, launch boats, and see the confluence from an observation platform.

Directions: From I-70 in St. Louis, take I-270 north and east to the last Missouri exit at Riverview Drive (exit 34). Drive north for 2.8 miles to the area entrance on the right. Take an immediate left to reach the visitor center.

Hours Open: The area is open daily from 6:00 a.m. to 10:00 p.m. from April 1 to September 30, and from 6:00 a.m. to 7:00 p.m. from October 1 to March 31. The visitor center is open from 8:00 a.m. to 4:00 p.m. on Saturday and Sunday and from 8:00 a.m. to 5:00 p.m. Wednesday through Friday. The visitor center is closed on Monday and Tuesday.

Facilities: The site offers nine exploration stations along the main road, a boat ramp, a fishing pier, canoe access, a wildlife viewing platform, a confluence observation platform, a hiking and biking trail, and restrooms. A visitor center offers information, exhibits, and interpretive programs.

Permits and Rules: Bicycles are allowed only on the paved road and the Confluence Trail. Horses are allowed only on roads open to vehicles. Dogs must be leashed. Hunting is allowed only under special regulations, in specific seasons, and in restricted zones.

For Further Information: Columbia Bottom Conservation Area, 801 Strodtman Road, St. Louis, MO 63138; 314-877-6019; www.mdc.mo.gov/areas/areas/bottom.

Other Areas of Interest

From the confluence observation platform at Columbia Bottom, you can look across the Missouri River to see **Edward "Ted" and Pat Jones–Confluence Point State Park**. Operated by the Missouri Department of Natural Resources, the site offers an interpretive kiosk, restrooms, and a .25-mile paved walkway to the confluence. From the intersection of Highways 270 and 367 north of St. Louis, go north on Highway 367 for 8.5 miles. Turn right on Riverlands Way and go 2.1 miles. Turn right on the gravel road and go 4.4 miles to the parking lot. The area opens daily at 8:00 a.m. and closes a half-hour after sunset. For more information, call 636-899-1135 or visit www.mostateparks.com. On Riverlands Way, you pass birding hotspot **Riverlands Migratory Bird Sanctuary**, operated by USACE. For more information, call 888-899-2602 or visit www.visitalton.com.

Columbia Bottom Conservation Area

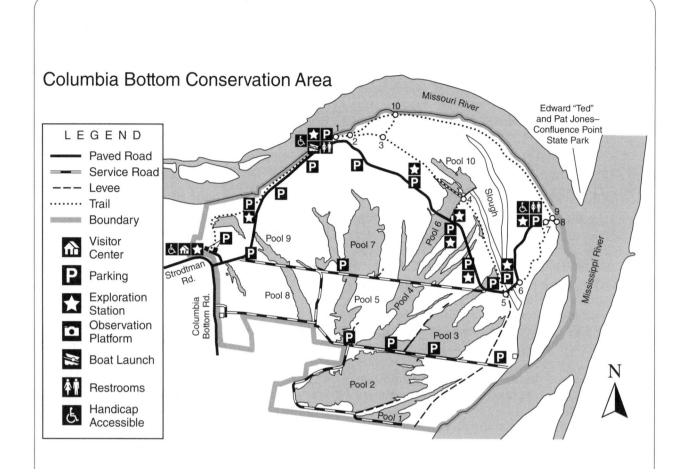

1. Start
2. Go straight
3. Go straight
4. Go straight
5. Road crossing
6. Interpretive sign
7. Parking lot
8. Observation platform
9. River's Edge Trail
10. Go straight

Confluence and River's Edge Trails

 Distance Round-Trip: 5.9 miles
Estimated Hiking Time: 2.5 hours

Plan your hike so that you can be on the River's Edge Trail at sunset. The water becomes a riot of reds, oranges, yellows, and peaches. White sycamore bark turns a rosy glow.

Caution: The Confluence Trail is open to bikers and hikers alike. The River's Edge Trail may have muddy sections after a rainfall. Also, take your mosquito repellent.

Trail Directions: Travel 1.5 mi. into the area and park in the lot for the boat ramp. Begin the Confluence Trail at the east end of the lot at the interpretive sign [1]. The mighty river in front of you began at the confluence of three streams in Montana and has traveled 2,312 mi. so far. At the end of this trail you will see the end of this river. The water continues, of course, but takes a new direction and a new name—the Mississippi.

You are on a wide, paved, flat trail with the Missouri River on your left and its expansive floodplain on your right. Here in the Mississippi Flyway, you are apt to see waterfowl and shorebirds anytime, but especially in spring and fall. Keep your eyes open for pelicans, swans, ducks, geese, and egrets. Go straight at the intersections at .16 mi. [2] and again at .44 mi. [3].

Among the jumble of young silver maple and willow trees, you see some massive cottonwood and sycamore trees in the bottomland forest on your left. Big trees like these are important to wildlife like bald eagles, for example, which require big trees to support their enormous nests. Bald eagles, in fact, have nested in the area in recent years. After passing a water-control structure, go straight at the intersection at 1.29 mi. [4]. Depending on the river level and recent rainfall, the slough on your left may or may not be wet. Abandoned river channels, or sloughs, often provide excellent shallow-water habitat for insects, amphibians, reptiles, fish, and other wildlife.

At 2.11 mi. [5], the trail crosses the main road and swings to the left on the other side. Cut through the parking lot on your left at 2.26 mi. [6] to check out the interpretive sign and the short boardwalk to the slough. Turn left when you return to the main trail. At 3 mi. [7], you find the parking lot for the confluence observation platform as well as an interpretive sign and restrooms. Step out onto the observation platform at 3.2 mi. [8] for some wonderful views of two mighty big rivers coming together to form an even bigger one.

Step off the north end of the platform to find the River's Edge Trail [9] literally at the river's edge. On your right, you have one splendid view after another as the Big Muddy accompanies you all the way back to the trailhead. Go straight at the spur at 5.06 mi. [10]. Turn right at the intersection with the Confluence Trail [2] to return to the parking lot.

- Give your legs a workout in the unusually rugged terrain of the Lincoln Hills.
- Hike next to Big Sugar Creek, with its alternating pools and riffles, gravel bars, and picturesque exposed bedrock and small bluffs.
- Listen for the loud and clear "Teacher! Teacher!" of the ovenbird and the even louder guttural, toneless clucks of the yellow-billed cuckoo.

Area Information

If Cuivre (pronounced "quiver") River State Park were in south Missouri, no one would find astonishing its rugged, wooded hills, deep valleys, clear-running creek, and karst features like caves, springs, and sinkholes—these are typical Ozark characteristics. But Cuivre River is surrounded by the glaciated plains of north Missouri. The park is situated at the southern edge of the Lincoln Hills, a band of uplifted limestone bedrock hills about 15 miles wide and 60 miles long that is responsible for the park's Ozark-like qualities.

Cuivre River was acquired in 1934 by the National Park Service as a recreation demonstration area and was primarily composed of abused farm areas. The site was developed to show the effects of good land use and provide an extensive recreation area for the people of St. Louis. Two of President Roosevelt's agencies, the Cilvilian Conservation Corps (CCC) and Works Progress Administration (WPA), built many of the park's facilities during the late 1930s. After World War II, Cuivre River was given to the state.

Cuivre River has largely recovered from its former abuses and now boasts three state natural areas and two state wild areas. Because of careful land stewardship and the ability of nature to heal itself, Cuivre River's story is one of success.

Directions: Cuivre River is northwest of St. Louis off Highway 61 north. From the intersection of Highway 47 and Highway 61 in Troy, take Highway 47 north for 3.1 miles. Turn north on Highway 147, which takes you to the visitor center in 2 miles.

Hours Open: The site is open year-round. The visitor center is open from April through October from 8:00 a.m. to 4:00 p.m. Monday through Friday, from 10:00 a.m. to 5:00 p.m. on Saturday, and from 11:00 a.m. to 6:00 p.m. on Sunday. The visitor center is open from November through March from 8:00 a.m. to 4:00 p.m. Monday through Friday, from 10:00 a.m. to 4:00 p.m. on Saturday, and from 11:00 a.m. to 4:00 p.m. on Sunday. The visitor center is closed on Thanksgiving, Christmas Day, and New Year's Day.

Facilities: The park offers a visitor center with exhibits, a campground, three group camps, an equestrian campground, an amphitheater, and picnic areas. Fishing, a boat ramp, and a swimming beach are available on 55-acre Lake Lincoln.

Permits and Rules: Horses are permitted only on designated equestrian trails. Bicycles are prohibited on all trails. Boats are restricted to using electric motors only. Pets must always be on leashes 10 feet long or shorter. Backpack camping is allowed on three of the park's longest trails, and campfires are restricted to designated backpack camps.

For Further Information: Cuivre River State Park, 678 State Road 147, Troy, MO 63379; 636-528-7247.

Park Trails

Mossy Hill Trail (👣👣, 1 mile). This trail follows a wooded valley and loops through an open forest with lots of mosses and reindeer lichen. It begins at the electric side of the campground.

Lakeside Trail (👣👣, 4 miles). This trail follows the entire shoreline of Lake Lincoln and offers views of many wildflowers. It is accessible from the boat ramp or swimming beach.

Big Sugar Creek Trail—South Loop (👣👣👣, 4.5 miles). This trail winds along several sections of Big Sugar Creek. Horses are allowed on this section, which may become unpleasant for hikers during wet periods.

Frenchman's Bluff Trail (👣👣👣, 2 miles). The trail begins behind the restrooms at the equestrian campground, located 1 mile west of the visitor center, and takes you on top of a 120-foot-high bluff with tremendous vistas of the Cuivre River Valley.

Cuivre River Trail (👣👣👣, 8 miles). This trail shares a trailhead with the Frenchman's Bluff Trail, traverses the entire length of Frenchman's Bluff, and descends into the Big Sugar Creek Valley. This is the main equestrian trail, along with the south loop of the Big Sugar Creek Trail.

Hamilton Hollow Trail (👣👣, 1 mile). See some of the largest trees in the park and a variety of wildflowers on this loop trail, which begins near the picnic shelter at the south end of the park.

Turkey Hollow Trail (👣👣, 1 mile). Look for the namesake of this trail, which begins and ends at Sugar Creek Valley Overlook, north of the visitor center.

Blazing Star Trail (👣👣, 2 miles). Hike through prairie, savanna, and woodland communities on this loop trail, which begins just south of the Prairie Trail on the east side of the park.

Prairie Trail (👣, .2 mile one-way). This linear trail begins at the Sac Prairie parking lot on the east side of the park and takes you into a restored prairie with native tallgrass prairie grasses and wildflowers.

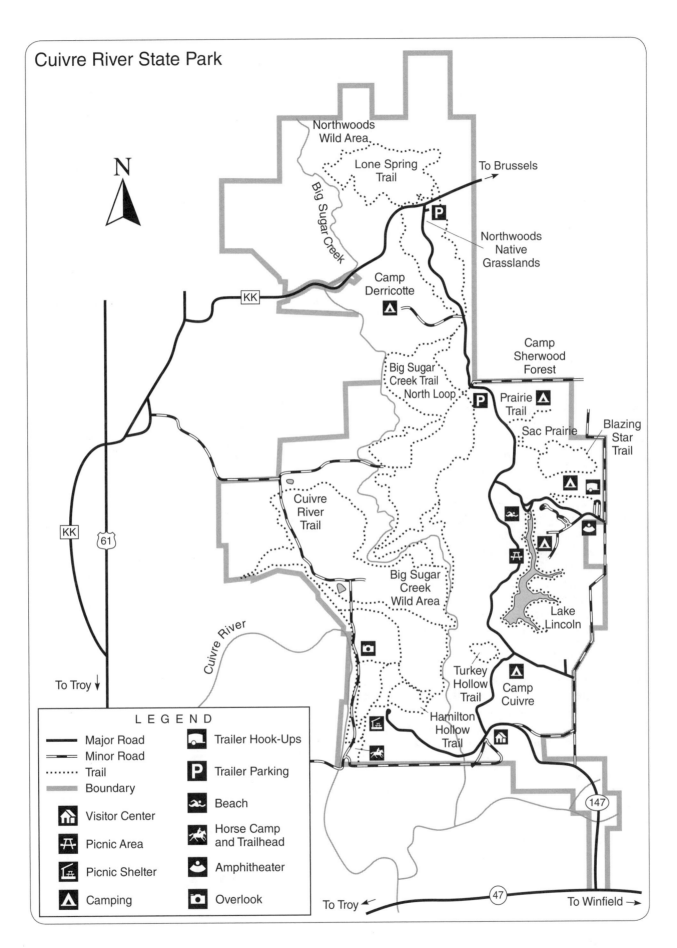

Cuivre River State Park

Lone Spring Trail

 Distance Round-Trip: 6 miles
Estimated Hiking Time: 2.75 hours

Even if you know exactly where it is and you walk right to it, the magical flow of a spring is always something of a surprise.

Caution: Watch for traffic when crossing Highway KK; you cross it four times.

Trail Directions: Park in the lot at the north end of the park at the intersection of Highway KK and the main park road. The north half of this trail loops through the Northwoods Wild Area.

Begin from the parking lot **[1]**, cross Highway KK, and continue on the other side. When you reach the intersection at .08 mi. **[2]**, turn left. This connector link is marked with white arrows that take you to the main trail. Immediately, you notice a landscape deeply scored. For thousands of years, water has cut through this limestone-laden area, draining into the Big Sugar Creek a half mile to the west. You pass hill after hill, each separated from the next by a deep V.

At .30 mi. **[3]** is a trail registration box. Please fill out a registration card before continuing. Turn right here to continue, following yellow arrows in a clockwise direction. As the whine of car tires on the highway fades behind you, several things let you know that you are approaching Big Sugar Creek. You will find yourself at the bottom of intersecting ravines, occasionally crossing small streams. The shade becomes denser, and the forest smells more like a greenhouse. Notice the plants; pawpaw, bloodroot, ginger, and golden seal let you know that you're in a shaded, moist, rich habitat.

A small, rocky stream soon appears on your right. Look for its small but lively inhabitants—whirligig beetles whirling on the surface and minnows schooling below. As you cross this stream at 1.05 mi. **[4]**, look downstream to see the wide, rocky bed of Big Sugar Creek. At the fork in the trail at 1.18 mi. **[5]**, bear right. Emerging from the base of this ridge is the lone spring **[6]** (1.20 mi.), which has a second, smaller outlet just 8 feet to the right after a rainy period. Look for ginger and jack-in-the-pulpit just above the spring.

Another karst feature, a sinkhole, appears next to the trail on the right at 1.24 mi. **[7]**. Caused by the partial collapse of a cavern below, sinkholes sometimes hold water. Pickerelweed Pond, a state natural area in the park, features a sinkhole pond. The forest shows off its mighty white oaks and sugar maples as you hike through the heart of the Northwoods Wild

Area. Ignore the spur to a camp at 1.46 mi. **[8]** and go straight. You cross several scenic streams and many ravines before reaching the connector link at 2.78 mi. **[9]**, where you go straight.

Cross Highway KK at 2.89 mi. **[10]**. Cross several more streams and cross the park road at 4.2 mi. **[11]** near the entrance to Camp Dericotte. You soon emerge into an open forest with a tall canopy and a floor covered in violets, ginger, and ferns. Cross a wide stream at 5 mi. **[12]** with moss-covered boulders and tiny sand beaches. Just on the other side, look for a plant about shin high with unusually wide, creased leaves. This is false hellebore, a plant rarely seen in bloom. Cross yet another stream and begin a hike uphill. Some ox-eye daisies will welcome you to Highway KK. Cross the highway at 5.54 mi. **[13]** and return to **[3]**, where you turn right to return to the trailhead.

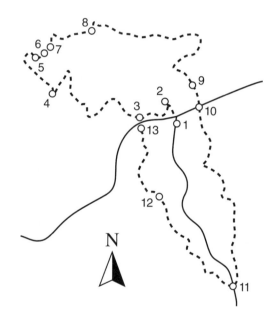

1. Start
2. Left turn
3. Trail registration
4. Small stream
5. Bear right
6. Lone spring
7. Sinkhole
8. Go straight
9. Go straight
10. Highway crossing
11. Park road crossing
12. Stream crossing
13. Highway crossing

North

Big Sugar Creek Trail— North Loop

 Distance Round-Trip: 3.75 miles
Estimated Hiking Time: 2 hours

After approaching what I thought was a stuffed animal lying in the trail, I discovered a fresh fawn, camouflaged perfectly in the dappled shade. I snapped a quick photo and hiked on, knowing that Mother was somewhere nearby, waiting for me to leave.

Caution: Horses are not allowed on the north loop of this trail, but they are allowed on the connector link.
Trail Directions: Park in the lot for the trailhead on the west side of the main park road, halfway between Camp Sherwood Forest and Camp Dericotte. Begin hiking straight out from the parking lot [1]. Find a trail registration box at .05 mi. [2] and fill out a card.

Continue straight on the wide, old roadbed of the connector link, an easy, long descent. Look for red-spotted purple and great spangled fritillary butterflies socializing on the trail. At the bottom, go straight at the intersection at .90 mi. [3], marked with an orange marker. From here, follow blue arrows going clockwise. Turn right at .97 mi. [4], where the white trail goes straight. Here is a thickly vegetated floodplain of Big Sugar Creek. Notice the winged stems of white crownbeard, which may reach 6 feet tall before flowering. At 1.14 mi. [5] is an unusual tree with broad leaves in the shape of tulips. This is a tulip tree, an Appalachian hardwood that grew so large that pioneers hollowed out single logs to make long, lightweight canoes.

Just after passing the tulip tree, you see Big Sugar Creek on your left. Contrasted with the muddy and silty streams typical of north Missouri, Big Sugar Creek runs crystal clear over gravel and exposed limestone bedrock. Begin ascending the bluff over the river. Large dolomite boulders on the left complete the Ozark-like scene and invite you to climb them. As you turn away from the creek, you enter an open forest crisscrossed with ravines and dominated by giant white oaks, sugar maples, and shagbark hickories. After you pass under a power line, the habitat becomes drier. Here are dittany, fragrant sumac, and pussytoes. The trail swings to the left at 1.82 mi. [6]. Pass under the power line again, and it's down you go!

Hike on a shaded slope covered with Christmas and maidenhair ferns. At the bottom you find a sheltered cove, with limestone ledges on each side of you. Ravines intersect everywhere, pulling you in all directions, and you may think that you've entered some type of geological crossroads. Cross an intermittent stream at 2.16 mi. [7]. You pass a pawpaw grove and some monster red oaks before you find a wet-weather spring in a ravine on your right.

Big Sugar Creek rolls right next to you at 2.52 mi. [8], where you can scan the slower pools for floating softshell turtles. Look carefully on rocks near the water for sunning water snakes. You see lots of their prey here—chubs, sunfish, and minnows. After you turn away from the creek, you cross a small tributary at 2.64 mi. [9] and hike along it for a while. Steep slopes on both the left and right shelter moisture- and shade-loving plants like jack-in-the-pulpit, bloodroot, and ginger. After passing under a power line, the trail puts you on top of a curving, dry ridgetop, and you may feel as if you're hiking on the back of a big snake, with slopes falling away on each side. Turn right at the intersection at 3.16 mi. [10] and cross a final stream at 3.37 mi. [11] beneath basswood and sycamore trees. Turn left when you return to the registration box [2] to finish your hike.

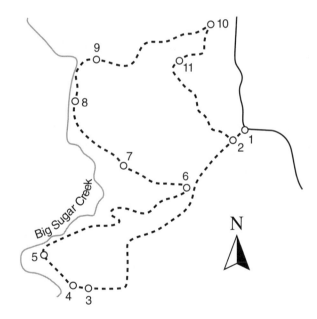

1. Start
2. Trail registration
3. Go straight
4. Right turn
5. Tulip tree
6. Swing left
7. Stream crossing
8. Big Sugar Creek
9. Stream crossing
10. Right turn
11. Stream crossing

North

- See the shelter cave that preserves evidence of human occupation as long ago as 9850 BP, the first archaeological site in the nation to be designated a national historic landmark.
- Find a sandstone pirate's plank and fantastic wet-weather waterfalls over undercut stone ledges.
- Hike next to a geological rarity—a sandstone cave.
- Find the six-spotted tiger beetle, a metallic green beetle that runs and flies just ahead of you on the trail.

Area Information

Caves in dolomite or limestone are common in Missouri (over 6,000 by last count), but sandstone caves, like Graham Cave, are rare. Graham Cave was formed when softer, more soluble dolomite dissolved away from underneath a more resistant layer of St. Peter sandstone, leaving an archlike cavity 120 feet wide and 16 feet high, extending about 100 feet into the hill. Two additional features of the cave—its location high enough on the hill to escape floods and its orientation almost due south, offering protection from northerly winter winds—set the stage for one of the greatest archaeological finds in the state.

Dr. Robert Graham came from Kentucky and settled in the area in 1816, buying rich bottomland along the Loutre River from Daniel Morgan Boone, one of Daniel Boone's sons, who became a property owner and land surveyor in the area with his father. In 1847 Graham bought the rocky tract that contained the cave, which remained in the Graham family. When archaeologists heard that the husband of Graham's great-granddaughter was bulldozing in the cave to enlarge it for his livestock, they persuaded him to stop and conducted excavations from 1949 through 1955. Their findings were astonishing—a 10,000-year record of almost continuous human habitation in the cave. This was the oldest material and the best-preserved deposit found until that time. Because of the significance of the site, portions have been left intact for future excavations.

Directions: From Danville, on I-70, take Highway TT west, which dead-ends at the park in 2 miles.

Hours Open: The site is open year-round from 7:00 a.m. to sunset.

Facilities: A campground, picnic areas, and playgrounds are available. Interpretive displays are located in the park office and in a shelter near the parking lot for the cave. A paved path leads from the parking lot to the cave. A boat ramp on the Loutre River offers access for boating and fishing.

Permits and Rules: Pets must always be leashed. As in all Missouri state parks, plants or animals may not be removed or damaged, although nuts, berries, and mushrooms may be collected for personal consumption.

For Further Information: Graham Cave State Park, 217 Highway TT, Danville, MO 63361; 573-564-3476.

Other Areas of Interest

Located on some scenic hills along the Missouri River, the little town of **Hermann** preserves the culture of Missouri's early German immigrants. Vineyards, wineries, antique shops, galleries, and bed-and-breakfasts abound, and festivals in May and October feature German music, food, and the art of wine making. For more information, call the Hermann Chamber of Commerce, 573-486-2313 or 800-932-8687.

Deutschheim State Historic Site, 109 West Second Street in Hermann, offers tours of two homes in the town's historic district. Tours of the Strehly House include the residence, the attached winery, and the first print shop in Hermann, which printed a German newspaper in the ground-floor shop. A fee is charged for the tours. For more information, call 573-486-2200.

Park Trails

Fern Ridge Trail (🥾🥾🥾, .3 mile). This trail begins at the west end of the parking lot for the cave. Find the trailhead sign behind the playground and near the restrooms. You hike alongside a fantastic wall of sandstone, covered with colorful lichens, mosses, and delicate ferns. You finish at the Graham Cave Trail, not far from the interpretive shelter. Don't miss this short but scenic trail!

Woodland Way Trail (🥾🥾, .4 mile). This trail connects the Indian Glade Trail with the picnic area near the park office. The picnic area has restrooms and drinking water.

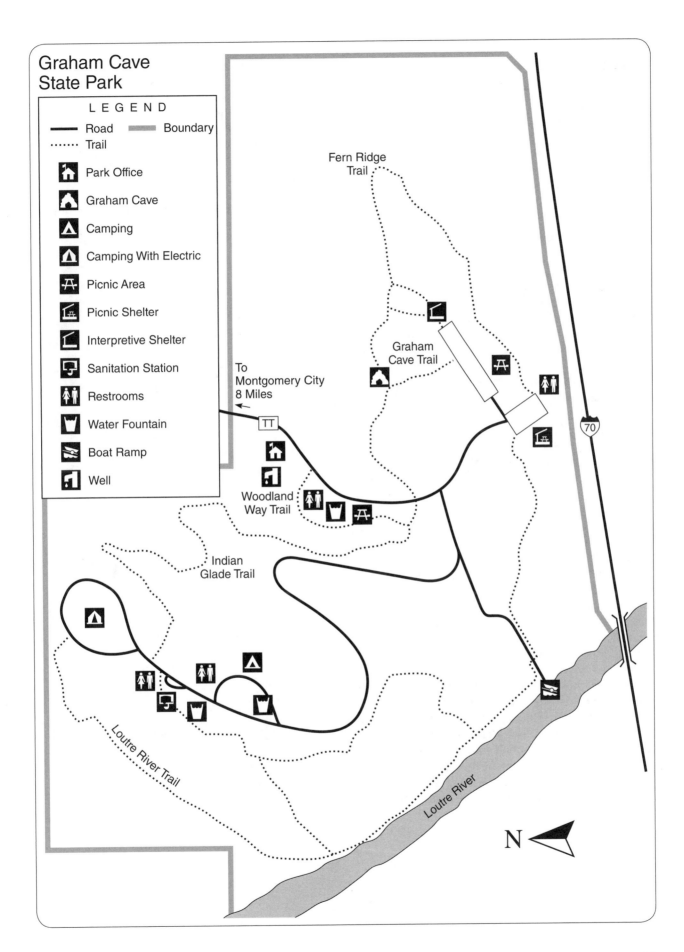

Graham Cave State Park

LEGEND

— Road ▬▬ Boundary
····· Trail

- 🏠 Park Office
- 🏕 Graham Cave
- ⛺ Camping
- ⛺ Camping With Electric
- 🪑 Picnic Area
- 🏠 Picnic Shelter
- 🏠 Interpretive Shelter
- ♿ Sanitation Station
- 🚻 Restrooms
- 🚰 Water Fountain
- 🚤 Boat Ramp
- 🔧 Well

Fern Ridge Trail

Graham Cave Trail

To Montgomery City 8 Miles

TT

Woodland Way Trail

Indian Glade Trail

Loutre River Trail

Loutre River

N

Graham Cave and Indian Glade Trails

Distance Round-Trip:
2.35 miles
Estimated Hiking Time:
1.5 hours

Archaeologically, Graham Cave is of national importance. Geologically, it is a rare and splendid example. Aesthetically, its elegant arch inspires wonder and delight.

Caution: Watch for traffic when crossing the main park road.

Trail Directions: Park in the lot for the cave and start the Graham Cave Trail at the east end of the lot [1]. Be sure to stop at the interpretive shelter at .02 mi. [2], which describes the site's archaeology, early people, geology, and natural communities. Continue the trail over a small wooden bridge. Turn left at the intersection with the Fern Ridge Trail at .09 mi. [3]. At .13 mi. [4], you hike over another wooden bridge and pass a beautiful wet-weather waterfall over an undercut rock bluff. After ascending the wooden steps, you soon reach the lawn in front of Graham Cave at .20 mi. [5]. Stand at the entrance to the cave. How does it feel to be on the front porch of a 10,000-year-old home? Imagine the generations of people who have stepped where you now stand. From here, you can hike down the paved path to finish the Graham Cave Trail and return to the parking lot. Otherwise, begin the Indian Glade Trail at the sign at the opposite end of the lawn.

In a few short steps, you are greeted by an amazingly contorted cedar tree. How's that for a lesson in resilience? After taking the wooden steps up, you find a small glade on your right at .27 mi. [6]. Prickly pear cactus is here, which produces big yellow blossoms in June and July. Can you find it? After crossing a small, wooden bridge, go up some steps and cross the main park road at .42 mi. [7]. The trail continues on the other side. Go straight at the intersection with the Woodland Way Trail at .46 mi. [8]. After crossing a small, wooden bridge, look for interesting plants along the trail, including shooting stars, maidenhair ferns, rattlesnake ferns, and a plant that looks like a fern but isn't—lousewort. After crossing another small, wooden bridge, you hike over a wet-weather waterfall

at .78 mi. [9]. Note how the rock ledge is eroded and undercut—a characteristic of sandstone. Sandstone erodes into some strange-looking shapes; check out the pirate's plank jutting out from the trail over the valley on your left at .84 mi. [10]. Cross another small, wooden bridge at .97 mi. [11]. After passing several rock outcrops on your right, you find what resembles an amphitheater of limestone at 1 mi. [12], dotted with mosses, lichens, and cliff brake. Reach the campground road at 1.17 mi. [13] and retrace your steps to return to the parking lot.

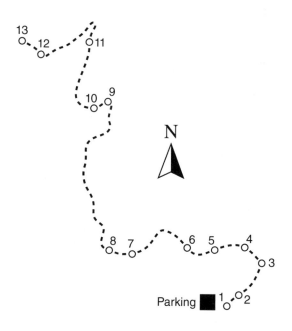

1. Start
2. Interpretive shelter
3. Left turn
4. Wet-weather waterfall
5. Graham Cave
6. Glade
7. Park road crossing
8. Go straight
9. Wet-weather waterfall
10. Pirate's plank
11. Wooden bridge
12. Limestone amphitheater
13. Campground road

North

Loutre River Trail

 Distance Round-Trip: 2.8 miles
Estimated Hiking Time: 1.5 hours

I pass a tropical pawpaw grove and descend onto the shadowy floodplain of the Loutre. Thick grapevines trail through the balmy air, suspended from the sprawling branches of enormous shagbark hickory trees. A spider monkey jumps from a treetop branch, startling a toucan, which lands just over my head. . . . No, not really, but it was easy to imagine.

Caution: Stay on the trail in the floodplain to avoid stinging nettles and poison ivy.

Trail Directions: Park in the lot for the cave and start the trail at the west end of the lot (opposite the interpretive shelter) **[1]**. Turn right at the intersection at .09 mi. **[2]** and continue through the thicket of eastern red cedar. Although wildlife uses cedar for shelter and food, cedar can quickly shade out nearly all other plant species, as you see here. Turn left on the paved road to the boat ramp at .29 mi. **[3]** and turn right just past the parking lot at .42 mi. **[4]** as the trail parallels the river. After hiking through a grassy field, you enter the woods at .56 mi. **[5]**. Go straight at this intersection.

As you follow the river, take one of several short spurs to the water. Sneak quietly to the river to improve your chances of seeing herons stalking in the shallows, teal or wood ducks gathering in slack water, or kingfishers perching on snags. On a warm summer day you will probably see a myriad of butterflies assembled on the sandy beaches near the water, looking for moisture and mates. If you see a brilliant green insect flying just ahead of you, you have discovered the six-spotted tiger beetle. They are plentiful on these sandy trails, their favorite haunts. As you get glimpses of the river through the trees, look for basking aquatic turtles or longnose gar floating just beneath the surface. Go straight at the intersection with the connector link at .72 mi. **[6]**. After the trail turns away from the river, you cross a small stream with undercut rock ledges and a beautiful wet-weather waterfall at .94 mi. **[7]**. Look in the pool for crayfish, camouflaged with the gravel. As you climb uphill, you pass a variety of interesting plants, including river oats, horsetail, and several wildflowers. Just after passing a private residence on your left, turn right at the intersection at 1.47

mi. **[8]**. Turn right again on the paved campground loop at 1.50 mi. **[9]**. At a trail sign just behind the restrooms and shower house, the trail enters the woods at 1.65 mi. **[10]**. Pick your way through these scenic woods over exposed boulders covered with lichens and mosses. Tall red oaks, ash, and sugar maples produce dense and welcome shade. Go straight at the intersection with the connector link at 1.90 mi. **[11]**. As you descend into the river bottom, you hike through several pawpaw groves, identified by trees from 5 to 15 feet high with exceptionally large leaves that fan out like fingers on a spread hand. The only tropical tree that lives in Missouri, the pawpaw produces a 4-inch peanut-shaped fruit in October that tastes like a banana. At 2.29 mi. **[5]**, turn left at the intersection to return to the trailhead.

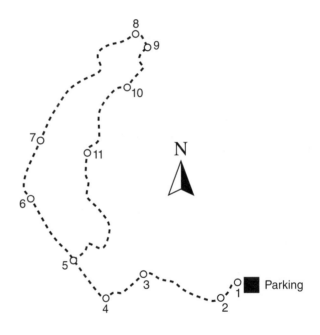

1. Start
2. Right turn
3. Left turn
4. Right turn
5. Go straight
6. Go straight
7. Wet-weather waterfall
8. Right turn
9. Right turn
10. Trail enters woods
11. Go straight

4. Mark Twain State Park and Historic Site

- Spy a giant aluminum butterfly, actually a hyperbolic paraboloid, from a Mark Twain Lake overlook.
- See the 420-square-foot cabin where a family of eight lived when Samuel was born.
- Spot the striking redheaded woodpecker in a lake cove "ghost forest."

Area Information

John and Jane Clemens moved from Tennessee and had lived in their two-room cabin in Florida, Missouri, for only six months before Samuel was born on November 30, 1835. Writing under his pen name, Mark Twain, Clemens later wrote, "I was postponed . . . to Missouri. Missouri was an unknown new state and needed attractions."

Established in 1924 to honor Monroe County's native son, Mark Twain State Park is the third oldest state park in Missouri and surrounds the historic site memorial museum. For decades, Mark Twain State Park consisted of rugged, forested hills overlooking the scenic Salt River, where Clemens spent his boyhood summers. But in 1983, 18,600-acre Mark Twain Lake was built, and now the park is reservoir based.

On seeing a picture of his birthplace cabin, Clemens wrote, "Heretofore I have always stated that it was a palace, but I shall be more guarded now." The soaring roof of Mark Twain Birthplace State Historic Site now protects this humble cabin, as well as a wealth of artifacts, exhibits, and Clemens family belongings in a museum, where visitors can come to contemplate Twain's wit, good-natured insight, and contribution to our national culture.

Directions: Travel east of Paris on Highway 154 for 12.3 miles. Turn north on Highway 107 for 2.7 miles. Turn east on Highway U for .4 mile to the historic site.

Hours Open: Hiking trails are open year-round except on Easter, Thanksgiving, Christmas Day, and New Year's Day. The park office is open daily from 7:30 a.m. to 4:00 p.m. from April 1 to October 31 and

Monday through Friday from 7:30 a.m. to 4:00 p.m. from November 1 to March 31. The historic site is open daily from 10:00 a.m. to 4:00 p.m. from April 1 to October 31 and Wednesday through Sunday from November 1 to March 31.

Facilities: The historic site offers a public reading room, museum exhibits, and tours for a small fee. The state park has campgrounds, a group camp, rental cabins, picnic areas, overlooks, and facilities for fishing, swimming, and boating.

Permits and Rules: Pets must always be leashed.

For Further Information: Mark Twain State Park, 20057 State Park Office Road, Stoutsville, MO 65283; 573-565-3440. To reach the historic site, call 573-565-3449. For rental cabins and camping reservations, call 877-422-6766.

Other Areas of Interest

Just across Highway U from the turnoff for the historic site is the **Florida Cemetery**, where several Clemens family members are buried, including Samuel's sister, Margaret, and an uncle, John Quarles. A red granite monument stands in **Florida, Missouri,** at the original site of the birthplace cabin, just east of the historic site on Highway U.

The **Union Covered Bridge** is one of only four covered bridges remaining in the state and Missouri's only surviving example of the Burr-arch truss system. The bridge is 5 miles west of Paris and 4 miles south on Highway C. For more information, call the historic site.

U.S. Army Corps of Engineers' **Clarence Cannon Dam** offers multiple water recreation facilities, campgrounds, and hiking trails along Mark Twain Lake. For more information, call 573-735-4097.

Park Trails

Barefoot Sam Trail (🐾, .60 mile). The hike begins at the end of the paved road to the Mark Twain Memorial Shrine and winds through an oak-savanna landscape on a peninsula between the lake and a cove.

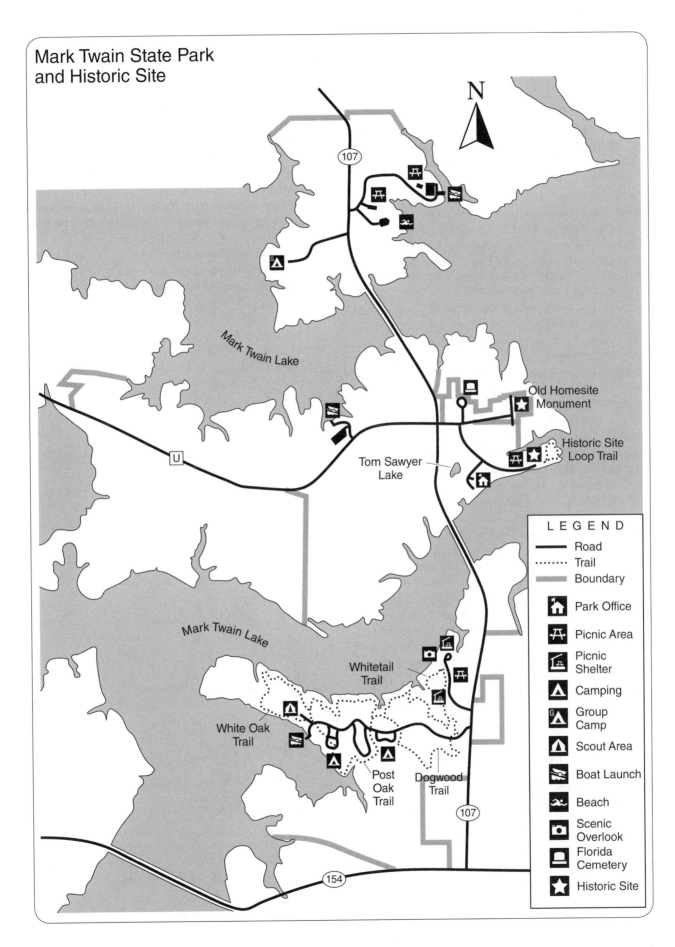

Mark Twain State Park
and Historic Site

N

107

Mark Twain Lake

Old Homesite
Monument

Historic Site
Loop Trail

U

Tom Sawyer
Lake

Mark Twain Lake

Whitetail
Trail

White Oak
Trail

Post
Oak
Trail

Dogwood
Trail

107

154

LEGEND

Road
.... Trail
Boundary

Park Office
Picnic Area
Picnic Shelter
Camping
Group Camp
Scout Area
Boat Launch
Beach
Scenic Overlook
Florida Cemetery
Historic Site

Whitetail and Dogwood Trails

   Distance Round-Trip: 3 miles
Estimated Hiking Time: 1.5 hours

Hike quietly when approaching the secluded lake cove and look for wood ducks, which nest in natural cavities of the dead standing trees. You'll see various woodpeckers, too. Scan the shoreline for deer, wild turkey, and red fox.

Caution: During wet periods the trail will be muddy in the numerous small stream crossings.

Trail Directions: Find the trailhead for both the Whitetail Trail and the Dogwood Trail near the scenic overlook in the Buzzard's Roost Picnic Area. Begin at the trail sign **[1]** and follow blue markers for the Whitetail Trail.

Once leveled by great sheets of ice, this area is more hilly and rugged than the surrounding level topography because of the carving action of the Salt River and its tributaries. The up-and-down hikes here are more reminiscent of the Ozarks than of north Missouri. At .03 mi. **[2]**, cross a small drainage stream and go straight at the intersection. Take the small spurs on your right to view Mark Twain Lake, created in 1983 by damming the Salt River. You can still see towering limestone bluffs carved by the river along some edges of the lake. The Buzzard's Roost area and other blufftop parts of the park that once overlooked the Salt River Valley now overlook this 18,600-acre lake, created for hydroelectric power and recreation. The trail reaches a fine lake overlook at .15 mi. **[3]**. Turkey vultures (nicknamed buzzards) often soar in wide circles here, quickly tilting their outstretched wings from side to side to maintain balance.

As you hike across the ends of these small ridges dissected by numerous drainage ravines, look for the orange-yellow blossoms of hoary puccoon from March to June. Later, you find the purple flower spikes of leadplant, so named for its ashy gray leaves. Purple prairie clover also thrives in the more open areas of these dry, rocky woods. Turn right at the intersection at .29 mi. **[4]** to begin the Dogwood Trail, where you follow yellow trail markers.

Go straight at the intersection at .37 mi. **[5]**. Look beyond the Highway 107 bridge at the lake overlook at .93 mi. **[6]** to see what looks like a giant aluminum butterfly, its wings spread in a graceful, wide V. This structure is the Mark Twain Birthplace Historic Site

building, specially engineered and constructed to protect the two-room clapboard cabin in which Samuel Clemens was born in 1835. Before or after hiking, be sure to stop at the historic site to see the cabin, a handwritten manuscript of *The Adventures of Tom Sawyer*, and other exhibits of Clemens's career. At 1.11 mi. **[7]**, you turn away from the lake and cross the campground road at 1.31 mi. **[8]**. Notice that the younger, brushier forest here of elm, locust, and multiflora rose looks quite different from the previous mature forest of oak, hickory, and maple. Turn left at the intersection at 1.43 mi. **[9]**. You pass several giant pin oak trees, whose small lower limbs point to the ground, before crossing the campground road again at 2.15 mi. **[10]**. After passing some sprawling white oak trees, you arrive at **[5]**, where you turn right. Turn right at the intersection at **[4]** to return to the Whitetail Trail. Ignore the spur on your right to the shelter houses and turn right again at the intersection **[2]** to return to the trailhead. Before you leave Buzzard's Roost, be sure to visit the CCC picnic shelter and lake overlooks.

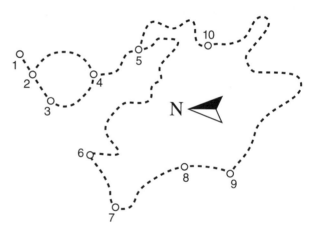

1. Start
2. Go straight
3. Overlook
4. Right turn
5. Go straight
6. Overlook
7. Left turn
8. Campground road crossing
9. Left turn
10. Campground road crossing

Post Oak and White Oak Trails

 Distance Round-Trip: 3 miles
Estimated Hiking Time: 1.5 hours

While hiking near the campground I came upon two furry baby red foxes, wrestling with each other on the trail. They didn't seem to mind me, but a bark from their nearby mother sent them scurrying into their den, tumbling over each other in their hurry.

Caution: During wet periods the trail will be muddy in the numerous small stream crossings.

Trail Directions: Find the trailhead for both the Post Oak and White Oak Trails on the main campground road near the shower house. Start the Post Oak Trail **[1]** at a sign for the trail and head north, toward the lake. As the trail approaches a cove, it swings to the left. This lake is fairly new, so many flooded trees have died but not yet fallen. Like many others, this cove is a ghost forest and a good place to look for the striking redheaded woodpecker, which prefers open, mature deciduous forests. The trail parallels the lake for a while, offering intermittent views of the lake on your right. Turn right at the white connecting link at .91 mi. **[2]**.

As you continue to hike along the lake, try to find a post oak leaf among the jumble of hickory, maple, and red oak leaves on the trail. Like white oak leaves, post oak leaves have rounded lobes. Unlike white oak leaves, the middle lobes of post oak leaves are almost square and give the leaf a crosslike appearance. Because post oak limbs are strong, settlers often used them as fence posts, thus giving the tree its name. After hiking past the last cove on the north shore of this peninsula, go straight at the intersection at 1.65 mi. **[3]** to begin hiking the south shore. From March through June, look for several patches of bluebells along the trail here, nodding their blue heads in the lake breezes.

Turn right at the white connecting link at 2.02 mi. **[4]** and you soon cross the paved road to the boat ramp. Go straight at the intersection at 2.10 mi. **[5]**. At 2.60 mi. **[6]**, you find a ridge knob with views of several lake coves. From here you can watch for ospreys in summer or bald eagles in winter. Also look for belted kingfishers, which often perch on dead trees over the water. Kingfishers sometimes hover before plunging in the water headfirst to catch fish, and they frequently announce their presence by a loud, rattling cry, often given while in flight. Turn right at 2.69 mi. **[7]**. Turn left at the intersection at 2.79 mi. **[8]** to return to the trailhead.

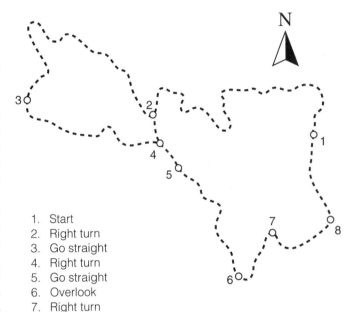

1. Start
2. Right turn
3. Go straight
4. Right turn
5. Go straight
6. Overlook
7. Right turn
8. Left turn

5. Battle of Athens
State Historic Site

- Walk around the 19th-century town of Athens, where a Confederate cannon (improvised from a hollow log) exploded with its first shot, where a 350-pound infantry captain (named Captain Small) successfully held the town's left flank despite his colleagues' defection, and where the Union forces (despite being besieged on three sides and being outnumbered four to one) won the battle and assured Federal control of northeast Missouri for the remainder of the Civil War.

- Find the rare snow trillium, a glacial relict, in abundance in the rich, moist soils of the Des Moines River Ravines Natural Area.

- Tour the restored Thome-Benning Home and see the holes in the walls where a Confederate cannonball ripped through the house and landed in the Des Moines River (or in Iowa) without hurting anybody.

- Come in March, April, or May to see acres (really) of blooming Dutchman's-breeches, many of them pink.

Area Information

Anxiety gripped northeast Missouri in 1861. Despite the proximity of powerful Union forces in Iowa and Illinois, many residents were pro-Southern, and the question of secession had divided the area. People were choosing sides, sometimes splitting families. Ambushes and assassinations had begun. As secessionist forces grew more numerous and bold, Union leaders resolved to unify their troops under a single command. At a July 4 rally in Kahoka, the First Northeast Missouri Regiment was born. David Moore, a storekeeper from Wrightsville, was named commander. Immediately, Moore began enlisting volunteers.

Moore chose Athens as the place to garrison his troops, confiscating the homes and businesses of the many Southern sympathizers who lived there. He and his 500 soldiers had not long occupied Athens before they were warned early on the morning of August 5 that an attack of 2,000 Rebel soldiers was imminent. Moore began lining up his troops to face the attack, and by 5:30 a.m. the Union Home Guard found themselves surrounded by the Confederate State Guard on three sides, with the wide and swift Des Moines

River at their backs. For two hours, cannons roared and muskets barked, finally leaving the Confederates retreating in such a hurry that they abandoned their horses and weapons.

Except for the old street grid and building foundations, it would be hard to tell that Athens was once a thriving town with 50 businesses. Apart from the cannonball hole and the history books, it would also be hard to tell that an important Civil War skirmish occurred here.

Directions: If you put your finger on a map on the northeasternmost tip of Missouri, Battle of Athens State Historic Site is under your finger. From Kahoka take Highway 81 north for 12 miles. Turn east on Highway CC for 3.9 miles and turn left at a sign for the site.

Hours Open: The site is open year-round. The park office is open from 8:00 a.m. to 5:00 p.m.

Facilities: A wooded campground, picnic area, and playground are at the site. Restrooms and drinking water are available in the campground, but not showers. Fishing and boating are available on a small lake or the Des Moines River. Guided tours of the Thome-Benning Home (Cannonball House) are offered year-round. Battle of Athens reenactments are held in early August every third year.

Permits and Rules: Pets must always be leashed.

For Further Information: Battle of Athens State Historic Site, Route 1, Box 26, Revere, MO 63465-9714; 660-877-3871; www.mostateparks.com/athens.htm.

Other Areas of Interest

The largest and best-preserved remnant of any Illinois Indian village is interpreted at **Iliniwek Village State Historic Site**. French explorers Louis Jolliet and Jacques Marquette estimated that 8,000 people were living at the village when they encountered it in 1673. Iliniwek is the only Illinois village found in Missouri so far. The historic site is 2 miles north of Wayland off Highway 27. Tours of the site can be arranged by calling the park staff at Battle of Athens State Historic Site at 660-877-3871.

Site Trails

Mill Ruins Trail (🥾, .25 mi. one-way). This U-shaped trail connects the Historic Trail with the Thome Mill Ruins and picnic shelter.

Battle of Athens State Historic Site

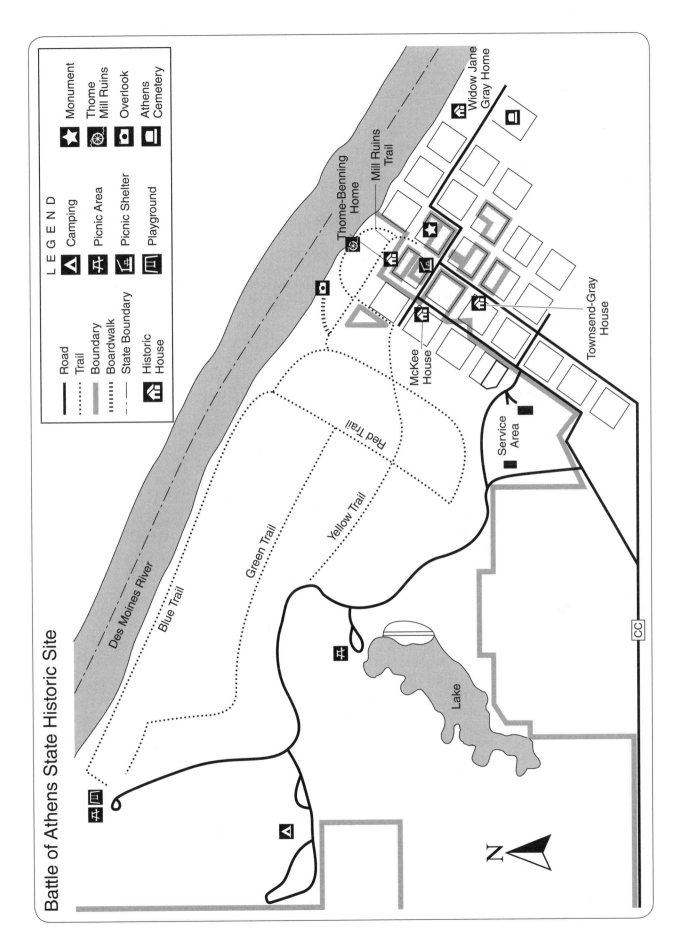

LEGEND

▲ Camping	★ Monument
🏕 Picnic Area	⚙ Thome Mill Ruins
🏠 Picnic Shelter	◉ Overlook
🎠 Playground	▥ Athens Cemetery

— Road
⋯ Trail
▬ Boundary
⋯ Boardwalk
—·— State Boundary
🏠 Historic House

Des Moines River

Thome-Benning Home

Mill Ruins Trail

Widow Jane Gray Home

Townsend-Gray House

McKee House

Service Area

Blue Trail

Green Trail

Yellow Trail

Red Trail

Lake

CC

N

Yellow–Red Historic Trail

   Distance Round-Trip: 1.75 miles
Estimated Hiking Time: 1 hour

Hike through Athens, a bustling pre–Civil War town now nearly ghostlike. Let your imagination run as you walk on the remnants of the old street grid next to the foundations of homes long gone, and see where an early Civil War showdown raged for almost two hours.

Caution: There are several stream crossings, and the Stallion Branch may be difficult to cross after a rainy period.

Trail Directions: As you enter the park, you see the signboard designating the trail at the edge of the forest where the road bends, just after you pass the driveway to the lake. There is no parking area at this trailhead, but you are allowed to park on the main park road. Be sure to keep vehicles on the pavement.

Begin at the trail sign with a yellow arrow [1]. If you are here in spring, you'll start among a profusion of blooming Dutchman's-breeches, anemone, and toothwort—a display that you'll find is not restricted to the trailhead! Go straight at the intersection at .05 mi. [2]. Turn right at .13 mi. [3] to begin the loop marked with red arrows. Turn left at .23 mi. [4], just before you reach a small, rocky stream. At .37 mi. [5], cross a small stream and continue the trail on the right. Go straight at the intersection at .44 mi. [6].

Cross the Stallion Branch at .53 mi. [7] and continue the trail on the other side. It was in the dense brush here, on August 5, 1861, around 5:30 in the morning that about 60 Union soldiers clashed with advancing Rebel forces and successfully held the west flank of Athens, then occupied by the Union Home Guard. At the Yellow–Red intersection at .57 mi. [8], turn right and walk up a hill. Soon you emerge in a large field. Turn to the right slightly and head for the McKee House, a white two-story home with red trim. This house [9] (.73 mi.) was used as headquarters for the Union forces during Colonel Moore's occupation of Athens. Turn left here. The cream-colored house at .81 mi. is the Thome-Benning Home, also called the Cannonball House [10] because it still bears the holes where a Confederate cannonball shot through it. Check here or at the park office if you are interested in a guided tour of the home. As you face the front of the Cannonball House, turn left on St. Louis Street to continue the trail.

Take the overlook boardwalk at .87 mi. [11] to see the ruins of the Thome Mill, once housing a gristmill, sawmill, and woolen factory. After the overlook, turn right on St. Louis Street and ignore the red trail sign on your right. Follow the edge of the field around until you see where you entered the field from the forest. Turn back into the forest here and hike down the hill. At 1.14 mi., you are back at the Yellow–Red intersection at [8].

Turn right here and cross the Stallion Branch again. At 1.26 mi., go straight at the intersection [12]. At 1.33 mi., turn left at the Des Moines River [13] and turn left again at the Blue–Red intersection [14] at 1.42 mi. Go straight at the intersection at 1.57 mi. [15], and soon you'll be back at [3], where you turn right to finish the trail.

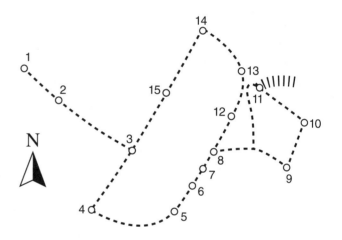

1. Start
2. Go straight
3. Right turn
4. Left turn
5. Stream crossing
6. Go straight
7. Stream crossing
8. Right turn
9. McKee House
10. Cannonball House
11. Overlook boardwalk
12. Go straight
13. Des Moines River
14. Left turn
15. Go straight

Green–Blue River Trail

 Distance Round-Trip: 1.75 miles
Estimated Hiking Time: 1 hour

From early on, you'll have fun with the roller-coaster pattern of ridge, stream, ridge, stream, ridge. . . . These steep slopes, called cove ravines, hide a botanist's paradise of unusually rich flora including many ferns, doll's eyes, and snow trillium, a glacial relict found nowhere else in the state.

Caution: The many streams may be difficult to cross after a rainy period.

Trail Directions: Drive to the end of the main park road and park next to the playground in the picnic area. The trailhead **[1]** is just across the road and is marked with a sign with a green arrow. The trail begins in a rolling, open forest among Ohio buckeye and big white oak and ash trees. Because of their unusual qualities and because they harbor rare and diverse plant life, 40 acres of these cove ravines have been designated as the Des Moines River Ravines Natural Area. You get to hike over the backs of these ravines now, and you'll see the ends of them later, next to the river. On the forest floor are wake robins, bloodroot, and trout lilies—all lovers of rich, moist woods. You might notice the many single, flowerless trout lily leaves. Flowers arise only from two-leaved plants. The plant is also known as thousandleaf because of the abundance of leaves and scarcity of flowers.

At .27 mi. **[2]**, cross the first of many small streams that have been eroding these cove ravines for eons. Between crossing streams and climbing ridges you will see entire groves of giant shagbark hickories on either side of the trail. You might not want to count them, but you cross no fewer than five more small streams before arriving at the intersection at .73 mi.

[3], where you turn left. Turn left again at .88 mi. **[4]**. For the next .75 mi., you hike between the Des Moines River and the ends of all those ridges that you just hiked over. You also get to see where all the water goes from the streams that you just crossed. In several places these streams widen at their mouths, no longer confined to the steep ravines of the forest, and large, moss-covered boulders become wet-weather waterfalls. The rare snow trillium, blooming in March, can be found on this section of the trail in abundance.

At 1.53 mi. **[5]**, a small spring erupts from under a rock with a gooseberry bush on top. Go up the wooden steps **[6]** at 1.65 mi. and emerge in a field. When you come to the pavement, turn left to return to the trailhead.

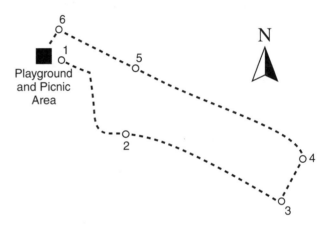

1. Start
2. Stream crossings
3. Left turn
4. Left turn
5. Spring
6. Wooden steps

- Visit the petroglyph site and see realistic depictions of opossum, deer, and snakes carved into sandstone as long as 1,500 years ago.
- Discover wolf trees on the Thousand Hills Trail.
- Near Forest Lake listen for the rattle of kingfishers, the clear whistles of osprey, and the mournful yodels of loons.
- Explore the trails in the forest and discover the reason for the park's name.
- Hike through a grove of rare trees in Missouri—the big-toothed aspen.

Area Information

Half of northern Missouri was once covered in prairie. Just west of Kirksville, however, lies a rugged belt of hills that runs north and south between rolling expanses of prairie lands. These hills supported a mosaic of mixed oak-hickory woodlands, tallgrass prairie openings, and savannas—grasslands with trees spaced much farther apart than they are in the forest. Remnants of these natural communities can be seen from the hiking trails of the park.

Many early settlers bypassed this rugged terrain, but a young doctor named George Laughlin developed a large farm here and named it Thousand Hills Farm. Later, the Laughlin heirs donated 1,100 acres of the old farm to the city of Kirksville to construct a freshwater reservoir for the town's growing population. Additional land was bought, and in 1952 a 600-acre reservoir was made by damming Big Creek. The whole tract was turned over to the state, which dedicated Thousand Hills State Park in 1953.

Directions: From Kirksville take Highway 6 west for 3.2 miles. Turn south on Highway 157 and go 2 miles to the park entrance.

Hours Open: The park is open daily from 7:00 a.m. to 10:00 p.m. from April 1 through October 31. It is open from 7:00 a.m. to sunset during the other months. The park office is open weekdays from 7:00 a.m. to 4:30 p.m.

Facilities: Forest Lake offers all kinds of water recreation, including sailing, waterskiing, canoeing, boating, and fishing. A swimming beach is located along the shore, as is a fully equipped marina from which visitors can rent many types of boats. The park includes a campground, rental cabins overlooking the lake, an interpretive shelter protecting the petroglyphs, numerous picnic areas, an amphitheater, and a dining lodge famous for its good food and scenic views of the lake.

Permits and Rules: Pets must always be leashed. Alcoholic drinks are prohibited on parking areas and swimming beaches in all state parks. Jet skis are prohibited on Forest Lake, and motorboat horsepower is limited to 90. Bicycles are permitted only on the Thousand Hills Trail.

For Further Information: Thousand Hills State Park, 20431 State Highway 157, Kirksville, MO 63501; 660-665-6995. For information about cabins, the marina, or the dining lodge, call 660-665-7119.

Other Areas of Interest

Wakonda State Park includes more than 1,000 acres of land that was once mined of sand and gravel and is now a recreational area featuring six lakes, a rare sand prairie, hiking, biking, swimming, fishing, and camping. Wakonda is 3 miles south of La Grange on Highway 61. For more information, call 573-655-2280.

Park Trails

Petroglyph Trail (🥾, .15 mile one-way). This linear trail winds along a pine-clad ridgetop and connects the petroglyph shelter with the closest campground.

Craig's Cove Loop Trail (🥾🥾🥾, 2.6 miles). This trail features some sprawling white oak trees along a picturesque western cove of Forest Lake. As you enter the park, turn right on Big Loop Trail Road just after you pass the park office. The trailhead is .2 mile ahead on your right. Park in the lot for the special-use shelter just across the road. The trail uses the same route as the Thousand Hills Trail for the first 1.3 miles and then splits off to the northwest at the dam. Follow blue trail markers for the Thousand Hills Trail and white trail markers for Craig's Cove Loop Trail.

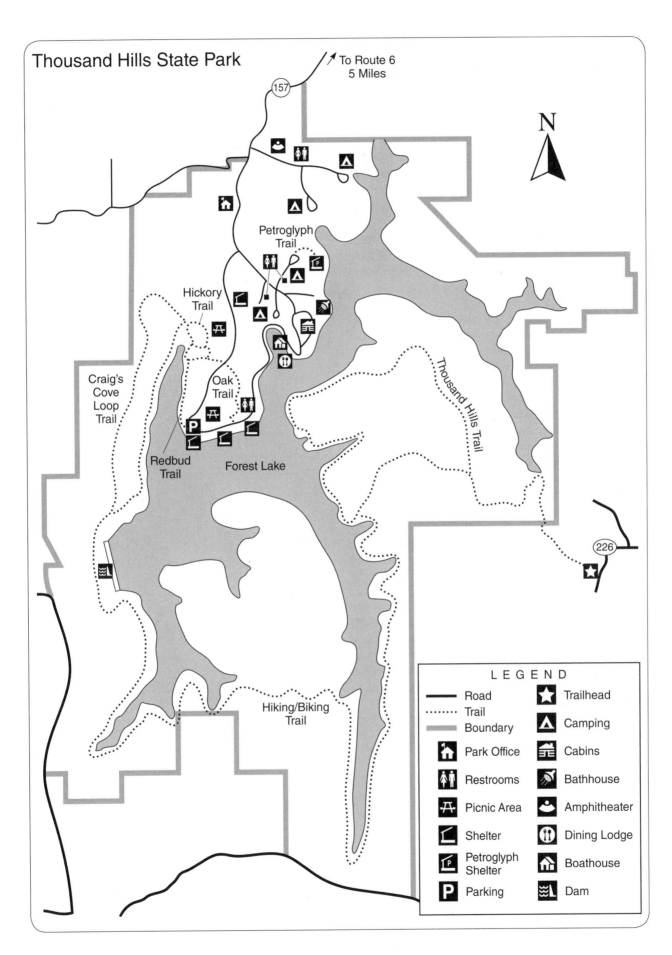

Thousand Hills State Park

To Route 6
5 Miles

157

N

Petroglyph Trail

Hickory Trail

Craig's Cove Loop Trail

Oak Trail

Redbud Trail

Forest Lake

Thousand Hills Trail

226

Hiking/Biking Trail

LEGEND

Road		Trailhead	
Trail		Camping	
Boundary			
Park Office		Cabins	
Restrooms		Bathhouse	
Picnic Area		Amphitheater	
Shelter		Dining Lodge	
Petroglyph Shelter		Boathouse	
Parking		Dam	

Redbud-Hickory-Oak Trails

 Distance Round-Trip: 1.5 miles
Estimated Hiking Time: 1 hour

You never know what you'll see at Thousand Hills State Park. While hiking these trails near Forest Lake I saw a pair of osprey, a pair of beaver, and three common loons yodeling and laughing at each other across the cove.

Caution: The trail near the lake will be muddy after a rain.

Trail Directions: As you enter the park, turn right on Big Loop Trail Road just after you pass the park office. Go .9 mi. and turn right into the parking lot. The trailhead for the Redbud Trail is at the north end of the parking lot.

Begin at the trail sign **[1]** for the Redbud Trail. Soon you hike between a western cove of Forest Lake and a grove of pines that whisper among themselves at the slightest breeze. Go straight at the intersection at .17 mi. **[2]**. As you hike, notice that the lake cove tapers into the woods, offering privacy for more secretive wildlife. Watch for osprey perching in large trees or hovering over the water, watching for fish. Because fish are their only prey, these elegant birds are also called fish hawks. You might notice some nearby trees chewed by beaver. Also look for herons stalking the shoreline shallows.

Cross a small stream at .35 mi. **[3]** and turn left. You find a stream splashing its way over several "falls" created by a series of large rock layers in the streambed at .45 mi. **[4]**. Go straight here and hike along the stream until the trail cuts away to the right and ascends a hill. Look and listen for woodpeckers in this second-growth forest of northern red oak, white oak, and shagbark hickory. Go straight at .65 mi. **[5]** and discover the reason for the park's name. In several places here you can count 10 or more hills, all seeming to come and go in different directions. Cross a small wooden bridge and turn left at the intersection at .77 mi. **[6]**.

When you reach the trail sign for the Hickory Trail, go straight and cross the park road at .88 mi. **[7]**. Con-tinue at the Oak Trail sign, just behind the restrooms. One of the common understory trees here is redbud. If you are here in April you won't be able to miss it— pink or lavender flowers cover almost every branch of the tree. The flowers make a slightly sweet (though not filling) trailside nibble. At 1.08 mi. **[8]**, you find a wooden bench. Turn right here and make your way down a short but steep hill. Walk toward the restrooms and go straight. At 1.16 mi. **[9]**, you meet the main park road, where you turn right and follow the road to return to the parking lot.

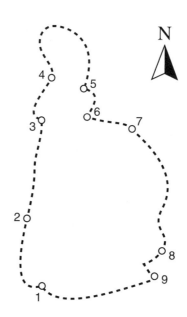

1. Start
2. Go straight
3. Left turn
4. Wet-weather waterfall
5. Go straight
6. Left turn
7. Road crossing
8. Wooden bench
9. Right turn

Thousand Hills Trail

Distance Round-Trip: 5 miles
Estimated Hiking Time: 2.5 hours

Savannas are grasslands interspersed with trees. Lacking a shrub layer, they form a parklike transition area where prairie and forest intermingle. Savannas need fire to maintain their composition. Missouri may have had 13 million acres of savanna before settlement, but today savannas are absent from most areas of the state.

Caution: The trail includes several stream crossings, and Big Creek may be impassable after heavy rain.

Trail Directions: This hiking and biking trail has two trailheads—one at the west end of the park at the Craig's Cove Loop trailhead and the other outside the park in Big Creek Conservation Area. If you use the trailhead inside the park, the trail is 26 mi., round-trip. As described here, the trail begins at Big Creek Conservation Area. To reach the trailhead at the conservation area, exit the park, turn right on Route 6, and go .7 mi. Turn right and go 2.3 mi. Turn right on Osteopathy Street and go 1.8 mi. Turn right on Michigan Street and go .3 mi. Turn left on Boundary Avenue and go 1.2 mi. Turn right at the sign for Rainbow Basin Ski Resort and go 1.2 mi., where the road dead-ends. Here are signs for Big Creek Conservation Area and the Thousand Hills trailhead.

Begin on a wide, mowed path **[1]**. You cross several streams and two wooden bridges. On these hilltops are remnants of hill prairies evidenced by native grasses such as big bluestem and Indian grass. At .33 mi. **[2]**, turn right at the intersection. Cross Big Creek at .50 mi. **[3]**.

A sprawling white oak marks a bend in the trail at .62 mi. **[4]**. These wolf trees have 180-degree-wide crowns that nearly reach the ground. Once monarchs of expansive savannas, wolf trees didn't have to compete for sunlight. The trees on the north-facing slope at .76 mi. are remarkable as well. These are the rare big-toothed aspen **[5]**. Turn left at the intersection at .92 mi. **[6]** and you soon pass another wolf tree on your left. The trail bends to the right when you reach the first cove of Forest Lake **[7]** (1.57 mi.), which has settled into such natural beauty that it's hard to tell that the lake is human-made. The trail follows the shore, offering a continuum of scenic views.

On your right at 1.83 mi. **[8]** is a prairie remnant. Although now choked with shrubs, sumac, and blackberries, native grasses still dominate the ground cover. Cross a small stream at the end of the lake cove and continue on your left. Turn right, away from the lake, at 2.78 mi. **[9]**. At 3.30 mi., you hike through a savanna remnant **[10]**. Notice that the old trees have wide-spreading limbs whereas the young, crowded trees must compete for sunlight. Turn left at the intersection at 3.97 mi. **[6]** to hike back to the trailhead.

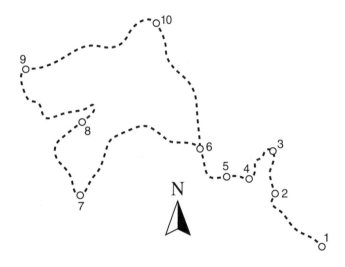

1. Start
2. Right turn
3. Big Creek
4. Wolf tree
5. Big-toothed aspen grove
6. Left turn
7. Forest Lake
8. Prairie remnant
9. Right turn
10. Savanna remnant

- Come for a hiking experience with the flavor of the Rockies. You won't just see these rugged, craggy, and scenic rock pinnacles—you'll hike on top of them!

- Zoom out and zoom in. Stand on top of the pinnacles for sweeping, majestic views and then get on your hands and knees to view the intricate, embedded fossils.

- See what a little stream can do to rocks. You'll find cliffs, arches, pinnacles, and a shelter bluff—all on one trail.

Area Information

We are familiar with river bluffs. An amorphous mass of rock is embedded in the surrounding landscape on one side and steeply carved on the other by moving water over time. But what happens when a bluff is carved on both sides? The pinnacles were formed as Silver Fork Creek doubled back on itself and pinched a mass of limestone between its channels. Another stream, Kelly Creek, became crowded in the process and added its erosional effects on the limestone. The results are peaks and points known as pinnacles. What is left of the original ridge is a geological grandpa 75 feet high and 1,000 feet long. Its craggy crest is only a few feet wide in spots, and erosional forces continue to enlarge two windows in its side, forming natural arches. Although these features may not be long in the world geologically, they'll likely be there when you arrive.

The Pinnacles Youth Park is owned by the Boone County Pinnacles Youth Foundation, which was established in 1965 to serve area youth. The area is managed by the foundation's board of directors, which consists of representatives from local youth agencies such as the Girl Scouts, Boy Scouts, and the 4-H program. Because of its significant geological features, the Pinnacles is designated a state natural area.

Directions: From the intersection of Highways 63 and I-70 in Columbia, go 13.9 miles north on Highway 63. Turn right on Pinnacles Road and turn right at the T. Go straight for .6 mile into the parking lot for the area.

Hours Open: The area is open year-round from 8:00 a.m. to sunset.

Facilities: Grills, picnic tables, and restrooms are provided. Three picnic shelters are available; priority is given to groups with reservations.

Permits and Rules: All dogs must be kept on a leash. Firearms, fireworks, glass containers, and intoxicants are prohibited. Primitive camping is allowed only by youth groups with reservations.

For Further Information: University of Missouri Extension of Boone County, 573-445-9792.

Other Areas of Interest

Rocky Fork Lakes Conservation Area, 6.9 miles south of the Pinnacles, includes 2,200 acres of forests, old fields, grassland, and savanna. The area has 20 fishing ponds, including 52-acre Rocky Fork Lake, which has a boat ramp. Activities include fishing, hunting, hiking, and bird-watching. The area has a wheelchair-accessible fishing dock and a firearms shooting range. The area is 7 miles north of Columbia, off Highway 63, on Peabody Road. For more information, call 573-445-3882.

Finger Lakes State Park is one of two state parks that allows off-road motorcycling and ATV use. The 1,129-acre park is reclaimed strip-mine land, and the old strip pits offer swimming, fishing, and canoeing. A picnic area and campground are available. Finger Lakes is also just south of the Pinnacles, off Highway 63, on Peabody Road. For more information, call 573-443-5315.

Pinnacles Trail

Distance Round-Trip:
2 miles
Estimated Hiking Time:
1.5 hours

It was in water, in the form of a shallow sea, where sediments formed this Burlington limestone around 290 million years ago. And it is water, in the form of streams, rain, and ice, that is wearing down the pinnacles today, reclaiming the rock and its embedded ocean animals.

Caution: This trail is not for the acrophobic, the fainthearted, or young children. Hikers must negotiate narrow, steep, and precipitous passages on the pinnacles.

Trail Directions: Start the trail at the trailhead sign **[1]** at the east end of the parking lot. Go downhill toward Silver Fork Creek. At .03 mi. **[2]**, turn right at the small picnic shelter on your left and follow the trail as it parallels the creek. Look at the rugged peaks just across the stream. Those are the pinnacles on which you will soon be hiking! Go straight at the trail intersection at .11 mi. **[3]**. Go straight at the spur on your right at .19 mi. **[4]**, which leads to a small picnic shelter. Just after crossing a wooden bridge and a rock outcrop on your right, go straight at the intersection at .24 mi. **[5]**. You are now on a short spur that dead-ends at a surprise at .29 mi. **[6]**—a shelter bluff, about 40 feet deep and 125 feet long, cut into the limestone bluff by the eroding power of Silver Fork Creek. The next geologic oddity that you encounter will be about 75 feet higher!

Return to the intersection at **[5]**, where you turn right and find a shallow spot to cross the stream. Climb the bank on the opposite side and turn left. Bear left at the fork in the trail at .51 mi. **[7]**, where you begin your climb. The views keep getting better as you continue the rugged and narrow trail on the spine of the pinnacles. You pass an eastern red cedar tree with a twisted trunk that seems to be growing straight out of the rock. As you pick your way carefully over the peaks, drink in the vistas. Then, if you zoom in for a close look at the rocks, you'll find that they are loaded with fossils. Many of these fossil disks are the remains of invertebrate ocean animals known as crinoids. The crinoid, by the way, is Missouri's state fossil.

When in doubt, look for the trail on the right side of each peak. Several holes have eroded in the pinnacles here, and you pass a natural arch at .70 mi. **[8]**. Across the stream, far below, you can see the picnic shelter that you passed earlier **[2]**. After passing the stump of an old cedar, bear right just behind one of the last pinnacles. Soon after the trail enters the forest, take the small spur on your left at .96 mi. **[9]**, which leads to an overlook of the craggy peaks that you just traversed. Although the trail continues into the woods to the north, it soon enters private property. The overlook at **[9]** is a good spot to turn around and retrace your steps to the parking lot.

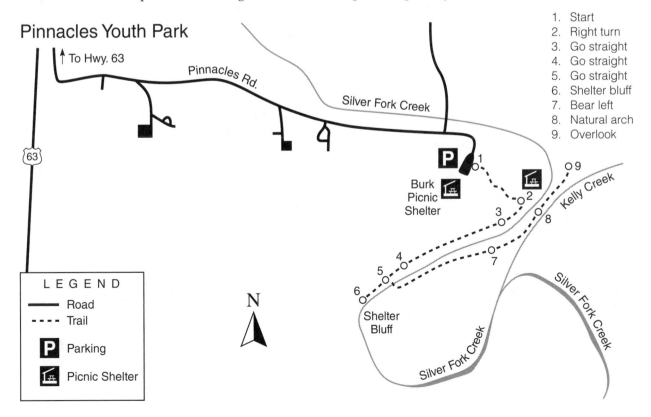

Pinnacles Youth Park

To Hwy. 63

Pinnacles Rd.

Silver Fork Creek

63

Burk Picnic Shelter

P

Kelly Creek

Silver Fork Creek

Silver Fork Creek

Shelter Bluff

LEGEND
— Road
- - - - Trail
P Parking
Picnic Shelter

N

1. Start
2. Right turn
3. Go straight
4. Go straight
5. Go straight
6. Shelter bluff
7. Bear left
8. Natural arch
9. Overlook

North

- Throw some diversity into your hiking and come hike "the Katy." It's scenic, flat as a board, and 225 miles long!

- Hike within a few feet of the mighty Missouri River while majestic river bluffs tower overhead.

- See the last remaining pictograph in the area painted by Native Americans on a sheer bluff face over the Lewis and Clark Cave.

- Wander through a 243-foot-long railroad tunnel constructed in 1892–93, the only tunnel on the Missouri-Kansas-Texas line.

- See Missouri's largest bur oak tree, a plant you have to hike *under* to appreciate.

Area Information

Katy Trail State Park, although it follows the Missouri River for most of its route, is itself a river of magnificence, history, and recreation. Built on the former corridor of the Missouri-Kansas-Texas (MKT, or "Katy") Railroad, the park is 225 miles long and only 100 feet wide. Of more than 1,000 rail-to-trail conversions in the nation, it is one of the longest, stretching from St. Charles to Clinton. The Katy is designed specifically for hikers and bicyclists.

Pre–Civil War Rocheport ("port of rocks"), a trailhead for the Katy Trail, began in 1825 as an important crossing on the Boone's Lick Road trade route. Rocheport thrived as a river and ferry port and became a key shipping point between St. Louis and St. Joseph. Farming, gristmilling, ice sales, and steamboat tourism were already in place when the MKT Railroad rolled into town in 1892, accelerating its economy. Rocheport now features shops, galleries, cafés, a museum, live entertainment, and several bed-and-breakfasts, and is on the National Register of Historic Places.

The Katy Trail parallels the river route taken by the Lewis and Clark expedition, which in 1804 stopped in the area of Rocheport and the Big Moniteau Bluffs. Clark's field notes on June 7 mention "Several Courious Paintings and Carveings [sic] in the projecting rock of Limestone." Hikers can still spy the remaining pictograph, a spot within a semicircle, visible above Lewis and Clark Cave.

Directions: Rocheport is west of Columbia off I-70. Take exit 115 and go north on Route BB for 2 miles into town. McBaine is southwest of Columbia. Take Highway 163 south for 3.4 miles. Take Highway K south an additional 7 miles. Turn right at McBaine at the sign for the park.

Hours Open: The trail is open only during daylight hours, year-round.

Facilities: Facilities at trailheads vary. Rocheport caters to trail users, offering bike rentals, cafés, and bed-and-breakfasts, as well as restrooms and drinking water. The McBaine trailhead has restrooms and drinking water.

Permits and Rules: All motorized equipment is prohibited on the trail except motorized wheelchairs. Also prohibited are horses, camping, rock climbing, and shooting. Pets must be leashed.

For Further Information: Katy Trail State Park, c/o Rock Bridge Memorial State Park, 5901 South Hwy. 163, Columbia, MO 65203; 573-449-7402 or 800-334-6946; www.mostateparks.com/katytrail/index.html. To find out about events at Rocheport, visit www.rocheport.com.

Other Areas of Interest

Diana Bend Conservation Area offers a short boardwalk trail, a waterfowl viewing blind overlooking a wetland, and a short hiking trail to an overlook of the Missouri River. The area can be accessed from the Katy Trail at the MKT Tunnel. For more information, call 573-884-6861 or visit www.mdc.mo.gov.

Les Bourgeois Winery is on Route BB, just 1 mile south of Rocheport, and offers wine tasting and a bistro situated on a bluff overlooking the Missouri River. For more information, call 573-698-2300 or visit www.missouriwine.com.

Hartsburg, another little river town revitalized by the Katy, offers hayrides, music, games, food, and tons of pumpkins at its popular fall pumpkin festival. Hartsburg is north of Jefferson City off Highway 63. For more information, call the Missouri Division of Tourism at 573-751-4133.

Park Trails

The Katy Trail provides infinite options for day hiking across the state, especially if a shuttle is available. Every mile on the trail is marked with a signpost. Trailhead mileage charts and brochures are available from the Missouri Department of Natural Resources.

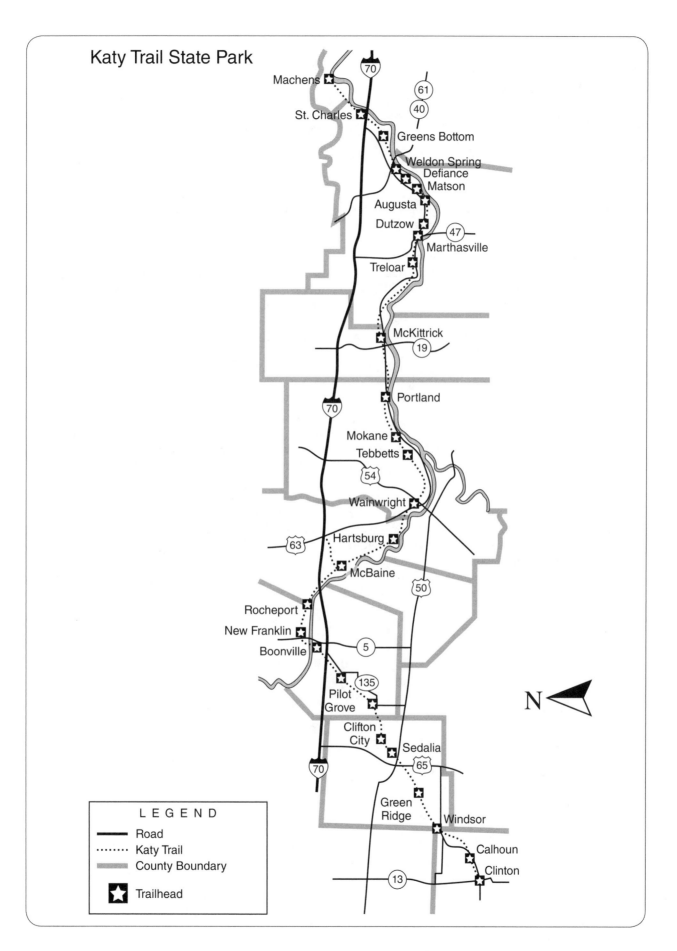

Katy Trail State Park

LEGEND
— Road
···· Katy Trail
━━ County Boundary
⭐ Trailhead

N

Historic Rocheport and MKT Tunnel

 Distance Round-Trip: 1.5 miles
Estimated Hiking Time: 45 minutes

Extend your hike on the Katy Trail. Bring your suitcase and stay at a bed-and-breakfast. Rocheport will charm you with its rich history, scenery, and hospitality.

Caution: You won't find too many people driving fast in Rocheport but be careful at street crossings anyway.

Trail Directions: As you enter Rocheport from the interstate, turn left on Pike Street and park in the lot for the Katy Trail. The hike begins **[1]** at the Katy Depot, which also serves as Rocheport City Hall.

Turn north on Pike Street, next to Trailside Café and Bike Rental. Turn left on Second Street, right on Clark Street, and left on Third Street. The School House Bed and Breakfast, at this corner, was built in 1914 as Rocheport's school for grades 1 through 12. The black slate floor of the entryway is made from the school's original blackboards. At .20 mi. **[2]** is Community Hall, erected as a Baptist church in 1860. Pass several antique shops and galleries and turn right on Lewis Street.

The small, curious building coming into view on your right, erected in 1870, is the last remaining icehouse in Rocheport **[3]** (.26 mi.). For business in the 1800s, as now, timing was everything. Ice blocks were cut from the Missouri River and Moniteau Creek in the winter and stored in icehouses between layers of sawdust and straw. Come summer, these icehouses held a lucrative commodity. The A-frame roof accom-

modated pulleys used to lift out the ice blocks. Turn right after returning to Third Street.

After one block turn left on Columbia Street. The United Methodist Church stands at .39 mi. **[4]**; its original building was constructed in 1844. Turn right on Second Street. The red granite stone on your left at .44 mi. **[5]** marks Rocheport as a major crossing on Boone's Lick Road, an important trade route from an area to the north, where the sons of Daniel Boone recovered salt from natural salt springs in the early 1800s. Deer and other animals frequently licked minerals from these areas, which thus were called licks. Across the street is the Christian Church **[6]**, erected in 1847. The home of river captain John Kaiser **[7]** (.48 mi.), built around 1830, stands at this corner on your left. It is one of the few buildings in town that survived the major floods of the mid-1800s, the Civil War raids of the 1860s, and a disastrous fire in 1922.

Cross this intersection, continuing on Second Street. Turn left on Moniteau Street. The Friends of Rocheport Historical Museum at .60 mi. **[8]** contains artifacts from the area's rich cultural past. Turn right on the limestone gravel of the Katy Trail. After crossing a wooden bridge over Moniteau Creek, you arrive at the yawning mouth of the MKT Tunnel at .76 mi. **[9]**. Hike through the tunnel to feel the drafts of cool air and see the original stonework, done in 1892 and 1893. To finish the trail, turn around toward Rocheport and stay on the Katy Trail until you return to the parking lot at the depot.

1. Start
2. Community Hall
3. Icehouse
4. United Methodist Church
5. Boone's Lick Road marker
6. Christian Church
7. Kaiser-Dimmit Home
8. Historical museum
9. MKT Tunnel

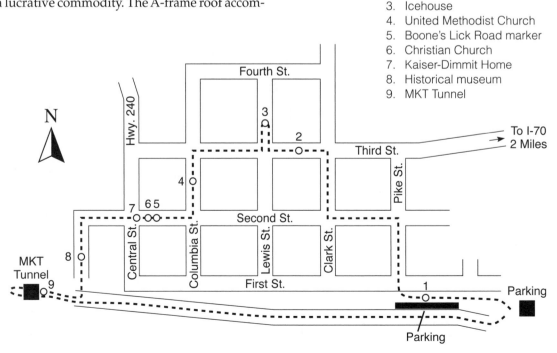

McBaine to Lewis and Clark Cave

 Distance Round-Trip: 9.75 miles
Estimated Hiking Time: 4 hours

The biggest bur oak, all the indigo buntings, and the cave were interesting, but it was the lone pictograph high on the smooth rock bluff that intrigued me most. Who painted it, and what does it mean? How did they get up there . . . on that tiny ledge?

Caution: Bring sunglasses and sunscreen (unless you are here in winter). The white limestone trail and the Missouri River reflect a lot of sunshine.

Trail Directions: Park in the lot for the Katy Trail in McBaine and begin hiking [1] on your right as you enter the trail. The terrain is easy, flat, and wide the whole way. The two advantages of this are that you'll not be surprised by hills at the end of the hike or (as long as you stay on the trail) come across ticks or chiggers.

The bridge over Perche Creek at .07 mi. [2] attests to the earnestness that railway engineers applied to bridge building. Handsome and strong, many of the bridges along the trail, built in the 1890s, remain today for use by hikers and bikers. The gravel roads at .20 mi. [3] lead to the constructed wetland cells that are the final stage of Columbia's innovative wastewater treatment program. After conventional treatment, the city's wastewater is pumped through a series of wetlands, where aquatic plants metabolize pollutants naturally. The clean water is then used to create wetland habitat for waterfowl at Eagle Bluffs Conservation Area. Hindman Junction at .25 mi. [4] is the intersection with the MKT Trail, which leads to downtown Columbia. Along the way, you pass several parks. The MKT Trail, also a recycled abandoned railway, is 8.9 mi. long.

As you continue, look through breaks in the trees into the large crop field on your left. Note the two trees in this field, a sycamore and a bur oak. Turn left onto the pavement at the intersection at 1.13 mi. [5] and keep your eyes on the tree on the left. This big field has a way of distorting your sense of proportion. The tree on the left, with the wider crown, may not look exceptionally large from a distance, but wait until you get under it. At nearly 500 years old, this is Missouri's state champion bur oak. Although a bur oak at Big Oak Tree State Park is nearly twice as tall, this tree has the widest trunk and crown [6] (1.28 mi.). Return to the main trail and turn left to continue. A plaque on the bridge at 3.48 mi. dates it at 1899.

Soon, the hill on your right becomes steeper, and bluff faces start to appear through the trees. By 4.19 mi., the Big Moniteau Bluffs [7] are overhead and straight up and down. Vines of Virginia creeper, grape, and trumpet creeper string their way across the bluffs, taking advantage of the abundant sunshine. Somehow, the mighty Missouri River suddenly appears on your left. When the bluffs on the right become taller, you are near your destination. Listen for rushing water; you will probably hear Lewis and Clark Cave before you see it. With its entrance hidden by trailside trees, the cave is at 5 mi. [8]. Although trail users are not allowed in the cave, you can stand at the entrance, feel the cave air, and see the ferns, liverworts, and mosses living just above the cave stream. An interpretive sign here describes pictographs found above the cave and at other nearby sites. Step back onto the trail and look above the cave. The last Big Moniteau Bluffs pictograph is here, a red boomerang with a dot above it. Possibly intended for ancient river travelers, perhaps a symbol marking the cave, its meaning is a mystery. A bench and some large rocks here make a good spot to rest. Retrace your steps to return to the trailhead.

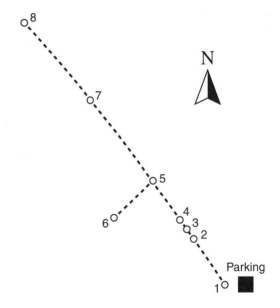

1. Start
2. Perche Creek bridge
3. Wetland cells
4. Hindman Junction
5. Left turn
6. State champion bur oak
7. Big Moniteau Bluffs
8. Lewis and Clark Cave

- Visit Missouri's first state historic site—a little town that was named for a river bluff and became an antebellum powerhouse.

- Bring a tree identification book; you'll see a mixed bag of trees on the Pierre A Fleche Trail.

- Walk around in a living-history river town where many early 19th-century buildings retain their original appearance and most of the town is a national historic landmark.

- Take a tour of the George Caleb Bingham Home, the Old Tavern, and the Old Courthouse, built in the 1820s. The one-room stone jail, built in 1873, has only held one prisoner!

Area Information

Arrow Rock's name first appeared in 1732 in French records as *pierre a fleche*, which referred to a nearby bluff along the river that was a landmark for American Indians and early explorers. Translated as "rock of arrows," the name probably refers to the fact that Native Americans gathered flint from the bluff to make arrow points and tools. The Osage Trace, an important American Indian trail, crossed the Missouri River here. Situated at the point where the main east–west route over land intersected the Missouri River, Arrow Rock became an early crossroads of all sorts.

Before the first settlers arrived, Arrow Rock was associated with the fur trade, Boone's Lick Trail, the Sante Fe Trail, and the Lewis and Clark Trail. In 1808 William Clark wrote in his journal that Arrow Rock was "a handsome Spot for a Town." Settlers from the east prompted a river ferry and increased growth for the town, and its citizens numbered over a thousand by the mid-1800s. Many prominent people became associated with Arrow Rock and played significant roles in the state's history. The town became the state's political power center and remained so until the Civil War.

Today, Arrow Rock is Missouri's grandparent, resting near the center of the state and waiting for people to visit. Many of the buildings look as if they haven't changed since they were built. Walking tours visit buildings throughout the town, most of which is a national historic landmark. The Old Tavern, built in 1834, still offers home-cooked meals to travelers.

The Lewis and Clark Trail of Discovery lies in the Jameson Island Unit of the Big Muddy National Fish and Wildlife Refuge, which was created in 1994. Operated by the U.S. Fish and Wildlife Service to conserve and protect fish and wildlife in and around the Missouri River in Missouri, the refuge consists of 10,000 acres of floodplains and adjacent lands.

Directions: Just west of Boonville, on I-70, take exit 98. Drive north on Highway 41 for 13 miles and turn right at the sign for the site. The visitor center and trailhead for the Pierre A Fleche Trail is accessed from this parking lot. To reach the Lewis and Clark Trail of Discovery trailhead, return to Highway 41 and turn right. Go .2 mile and turn right on Van Buren Street. Drive .4 mile and turn left at the T intersection. Go .1 mile and turn right at a sign for the Big Muddy National Fish and Wildlife Refuge. The parking lot is .2 mile farther.

Hours Open: The visitor center is open daily from 10:00 a.m. to 5:00 p.m. in summer (June 1–August 31); from 10:00 a.m. to 4:00 p.m. daily in spring and fall; and from 10:00 a.m. to 4:00 p.m. Friday through Sunday in winter (December 1–February 28). The campground and lake area close at 10:00 p.m.

Facilities: A visitor center with exhibits, a campground, and picnic areas are available on the site. Fishing is available at Big Soldier Lake near the campground. Guided tours of the historic buildings are available for a fee. The community offers historic tours, bed-and-breakfasts, antique shops, restaurants, and a summer theater.

Permits and Rules: Bikes and horses are not allowed on the trail. Swimming is not allowed in the lake. Pets must always be leashed.

For Further Information: Arrow Rock State Historic Site, P.O. Box 1, Arrow Rock, MO 65320-0001; 660-837-3330 (visitor center); 660-837-3200 (tavern); 660-837-3311 (theater). Big Muddy National Fish and Wildlife Refuge, 4200 New Haven Road, Columbia, MO 65201; 573-876-1826 or 800-611-1826; www.fws.gov/midwest/bigmuddy.

Other Areas of Interest

Boone's Lick State Historic Site is the site of the salt-manufacturing business once owned and operated by Daniel Boone's sons, Daniel and Nathan Boone. Recovering salt from natural salt springs, or "licks," the Boones began one of the earliest centers of industry in central Missouri in 1805. A trail leads to the salt springs. The site is 12 miles northwest of Boonville, off Highway 87, on Highway 187. For more information, call Arrow Rock State Historic Site.

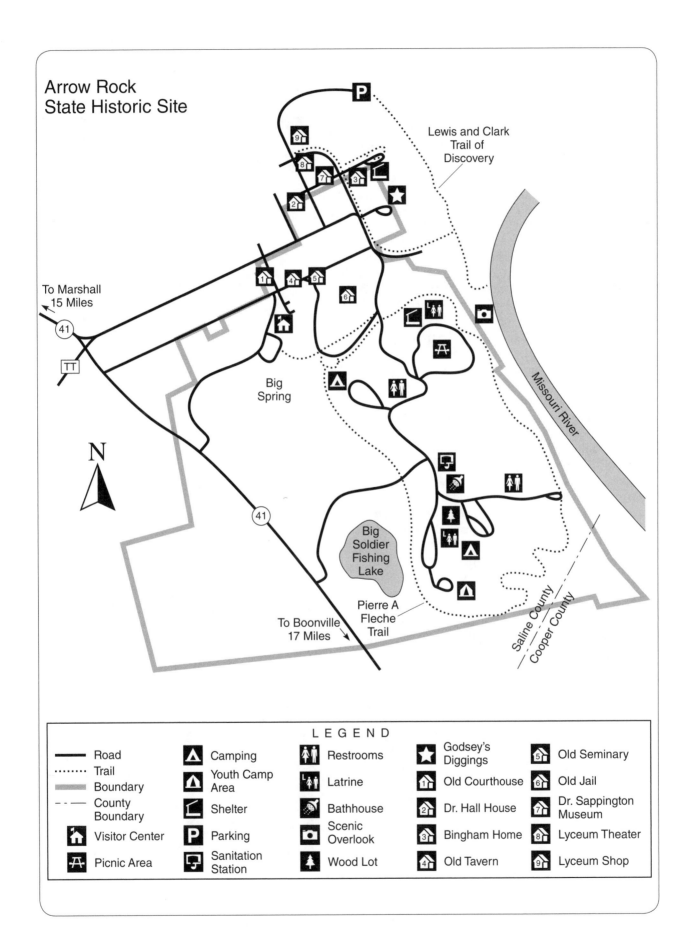

Arrow Rock
State Historic Site

Lewis and Clark
Trail of
Discovery

To Marshall
15 Miles

41

TT

N

Big
Spring

Big
Soldier
Fishing
Lake

Missouri River

Pierre A
Fleche
Trail

To Boonville
17 Miles

Saline County
Cooper County

L E G E N D

—— Road	Camping	Restrooms	Godsey's Diggings
···· Trail	Youth Camp Area	Latrine	Old Courthouse
Boundary	Shelter	Bathhouse	Dr. Hall House
County Boundary	Parking	Scenic Overlook	Bingham Home
Visitor Center	Sanitation Station	Wood Lot	Old Tavern
Picnic Area			

Old Seminary

Old Jail

Dr. Sappington Museum

Lyceum Theater

Lyceum Shop

Pierre A Fleche Trail

 **Distance Round-Trip:** 1.5 miles
Estimated Hiking Time: 45 minutes

Who is this Pierre A. Fleche, anyway?

Caution: Be careful when crossing the paved park roads.

Trail Directions: Park in the lot for the visitor center; the trailhead is at the edge of the lot. Begin at the sign for the trail [1] and follow the green arrows on this trail. The trail begins in a mixed forest, among Osage orange, hackberry, shingle oak, and cedar. After crossing a couple of intermittent streams, you cross a paved road at .12 mi. [2].

The trail soon intersects another paved road. WPA workers constructed the European-style, triple-arched, stone bridge in front of you around 1936. Cross this bridge at .20 mi. [3] and turn left at the trail sign, just on the other side. Notice the abundant jewelweed, with cornucopia-shaped orange blossoms, in the spring branch.

When you approach a small, wooden bridge on your left, take the spur on your right at .30 mi. [4]. When you enter the open field of the picnic area, turn left on the pavement and stop at the overlook at .37 mi. [5]. The ceaseless flow of muddy water below you is the Missouri River, the dominant geographic feature of the region. Descend the hill to your right and reenter the forest at the trail sign. You then cross a wooden bridge. After passing through a glade remnant, turn left on the wide, mowed path at .54 mi. [6]. Soon you pass the tip of the campground loop. When you reenter the woods, you spy a few more trees; here are slippery elm, honey locust, and persimmon.

As the trail begins some switchbacks, notice the unusual contours of the water-sculpted bedrock in the stream crossing at .72 mi. [7]. The deep Vs of the terrain show the effects of draining water as well. Go straight at the connecting link on your right at 1.04 mi. [8]. Take the spur on your left at 1.11 mi. [9] to sneak behind some willows. Scan the lake for bulging eyes of bullfrogs, pointed snouts of aquatic turtles, and bobbing coots.

Turn left after returning to the main trail and cross a paved road at 1.20 mi. [10]. As you cross a wooden bridge at 1.28 mi. [11], notice the stone slabs on each side of the stream bank—remnants of a much older bridge. At 1.4 mi. [12], cross a small stream and turn right to find Big Spring, a watering stop for early travelers on the Santa Fe Trail. Turn left on the paved road here to return to [2], where you turn left to return to the trailhead.

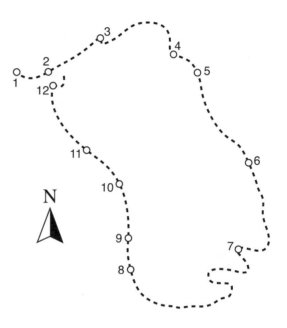

1. Start
2. Road crossing
3. Stone bridge
4. Right turn
5. Missouri River overlook
6. Left turn
7. Bedrock stream
8. Go straight
9. Spur to lake
10. Road crossing
11. Old bridge
12. Big Spring

Lewis and Clark Trail of Discovery and Arrow Rock Historic River Landing Trail

 Distance Round-Trip: 1.85 miles
Estimated Hiking Time: 1 hour

"The agitation was so great that the water was all muddy and could not get clear." —Father Jacques Marquette, 1673, in the first written description of the Missouri River

Caution: The last 100 feet of the trail to the river may be muddy or impassable because of rain or high river level. Bring your mosquito repellent.

Trail Directions: Park in the lot for the trailhead, where you'll find an information kiosk. Walk around the yellow gate at the end of the parking lot and turn right at the three-way intersection. Begin at the sign for the trail **[1]** on a flat, gravel path that follows an old levee. As you hike, look for cone-shaped stumps along the trail—sure signs that beavers live nearby. Ironically, one of the interpretive signs near a bench at .15 mi. **[2]** explains that beavers were exploited for their fur and had already been trapped out of the area when Lewis and Clark came through here in 1804. The explorers had to travel another 200 mi. upstream before they found the first signs of the valuable rodents. Today, beavers have made a dramatic return and are common along Missouri's rivers and streams.

At .34 mi. **[3]**, you find wooden steps on your right leading to a bridge and trail. Go straight here. Soon, you pass a bench and an interpretive sign that explains the benefits of floodplains, which serve as wildlife habitat and natural flood control. The Big Muddy itself soon appears in breaks in the dense stands of young box elder, willow, and silver maple trees. If the ground is not too muddy, hike on out to the edge of the water at .75 mi. **[4]** and throw rocks, do a little beach combing, or watch for wildlife. Deer and turkey are common here, and bald eagles, shorebirds, and waterfowl use the river as a corridor for migration and travel.

After your visit with the river, retrace your steps to the intersection at **[3]**, where you turn left and cross a wooden bridge. You are now hiking on the Arrow Rock Historic River Landing Trail, which once connected the river to Arrow Rock. By 1849 as many as 58 steamboats were traveling the river in the area, loaded with passengers, produce, and goods. Commercial traffic from the landing to Main Street was constant from March through October, and the riverfront was the economic engine of the town. After passing a trail kiosk, turn right on the paved road at 1.29 mi. **[5]**.

At 1.37 mi. **[6]**, you reach a brush-filled ditch, known as Godsey's Diggings, which is all that remains of the town's attempt in 1842 to connect Main Street with the river. By 1844 the project was abandoned. At 1.40 mi. **[7]**, you reach George Caleb Bingham's home on your right. A self-taught artist, Bingham is considered one of the greatest American painters of the 1800s. Beginning his career as a portrait artist in Franklin and Arrow Rock, Bingham painted scenes of frontier life along the Missouri River. He later became involved in politics and eventually was a professor of art at the University of Missouri at Columbia. Turn right just past the Bingham home and take the spur to an overlook and interpretive sign at 1.46 mi. **[8]**. Back on the main road, turn right to continue. Just after passing the Lyceum Shop and Theater, turn right on a gravel road at 1.61 mi. **[9]** at a sign for the refuge. Follow the road until you return to the parking lot.

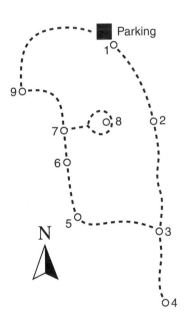

1. Start
2. Bench
3. Go straight
4. Big Muddy
5. Right turn
6. Godsey's Diggings
7. George Caleb Bingham Home
8. Overlook
9. Right turn

10. Van Meter State Park

- Hike on a trail with a 100-year-old cemetery at one end, a 1,300-year-old cemetery at the other, and mysterious, prehistoric earthworks in between.

- Learn about the Missouri Indians, who built their principal village on the steep, loess ridgetops that are now within and near the park, and who gave the state and the river its name.

- Visit the Oumessourit Natural Area, a highly diverse area and one of the few remaining natural wetlands along the Missouri River.

- Walk around the Burial Mounds—three large, earthen mounds constructed as burial monuments to the dead.

Area Information

The Missouri Indians were probably living for 300 to 400 years on the loess hills and ridges above the Missouri River before they were noted by the first Europeans who ventured into what is now Missouri. The first historical mention came in 1673, when two Frenchmen, Father Jacques Marquette and Louis Jolliet, drew a map of their village's location and recorded their name as *Oumessourit*, which, loosely translated, means "people of the big canoes." *Oumessourit* evolved into *Missouri*, and so it was that a group of people, a major river, and a state were named.

In the early 1700s, as many as 5,000 Missouri Indians may have lived on the ridges in and near the park. The Missouri were described as a friendly and proud people who farmed, fished, hunted, and gathered their food from the rich floodplain and uplands alike. But the Missouri were not the first people to live here. Although the Old Fort has been revealed to be associated with the Oneota (prehistoric Missouri Indians), the Burial Mounds predate these people, and archaeological research here indicates that American Indians may have inhabited this area as early as 10,000 BC.

When the Missouri lived here the landscape looked very different from how it does now. Prairies or savannas capped many of the ridges, which commanded distant views of the great river valley. Natural marshes, wet prairies, and other rich wetlands covered the vast floodplain.

Today, however, the park offers a peaceful, natural landscape in an urbanizing world. It preserves unusually steep ridges of loess, rich forests of red oak, sugar maple, and black walnut, and a diverse natural marsh in the Missouri River floodplain. Although the park contains a beautiful lake and shady, spacious picnic areas, the most special parts of the park are the sacred ones. Hike up to one of them and imagine the lives of the early Missourians.

Directions: From Marshall, take Highway 41 north for 7.3 miles. Turn west on Highway 122 and go 4.7 miles to the visitor center (cultural center) on the right.

Hours Open: The park is open year-round from 8:00 a.m. to sunset. The visitor center is open from 10:00 a.m. to 4:00 p.m. Monday through Saturday and from 1:00 p.m. to 5:00 p.m. on Sunday. From November through March the visitor center is closed on Monday, Tuesday, and Wednesday.

Facilities: Missouri's American Indian Cultural Center interprets the state's Native American history through exhibits, artwork, and an audiovisual room. The park also offers a campground and picnic areas. Fishing and boating (carry-on only) are available on Lake Wooldridge.

Permits and Rules: Strict federal and state laws prohibit the disturbance of archaeological sites and artifacts. Digging, or otherwise disturbing the area, is prohibited. Boat motors on Lake Wooldridge are restricted to trolling motors. Swimming is not allowed. Horses, bikes, and ATVs are not allowed on the trails. Do not pick the wildflowers. Pets must always be leashed.

For Further Information: Van Meter State Park, Route 1, Box 47, Miami, MO 65344; 660-886-7537.

Park Trails

Lake View Trail (🥾🥾, .75 mile). Park in the lot for Lake Wooldridge. This trail follows the west shoreline of the lake and offers great opportunities to see a variety of wildlife. The trail shares a trailhead with the Loess Hills Trail. The road to the lake (1.4 miles long) is closed to vehicles from November 1 to March 31, although it is always open for hiking.

Missouri River Overlook Trail (🥾, .30 mile). Park in the lot for Lake Wooldridge. The trail begins at the north end of the lot, follows a wooded ridge, and ends with a vista of the Missouri River bottoms.

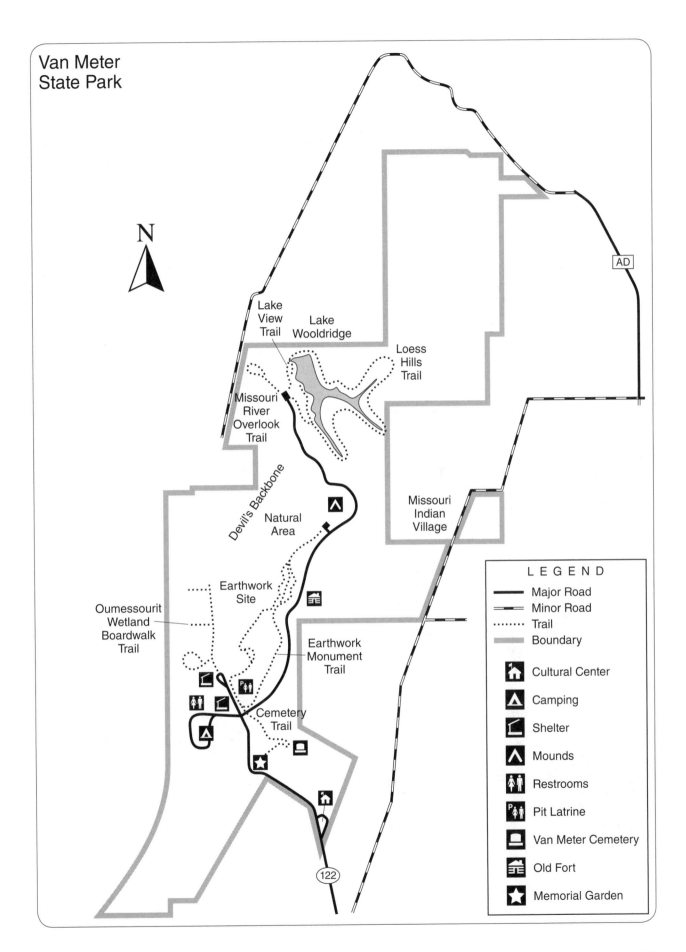

Van Meter State Park

N

Lake View Trail

Lake Wooldridge

Loess Hills Trail

Missouri River Overlook Trail

Devil's Backbone

Natural Area

Missouri Indian Village

Earthwork Site

Oumessourit Wetland Boardwalk Trail

Earthwork Monument Trail

Cemetery Trail

AD

122

LEGEND

━━━	Major Road
━╪━	Minor Road
⋯⋯	Trail
▬▬	Boundary
🏠	Cultural Center
🅰	Camping
◪	Shelter
⋀	Mounds
👫	Restrooms
🅿	Pit Latrine
▭	Van Meter Cemetery
⛩	Old Fort
★	Memorial Garden

Earthwork Monument Trail

 Distance Round-Trip: 2 miles
Estimated Hiking Time: 1.75 hours

After stepping into one of the 3,000-foot-long ditches dug by the early Missouri Indians, I imagined myself helping dig it, sweating, and doing my share with my bison scapula shovel. Then, I tried to imagine why.

Caution: Digging or otherwise disturbing archaeological sites is prohibited.

Trail Directions: If possible, stop in the visitor center before your hike; an understanding of the area's history will help you appreciate the prehistoric archaeological sites that you will see on this trail. From the visitor center, enter the park and turn right at the picnic shelter, toward Lake Wooldridge. Park in the lot for the Burial Mounds, located 1.3 mi. from the visitor center.

Before you begin, notice the earthen mounds to the northeast of the parking lot. The Native Americans of the Late Woodland period built these as burial monuments to honor people with high status. The mounds were probably constructed between 1,100 and 1,600 years ago by people who lived on the loess ridges all around you.

Begin the trail at the wooden gate **[1]**. Look around the gate for wahoo, a shrub with four-lobed seedpods that turn deep red in the fall. Native Americans found many uses for this shrub, including medicine for sores, lotion for eyes, and wood for arrows. You are now entering Van Meter Forest Natural Area, a 114-acre part of the park designated for its rugged ridges of loess (known as the Pinnacles) and a rich, diverse forest, with remnants of old-growth forest in deep ravines. Continue on a wide roadbed. The tall, spiked wildflower here with star-shaped, blue flowers is tall bellflower, a plant that prefers borders of woods and stream bottoms.

Soon, an expansive field opens before you on this ridgetop. Widely spaced trees and a manicured lawn may make you think that you've entered a picnic area, but there are no tables. You have entered an archaeological earthwork site **[2]** (.12 mi.) of encircling rows of parallel ditches and embankments. Originally thought to be built around 2,000 years ago by Hopewell people, excavations have revealed that it was built by the Missouri Indians, who lived on these ridgetops as recently as 300 to 600 years ago. Despite being known to scientists as early as 1872, reasons for this massive and complex structure are still unknown. Walk around the earthwork site to appreciate its scale, slowly making your way to its opposite end.

At the south end of the earthworks, take the trail to the far left of the bench that you find at .36 mi. **[3]**. This trail takes you down from the top of the Pinnacles and skirts some of its steep sides. Notice the dense and diverse understory that thrives in this rich soil. Thick grapevines climb from pawpaw groves to limbs of immense red oak, walnut, and hickory trees. Various wild nuts lie scattered on the trail as if someone spilled a bag of big marbles.

At the bottom of the hill, cross the small, wooden bridge at .80 mi. **[4]** that leads into the picnic area. Before you reach the paved road, turn left and cross the road that you drove on to reach the Burial Mounds **[5]** (.83 mi.). Look for a small asphalt sidewalk leading up a hill into the forest at .85 mi. **[6]** and take this trail. After climbing a steep loess hill, you reach the Van Meter family cemetery at the top at 1.06 mi. **[7]**. The Van Meters lived here for a century before they donated this land to the state for the park. Return to **[5]**, where you can take the road up the hill to the trailhead, or return to **[4]** to retrace your steps through the earthwork site.

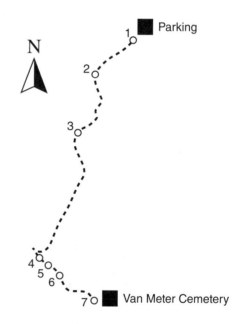

1. Start
2. Earthworks
3. Left turn
4. Wooden bridge
5. Road crossing
6. Small sidewalk
7. Van Meter Cemetery

Loess Hills Trail

Distance Round-Trip: 2 miles
Estimated Hiking Time: 1 hour

You'll see some grapevines as big around as trees, looming through the dark woods and hanging from the limbs of giant red oaks. If you listen carefully, you can hear the faint rustle of the wind in the upper canopy. Down here, there's little breeze to be had.

Caution: Unless you are here in winter, use some repellent for mosquitoes and biting flies.

Trail Directions: Park at the end of the main park road, at Lake Wooldridge, located 2 mi. north of the visitor center. This trail shares a trailhead with the Lake View Trail. Begin at the sign for the trail **[1]**, in the corner of the parking lot, and plunge into a junglelike forest. The windblown glacial dust (loess) that covers much of this area is fertile soil that produces immense trees and a dense understory.

At .09 mi. **[2]**, you cross a small, wooden bridge. Go straight at .16 mi. **[3]**, where the Lake View Trail continues on the left. As you cross another bridge, notice the ferns below, with long, gracefully arching fronds. Cat briars and grapevines connect the understory with the overstory, and large pawpaw leaves virtually eliminate the possibility that a ray of sunshine will reach the forest floor. Notice the puffy, yellow-green lanterns of American bladdernut as the trail swings to the left. At .30 mi. **[4]** is a small boardwalk over a marshy area. Notice the jewelweed below, a water-loving plant that produces orange, cone-shaped flowers. Later in the summer, when many plants get older and tougher, deer feed more heavily on jewelweed, which remains soft and juicy.

Go up some steps and enter a higher, more open forest. Notice the alligator-hide-like bark of the persimmon tree. At .68 mi. **[5]**, as the trail bends left, you cross two more small boardwalks over a slough area, which may hold some standing water. You climb higher again and emerge into the opening of an old field at .88 mi. **[6]**. Now you get to see the sun and feel the breeze again! Look for the iridescent blue-indigo bunting. Listen for the song of the field sparrow, which sounds like a dropping Ping-Pong ball, and the buzz of flying grasshopper wings as you hike on a wide, mowed path through this old pasture or hay field, now grown up in sumac, fescue, and blackberry briars. You reach a bench at 1.12 mi. **[7]**. As you continue, dragonflies zip figure eights over the trail, and black-eyed susans and purple ironweed brighten the way.

After you reenter the forest, some views of the lake open on your left. Duckweed covers the coves in the foreground, and the steep, wooded, loess hills frame the lake in the distance. Look for rough-leaved sun-

flowers and the star-shaped blue flowers of tall bellflower. At 1.75 mi. **[8]**, you walk out into the clearing of the lake dam. Hike over the dam. At 1.8 mi. **[9]**, you reach a signed intersection with the Lake View Trail; go straight here. Ignore the spur on the right at 1.92 mi. **[10]** and go straight to return to the trailhead.

1. Start
2. Wooden bridge
3. Go straight
4. Boardwalk
5. Two boardwalks
6. Old field
7. Bench
8. Dam
9. Go straight
10. Go straight

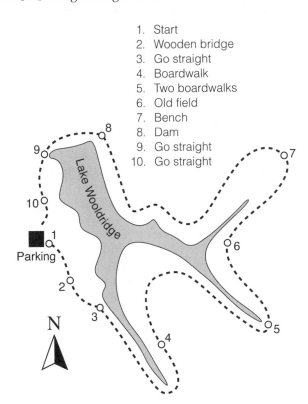

Oumessourit Wetland Boardwalk Trail

 Distance Round-Trip: 1 mile
Estimated Hiking Time: 45 minutes

Wetlands are extreme habitats. They are the richest, most diverse, and perhaps most important of all ecosystems. Ironically, they require both flood and fire to keep them alive.

Caution: Stay on the trail to avoid stinging nettle. The trail may be muddy in spots after a rainfall; check with park staff for conditions. Unless you are here during the winter, repellent for mosquitoes and biting flies is advised.

Trail Directions: Drive on the park road to the loop behind the small picnic shelter and park near the shelter house. The trail begins [1] next to the shelter, where there are interpretive signs at the trailhead. A brochure about the area may be available here. There are two forks to this trail—the Marsh Loop fork and the Spring-Bluff fork—each of which highlights different areas of the Oumessourit Natural Area, one of the best remaining examples of natural floodplain marshes and forests in the state. The Oumessourit Natural Area, one of over 170 state-designated natural areas, includes a wide array of native Missouri River floodplain ecosystems, including marsh, wet meadow, fen, bottomland, and upland forests.

Just past the interpretive signs, monstrous cottonwood and sycamore trees welcome you to the bottomland forest. Taking advantage of the moist and extremely fertile soil of the floodplain, bottomland trees can reach enormous proportions. Turn left at the intersection at .03 mi. [2] to begin the Marsh Loop. At a bench, turn right at the intersection at .15 mi. [3] to hike onto the boardwalk. Although the Missouri River is now 2 mi. away, it created the marsh in which you are now hiking. Until it was channelized, the Missouri meandered back and forth across its floodplain, creating multiple channels, oxbow lakes, sloughs, and marshes—a diversity of high-quality habitats. Unfortunately, only about 10 percent of Missouri River wetlands still remains. As you continue on the boardwalk, notice the variety of plants living in the marsh. Over 120 native plants live in the wetland, including rare species such as tufted loosestrife and star duckweed. The Missouri Indians used many resources from the marsh, including American lotus and arrowhead for food, cattails and rushes for lodge thatching, and mud for making clay pots. At .26 mi., you return to the bench, completing the loop.

Now return to [2] and turn left to begin the Spring-Bluff fork. After passing a bench, bear left at the intersection, ignoring the service road on your right at .45 mi. [4]. Notice the steep sides of the hill on your right. The trail passes between the marsh on your left and a ridge of loess (fine, wind-swept glacial soil) on your right. At .61 mi. [5], take the small boardwalk spur on your left to watch and listen for some of the many animals that live in the wetland. Some of the creatures, like frogs, have distinctive calls and can be heard from a great distance. Most others are quiet and are much more secretive, like the marsh pond snail, which lives in only two other places in Missouri, and the mosquitofish, the only Missouri fish that bears live young. Other marsh animals that the Missouri Indians used are otter, beaver, turtle, muskrat, fish, and swan. Return to the main trail and turn left.

At .71 mi. [6], you reach a bench, an interpretive sign, and a spring. Although small, the spring was a reliable, year-round source of water for the Van Meter family between the 1840s and 1930s. Before that, it was likely a source of water for the Missouri Indians. At .75 mi. [7], you reach another bench and another small boardwalk spur on your left into the marsh. After taking in some final views of the marsh, return to the main trail and turn right to return to the trailhead.

1. Start
2. Left turn
3. Right turn
4. Bear left
5. Boardwalk spur
6. Spring
7. Boardwalk spur

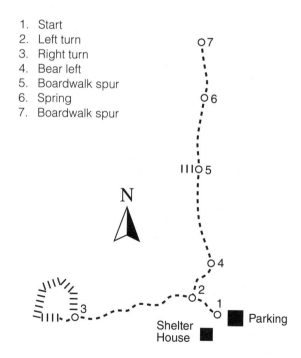

11. Pershing State Park

- Hike an educational, award-winning trail—an outdoor visitor center that you absorb as you go.
- Bring your binoculars to help you make out the red eye of the red-eyed vireo or the black bill of the black-billed cuckoo. Over 100 birds make their homes here.
- Hike in rare, natural wetland communities—bottomland forests, wet prairies, marshes, and swamps.
- Feel the spongy stalks of river bulrush, a marsh plant that gets its oxygen from its stalks instead of its roots.
- From an observation tower, feel the breeze on your face from across the largest natural wet prairie in northern Missouri—1 mile wide and 2 miles long.

Area Information

Growing up in the 1860s and 1870s in Laclede, Missouri, John J. Pershing found nuts and hunted in the wild countryside around his home, fishing and swimming in nearby Locust Creek. Later, he became the commanding general of the American Expeditionary Forces during World War I, eventually becoming the highest ranking military officer in American history.

In 1930 a ranch southwest of Laclede, still rich with its tall forests, open prairies, and wild streams, was chosen as a memorial park to the still-living hero. The state acquired initial park acreage in 1937 for Pershing State Park, which now totals 2,909 acres. Creators of the educational Wetland Boardwalk won a Renaissance Award from the Missouri Department of Natural Resources, which acknowledges outstanding works within Missouri state parks.

A major portion of the park is in the Locust Creek floodplain. Annual flooding and other natural processes of the meandering, unchannelized river here have formed a wealth of wetland habitats. Oxbow lakes, sloughs, and swamps form and re-form. Entire communities of plants inhabit wet prairies and marshes. The old-growth bottomland forest is one of the highest quality forests in the state and has been officially designated a state natural area. In the 1870s this area would have been wildland typical of north Missouri. Today, however, surrounded by human-made drainage ditches, channelized rivers, and seemingly endless miles of row crops, the park is a rare gem.

Directions: Pershing State Park is on Highway 130, 2 miles southwest of Laclede.

Hours Open: The site is open year-round.

Facilities: The park offers a campground, picnic areas, and four small lakes for swimming and fishing. Fishing is also available in Locust Creek.

Permits and Rules: Pets must always be leashed. Boats with electric motors are allowed on the lakes but must be carried on.

For Further Information: Pershing State Park, 29277 Highway 130, Laclede, MO 64651; 660-963-2299.

Park Trails

Oak Ridge Trail (🥾🥾🥾, .75 mile). This trail begins at the end of the campground loop, between campsite #14 and the restrooms. You pass a shrub swamp, Christmas ferns, and hilly, open woods before reaching the picnic shelter near the War Mothers Statue.

Canfield Savanna Trail (🥾🥾🥾, .75 mile). This trail begins across the road from the shower house in the campground and quickly transports you into a restored savanna, complete with native tallgrass prairie grasses and huge white oak trees with sprawling branches. You finish at the parking lot for the iron bridge and the Wetland Boardwalk Trail.

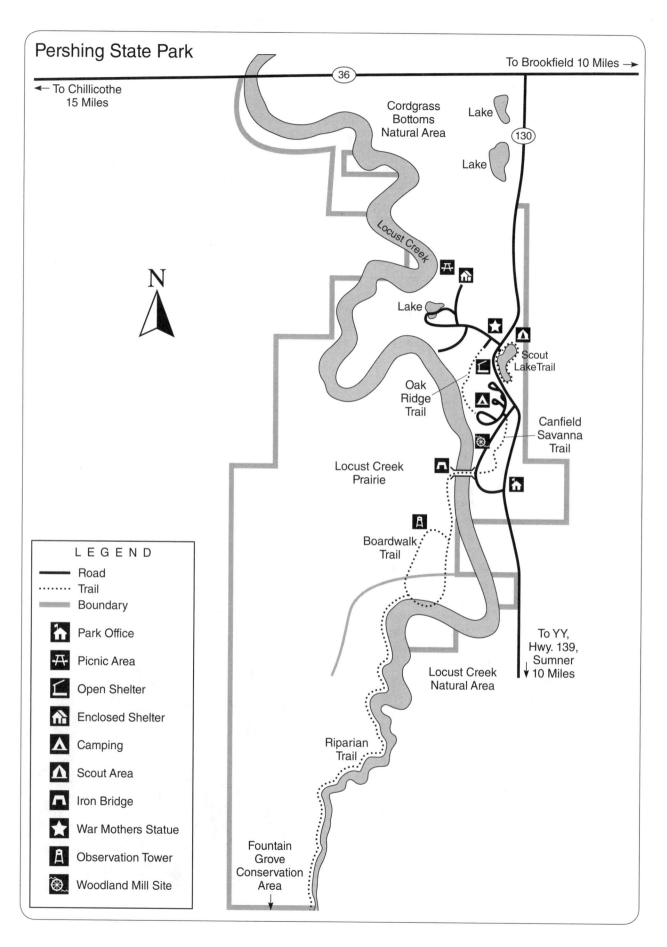

Pershing State Park

← To Chillicothe
15 Miles

36

To Brookfield 10 Miles →

130

Cordgrass
Bottoms
Natural Area

Lake

Lake

Locust Creek

N

Lake

Scout
Lake Trail

Oak
Ridge
Trail

Canfield
Savanna
Trail

Locust Creek
Prairie

Boardwalk
Trail

To YY,
Hwy. 139,
Sumner
10 Miles

Locust Creek
Natural Area

Riparian
Trail

Fountain
Grove
Conservation
Area

LEGEND

Road
Trail
Boundary
Park Office
Picnic Area
Open Shelter
Enclosed Shelter
Camping
Scout Area
Iron Bridge
War Mothers Statue
Observation Tower
Woodland Mill Site

Wetland Boardwalk Trail

 Distance Round-Trip: 1.5 miles
Estimated Hiking Time: 1 hour

The observation tower lets you view the largest remaining wet prairie in northern Missouri. Sedges make it a vibrant sea of green in spring, and 12-foot-high wildflowers splash it with yellow and gold by fall.

Caution: The trail is wheelchair accessible, but seasonal flooding sometimes leaves it underwater. Check with park staff for conditions. Unless you are here during winter, repellent for mosquitoes and biting flies is advised. Also, stay on the boardwalk to avoid abundant stinging nettle and poison ivy.

Trail Directions: Park near the interpretive signs in the parking lot for the boardwalk trail, across the main park road from the park office. The trail begins **[1]** at the iron bridge over Locust Creek. The portion of Locust Creek that runs through the park is one of the only sections of sizable streams in north Missouri that has not been channelized. Flowing and meandering along its natural course, the creek's periodic flooding is the single most important influence on the landscape of the park.

After crossing the bridge you find one of the many interpretive signs on the boardwalk that explain wetland communities, their formation, and the plants and animals that depend on them. The natural levee at .19 mi. **[2]** was formed by the creek's deposition of sand. The slightly higher elevation and well-drained sandy soil provide a drier habitat for plants than saturated soil does. The elevation drops slightly at .37 mi. **[3]**. Water stands on the ground for much of winter and spring here, leaving little oxygen in the soil. Specially adapted plants and trees in this bottomland forest include knotweed, pin oak, shellbark hickory, and swamp white oak.

A wooden bench at .41 mi. **[4]** makes a great place to stop and listen for the cooing of black-billed cuckoos or the buzzing, rising trill of the northern parula. Resident and migrating birds alike find an oasis in this towering forest. Go straight at the intersection at .44 mi. **[5]**. Another wetland community, a shrub swamp, is at .59 mi. **[6]**. Plants that live here, like duckweed and tickseed, have extraordinary adaptations to cope with the abundance of water and the scarcity of oxygen. You reach an overlook of Locust Creek at .84 mi. **[7]**.

At the entrance to the 1,040-acre wet prairie **[8]** (1 mi.) an interpretive sign explains that, paradoxically, the other major natural force that maintains these wetlands besides flooding is fire. The observation tower at 1.09 mi. **[9]** lets you experience the vastness of the prairie, home to wild iris, false dragonhead, and saw-toothed sunflower. Note the water-filled oxbow of Locust Creek transformed to a marsh **[10]** at 1.15 mi. Feel the spongy stalks of the river bulrush, specially adapted for gathering oxygen from the air. At 1.26 mi., you return to the intersection at **[5]**, where you turn left to return to the bridge.

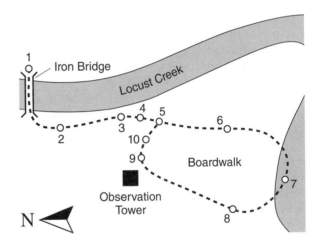

1. Start
2. Natural levee
3. Bottomland forest
4. Wooden bench
5. Go straight
6. Shrub swamp
7. Locust Creek overlook
8. Wet prairie
9. Observation tower
10. Marsh

Scout Lake Trail

🐾 **Distance Round-Trip:** .5 mile
🐾 **Estimated Hiking Time:** 15 minutes

Spend a quiet 15 minutes strolling around this picturesque little lake and watch the small natural dramas unfold. A katydid jumps into the lake from near your feet, and a bluegill inhales it with a slurp. A shagbark kerplunks a nut into the water from an overhanging limb, sending a nearby squirrel racing across dry leaves.

Caution: Stay on the trail to avoid damage to fragile mosses and lichens.

Trail Directions: Park in the lot for the small lake on the left, 1.3 mi. into the park off Highway 36. Begin at the parking lot [1] and follow the trail counter-clockwise around the lake. As you begin the section between the lake and the park road, scan the water for wood ducks or teal huddled in small coves. Look for green herons perched motionless on tree limbs or exposed tree roots near the water, and watch for red-eared sliders and other aquatic turtles basking on logs. Near the parking lot, you can find evidence of beaver teeth on trees near the water.

In spring or summer, you may be surprised by frogs springing into the water beside you, later exposing bulging eyes between floating leaves of aquatic plants. At .12 mi. [2], you cross a wooden bridge over the end of the lake. Look in the water for young largemouth bass chasing schools of small bluegill in the shallow water. Watch for zipping dragonflies, hovering nearby and landing on the bridge railing.

Just after crossing another wooden bridge, you enter a forest of mixed oak and hickory. Mounds of reindeer lichen grow between rounded tufts of moss that bubble up from the forest floor like pincushions at .17 mi. [3]. Reindeer lichen, like all lichens, is a composite organism formed from fungi and algae, although the lichen formed does not resemble either of the components. The fungus maintains a moist habitat for the algae, which produces food by photosynthesis that both organisms use. This mutually advantageous relationship is known as symbiosis. On rainy and humid days, reindeer lichen is soft and spongy. On sunny, dry days, it is brittle and crunchy.

Cross another wooden bridge at .18 mi. [4] and notice all the beaver stumps nearby. Look for fragrant sumac and leadplant near the trail—two plants that prefer dry, upland habitats. If you are here in early spring, look for wine red, fernlike leaves of lousewort or wood betony. This plant produces stalks of yellow blossoms in April and May. At .24 mi. [5], you cross another wooden bridge over a drainage stream to the lake. Notice the Christmas ferns lining the drainage. Named because they are green at Christmas, Christmas ferns are actually green all year long. Turn left at the intersection with a gravel road at .27 mi. [6] and turn left again at the elevated wooden bridge at .30 mi. [7].

Just after crossing yet another wooden bridge, ignore the two spurs on your right that lead to a picnic area at .39 mi. [8] and go straight at both of them. You wind through the woods between the lake and park road before returning to the parking lot and finishing your lake hike.

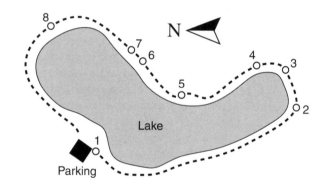

1. Start
2. Wooden bridge
3. Reindeer lichen
4. Beaver stumps
5. Wooden bridge
6. Left turn
7. Left turn
8. Go straight

North

Riparian Trail

Distance Round-Trip: 12.8 miles
Estimated Hiking Time: 6 hours

Spend some time next to Locust Creek and celebrate its meanders. As it wanders in its floodplain, it creates oxbow lakes, sloughs, natural levees, shrub swamps, marshes, and wet prairies, not to mention the grand and massive trees of its rich, bottomland forests.

Caution: Seasonal flooding may leave parts of the trail underwater or extremely mucky. Check with park staff for conditions. Also, unless you are here during winter, repellent for mosquitoes and biting flies is advised.

Trail Directions: You may cut your hiking distance in half by arranging for a pickup where this linear trail ends—in the parking lot in the northeast corner of Fountain Grove Conservation Area. The Riparian Trail uses the Wetland Boardwalk Trail for the first .7 mi. Park in the lot for the Wetland Boardwalk Trail. Begin **[1]** at the iron bridge over Locust Creek. Turn left at the end of the iron bridge and go straight at the intersection at .29 mi. **[2]**. The Riparian Trail begins at a bend in Locust Creek at .66 mi. **[3]**.

Several views of Locust Creek appear, including one at 1.4 mi. **[4]**. Along with massive sycamore and cottonwood trees along the trail, look for ash trees, which can be identified by uniform bark, lack of lower limbs, opposite leaves, and gentle curves in the trunk. As you approach the 2 mi. marker **[5]**, you hike through some lower-lying land, which may be puddled or mucky. The trail may be wet for about .5 mi. One of the most common plants along the trail here is stinging nettle, which is about thigh high, has broad leaves with serrated edges and pointed tips, and often forms dense stands next to streams. Look for hairlike spines along the stem and under the leaves, which break off when you rub against them. If you walk through stinging nettle while wearing shorts, you'll quickly get the sensation that your skin is on fire. Despite its pain-inflicting qualities, nettle has been used as a soup, pot herb, tea, fiber, and an herbal medicine for a long list of ailments.

At 3.9 mi. **[6]**, turn right at the intersection with a wide path. You are hiking along the boundary between Department of Natural Resources and Department of Conservation properties. Just after a sharp bend in the river on your left, turn left into the woods at 4 mi. **[7]**. You are now entering Fountain Grove Conservation Area. At 4.53 mi. **[8]**, you hike next to an oxbow lake. Oxbow lakes are old river channels, abandoned when the river changed course. Though they may not be con-

nected with the river any longer, they often still hold water. Approach quietly and watch for wood ducks or other waterfowl. After crossing a wooden bridge, turn left at the intersection at 4.77 mi. **[9]**. At 5 mi. **[10]**, you cross a footbridge over Hickory Branch. Funded by the Missouri Conservation Heritage Foundation, this bridge allows trail connection between two important wetland areas. Turn right on top of the levee at 5.2 mi. **[11]** and go straight at all intersections. The expanse of Fountain Grove soon opens on your left. Originally including 3,433 acres in the 1940s, Fountain Grove was the first wetland area developed by the Department of Conservation. Now containing over 7,000 acres, the area is an important stop for a variety of wildlife and is managed to provide diverse wetland habitats, including marshes, bottomland forests, lakes, and sloughs. Stay on the levee until the trail makes a turn to the left at 6 mi. **[12]**. Continue on the levee until you reach the parking lot at 6.4 mi. **[13]**.

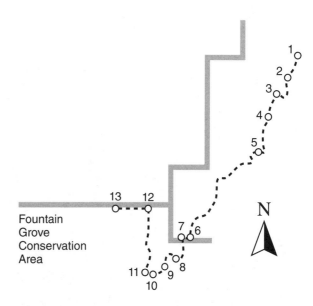

1. Start
2. Go straight
3. Riparian Trail begins
4. Locust Creek
5. 2 mi. marker
6. Right turn
7. Left turn
8. Oxbow lake
9. Left turn
10. Footbridge
11. Right turn
12. Left turn
13. Parking lot

- Meet the Kentucky coffee tree—the only tree in Missouri whose compound leaves grow up to 3 feet long.
- How can you tell a possum track from a raccoon's? Brush up on your wildlife tracks and then test your skills on the River Forks Trail.
- See the ruins of the home built by Dr. William Preston Thompson in 1833.
- Look around for the occasional ostrich in the forest (ostrich fern, that is).

Area Information

With its winding and shaded entrance road, wooded hillsides, and picturesque lake, Crowder State Park poses a classic park landscape and serves as a scenic memorial to Major General Enoch H. Crowder, the Missourian who founded the nation's Selective Service System, better known as the military draft.

Crowder State Park, with its hilly forests, steep-walled valleys, and well-shaded sandstone ledges, is a natural attraction in northern Missouri, a region that has been converted mainly to agricultural uses. The rugged drainages of the adjoining Thompson River probably helped protect the thick forests from the saw and the plow.

Today, under the protection and management of the state park system, mature and sprawling white oak, red oak, and sugar maple thrive in the glacial till and loess soil of the park. Giant cottonwoods tower in the bottomland forests along the Thompson River, and yellow lady slipper orchids and ferns adorn moist, rocky ledges.

Directions: From Trenton go 4 miles west on Highway 6. Take Highway 146 west for 1 mile. Turn right on Highway 128 into the park.

Hours Open: The park is open daily from sunrise to 10:00 p.m.

Facilities: All types of campsites are available at Crowder, including primitive camping for scout groups and a large group camp with enclosed buildings. Crowder Lake offers fishing, boating, swimming, a sandy beach, and a nearby bathhouse. The park contains numerous picnic areas, an enclosed shelter, grills, playground equipment, and a paved tennis court.

Permits and Rules: No gas-powered motors are allowed on Crowder Lake, but electric motors are permitted. Pets must always be leashed. Horses are allowed only on the Thompson River Trail. Bicycles are allowed on all trails except the Redbud Trail. Trails are closed to bikers and equestrians when conditions are wet. To check the daily trail status, call the dedicated hotline: 660-359-0900. All trails are always open for hiking.

For Further Information: Crowder State Park, 76 Highway 128, Trenton, MO 64683; 660-359-6473.

Park Trails

Redbud Trail (👣👣👣, 2 miles). Park in the special-use area across the road from the park office. The trail has several stream crossings and limestone shelves on hillsides with wild ginger and maidenhair ferns. Exit the trail at the tennis court and walk uphill (right) toward the trailhead.

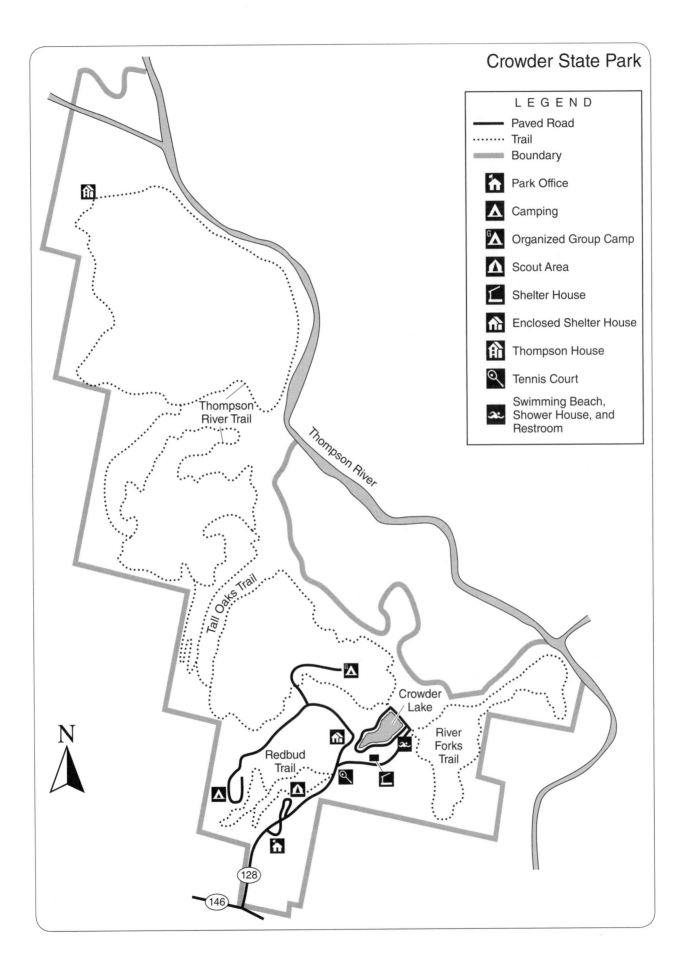

Crowder State Park

LEGEND

———	Paved Road
·········	Trail
▬▬▬	Boundary
🏠	Park Office
⛺	Camping
⛺ᴳ	Organized Group Camp
⛺	Scout Area
⌐	Shelter House
🏠	Enclosed Shelter House
🏠	Thompson House
🔍	Tennis Court
🏊	Swimming Beach, Shower House, and Restroom

Thompson River Trail

Thompson River

Tall Oaks Trail

Crowder Lake

River Forks Trail

Redbud Trail

N

128

146

River Forks Trail

 Distance Round-Trip: 2.5 miles
Estimated Hiking Time: 1.25 hours

Human fishers know that river confluences are good places to fish. Animal anglers know it, too. At the two-river junction on this trail I saw an osprey plunge completely underwater, feet first. Soon it emerged and pulled itself (and its finny prey) back into the air with long, powerful wing strokes. A belted kingfisher chattered by just then, as if in congratulations.

Caution: The first mile of this trail will be muddy after wet weather.

Trail Directions: Park at the swimming beach parking lot at the northeast corner of Crowder Lake and find the trailhead [1] near the northeast corner of the lot. The trail starts as a wide dirt path lined with tall black walnut, sugar maple, basswood, and sycamore trees, spreading a beautiful canopy over the trail. Look for animal tracks on the trail; no matter what time of the year you are here, this part of the trail will probably be well trod by white-tailed deer. North Missouri is known for its large numbers of deer, and this trail, which parallels crop field and forest edge, is a likely wildlife highway.

Look on your left at .51 mi. just a few feet off the trail for several trees with flaky, papery bark. These are Kentucky coffee trees [2]. Early settlers ground the seeds of this tree to make a passable (though not very popular) substitute for coffee. With compound leaves up to 3 feet long, the Kentucky coffee tree produces the largest leaf of all Missouri trees.

Enjoy the view at .86 mi. at the junction of the Thompson River with the Weldon Fork [3]. This is a likely spot to see wood ducks taking to the air, crying, "Weet! Weet! Weet!" Also look for statuesque shorebirds in the shallows. Nearby dead trees provide favorite perches for belted kingfishers and osprey. If the water is low, the muddy river bed would be another good place to look for animal tracks. Deer,

heron, raccoon, coyote, and mink are likely. Note the multitude of young trees on the river banks—willows, cottonwoods, and sycamores. These trees are natural erosion controllers. Turn right, uphill, to continue the trail.

Turn right at the switchback at .98 mi. [4] and find a shagbark hickory [5] at 1.36 mi. At 1.53 mi. [6], turn right and begin to go downhill. At 1.73 mi. [7], you cross an intermittent stream. Turn right at the intersection at 1.97 mi. [8] to find some picnic tables from an old camp. Continue on the right to find your way back to the trailhead.

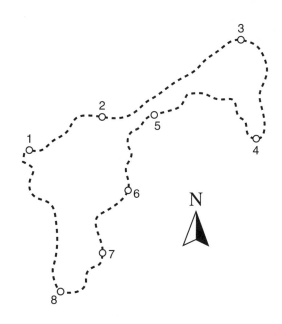

1. Start
2. Kentucky coffee trees
3. River junction
4. Right turn
5. Shagbark hickory
6. Right turn
7. Stream
8. Right turn

Tall Oaks Trail

 Distance Round-Trip: 3.6 miles
Estimated Hiking Time: 2 hours

On this trail the landscape will change channels on you and your feet. You will hike next to a lake, under tall oaks, through a hay field, into a creek bottom, and back to the lake. Enjoy the diversity!

Caution: The trail will be muddy in the stream bottom after a rain and stinging nettles encroach the trail there; long pants are in order. Intermittent streams crossing the trail may not be dry. Watch for traffic at park road crossings.

Trail Directions: Park in the swimming beach parking lot. Walk across the dam of Crowder Lake and find the trailhead **[1]** at the northwest corner of the lake. Begin the trail to the left of the trail sign. Stop for a moment and listen for the sound of beaver teeth in wood—at least one beaver in the area has a habit of dropping trees right across the trail! You will find some beaver stumps at .08 mi. **[2]**.

Cross a couple of intermittent streams and go straight when a road crosses the trail at .22 mi. **[3]**. Go straight also at the spur on the left at .50 mi. **[4]**. A remarkable example of a bent tree is on your right at .53 mi. **[5]**. Note how the trunk grows horizontally while all the limbs grow straight up. When it was a sapling, this tree was probably bent over when a larger tree (now rotted away) fell on it and trapped it. The bent tree survived in its sideways condition and still grows that way today, a testimony to its resilience.

Go straight at the road crossing at .73 mi. **[6]**. The forest soon has a different look and feel. Walk under towering oaks with broad, creeping limbs. See the twisted bark of old trees, some with lightning scars, and notice the trunk cavities at their bases, filled with black, tannic water. Soon you find yourself on a shelf, with a rocky stream below you on your left and a rocky slope ascending on your right. At 1.38 mi. **[7]**, you come across a rugged limestone wall in the forest. Note how the rocks fracture into flat, stepping-stone shapes. Early settlers used these natural foundation stones for their buildings.

At 1.58 mi. **[8]**, you emerge into a large hay field—a good place to look for deer beds and soaring hawks. Follow the mown path through the field and reenter the forest at 1.74 mi. **[9]**. Ignore the intersecting paths near the power line and continue straight. Soon you cross a log bridge at 1.99 mi. **[10]** and enter a stream bottom. Check out the monstrous cottonwood tree at

2.21 mi. **[11]** with grooves in the bark so deep that you can lay your finger inside. Cross a gravel road at 2.92 mi. **[12]** and continue straight. Finally, you climb out of the creek bottom, the trail opens up again, and you find yourself on another shelf at 3.3 mi. **[13]**, skirting a hill on your right. Find a gigantic black maple at 3.36 mi. **[14]**, which will probably require two people's arms to encircle it.

Turn right at the intersection at 3.37 mi. **[15]** and start counting your steps. At about 25 paces, take the small trail on the left **[16]** (3.39 mi.). (If you come out at the brown buildings of the group camp you missed this last turn.) Go straight at an intersection at 3.47 mi. **[17]** and soon you will be back at the trailhead.

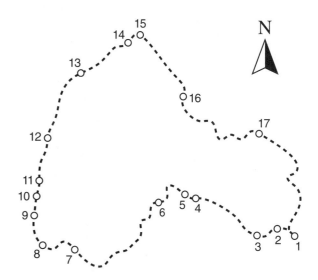

1. Start
2. Beaver stumps
3. Go straight
4. Go straight
5. Bent tree
6. Go straight
7. Limestone wall
8. Hay field
9. Reenter forest
10. Log bridge
11. Cottonwood
12. Road crossing
13. Shelf
14. Black maple
15. Right turn
16. Left turn
17. Go straight

Thompson River Trail– North and South Loops

 Distance Round-Trip: 9.6 miles
Estimated Hiking Time: 4.5 hours

Hike both of these loops to experience the contrasting and delicious flavors. On the North Loop are the intriguing antebellum cemetery and home, monstrous cottonwood trees, and the Thompson River. On the South Loop, you'll think that you're in the Ozarks—steep ravines, exposed rocks, and views of distant, wooded ridges.

Caution: In the floodplain, stay on the trail to avoid stinging nettles.

Trail Directions: Although this trail can be accessed by connector links from the Tall Oaks Trail, directions here begin from the equestrian trailhead on the northwest end of the park. To reach the equestrian trailhead, go west from the park entrance 1.3 mi. on Highway 146. Turn right (north) on NW 52nd Avenue and go 2 mi. Turn right (east) on Dove Lane, which dead-ends in the parking lot for the trailhead. Start the trail at the end of the lot and go straight at the first intersection [1] to start the North Loop going clockwise. You begin in a wide, flat field where native vegetation of tallgrass prairie grasses and wildflowers is being restored. Turn left at the trail marker at .28 mi. [2] and follow red marks on the North Loop. At .43 mi. [3], you find the Thompson family cemetery, marked by a wooden fence. Dr. William Preston Thompson, for whom the nearby river is named, was one of Grundy County's first white settlers. Dr. Thompson, who died in 1848, is buried here, along with several family members. Some grave markers are carved monuments, whereas others are natural stones placed on end. From here, you enter the woods and hike along a ridgetop, populated by hickory, oak, redbud, and mulberry. Just after you enter an old field, the trail swings to the right at .89 mi. [4]. At 1.02 mi. [5], take the spur to the left to view the grand, two-story brick Thompson House at 1.12 mi. [6]. Complete with an ancient maple tree and what looks like a root cellar in the yard, the house was built in 1833. Supposedly, clay for the bricks was taken from a nearby creek and fired on the site. It is said that Dr. Thompson used part of the lower level of the house for his practice. Return to [5] and turn left to continue the trail.

Notice how flat the terrain becomes as you enter the floodplain of the Thompson River. Look ahead to see monstrous cottonwood trees. Characteristically, their leaves shimmer in the slightest breeze because of their semiflattened stems. At 1.68 mi. [7], you get to greet these giants up close and get your first view of the river. The sandy trail parallels the river for a while as you hike under hackberry, walnut, basswood, and silver maple trees. Note the giant cottonwood next to

the trail at 2.15 mi. [8] with fissures in its bark so deep that you can place your fingers inside. Watch out for that hairy vine climbing the trunk—it's poison ivy.

The north-facing hillsides on your right are a favored habitat for sugar maple trees. If you're here in fall, these hills will be awash in brilliant oranges, reds, and yellows. As the trail turns away from the river, you enter an old field with young willow, sycamore, and river birch trees. Head for the hills. The trail soon enters the woods among hickory and maple trees. Turn left at the intersection at 3.25 mi. [9]. Turn left at the intersection with the white connector at 3.44 mi. [10]. Follow white blazes now as the trail crosses an intermittent stream several times before taking you uphill. Turn left at the intersection at 4.34 mi. [11] to begin the South Loop, where you follow green blazes. The trail drops abruptly on your left side, giving you fine views of open woods and distant ridges. Rich glacial soils produce stately stands of bur oak, basswood, maple, and white and red oak. Turn right at 6.33 mi. [12], ignoring the intersecting trail. Go straight at the intersection with an old road at 6.47 mi. [13]. Turn right at the intersection with the Northwest Passage connector at 6.75 mi. [14]. Enjoy the view as you look down the scenic ravine at 7.28 mi. [15]. Turn right at the intersection with the Steep Creek connector at 7.55 mi. [16]. Emerge from the woods into the bright sunlight of an old field. When you reenter the woods, turn left at [11] to take the white connector back to the North Loop. Turn left again at [10]. You climb steadily through the woods now before you return to the prairie under restoration and the parking lot.

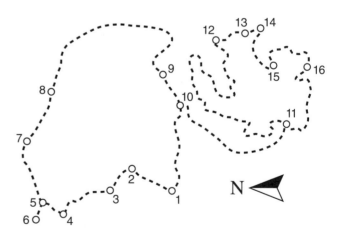

1. Start
2. Left turn
3. Thompson cemetery
4. Right turn
5. Spur to Thompson House
6. Thompson House
7. Thompson River
8. Giant cottonwood
9. Left turn
10. Left turn
11. Left turn
12. Right turn
13. Go straight
14. Right turn
15. Scenic ravine
16. Right turn

North

- Enjoy the solitude and beauty of a forested oasis in the midst of rolling farmland.
- Hike next to some limestone shelves in Deer Creek, a site believed to be a Mormon trail crossing of the early 19th century.
- Discover the beauty and utility of the Osage orange tree.
- Stand in a thicket of American bladdernut.

Area Information

While hiking one of the forest trails at Wallace State Park, you can readily imagine that you are in the Ozarks, where rugged and rocky terrain is the norm and trails intersect dozens of small, rocky streams. But you are in the glaciated plains of northwest Missouri, where fertile farmlands dominate the landscape. And you are only an hour's drive from the heart of Kansas City.

Wallace was only the second state park, after Mark Twain, to be acquired north of the Missouri River, where land was considerably more expensive than it was in the Ozarks. Bought from the Wallace family in 1932, the park became one of the first recreational areas in northwest Missouri. The area is rich in the history of the Mormons, who flooded by the thousands into the surrounding counties after Joseph Smith arrived in March 1838 and proclaimed Far West, only 4 miles east of the Wallace farm, their new gathering place. Far West quickly became second in population among western Missouri cities, until non-Mormon settlers drove the Saints to Nauvoo, Illinois, and later to the Great Salt Lake in Utah.

Today, Wallace State Park preserves about 500 acres of forested hills, including a mile of the valley of Deer Creek. The hillsides are covered with white, black, and red oaks, as well as hickory, black walnut, and redbud trees. A turkey vulture roost and nest site are located just south of Lake Allaman. Common springtime plants include trout lilies, mayapples, touch-me-nots, and Dutchman's-breeches.

Directions: Travel 5.6 miles south of Cameron on Interstate 35. Turn left on Highway 69 south and go .5 mile. Turn left on Highway 121 and go 1.2 miles to the park entrance.

Hours Open: The park gates are open between 7:00 a.m. and 10:00 p.m. year-round. Trails and picnic areas close at sunset.

Facilities: The park offers four campgrounds, including sites with and without electricity and sites for organized travel camping groups. Lake Allaman offers fishing, boating for carry-on boats only, and a sandy beach for swimming. Shady picnic areas abound.

Permits and Rules: Pets must always be leashed. Electric motors only are allowed for boats, and horses are prohibited on all trails.

For Further Information: Wallace State Park, 10621 NE Highway 121, Cameron, MO 64429; 816-632-3745.

Other Areas of Interest

Trice-Dedman Memorial Woods, a 60-acre remnant old-growth oak woodland, is one of the best examples of presettlement forest in northwest Missouri. A 1-mile hiking trail leads the visitor through an impressive stand of white oaks, many of which are 175 years old. The preserve is owned by the Nature Conservancy and managed by the Missouri Department of Natural Resources. For more information, call Wallace State Park at 816-632-3745 or the Nature Conservancy at 314-968-1105.

Watkins Mill State Park provides a scenic area for recreation, including a 4-mile paved biking and hiking path around Watkins Mill Lake. **Watkins Woolen Mill State Historic Site**, a national historic landmark, is the only 19th-century American woolen mill with its original machinery still intact. For more information, call 816-296-3357 or 816-580-3387.

Park Trails

Rocky Ford Trail (👣👣, .75 mile). Hike next to Deer Creek and see large limestone shelves in the streambed that serve as a crossing, or ford. The shelves at .28 miles are thought to be a Mormon trail crossing from the early 19th century.

Skunk Hollow Trail (👣👣, .5 mile). This pleasant, shady trail takes you by some large shagbark hickories and an intermittent stream with a small waterfall (when wet). Park at the entrance to the travel campground and walk to the trailhead near campsite #80.

Wallace State Park

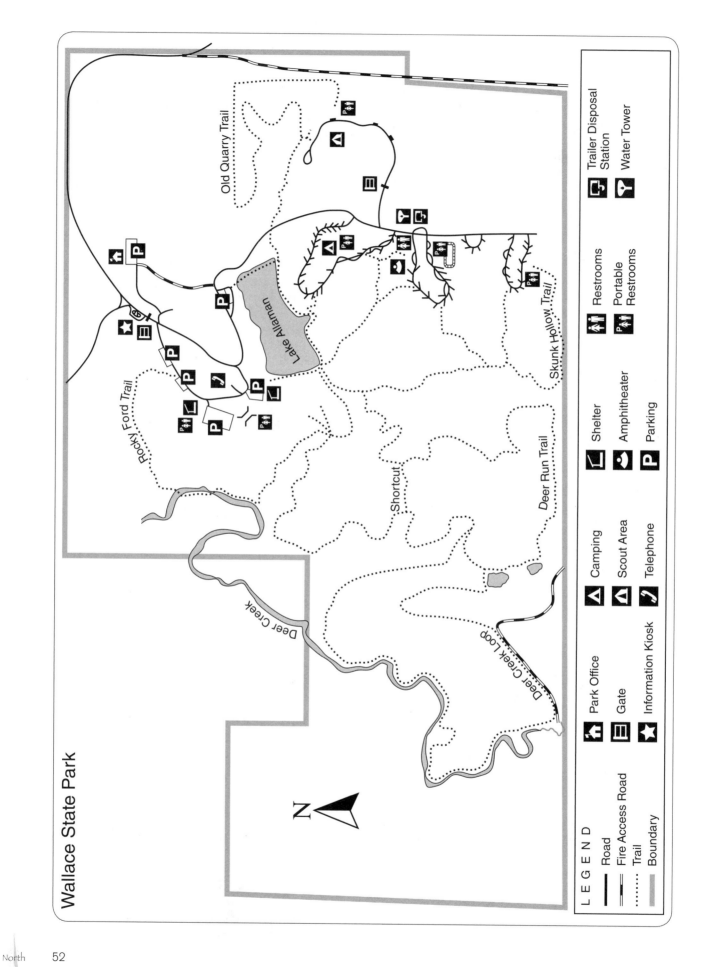

LEGEND

—	Road
⊢	Fire Access Road
⋯	Trail
▬	Boundary

- Park Office
- Gate
- Information Kiosk
- Camping
- Scout Area
- Telephone
- Shelter
- Amphitheater
- Parking
- Restrooms
- Portable Restrooms
- Trailer Disposal Station
- Water Tower

Old Quarry Trail
Rocky Ford Trail
Lake Allaman
Shortcut
Deer Creek
Deer Run Trail
Skunk Hollow Trail
Deer Creek Loop

N

Deer Run Trail

Distance Round-Trip: 3.5 miles
Estimated Hiking Time: 1.5 hours

The pawpaw is Missouri's only tropical tree. When you walk under a grove of them, you can easily imagine that you are somewhere where palm trees grow, too. The handsome leaves—oval, pointed at the tip, and up to 12 inches long—fan out from stems like fingers from hands (just as many palms do).

Caution: Several streams may be difficult to cross after heavy rains.

Trail Directions: Park at the picnic shelter at the northwest corner of Lake Allaman and walk across the dam. The trailhead is at the southwest corner of the lake. Two opportunities for shortcuts on this trail provide length options of 1, 2, or 3.5 mi. Deer footprint signs guide you around the 2 mi. route.

Begin at the trailhead **[1]** and turn right at the first intersection at .04 mi. **[2]**. Soon you come to an intermittent stream **[3]** (.08 mi.). You are likely to see a patch of jewelweed by the stream if you are here during spring or early summer. If you are here in late summer, however, don't be surprised to see only bare stalks—jewelweed is one of the white-tailed deer's favorite late-summer foods.

Take a few steps and identify a stately bur oak on your left **[4]** (.10 mi.). This one is particularly easy to identify because it has a label on it. When bur oaks aren't labeled, you can identify them by their characteristic acorn, which is broad, has a scaly cap, and has a hairy fringe around the outside of the cap. The bur oak prefers bottomland soils and produces the largest acorn in Missouri. Look up as you walk under a pawpaw grove at .18 mi. **[5]** to experience the delightful illusion of walking under so many palm trees.

Find a wooden bench at .21 mi. **[6]** and decide whether to take the shortcut option at .23 mi. **[7]**. Go straight to continue the trail and find another bench at .63 mi. **[8]**. You come upon two ponds on the left at .90 and .95 mi. **[9]**. The elevated nest boxes in the second pond are for wood ducks, undoubtedly one of the most brilliantly colored birds in North America. Once nearly extirpated from Missouri, the wood duck is now one of the state's most common waterfowl.

Just after you pass the second pond you can turn right at the intersection **[10]** (.96 mi.) to return to the trailhead. Turn left here to continue the trail and begin the Deer Creek Loop. At the intersection at 1.37 mi. **[11]**, turn right and soon you will be hiking next to Deer Creek. Note the large black locust tree on your right at 1.75 mi. **[12]**. The black locust has only small spines on its twigs, whereas the similar honey locust has clusters of long spines on its bark. Because black locust wood is extremely hard and durable, colonists and settlers used it for fence posts and corner posts for buildings.

Just after you cross a small, wooden bridge at 2.23 mi. **[13]**, a thicket of American bladdernut grows on both sides of the trail. This shrub has compound leaves with three leaflets and curious, three-lobed hanging lanterns, encapsulating shiny seeds. Even after the leaves fall, the capsules hang on until midwinter. Note the patch of maidenhair ferns on your right and turn left at the intersection at 2.51 mi. **[14]**. Meet the shortcut intersection at 2.72 mi. **[15]** and go straight. Find a bench at 3.01 mi. **[16]** and ignore the spur to the creek. At the five-way intersection at 3.19 mi. **[17]**, take the extreme right trail. Turn left at the intersection at 3.30 mi. **[18]** to return to the trailhead.

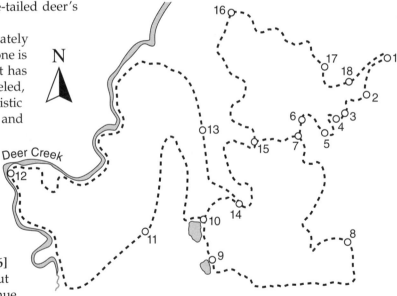

1. Start	10. Left turn
2. Right turn	11. Right turn
3. Stream	12. Black locust
4. Bur oak	13. Wooden bridge
5. Pawpaw grove	14. Left turn
6. Bench	15. Go straight
7. Go straight	16. Bench
8. Bench	17. Right turn
9. Two ponds	18. Left turn

Old Quarry Trail

 Distance Round-Trip: 1.25 miles
Estimated Hiking Time: 45 minutes

In October I found dozens of hedge apples lying on the ground near the trailhead. I watched a big fox squirrel tear into one, rolling it around and ripping it to shreds. Proportionately, this would be like a person eating something the size of, say, a kitchen stove.

Caution: Don't stand under an Osage orange tree on a windy day in October. Osage oranges can be bigger than Texas grapefruit, and much harder.

Trail Directions: Park outside the gate at the scout area and walk down the gravel road a quarter of a mile to find the trailhead on the right. It's OK to hike this trail even if the scout area is being used. As you begin, notice all the Osage orange trees in the scout area and across the road from the trailhead. Archery bows made from the wood of these trees were highly prized by the Osage and other Native Americans and were traded in distant regions where the Osage orange doesn't grow. Early settlers fenced the plains and prairies with rows of these spiny trees before the introduction of barbed wire. They also extracted a yellow dye for clothing from the root bark. The tree is still used today for archery bows and fence posts. The fruits, heavy yellow-green balls, are eaten by wildlife as well as livestock, giving rise to two other common names—hedge apple and horse apple.

Begin the trail at the trailhead **[1]** and turn right at the first intersection at .02 mi. **[2]**. At .12 mi. **[3]**, the dangerous-looking tree on your left with long, clustered spines on its bark is the honey locust, so named for the sweet, edible pulp found in the seedpods around the seeds.

Come to the shortcut at .15 mi. **[4]** and turn left to continue the trail. If you count about 125 paces from this intersection, you'll find the trail's namesake, an old quarry at .22 mi. **[5]** on the left. Long ago on this small rock outcrop a local settler might have pried out enough limestone rocks to make a small building foundation or fruit cellar entrance. You won't find any titanic bulldozers or earth movers at this quarry. In fact, you may have to look hard to see the quarry at all.

Note the big white oak tree at .24 mi. **[6]**. Both Native Americans and wildlife preferred white oak acorns because they ripen in a single season and have a mild flavor. The acorns of the red oaks, on the other hand, are bitter and require two years to mature. You can identify the white oak in winter by noticing that the bark on the upper limbs is usually flakier than the bark on the trunk.

At .34 mi. **[7]**, the trail takes you to the edge of a hay field, a good place for deer to graze and sleep and for turkeys to come out of the woods to find grasshoppers and other insects. Turn right to follow the trail along the edge of the forest.

Turn right at .51 mi. **[8]** to reenter the forest. Pass the shortcut at .53 mi. **[9]** and go straight. Cross a small wooden bridge at .60 mi. **[10]** and finish the trail at the scout area at .66 mi. **[11]**. From here, take the gravel road to the right to return to the trailhead (.72 mi.) or turn left to return to your car. Although the trail is only .75 mi. long, include the .25 mi. trip each way from your car to make the trail 1.25 mi. long, round-trip.

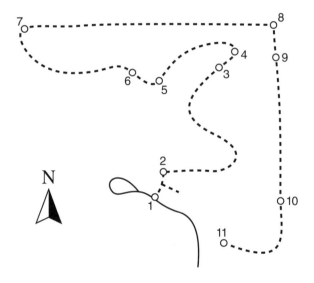

1. Start
2. Right turn
3. Honey locust
4. Left turn
5. Old quarry
6. White oak
7. Right turn
8. Right turn
9. Go straight
10. Wooden bridge
11. Scout area

14. Weston Bend State Park

- View the Missouri River and the Kansas plains and hike on a blufftop trail at the same time.
- Meet loess (pronounced "luss").
- Hike down to the state's second largest river, the Missouri, and meet the Big Muddy at its own level.
- Bring your camera and enjoy expansive views of the Missouri River and some of the state's best fall colors as well.

Area Information

In the late 1830s, the town of Weston, Missouri, sprung up and grew rapidly. Settlers quickly discovered that the soil of the surrounding river hills was extremely fertile. This fine-grained soil, called loess, was ground up by retreating glaciers and deposited by the wind. The two main plantation crops of the antebellum upper South were tobacco and hemp, and both crops flourished in Weston's windblown, silty soil.

Located at a natural harbor on the great bend of the Missouri River now known as Weston Bend, Weston became a major river port. Trade was established with Fort Leavenworth, just across the river, and Weston became a major outfitting station for settlers heading west. Steamboat traffic added to the commercial boom. Tremendous quantities of tobacco and hemp were exported, and by 1858, Weston was recognized as the largest hemp port in the world.

The hemp industry died in the late 1800s, but the tobacco economy still flourishes today. Four tobacco-drying barns are still standing in Weston Bend State Park. One of them has been converted to a picnic shelter, and another is used to teach visitors about tobacco production and the state's tobacco heritage.

Directions: The park is on the Missouri River, just northwest of Kansas City and 3.1 miles south of Weston on Highway 45.

Hours Open: The park is open year-round from sunrise to sunset. The park office is open from 8:00 a.m. to 4:30 p.m. year-round.

Facilities: The park features views of the Missouri River from an overlook that is accessible to persons with disabilities. The park offers a campground, picnic tables, shelter houses, and playground equipment. Fishing is available in the Missouri River.

Permits and Rules: Bicycles are restricted to paved areas. Horses, roller skates, and skateboards are prohibited in all areas. Pets must always be leashed.

For Further Information: Weston Bend State Park, 16600 Highway 45 North, Weston, MO 64096; 816-640-5443.

Other Areas of Interest

Visit the natural Missouri River oxbow lake that William Clark named Gosling Lake in 1804 for its abundance of waterfowl. The oxbow lake is located at **Lewis and Clark State Park**, which commemorates one of the most successful exploratory journeys of all time, the Lewis and Clark expedition. The park is 20 miles southwest of St. Joseph, on Highway 138. For more information, call the park at 816-579-5564.

Park Trails

Missouri River Trail (, .5 mile). Park in the lot for the North Ridge Trail. Walk around the iron gate, over the gravel road, and find the trailhead on the other side of the railroad tracks. This trail offers the opportunity to stand next to the Missouri River.

North Ridge Trail (, 2 miles). This trail ascends a hill into the forest and winds through some thickets on the ridgetop.

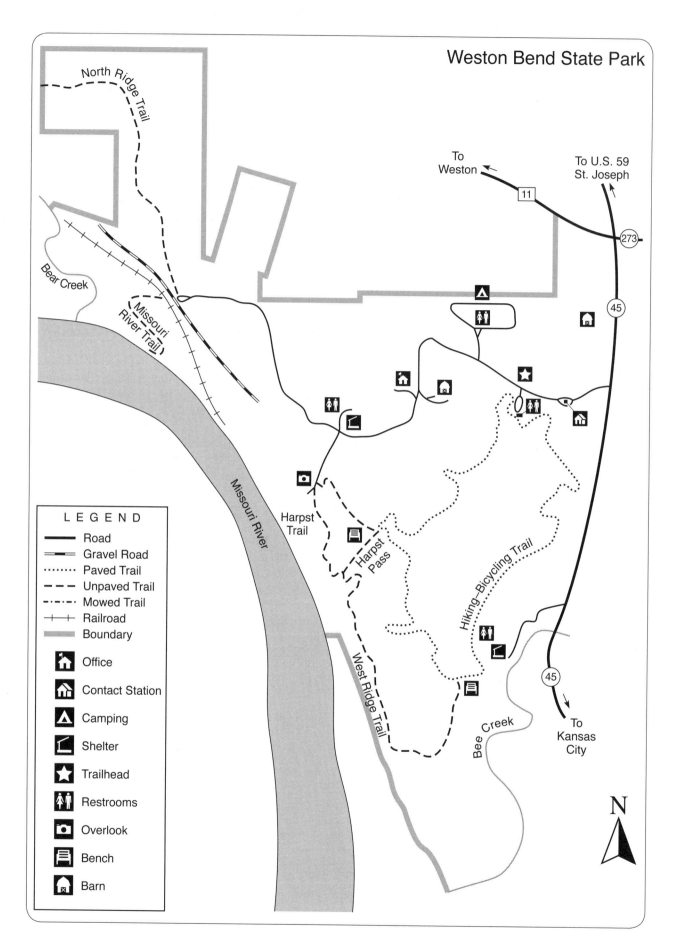

Weston Bend State Park

LEGEND

Road	
Gravel Road	
Paved Trail	
Unpaved Trail	
Mowed Trail	
Railroad	
Boundary	
Office	
Contact Station	
Camping	
Shelter	
Trailhead	
Restrooms	
Overlook	
Bench	
Barn	

North Ridge Trail

Bear Creek

Missouri River Trail

Missouri River

Harpst Trail

Harpst Pass

West Ridge Trail

Hiking–Bicycling Trail

Bee Creek

To Weston

To U.S. 59 St. Joseph

11

273

45

45

To Kansas City

N

West Ridge and Harpst Trails

 Distance Round-Trip: 2.5 miles
Estimated Hiking Time: 1.25 hours

Although some hiking trails have an overlook or two, this trail is an overlook. For the first mile, the trail is lined with dozens of views of the state's second largest river, the Missouri, and the Kansas plains beyond. Vistas explode in front of you while you hike, and the views keep getting better as you go.

Caution: Stay on the trail because the soil here (loess) is crumbly and easily eroded. Also, watch for bicycle traffic when the trail joins the Hiking–Bicycling Trail.

Trail Directions: Park in the lot for the overlook and find the trailhead about 30 yards up the asphalt path leading to the overlook. (Don't forget to stop at the overlook, too.) Begin at the trail board **[1]**. If you are here in fall, you will soon find yourself under a blinding barrage of yellow sugar maple leaves over the trail and on both sides of it. If you are here in summer, you will enjoy the dense shade that these leaves provide. Ignore the occasional side spurs and follow the blue arrows on this trail.

At .31 mi. **[2]**, come to a four-way junction. Take a left to complete the Harpst Pass and Harpst loop (1 mi.) and return to the trailhead. To continue the West Ridge Trail, go straight. Take a look at the purplish white, arching canes on both sides of the trail at .33 mi. **[3]**. These are wild raspberry vines. If you are here in June or July look closely for the purplish black berries, highly prized for making jelly, pie, syrup, wine, or for nibbling trailside!

Hike among many mature sugar maple trees with flaky bark and knobby, outreaching limbs. The bluff on your right is so steep that you can look down on the tops of some of these big trees. The best (and unique) feature of this trail is that you can enjoy overlook views of the Missouri River and hike at the same time. You are even traveling in the same direction as the river, although the water is moving a little faster than you are. Turn right at the small overlook spur at 1 mi. **[4]** for the best view of all. The Kansas plains seem to go on forever, with the horizon interrupted

only by an occasional church steeple surrounded by a cluster of rooftops. Wheat fields lie between patches of trees. If it weren't for the flatness, you'd think that you were on a peak in the Alps, looking down on so many European hamlets.

After you return to the main trail, you hike downhill and away from the river. See how the dark, rich loess soil erodes into straight-up-and-down ravine sides as you descend. At 1.33 mi. **[5]**, you are in a cool, lush valley. See how the plants grow thicker and taller here than they do on the dry ridgetop. At 1.53 mi. **[6]**, turn left on the asphalt, where the West Ridge Trail meets the paved Hiking–Bicycling Trail. Find a red bench at 2 mi. **[7]**. At 2.25 mi. **[8]**, leave the paved trail and walk behind the yellow bench. Follow the signs to take the Harpst Trail and complete the West Ridge loop.

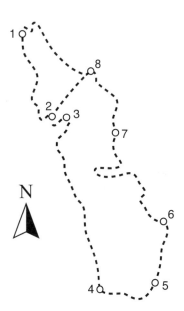

1. Start
2. Go straight
3. Wild raspberries
4. Overlook spur
5. Valley
6. Left turn
7. Red bench
8. Yellow bench

North

Hiking–Bicycling Trail

 Distance Round-Trip: 3 miles
Estimated Hiking Time: 1.5 hours

It was fall. The sky was a bleary gray, and had been for days. Yet every time I hiked under some sugar maples, with their stunningly bright yellow leaves, I thought for sure that the sun had finally come blasting through the clouds.

Caution: Watch out for bicycles. Bicyclists are restricted to counterclockwise use on this trail, so at least you'll know from which direction to expect them.

Trail Directions: The parking lot for this trail is .3 mi. from the park entrance, on the left. This paved trail includes mileage markers every .25 mi., so it offers a good opportunity to check the accuracy of your pedometer. The trail is accessible to people with disabilities, although it climbs some fairly steep hills.

Begin the trail at the west side of the parking lot **[1]**. Start in some open woods with a small stream on your right. Cross a small bridge at .20 mi. **[2]**. You pass several interesting trees in this section. The tree at .45 mi. **[3]** with six trunks is a black cherry. The small cherries are black when ripe and are a favorite among robins, orioles, and catbirds. Note the remarkable cottonwood tree on your left at .53 mi. **[4]**. The tree that looks like a porcupine at .63 mi. **[5]** is the honey locust, which is responsible for the dark brown, curlicue seedpods that you often see on trails. The tree on your right at .73 mi. **[6]** with the orange bark and spiny branches is the Osage orange tree.

At .82 mi. **[7]**, you reach a yellow bench, along with the Harpst Pass and Harpst Trail intersection. If you are here in fall, keep your eyes (and nose) open for clusters of small, wild grapes that have fallen onto the trail from the vines above. The grapes are fragrant when ripe, and tasty, too! At 1.0 mi. **[8]**, see the octopus-tangle of grapevines on your left. If you are lucky enough to find some ripe grapes, you could sit on the red bench at 1.1 mi. **[9]** to eat them.

Find a white bench and the West Ridge Trail intersection at 1.53 mi. **[10]**. Find another red bench at 1.77 mi. **[11]**. An outcrop of boulders at 1.85 mi. **[12]** underneath a sugar maple canopy provides some good photographic subjects, with or without people. The last bench is blue, at 2.17 mi. **[13]**.

Soon, you enter another landscape. The maple and cottonwood canopy gives way to open sky. You walk uphill and begin to feel a breeze on your face as you walk out onto some Missouri River loess hills. At 2.5 mi. **[14]**, the hilltop prairie goes on in both directions as far as the eye can see. Watch for kestrels, hovering while searching for mice in the grass below. Look for cottontail rabbits bounding into thickets of blackberry and sumac. The last part of the trail winds through the prairie before it returns you to the parking lot.

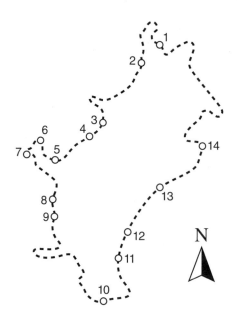

1. Start
2. Bridge
3. Black cherry tree
4. Cottonwood tree
5. Honey locust tree
6. Osage orange tree
7. Yellow bench
8. Grapevines
9. Red bench
10. White bench
11. Red bench
12. Boulders
13. Blue bench
14. Hilltop prairie

15. Squaw Creek National Wildlife Refuge

- Hike where the ruckus of half a million snow geese and ducks replaces the sound of hiking boots shuffling through dead leaves.

- Bring your binoculars and bird field guides to help you identify everything from pintails to gadwalls, dowitchers to snipe, pheasants to snow geese, as well as an occasional swan.

- From an observation tower scope out the refuge, where white pelicans are the first heralds of fall in September and 300 bald eagles arrive by early winter.

- Hike on a loess bluff hill, a rare geologic formation of wind-deposited soil from the past glacial period.

Area Information

Unique wildlife viewing and hiking opportunities abound at Squaw Creek. One of four national wildlife refuges in Missouri, Squaw Creek was established in 1935 by President Franklin D. Roosevelt as a resting and feeding area for migratory birds and other wildlife. The 7,178-acre refuge includes a mosaic of wildlife habitat—open marsh, moist soil, flooded timber, cordgrass prairie, and forest.

Squaw Creek's main attraction is the migratory waterfowl that stop over every spring and fall in phenomenal numbers. During peak season, sometime in November or December, as many as 450,000 snow geese and 100,000 ducks feed and rest in the vast marshes. The diversity of habitat promotes a diversity of species—321 species of birds have been identified here so far. Come in spring for the best shorebird viewing. Come in fall to see pelicans, geese, ducks, and eagles.

Overlooking the refuge from the east like ancient guardians of the flocks are the rare loess bluff hills. Loess (a fine-grained fertile soil deposited by the wind) in itself is not uncommon, but these steep-sided mounds of loess are found in only a few other places in the world. In the words of early 20th-century natural historian Bohumil Shimek, the loess bluff hills "appear like a giant swell of a stormy sea which has been suddenly fixed." To make them even more exceptional, on top of these bluffs are some of the last remnants of the once vast native prairie.

One way to enjoy Squaw Creek's variety of landscapes and wildlife is to drive its auto tour route. Another way is to hike its trails. One of the trails leads you to an observation tower in a marsh, where you can see bald eagles keeping watch for sick and injured waterfowl. Another takes you to the top of a loess bluff hill, where you can hear the wind in the native prairie grasses as you look out over the bustling refuge.

Directions: Drive about 35 miles northwest of St. Joseph on I-29. Take exit 79 and then Highway 159 south. The visitor center is about 2.25 miles farther on your left.

Hours Open: The refuge is open sunrise to sunset, year-round. The visitor center is open Monday through Friday from 7:30 a.m. to 4:00 p.m. year-round and on weekends from 10:00 a.m. to 4:00 p.m. in spring and fall.

Facilities: The refuge offers a visitor center, a 10-mile auto tour route, several observation towers (including some that are accessible to persons with disabilities and some with scopes), and a picnic area.

Permits and Rules: Camping, overnight parking, collecting, and firearms are prohibited. Fishing is permitted. Pets are allowed but must be on a leash.

For Further Information: Refuge Manager, Squaw Creek National Wildlife Refuge, Highway 159 South, Mound City, MO 64470; 660-442-3187.

Other Areas of Interest

Camping is available at **Big Lake State Park**, 8 miles west of Squaw Creek. The park also offers a swimming pool, cabins, and a modern motel. For more information, call 660-442-3770.

St. Joseph is home to the Pony Express Stables, Jesse James Home Museum, and hosts of other museums, theaters, mansions, and historic attractions. For more information, call 660-232-4626.

Site Trails

Mike Callow Memorial Trail (, .25 mile one-way). This trail is dedicated to former Squaw Creek Refuge employee Mike Callow, who was killed in an airplane accident while conducting a waterfowl survey in Washington in 1998. The flat, paved trail is accessible to people with physical disabilities. It begins in the southwest corner of the parking lot for the visitor center and connects with the Connector Link to the Loess Bluff Trail to make a 1-mile loop. A memorial is located at the end of the trail.

Connector Link (, .25 mile one-way). This link joins near the end of the Mike Callow Memorial Trail and quickly takes you up a steep loess bluff to connect with the Loess Bluff Trail at the overlook.

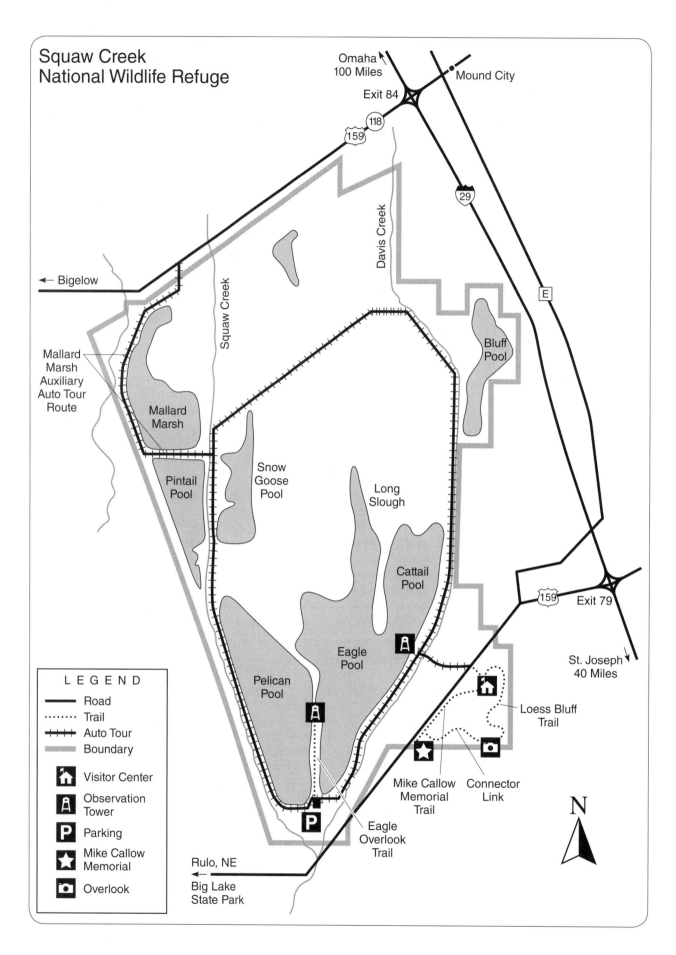

Squaw Creek
National Wildlife Refuge

Omaha
100 Miles

Mound City

Exit 84

159 118

Bigelow ←

Davis Creek

Squaw Creek

29

E

Bluff
Pool

Mallard
Marsh
Auxiliary
Auto Tour
Route

Mallard
Marsh

Pintail
Pool

Snow
Goose
Pool

Long
Slough

Cattail
Pool

Pelican
Pool

Eagle
Pool

159 Exit 79

St. Joseph
40 Miles

Loess Bluff
Trail

Connector
Link

Mike Callow
Memorial
Trail

Eagle
Overlook
Trail

LEGEND

——— Road
.... Trail
++++ Auto Tour
——— Boundary

Visitor Center
Observation Tower
Parking
Mike Callow Memorial
Overlook

Rulo, NE
Big Lake
State Park

N

North   60

Loess Bluff Trail

Distance Round-Trip: 1 mile
Estimated Hiking Time: 45 minutes

Early on, you may notice nothing unusual about this trail. A gray squirrel scurries over dry oak leaves. A crow calls somewhere overhead . . . but wait. The 191 limestone steps near the end will kick your heartbeat into overdrive as they lift you to the top of one of Missouri's rarest natural features—a loess bluff prairie remnant.

Caution: Loess is crumbly and easily eroded. Stay on the trail, especially on the blufftop.

Trail Directions: You might want to stop in the visitor center and pick up a trail guide, which explains interesting features noted on the trail with numbered posts. Begin the trail at the signboard **[1]** directly behind the visitor center. Ignore spurs to the left and right at .03 mi. **[2]** and continue straight. At .04 mi. **[3]**, you find a planted plot that previews some of the plants found on the trail at the blufftop. The Indian grass, little bluestem, and sideoats grama found here are a sample of plants found in the vast prairies that covered about a third of the state during presettlement times. A folk remedy for warts is to soak the wart in water that's been standing in a cavity of a tree. You may find the ingredient for this remedy in a tree cavity on your left at .13 mi. **[4]**, which is, incidentally, about the size of a witch's cauldron.

Continue under many black walnut, hackberry, and pawpaw trees, start to climb uphill, and find a wooden bench at .24 mi. **[5]**. At .30 mi. **[6]**, you reach the first of the 191 limestone steps that will take you to the loess blufftop. These stones were carried by hand by CCC workers, who built the trail in 1936. As you ascend, you may find some of the light-colored steps dotted with small blue, waxy berries. These are the fruit of the eastern red cedar, the only evergreen tree native to northwest Missouri. Because of its abundance, its evergreen nature, and its aroma, the cedar was (and still is) a popular choice for a Christmas tree.

At the blufftop (after step #191) you may find a good use for the bench in the stone shelter at .42 mi. **[7]**. As you continue, notice how the aspect of a slope (its position in relation to direction) influences its vegetation. Prairie grasses and forbs dominate the left side of the trail because these south-facing slopes receive lots of sunlight and are warmer and drier. Conversely, trees dominate the shadier, damper north-aspect slopes on the right.

The overlook at .50 mi. **[8]** offers unusual vistas in all directions. Use the free viewing scope to look out over the Squaw Creek Refuge. From here, on a clear day, you can look across the refuge into Nebraska and, farther south, into Kansas. Look behind you at the loess hills, which occur in only a few places on earth. The sunny slopes grow vigorous stands of native prairie grasses, which turn a warm orange-brown in the winter. The backbone ridges seem to hold back the crowded trees on the other side like electric fences hold back cattle. Relax and enjoy the sights. Retrace your steps to return to the trailhead, or continue down the spine of the loess bluff on your left to use the Connector Link to connect with the Mike Callow Memorial Trail, which takes you back to the parking lot.

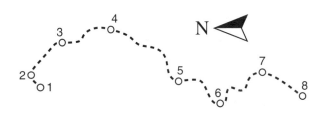

1. Start
2. Go straight
3. Native grasses
4. Tree cavity
5. Bench
6. Limestone steps
7. Stone shelter
8. Overlook

North

Eagle Overlook Trail

 Distance Round-Trip: 1.35 miles
Estimated Hiking Time: 45 minutes

You will feel as if you stepped into a wildlife movie as you hike out into a 1,500-acre marsh on a narrow strip of land and watch the nature scenes unfold. American lotus looms for what seems like miles, and a large crayfish scuttles away as you approach the water. You are looking for bald eagles perching in nearby trees when you spot a white pelican, silently and gracefully passing just overhead.

Caution: This trail is on a levee that is about 2 mi. along a 10 mi. auto tour route around the refuge. The road is one-way, so if you take your vehicle to get to the trailhead be sure that you have enough fuel to go the distance. The auto route will take at least a half hour.

Trail Directions: Because of the trail's short length, mileage distances will not be given here.

Pick up an auto tour guide from the visitor center and locate the route, which begins across Highway 159 from the visitor center. Drive (or hike) about 2 mi. (going clockwise) along the auto tour route, which is a gravel road that goes around most of the refuge. You will find the trail signboard just past the Eagle Pool water-control gates on the right, on a levee between Eagle and Pelican pools. Parking is available here along the side of the road.

Observing the refuge from an overlook or from the road is interesting, but this trail goes further and gives you the privilege of hiking into the refuge. As you hike on this skinny isthmus, glance often into the skies. You may watch a dozen teal glide down and make an elegant water-ski landing, or you may witness a thousand snow geese boil up like a loud, gray cloud, take flight for a few confusing moments, and quietly settle back down.

Begin at the signboard **[1]**. Probably one of the first things you notice is the great number of brushy, domed muskrat houses **[2]** in the water on both sides of the trail. The walls of these houses are made of nearby aquatic vegetation, are about 1 foot thick, and

keep the inside cool in summer and warm in winter. The muskrat enters the dry interior of the house through an underwater tunnel. Keep watch for ducks, geese, eagles, snakes, turtles, and other animals that commonly use the houses for basking or idling.

Some of the aquatic plants nearby that wildlife use for food and shelter are arrowhead, cattail, and river bulrush. The American lotus **[3]**, found in the water on both sides of the trail, has plate-sized leaves that lie on top of the water and a large, dish-shaped seedpod. If you are here during summer, look for the radiant, saucer-sized yellow blooms. Some lotus seeds found in the Orient have the distinction of being the oldest, still viable seeds in the world—over 900 years old.

As you continue the trail, notice the odd loess bluff hills **[4]**, which dominate the horizon on the right. From this distance, the warmer, drier southern slopes look shaved, contrasted with the northern slopes, which are crowded with trees. These hills are made of silty soil that was deposited by the wind after being ground finely by retreating glaciers. Loess bluff hills are found in only a few places on earth.

At the end of the trail is an observation tower **[5]**, which is a good vantage point to watch ducks, geese, deer, coyotes, and an occasional swan. Further hiking on the levee is prohibited, so you must retrace your steps to return to the trailhead. On the way back, check the shore next to the water for a highway of muskrat, raccoon, and other wildlife tracks, as well as burrowing crayfish tunnels.

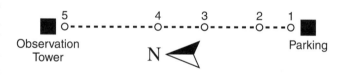

1. Start
2. Muskrat houses
3. American lotus
4. Loess bluff hills
5. Observation tower

Southeast

The southeast region of Missouri comprises the area south of
Highway 70 and east of Highway 19.

Topography

In almost every way possible, this part of Missouri is
the most diverse. It contains the highest and lowest
points in the state and areas of the most relief and
the least. It contains the oldest exposed land mass
and the youngest. Desertlike glades are home to the
dwarfed, scrubby trees, while swamps and wet forests
in the Bootheel produce some of the largest trees in
the nation. Topographically, the region can be divided
into three areas—Ozark, Ozark border, and Mississippi Lowlands.

The Ozark Highlands, which cover almost the
lower half of Missouri (40 percent of the state),
compose the western half of the southeast region
of Missouri. The Ozarks are an unglaciated area of
greater relief and elevation than surrounding areas.
Characteristic features include steep topography,
thin, rocky, residual soils, deep erosion by streams,
and extensive forests. While glaciers, seas, or floods
repeatedly covered surrounding areas, the Ozarks
have remained exposed for 250 million years. The
St. François Mountains, in the center of the southeast
region, are igneous in origin and considered the
geologic core of the Ozarks. Exposed granites and
rhyolites are around 1.5 billion years old—some of
the oldest rocks on the continent.

The Ozark border, an area along the lower Missouri and Mississippi Rivers, is a transition zone
between the Ozarks and the big rivers. The rugged
hills resemble the Ozark landscape, but the soils are
influenced by the rivers and are much deeper and
more productive. The Mississippi Lowlands, often
referred to as the Bootheel region, are a sharp contrast
to the rugged, rocky Ozarks. Except for Crowley's
Ridge, a disjunct series of forested, low hills that

rise in a diagonal line just above the Bootheel, the
Mississippi Lowlands are a flat, alluvial plain with
slight relief. Once the northern boundary of the Gulf
of Mexico, much of the area is less than 100 meters
above sea level. Missouri's lowest point occurs at the
Bootheel's southwest tip.

Major Rivers and Lakes

The southeast region is bordered on the north by the
Missouri River and on the east by the Mississippi
River. The St. Francis River carries the distinction of
forming the western boundary of the Bootheel. Nearly
all the region's rivers are rock bottomed and clear, and
most are popular for floating and fishing. At the top of
the region, the Meramec River is the most biologically
diverse in the Midwest. The Current and Jacks Fork
are managed by the National Park Service as the Ozark
National Scenic Riverways because of their high-
quality waters, scenic beauty, and recreation opportunities. The Eleven Point, farther south, is another
spring-fed, scenic river favored by canoeists. To the
east, the Black, St. Francis, and Castor Rivers begin
in the St. François Mountains and include sections of
shut-ins, where rushing water sculpts and polishes
igneous boulders in the streambed. National and
regional kayak races are held on the St. Francis River
in spring. The Bootheel is a massive grid of channels
built to drain the low-lying area for agriculture, and
the lower end of the Castor River was channelized to
serve as a drainage canal.

The region includes two reservoirs—Clearwater
Lake, formed by impounding the Black River, and
Wappapello Lake, an impoundment of the St. Francis
River. The swamps, marshes, and other wetlands at
Mingo National Wildlife Refuge were formed in an

abandoned channel of the Mississippi River when the river shifted east about 18,000 years ago.

Common Plant Life

With the exception of prairies, virtually every plant and forest community in Missouri can be found in this diverse region. The Ozarks have been altered the least, and presettlement vegetation of pine and pine-oak forests still dominate. Much of the Ozark border has been converted to pastures and crop fields, but fragmented forests and forested bottomlands still persist. The Mississippi Lowlands lost almost all their original natural communities of extensive swamps, bottomland forests, and associated wetlands. Starting around 1900, bottomland forests were cleared and canals were constructed to drain the swamps for fields of soybeans, wheat, corn, rice, and cotton. The conversion was almost total. Today, only tiny fragments of swamp and bottomland forest are preserved. Except for the Bootheel, the southeast and south-central regions are the most heavily forested in the state. Besides mixed forests of oak, pine, and hickory, sheltered cove ravines along the Mississippi River hide trees more typical of Appalachian habitats—cucumber tree, tulip tree, and American beech.

Dry igneous forests and glades characterize the St. François Mountains and include blackjack oak, post oak, black hickory, and shortleaf pine. Common plants are Indian grass, little bluestem, buttonweed, reindeer lichen, sundrops, milkwort, and fameflower. Dolomite glades are common on the hills of the Ozarks and Ozark border and include little bluestem, sideoats grama, prairie dropseed, black-eyed susan, Missouri evening primrose, calamint, and yellow coneflower. Gravel-bar communities in the Ozarks commonly include shrubs like witch hazel, buttonbush, ninebark, swamp dogwood, and black willow, as well as wildflowers like blue star, cardinal flower, and mistflower. Bald cypress, tupelo gum, water hickory, and pumpkin ash dominate Bootheel swamps. Wet bottomland forests include bur oak, swamp white oak, water oak, swamp cottonwood, deciduous holly, swamp rose, and lizard's tail.

Common Birds and Animals

Many animals that use glades live in adjacent forests, but several have adapted to live in the dry, desertlike habitat. While on glades with large rocks, look for eastern collared lizards, which turn bright blue and green (males) during breeding times. Other glade reptiles include the fence lizard, six-lined racerunner, eastern coachwhip snake, and flathead snake.

Birds commonly seen in upland forests are wild turkey, great horned owl, screech owl, various woodpeckers, yellow-throated warbler, nuthatch, summer tanager, titmouse, and red-eyed vireo. Other animals include the bobcat, gray fox, white-tailed deer, raccoon, opossum, squirrel, chipmunk, and various bats. Black bears are slowly returning to Missouri by expanding their range from Arkansas and are occasionally seen in more remote portions of the Ozarks.

Birds of bottomland forests and swamps include the barred owl, teal, ruddy duck, great blue heron, green heron, pileated woodpecker, Louisiana water thrush, prothonotary warbler, and cerulean warbler. Other animals include the muskrat, beaver, raccoon, water snake, river cooter, painted turtle, and stinkpot.

Climate

The Bootheel area has the highest average temperature and precipitation in the state. Bootheel temperatures average 60 degrees F in spring, 79 degrees F in summer, 60 degrees F in fall, and 34 degrees F in winter. Precipitation here averages 51 inches annually. The rest of the southeast region's temperatures average 57 degrees F in spring, 78 degrees F in summer, 58 degrees F in fall, and 31 degrees F in winter. Precipitation varies greatly from top to bottom of this region; the average is 44 inches annually.

Finally, it is noteworthy that Taum Sauk Mountain, the state's highest point, is high enough to have a microclimate of its own. Its winter weather is like that of Kirksville in northeast Missouri, and summer temperatures rarely reach 90 degrees F.

Best Features

- Incredibly huge trees at Big Oak Tree State Park
- Forested swamps in the Bootheel
- Large and fabulously decorated caves
- Vast igneous glades with astounding vistas
- Mina Sauk Falls, the state's highest waterfall
- Refreshing water and scenic beauty of Johnson's Shut-Ins
- Numerous beautiful springs, including the largest single-outlet spring in the nation

16. Big Oak Tree State Park

- Stand beneath six state champion trees, two of which are national champions.
- Find yourself in the heart of a genuine swamp (from the convenience of a wheelchair-accessible boardwalk).
- Find the tallest tree in Missouri.

Area Information

In many ways, no other Missouri park can boast what Big Oak Tree can. Within the 1,005 fertile acres of the park are enormous trees, six of which are state champions (the largest individuals of their species). Of these six state champions, two of them, the pumpkin ash and the persimmon, are national champions. With a tree canopy averaging 120 feet and with several trees more than 140 feet tall, the park is often called the Park of Champions.

Big Oak Tree State Park is one of the last remaining examples of the vast bottomland forest that once covered 2 million acres of the Bootheel region. Standing like an island in the midst of a vast agricultural area, it is registered as a national natural landmark. Also, a 940-acre part of the park is a Missouri natural area. Missouri natural areas are permanently protected and managed to preserve their natural qualities.

Big Oak Tree showcases the bottomland forest and swamp. These two communities, now two of the rarest types in Missouri's natural landscape, depend on periodic flood cycles. The park also includes an 80-acre portion that is virgin wet-mesic bottomland forest.

Majestic trees—giant oak, hickory, bald cypress, and swamp cottonwood—dominate the scene. The rich soils support patches of giant cane, which can reach 25 feet in height, and poison ivy vines as big around as a person's leg. The swamp rabbit, a rare species, lives in the area. Big Oak Tree has a national reputation among bird-watchers.

Directions: Follow Highway 102 south of East Prairie for 14 miles. Signs direct you to the park office and the park.

Hours Open: The site is open year-round and designed for day use. It is not accessible during flood periods. Call the park before you come to ensure that you will have access to the park. Generally, the interpretive center is open from 10:00 a.m. to 3:00 p.m. Monday through Friday.

Facilities: Big Oak Tree State Park features an interpretive center; an interpretive boardwalk into the swamp; picnic shelters; and boating, canoeing, and fishing on 22-acre Big Oak Lake.

Permits and Rules: Except for special youth outings, camping is not allowed. Pets must always be leashed.

For Further Information: Big Oak Tree State Park, 13640 South Highway 102, East Prairie, MO 63845; 573-649-3149.

Other Areas of Interest

Just to the east of Big Oak Tree State Park is **Towosahgy State Historic Site**, which preserves the remains of a Native American village. Inhabited between AD 1000 and AD 1400 by people of the Mississippian culture, the village was also an important ceremonial center. Interpretation for the site is planned. For more information, call 573-649-3149 (Big Oak Tree State Park).

The **Hunter-Dawson Home State Historic Site** is a 15-room mansion that reflects the lifestyle of Missouri Bootheel gentry before the Civil War. The home features Georgian, Greek revival, and Italianate architecture; original furniture; nine fireplaces; and guided tours. For more information, call 573-748-5340.

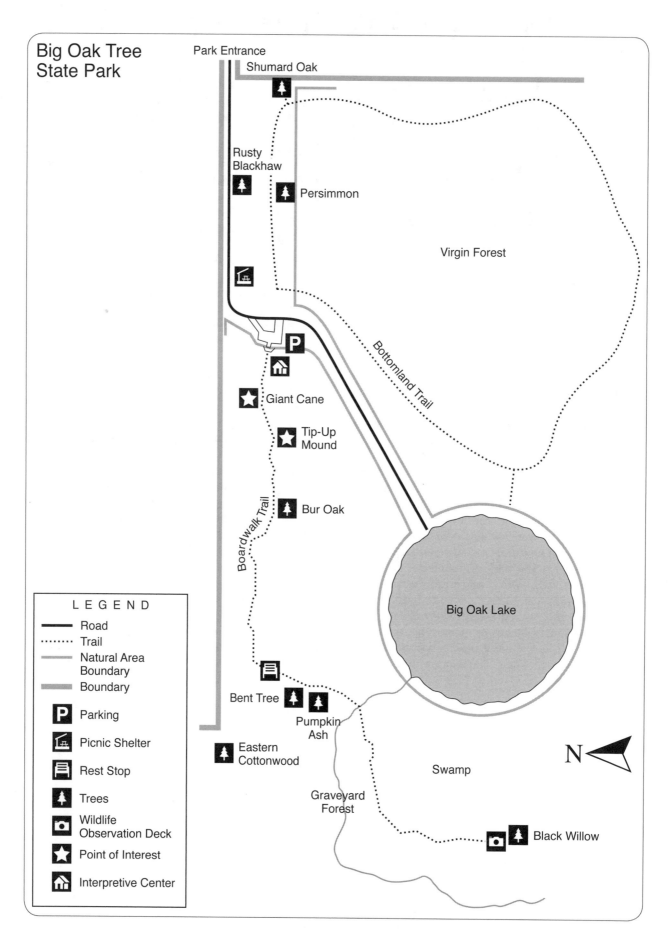

Big Oak Tree State Park

Park Entrance

Shumard Oak

Rusty Blackhaw

Persimmon

Virgin Forest

Bottomland Trail

Giant Cane

Tip-Up Mound

Boardwalk Trail

Bur Oak

Big Oak Lake

Bent Tree

Pumpkin Ash

Eastern Cottonwood

Swamp

Graveyard Forest

Black Willow

N

LEGEND

——	Road
······	Trail
——	Natural Area Boundary
——	Boundary
P	Parking
	Picnic Shelter
	Rest Stop
	Trees
	Wildlife Observation Deck
★	Point of Interest
	Interpretive Center

Boardwalk Trail

  Distance Round-Trip: 1.25 miles
  Estimated Hiking Time: 1 hour

A pileated woodpecker pierces the swamp air with a shrill cry, a barred owl's "who-cooks-for-you?" resonates between tree trunks, and unexplained splashes in the calm water remind you that you are not alone.

Caution: Swamps are notorious for mosquitoes; bring repellent. Also, be sure to call the park before you visit. The whole park floods once or twice a year, sometimes placing the boardwalk 10 feet under water!

Trail Directions: The trailhead **[1]** is in the southwest corner of the parking lot for the boardwalk and interpretive center. This is a self-guiding trail, so pick up a trail guide, which explains points of interest labeled along the trail. Note, however, that numbered features on the trail do not correspond to numbered features in this book.

After a few steps you come upon the pentagonal interpretive center **[2]** on your left. Built 19 feet off the ground, it testifies to the regular floods that have maintained for centuries this now-rare natural community. The center houses a cross section of a 400-year-old bur oak, the park's namesake. Walk under a gigantic pawpaw tree (Missouri banana) leaning over the boardwalk and you come upon a stand of giant cane at .05 mi. **[3]**. The cane in this park provides nesting habitat for the Swainson's warbler. At .13 mi. **[4]**, look for a tip-up mound on the left. When a tree falls over, its roots bring to the surface these large mounds of soil. In poorly drained soils like these, such depressions are often filled with water.

At .15 mi. **[5]**, look up. The massive branches of the tallest tree in Missouri tower 142 feet over your head. This bur oak, with a trunk circumference of 17 feet, 7 inches, is a remaining example of the impressive giants that formerly spread over 2 million acres of lowland area in Missouri's Bootheel.

Two wooden benches at .34 mi. **[6]** mark the halfway point on the boardwalk. At .41 mi. **[7]**, look on the left for what look like wooden stalagmites growing from the forest floor. These are knobby growths from the root systems of bald cypress trees. Although their function is not known for certain, it is thought that these growths, called knees, serve as oxygen-absorbing structures for the trees. Also notice that the cypress trunks are buttressed. Their flared trunks keep them from falling over in the saturated, mucky soil.

At .43 mi. **[8]**, you will see the largest pumpkin ash tree in the nation. If you haven't seen standing water yet, you probably will soon. Characteristic plants in the swamp include buttonbush, swamp privet, young water locust, and black willow trees. The green scum on the water is actually millions of floating duckweed plants.

At the end of the boardwalk at .60 mi. **[9]** are the state champion black willow tree and two wooden benches. If you hear something like a loud, lone monkey, it is probably the state's largest woodpecker, the pileated. If you hear a hoarse and abrupt "Bwaaawk!" it is probably the great blue heron. Also look for wood ducks skimming through the duckweed and turtles lying on little log islands. Retrace your steps to return to the trailhead.

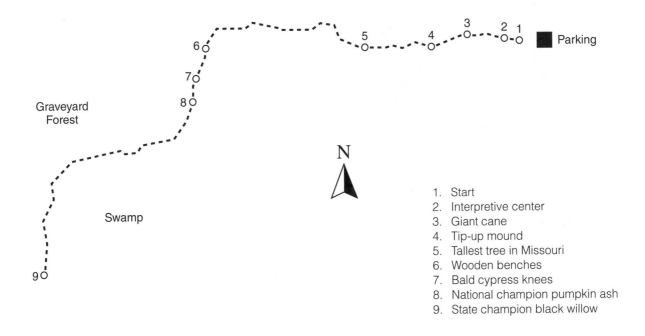

1. Start
2. Interpretive center
3. Giant cane
4. Tip-up mound
5. Tallest tree in Missouri
6. Wooden benches
7. Bald cypress knees
8. National champion pumpkin ash
9. State champion black willow

Southeast

Bottomland Trail

   Distance Round-Trip: 1.4 miles
Estimated Hiking Time: 1 hour

This trail brings you right up to some of the largest trees in the state and nation. Have you heard of the Druids, the ancient people who worshipped trees? You may not feel like worshipping these trees after you finish this trail, but I guarantee that you will not leave unaffected by them.

Caution: Be cautious about admiring the towering tops of these giant trees and walking at the same time; poison ivy and stinging nettle are common on both sides of the trail. As with the Boardwalk Trail, be sure to call the park before you come to make sure that it isn't flooded. Also, if you forget mosquito repellent on all your other hikes this year, don't forget it on this one.

Trail Directions: Find the Bottomland Trail sign **[1]** directly across the road from the parking lot for the Boardwalk Trail. You are about to enter what is probably the highest concentration of Big (capital *B*) trees in the state. Nickname this trail the Trail of Giants.

After only a few steps, notice the big tree on your right with the bark that pulls away from the trunk in thin strips **[2]**. This tree is a shellbark hickory. The nuts, the largest of all Missouri hickories, are almost as large as baseballs. At .17 mi. **[3]**, you encounter the state champion swamp chestnut oak. Its trunk is over 20 feet around, and it stands 142 feet high. These trees have a way of making you feel mighty small.

At .29 mi. **[4]** is a small spur on your right that takes you to Big Oak Lake. Turn left to continue the trail. At .48 mi. **[5]** is a bald cypress tree whose trunk is starting to flare at the base. Just 5 feet away is a pumpkin ash with a trunk circumference of over 11 feet. Notice the uniform, deep grooves of the ash bark. Take a few more steps and contrast the ash bark with the bark of the big tree on your left **[6]** (.50 mi.). This tree is a hackberry showing its characteristic bark—an extremely smooth background with corky, raised bumps. The hackberry's fruit, similar to wild black cherries, is a favorite of songbirds.

If you are here on a breezy day you may notice white, fleecy tufts in the air or in puffy piles on the trail. These are the seeds of the cottonwood tree, and at .63 mi. **[7]** is a cottonwood with a circumference of over 12 feet. Sometimes these seeds travel for miles on the wind, filling the summertime air with what looks like snow.

Look closely around the cypress knees and you may see what look like little mud smokestacks. These are the burrow entrances, or "chimneys," of the devil crayfish. The burrows extend to groundwater, sometimes to a depth of 15 feet.

Walk under a giant sweet gum tree at .72 mi. **[8]** (look for the spiky "gumballs" on the trail) and find the state champion possum haw (also called deciduous holly) about 20 yards off the trail on your right at .78 mi. **[9]**. Walk through a stand of native cane (bamboo) at .83 mi. **[10]** and exit the forest at 1.13 mi. **[11]**. Take the short spur on your right to visit the state champion shumard oak tree **[12]** and then retrace your steps to the forest exit. Follow the mown path through the picnic area and look at the giant persimmon tree on your left at 1.26 mi. **[13]**. With a trunk circumference of 6 feet, 9 inches, this is the largest persimmon tree in the country. Continue the path and finish the trail back at the trail sign.

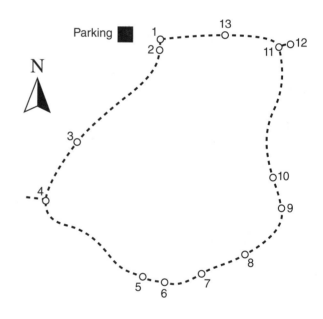

1. Start
2. Shellbark hickory
3. State champion swamp chestnut oak
4. Spur to lake
5. Bald cypress
6. Hackberry
7. Cottonwood
8. Sweet gum
9. State champion possum haw
10. Native cane
11. Forest exit
12. State champion shumard oak
13. National champion persimmon

- Stand on 600-foot-high Mississippi River blufftops with spectacular views of Ol' Man River and the Illinois floodplain.
- Get your blood pumping on some beautiful trails with some serious topographic relief.
- Look for doll's eyes.
- Find a cucumber magnolia.

Area Information

The natural resources and scenic beauty of the Trail of Tears State Park are easy to appreciate. Rich, moist forest bottoms contrast with sharp ridges and deep ravines. Blufftop overlooks offer dramatic views of the Mississippi, Missouri's largest river. The mixed hardwood forests of the park have been preserved with much of their original integrity, and two areas with special designations, Indian Creek Wild Area and Vancill Hollow Natural Area, offer their own natural features. One of these is a rare forest containing American beeches, tulip trees, and cucumber magnolia, species more characteristic of the Appalachian Mountains than of the Ozarks.

But the park has a more somber cultural history. When the federal Indian Removal Act was passed in 1830, 13,000 Cherokee Native Americans were forced to leave their ancient homelands east of the Mississippi River and travel 1,200 miles to reservations in the west. During the bitter winter of 1838–39, a quarter of the entire Cherokee tribe died. "Trail of Tears" refers to routes used during this forced exodus. The main purpose of the park interpretive center is to teach visitors about this tragedy.

Directions: Trail of Tears State Park is on the Mississippi River, just north of Cape Girardeau. Go 10 miles east of Fruitland on Highway 177.

Hours Open: The site is open year-round. The park gate opens at 7:00 a.m. daily; note the closing time when you enter. From April through September, the visitor center is open from 9:00 a.m. to 5:00 p.m. Monday through Saturday and from noon to 5:00 p.m. on Sunday. In October, the visitor center is open from 9:00 a.m. to 5:00 p.m. Thursday through Saturday. From November through March, the visitor center is open on Saturday from 10:00 a.m. to 4:00 p.m. and on Sunday from noon to 4:00 p.m.

Facilities: The park offers a visitor center, amphitheater, and picnicking; camping (including electric, nonelectric, and camping for special groups and backpackers), boating, and fishing on the Mississippi River; and boating, fishing, and swimming on 20-acre Lake Boutin. Most trails are for hikers only, but the Peewah Trail is open to hikers, backpackers, and equestrians.

Permits and Rules: Camping by backpackers on the Peewah Trail is allowed, but campfires are prohibited there. Bicycles are prohibited on all trails. Boats with electric motors only are allowed on Lake Boutin. Pets must always be leashed.

For Further Information: Trail of Tears State Park, 429 Moccasin Springs Road, Jackson, MO 63755; 573-290-5268.

Other Areas of Interest

Visit the **Burfordville Bridge**, the oldest of only four covered bridges remaining in the state. It is located at **Bollinger Mill State Historic Site**, off Highway 34, near Burfordville. Picnicking is available near the covered bridge, and guided tours of the mill are offered for a fee. For more information, call 573-243-4591.

Park Trails

Nature Trail (👣👣, .5 mile). This loop trail, which begins behind the interpretive center and travels behind the seats of the amphitheater, has many pawpaws and ferns.

Lake Trail (👣👣👣, 2 miles). See some giant tulip trees and hike next to Lake Boutin. Begin at the shower house at the nonelectric campground loop and finish across the road from the shower house.

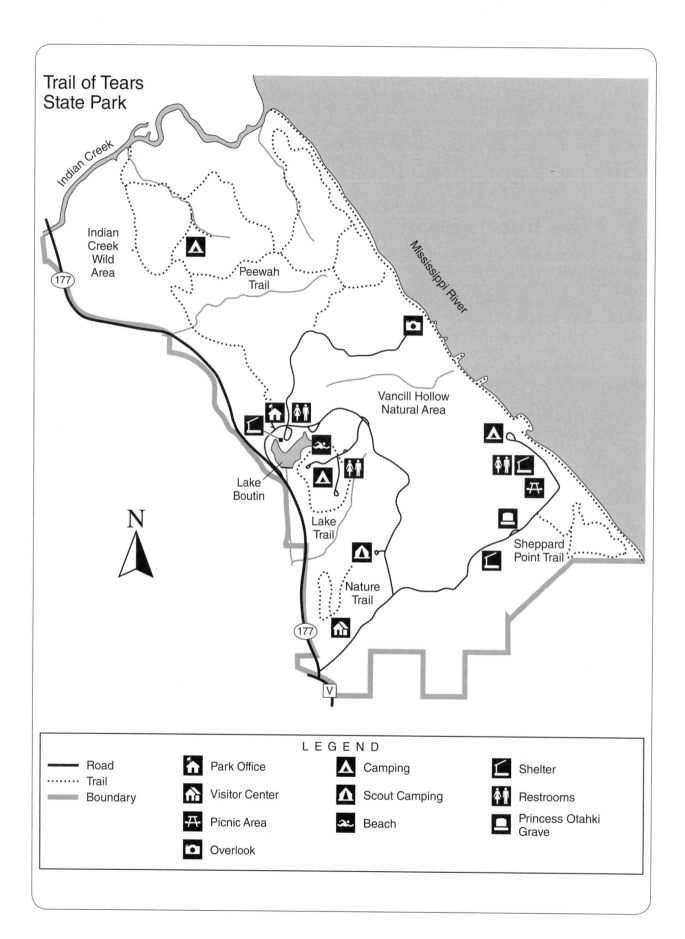

Trail of Tears State Park

Indian Creek

177

Indian Creek Wild Area

Peewah Trail

Mississippi River

Vancill Hollow Natural Area

Lake Boutin

Lake Trail

N

Nature Trail

Sheppard Point Trail

177

V

L E G E N D

—— Road		Park Office	Camping		Shelter
···· Trail		Visitor Center	Scout Camping		Restrooms
—— Boundary		Picnic Area	Beach		Princess Otahki Grave
		Overlook			

Sheppard Point Trail

Distance Round-Trip:
2 miles
Estimated Hiking Time:
1.25 hours

Hike this trail in an hour and a half or less and you will be in for a real sweat-er. The naturalist in the visitor center told me that she had it down to 45 minutes!

Caution: The four intermittent streams that cross the trail may be wet. The scenic overlook is perched on some high bluffs. In addition, some steep ascents have loose rocks.

Trail Directions: The trailhead sign **[1]** is at a small parking area, just off the main road, northeast of Princess Otahki's grave. The trail begins just left of this sign. At .08 mi. **[2]**, stop to look at the unusual ferns on your right. These are broad beech ferns, the only ferns in Missouri whose central stem (rachis) is winged throughout its entire length.

The large trees with smooth bark are beech trees. At .11 mi. **[3]**, look at the leaves on the big tree on the left side of the trail. The leaf shape gives the tree its name—the tulip tree. Another tree on this trail in the same family as the tulip tree is the cucumber magnolia, so named because its fruit is green and erect when developing. The leaves of the cucumber magnolia look like pawpaw leaves, but they are not as pointed and they do not have the pawpaw leaves' unpleasant odor. The higher rainfall here, the protective high bluffs, and the deep ravines combine with the winter-ameliorating effects of the Mississippi River to produce a climate and habitat more typical of Tennessee, North Carolina, and Virginia. Unless you are accustomed to hiking in the Appalachian region of the United States, these three trees may not be familiar to you.

These beautiful ravines cut through moist, rich soil. On this trail you see a lot of wild ginger, bloodroot, jack-in-the-pulpit, and Christmas ferns. If you come in August or September, look for doll's eyes on both sides of the trail. This medium-large plant has strange-looking fruit—pure white balls the size of large peas, held erect on red stems. There are even black pupils in the eyes!

At .27 mi. **[4]**, turn left and follow the yellow arrows. You reach a giant sassafras tree at .44 mi. **[5]**. Just for fun, put your outstretched hands around the base—it will take more than four hand-lengths to span it! In the early 1500s, Spanish explorers mistook the aromatic sassafras for a cinnamon tree, and it became a major colonial export, second only to tobacco. Before sassafras oil was found to be a potential carcinogen in the 1960s, the fragrant oil was used commercially to flavor root beer, chewing gum, and toothpaste.

Cross a couple of intermittent streams at .70 mi. and .76 mi. **[6]** and find a lot of jewelweed, a favorite flower of hummingbirds. You are close to the Mississippi now, and from here you begin a steep ascent to the blufftops.

At .90 mi. **[7]**, reach a flat boulder that offers a magnificent view of the largest river in the state and its Illinois floodplain. In winter look for soaring bald eagles. During summer months you can spot the graceful and rare Mississippi kite, gliding and swooping for insects.

Begin your descent back to water level and find a couple more intermittent streams at 1.03 mi. and 1.13 mi. **[8]**. Enjoy the flat walking in the stream bottom because at 1.31 mi. **[9]** the trail makes another steep incline. Some small, loose rocks here cause unsure footing. At 1.49 mi. **[4]**, you reach the intersection that you came across earlier. Bear left to retrace your steps and return to the trailhead.

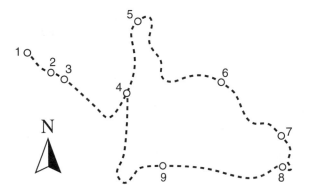

1. Start
2. Broad beech ferns
3. Tulip tree
4. Left turn
5. Giant sassafras tree
6. Intermittent streams
7. Boulder overlook
8. Intermittent streams
9. Rocky incline

Peewah Trail

Distance Round-Trip:
8.75 miles
Estimated Hiking Time:
4.75 hours

Peewah is a Native American word meaning "come follow in this direction." Actually, following someone on this trail wouldn't be a bad idea—then you wouldn't have to carry a spiderweb stick.

Caution: The steep ascents have some loose footing, and the overlooks are on high bluffs. Stinging nettles encroach on the trail in creek bottoms, and the intermittent streams may be wet.

Trail Directions: Find the parking lot for the Peewah trailhead on Overlook Road, about halfway between Lake Boutin and the overlook. Hikers are encouraged to register at the trailhead before they begin, especially if they plan to stay overnight. Two backpack camps are located on this trail.

Begin at the trailhead [1]. If you are here in late August, September, or October, you might as well pick up a stick right now and practice waving it in front of you, because harmless spiders have a propensity for building extensive webs about face high. Don't turn back, though—the blufftop views are worth a little arachnid annoyance.

Follow the yellow arrows until you come to the yellow–green intersection at .33 mi. [2], where you turn right. This spur, marked by green arrows, takes you to a tremendous bluff overlook. Go straight at the intersection at .65 mi. [3] to continue to the overlook. At the overlook [4] (.69 mi.), take your time to gaze at the mighty Mississippi and Illinois land beyond. When you are ready to move, retrace your steps to the yellow–green intersection [2] and turn right to follow the yellow arrows.

At 1.09 mi. [5], you come to the yellow–yellow intersection, where you turn left. At 1.60 mi. [6], you reach the yellow–red intersection. Turn right to continue the yellow loop to find more exercise and more overlooks.

Cross a couple of intermittent streams and watch out for stinging nettles encroaching on the trail. At 2.40 mi. [7], you step into a streambed. The continuing trail may be hard to see, but it is directly across the stream from the bank where you are standing now.

Climb the hill to the blufftop, where spectacular views of the Mississippi begin

to emerge on your left. At 3.83 mi. [8], take the spur to the left to find a 600-foot overlook with the most impressive views of all [9] (3.93 mi.). In winter look for bald eagles perched in large trees near the river.

Backtrack on the spur to return to [8] and complete the yellow loop by turning left. At 4.36 mi., ignore the intersecting green path on your left and continue to 4.43 mi. [5] to the yellow–yellow intersection where you were earlier. If you are officially tuckered, go straight to return to the trailhead. If you are ready for more, turn right.

Come to the yellow–yellow intersection at 4.84 mi. [6]. In just a few steps you come to the red–red intersection [10] (4.86 mi.), where you bear left to begin the red loop. At 5.54 mi. [11] is the white connector intersection. Turn right to shorten the red loop or bear left to continue it. At around 6 mi., you hike under some majestic tulip trees. You are now in the Indian Creek Wild Area. At 6.47 mi. [12] is a white spur to Indian Creek. Bear right to continue the red loop. Cross a streambed at 6.65 mi. [13], pass the white connector at 6.95 mi. [14], and finish the red loop back at [10] (7.86 mi.). Turn left to return to the yellow loop, turn right at [5] (8.28 mi.), and turn right again at [2] (8.38 mi.) to return to the trailhead.

1. Start	8. Spur to overlook
2. Right turn	9. Overlook
3. Go straight	10. Bear left
4. Overlook	11. White connector
5. Left turn	12. Spur to Indian Creek
6. Right turn	13. Streambed
7. Streambed	14. White connector

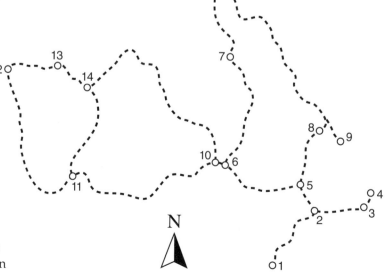

- Walk up to the Arch, feel its warm stainless steel sides, and experience Arch vertigo for yourself.
- Ride in a five-person capsule to the top of the 630-foot-tall Arch, the tallest human-made monument in the Western Hemisphere. On a clear day, get a 25-mile view.
- Hike past grizzly bears, polar bears, gazelles, and a southern pudu, the world's smallest deer, which is only shin high when standing!

Area Information

In 1764, Pierre LaClede, a French trader from New Orleans, set up a post on the Mississippi River just a few miles south of where the Missouri River flows into the Mississippi from the west. He chose a good spot. St. Louis was a thriving fur-trading settlement by the time President Thomas Jefferson bought the Louisiana Territory from France. In 1804 Lewis and Clark began their exploration of the unknown West from St. Louis and returned with reports of the new land's wealth. Land-hungry settlers in the East flocked to St. Louis and outfitted for journeys west, and St. Louis became, literally and commercially, the gateway to the West.

In 1947 a national architectural competition was held to create a design for the Jefferson National Expansion Memorial, a monument to commemorate Thomas Jefferson's purchase of the Louisiana Territory and the wave of westward expansion that followed. An ambitious design by Eero Saarinen was chosen—the mightiest freestanding arch ever built, taller than any symbolic monument except the Eiffel Tower. Remarkably, no inner frame or skeleton holds up the Arch; its steel panels, composed of equilateral triangles, bear the Arch's entire weight. The National Park Service administers the Arch grounds and museum.

Forest Park, dedicated in 1876 as a carriage park, was the site for the 1904 World's Fair, an event that attracted 20 million visitors. Over 1,500 plaster-of-paris buildings were constructed for the fair. The second largest urban park in the nation, Forest Park is used by over 10 million visitors a year, who come to its lawns, lakes, museums, and zoo to play and relax.

Directions: Take any major highway in Missouri east toward St. Louis and you'll end up at the Arch. On I-70 east, take exit 250A. Follow signs to the Arch or the riverfront. Forest Park is 4 miles west of the Arch on I-64/Highway 40. Take Hampton Avenue north into the park and follow the signs to the art museum.

Hours Open: The Arch grounds are open from 6:00 a.m. to 11:00 p.m. year-round. The visitor center and museum are open daily from 8:00 a.m. to 10:00 p.m. in the summer and from 9:00 a.m. to 6:00 p.m. in the winter. A 10:00 p.m. curfew is enforced in Forest Park. The St. Louis Zoo is always free and is open daily from 9:00 a.m. to 5:00 p.m., except for Christmas Day and New Year's Day.

Facilities: The visitor center underneath the Arch offers tram rides to the top, the Museum of Westward Expansion, two theaters, and a bookstore. Ranger-led tours of the Old Courthouse are available. Forest Park facilities include a skating rink, tennis courts, a science center, golf courses, a musical theater, a conservatory, boat rentals, a zoo, an art museum, fishing, and sledding.

Permits and Rules: Smoking or pets are not allowed in the Arch visitor center or Old Courthouse. While on Arch grounds, pets must be leashed.

For Further Information: Jefferson National Expansion Memorial, 11 North Fourth Street, St. Louis, MO 63102; 314-982-1410. For information about Forest Park, call 314-535-1503 or 314-367-7275.

St. Louis

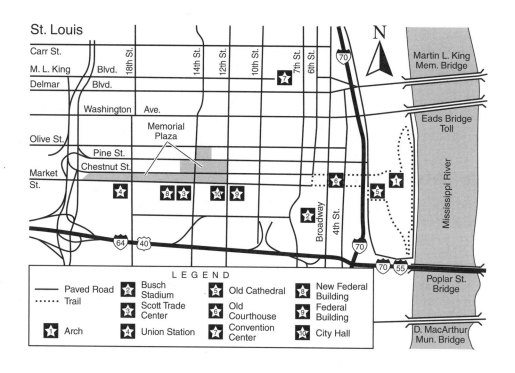

L E G E N D

— Paved Road
··· Trail

⭐1 Arch

⭐2 Busch Stadium
⭐3 Scott Trade Center
⭐4 Union Station

⭐5 Old Cathedral
⭐6 Old Courthouse
⭐7 Convention Center

⭐8 New Federal Building
⭐9 Federal Building
⭐10 City Hall

Forest Park

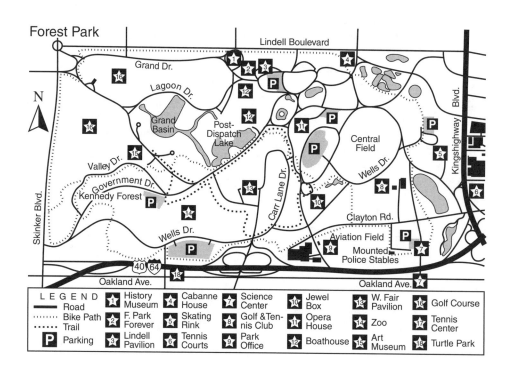

L E G E N D

— Road
···· Bike Path
··· Trail
🅿 Parking

⭐1 History Museum
⭐2 F. Park Forever
⭐3 Lindell Pavilion

⭐4 Cabanne House
⭐5 Skating Rink
⭐6 Tennis Courts

⭐7 Science Center
⭐8 Golf & Tennis Club
⭐9 Park Office

⭐10 Jewel Box
⭐11 Opera House
⭐12 Boathouse

⭐13 W. Fair Pavilion
⭐14 Zoo
⭐15 Art Museum

⭐16 Golf Course
⭐17 Tennis Center
⭐18 Turtle Park

Arch Area

Distance Round-Trip: 2 miles
Estimated Hiking Time: 1.25 hours

Hold both ends of a necklace about 9 inches apart, allowing the loop to hang freely. You are holding a catenary curve—the exact design (though upside-down) of the Arch.

Caution: Cross streets with care and only at corners; Memorial Drive is a major artery.

Trail Directions: Park in the garage for the Arch or in one of the lots along the river. A fee is charged for parking. Begin your hike at the north leg of the Arch [1], a good place to pat its stainless steel sides. (You'll see many people doing this.) Feel the warmth of the steel. As the two legs of the arch were being built, engineers took measurements at night to avoid variations caused by the sun's heat. Now look up. If there are any clouds at all, you'll be able to experience Arch vertigo, the remarkable illusion that the monument is falling over. In reality, the Arch sways a little in the wind, but only as far as 4 inches off center since it was built in 1965.

Hike northward, away from the Arch, along a curved walkway lined with ash trees. Bear right at two forks in the trail. Step out onto the William Clark overlook at .23 mi. [2]. The Eads Bridge, the first one on your left, was completed in 1874 and was St. Louis's first bridge over the Mississippi. Granite for its massive piers came from quarries in the Elephant Rocks area, south of Potosi. The silver ship in front of you, the *Admiral*, was once the largest river excursion ship in the nation. It is now permanently moored as part of a casino.

Turn right, descend the steps, and walk under some bald cypress trees. You reach the grand staircase at .44 mi. [3], a favorite place for meeting, sunning, and watching activities by the water. Continue straight and pass some steamboat replicas moored to the levee that serve as excursion ships and restaurants. Just past the cruise ships, ascend the steps and walk across the walkway. Climb a final set of steps to reach the Meriwether Lewis overlook at .83 mi. [4], with great views of the river, the Arch, and the assembly of skyscrapers behind it.

Turn around, descend the first set of steps, and turn left. Turn right at the fork at .93 mi. [5] and walk toward the Arch. Just before reaching the south leg, turn left, toward the cathedral with the green steeple. This is the Basilica of St. Louis, the King, and is affectionately known as the Old Cathedral [6] (1.20 mi.). The oldest Catholic church west of the Mississippi, the cathedral was founded in 1770. It's OK to step quietly inside. From here, turn right on Memorial Drive, pass the Old Cathedral Museum, and turn left onto Market Street. Luther Ely Smith Plaza, on your right, was named for the St. Louisan who proposed the memorial in 1933 that is now realized as the Arch. Cross 4th Street and enter the Old Courthouse if it is open.

The Old Courthouse [7] (1.4 mi.), the site of slave auctions and the Dred Scott trial, is interpreted by museum galleries and ranger-led tours. Walk under the magnificent rotunda and exit the building opposite the side you entered. Just across Broadway is a red granite monument marking the beginning of Boone's Lick Road [8] (1.5 mi.), the nation's first westward trail on this side of the Mississippi. Walk through Kiener Plaza toward the fountain with the bronze statue, *The Runner*, in its center [9] (1.6 mi.). At the far side of the fountain, turn and face the Old Courthouse for an unexpectedly splendid view of the Arch, which has a way of complimenting its surrounding structures, both old and new. Turn right on Chestnut Street, which borders Kiener Plaza on the north. Stay on Chestnut until it leads you to the north leg of the Arch, where you started.

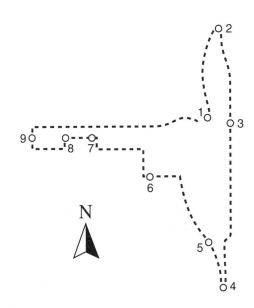

1. Start
2. William Clark overlook
3. Grand staircase
4. Meriwether Lewis overlook
5. Right turn
6. Old Cathedral
7. Old Courthouse
8. Boone's Lick Road monument
9. *The Runner*

Forest Park

 Distance Round-Trip: 2.5 miles
Estimated Hiking Time: 1.5 hours

I liked watching the polar bears' antics and strolling through the 1904 Flight Cage, but I liked the southern pudu best, a 14-inch-high deer that makes its living pushing over small trees!

Caution: Watch for bicycle and car traffic, and don't feed the bears (or the hammerkops)!

Trail Directions: Park on any of the streets near the art museum (parking is free) and begin your hike at the statue of Saint Louis on his horse, in front of the art museum [1]. As you face the lake at the bottom of the hill, the Grand Basin, turn right and hike down Fine Arts Drive. Just after you cross the paved bicycle path, make a gentle curve to your right through the shaded park and look for a building with blue tiles and animal figures on its side. This is the zoo entrance.

Enter the St. Louis Zoo at the Living World Entrance, which has educational, interactive exhibits [2] (.30 mi.). (If the zoo is closed, walk around to the zoo Hampton exit at its southeast end to resume the hike.) Walk through the Living World and go down the steps outside. Turn left on the main zoo path to the Bear Pits [3] (.44 mi.). Pass the black bears, spectacled bears, grizzly bears, and polar bears, and remain on the main zoo path. Pass the Kiener Memorial Entrance on your left and make your way toward the black walk-through bird cage. Enter the 1904 Flight Cage at .70 mi. [4].

Built by the Smithsonian Institution as an attraction for the 1904 World's Fair held in Forest Park, the continuing popularity of the giant cage led to its purchase by St. Louis and eventually to the formation of the St. Louis Zoo in 1913. Look for white-faced whistling ducks and white-headed buffalo weavers. You can't miss the pink flamingos; they're pink and loud.

Turn left at all forks in the trail after exiting the Flight Cage and arrive at the antelope fields on your right at .80 mi. [5]. Here are gazelles, kudus, and the southern pudu, the world's smallest (and one of its rarest) deer, standing only 14 inches high. Stay on the main path until you reach the Hampton exit at .95 mi. [6], where you exit the zoo, cross Concourse Drive, and continue on Carr Lane Drive. Turn right at 1.04 mi. [7] on Wells Drive and turn left on McKinley Drive.

Take the sidewalk to the art-deco glass house on your right. This structure is the Jewel Box [8] (1.32 mi.), a 1936 greenhouse must-see for anyone interested in houseplants or botany.

Return to McKinley Drive, continue on your right, and go through several intersections. The building on your right, just as you cross a canal, is the Municipal Theater, better known as the Muny [9] (1.67 mi.). This structure has been an outdoor theater since 1919 and has hosted such entertainers as W.C. Fields, Grace Kelly, and Bob Hope. Curve to the left onto Government Drive. The lake on your right is Post-Dispatch Lake [10] (1.88 mi.), where boats of all types are available for rent when weather permits. The shelter on the hilltop on your left is the World's Fair Pavilion, often used, like the Jewel Box, for weddings and other special events. Cross Washington Drive and stay on Government. Turn right at 2.21 mi. [11] on Fine Arts Drive to return to the saint.

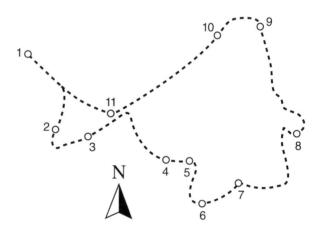

1. Start
2. Zoo entrance
3. Bear Pits
4. 1904 Flight Cage
5. Antelope fields
6. Hampton exit
7. Right turn
8. Jewel Box
9. The Muny
10. Post-Dispatch Lake
11. Right turn

19. Rockwoods Reservation

- Hike in an Ozark-like pocket of natural beauty, right in St. Louis County!
- Find evidence of historic quarrying operations in the woods.
- Hike on a suspension bridge over a scenic woodland stream.

Area Information

Imagine a rugged, wooded area with springs, streams, caves, protected valleys, and a rich diversity of plant, tree, and animal life. Now imagine removing all the marketable trees, leaving stripped and eroding hillsides. Imagine spending 70 years dynamiting the rock outcrops, altering the forest floor to build a railroad, constructing a mining community, and removing as much marketable rock, clay, and gravel as possible. Such is the story, or part of the story, of Rockwoods Reservation.

After the Glencoe Lime Company went bankrupt in 1938, the 1,800-acre area became one of the first properties of the newly formed Missouri Conservation Commission. Mining-town houses and structures were removed, along with the railroad tracks. Trees were planted and educational trails were constructed. The old company store was converted into a wildlife exhibit museum, and rehabilitated wildlife on display became a popular attraction. Tens of thousands of visitors came to hike the trails, see the animal exhibits, and picnic. In 1954 the Rockwoods Reservation Conservation Education Center was constructed at its current site.

Now imagine a place where the altered land is protected and healing, the trees have grown back, and people from the surrounding urban area can come for solitude in a peaceful setting to reconnect with the natural world. This is another part of Rockwoods' story. Audubon Missouri has designated Rockwoods as an important bird area (IBA), and the Department of Conservation operates it as a site for conservation education through the education center, hiking trails, and naturalist-led interpretive programs.

Directions: From I-44 in Eureka, take Highway 109 north 3.8 miles to the conservation sign at Woods Avenue. Turn left and then right on Glencoe Road. Travel 1.5 miles to the education center on the left.

Hours Open: The gate to the area opens at 5:00 a.m. and closes at 10:00 p.m. daily. The trails open at sunrise and close a half-hour after sunset daily. The education center is open from 8:00 a.m. to 5:00 p.m. Monday through Friday, except for state holidays.

Facilities: The site offers an education center with exhibits, information, and demonstration areas. There are picnic areas and restrooms. Programs about Missouri's fish, forest, and wildlife resources are available by advance registration for organized groups. Camping is available to organized youth groups by reservation only.

Permits and Rules: Because of potentially hazardous areas, hiking is permitted on designated trails only. Pets and horses are prohibited. Bicycling is allowed only on roads. Climbing and rappelling is by special-use permit only. Mushrooms may be taken for personal use, but digging, cutting, or removing other vegetation is prohibited.

For Further Information: Rockwoods Reservation, 2751 Glencoe Road, Wildwood, MO 63038; 636-458-2236.

Site Trails

Prairie Trail (, .25 mile). This trail winds through an area planted in native prairie grasses and wildflowers. It shares a parking area with the Lime Kiln Loop Trail, which is about .75 mile into the area.

Lime Kiln Loop Trail (, 3.2 miles). Winding through the central part of the property, this is the most rugged trail on the reservation. One of the older lime kilns still stands near the trailhead.

Turkey Ridge Trail (, 2 miles). Get your exercise as you hike up a ridge, down into a valley, and up onto a ridgetop again. The trailhead is at a parking lot near the northeast corner of Woods Avenue and Highway 109.

Green Rock Trail (, 10 miles one-way). This linear trail winds through the southwest portion of the site before continuing into Greensfelder County Park and Rockwoods Range. Park at the Cottonwood Picnic Area at Rockwoods Reservation, in Greensfelder County Park, or at Rockwoods Range.

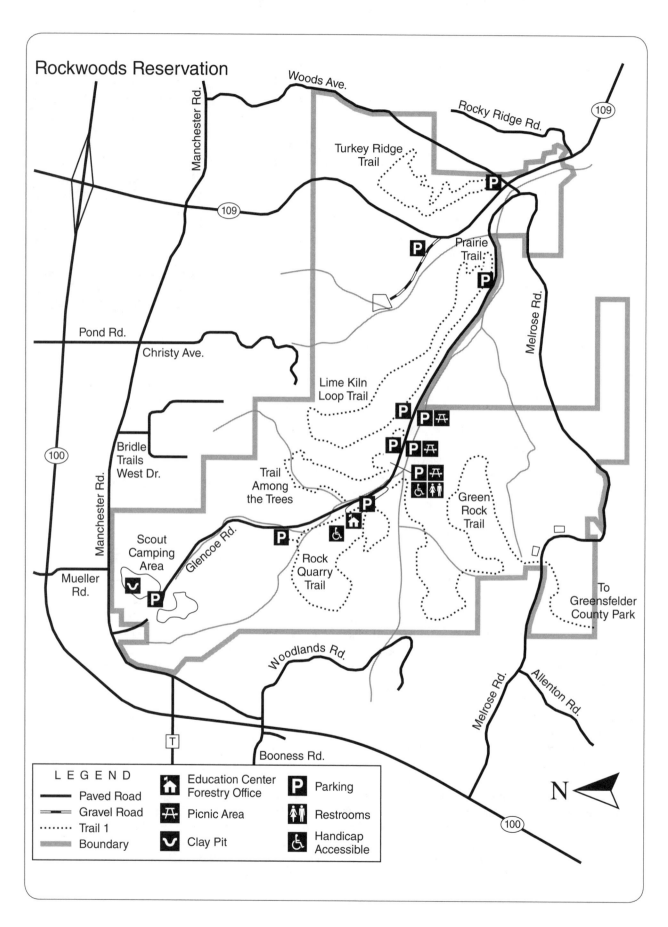

Rockwoods Reservation

Woods Ave.

Rocky Ridge Rd.

109

Manchester Rd.

109

Turkey Ridge Trail

P

P

Prairie Trail

P

Melrose Rd.

Pond Rd.

Christy Ave.

Lime Kiln Loop Trail

P **P** 🏕

100

Manchester Rd.

Bridle Trails West Dr.

P **P** 🏕

Trail Among the Trees

P **P** ♿ 🚻

Green Rock Trail

Scout Camping Area

Glencoe Rd.

P 🏠 **P**

♿

Rock Quarry Trail

To Greensfelder County Park

Mueller Rd.

Woodlands Rd.

Melrose Rd.

Allenton Rd.

100

T

Booness Rd.

L E G E N D

——	Paved Road
⊢⊣	Gravel Road
·····	Trail 1
▬▬	Boundary

🏠 Education Center Forestry Office

🏕 Picnic Area

ᴗ Clay Pit

P Parking

🚻 Restrooms

♿ Handicap Accessible

N

Trail Among the Trees

Distance Round-Trip: 2 miles
Estimated Hiking Time: 1.25 hours

Go on a scavenger hunt to find evidence of a major quarrying operation that occurred in this area between 1868 and 1938. You may have to look closely; this trail is a testimony to nature's amazing powers of resilience and healing.

Caution: To avoid potentially hazardous areas, stay on designated trails only. Also, be careful when crossing Glencoe Road and use the gravel path to return to the trailhead.

Trail Directions: Park in the parking area for the education center and offices. The trail begins across Glencoe Road from the offices, at a sign for the trail. An interpretive brochure about the trail is available at the trailhead or at the education center. Numbered stops in the brochure and on the trail do not correspond to numbered features here.

As you begin the trail [1] you cross the first of many small, wooden bridges over Hamilton Creek, a scenic woodland stream. Not far after the bridge, ignore the spur on your left and continue on the paved trail. One of the first clues to past quarrying operations, now camouflaged by moss, appears on your right at .08 mi. [2]. Notice the remnants of a stone wall. Was the wall built to construct a roadbed? Was the ditch part of a road, too? Beginning in the 1870s and continuing into the 1930s, the Glencoe Lime Company extracted Kimmswick limestone from these hills and processed it in kilns to make lime for cement and for agriculture. Keep an eye out for more evidence of past quarrying as you continue.

At .16 mi. [3], cross the stream on some stones that still bear drill marks. Across the stream, you ascend some wooden steps. At the top you encounter a rock cliff face. Turn right here at .23 mi. [4]. As you approach a bench on your right at .27 mi. [5], look at the cliffs on your left. They look natural enough now, with lichens, mosses, and other plants growing on and around them. These cliffs were made, however, when huge limestone beds were drilled and blown apart with dynamite. Look closely to see drill marks and holes in some of the rocks.

More clues appear just ahead at .33 mi. [6], where you can see remnants of an old railroad bed as a small ridge on your right. A small-scale rail line was built to haul limestone from the quarries to the kilns. Animals like mules or donkeys pulled hopper cars along the rails. Notice the piles of discarded rocks, too. After you cross the creek twice more, first on a stone bridge and then on a wooden one, you may be surprised by the grand cliff that pops out of the woods on your left.

Just past the cliff at .45 mi. [7], ignore the spur on your left and turn right. After going down some wooden steps you find a huge, blocky boulder adorned with water-loving plants like hydrangea and mosses. Cross a suspension bridge over the stream at .50 mi. [8] and revel in the beauty of this healing landscape.

The trail now zigzags up a slope adorned with grand trees and Christmas ferns. You go over two more small, wooden bridges before finding a bench at .71 mi. [9]. At 1.25 mi. [10], the pavement ends and you step out onto the rocks of a gladelike opening, complete with a bench and an overlook of the surrounding wooded hills. After passing another quarry site on your left, you make a long, gentle descent along some beautiful rock outcrops. Just before reaching the parking lot, look on the left side of the trail at 1.53 mi. [11] for a piece of the old railroad rail. At 1.56 mi. [12], cross Glencoe Road and turn right on a gravel path to return to the trailhead.

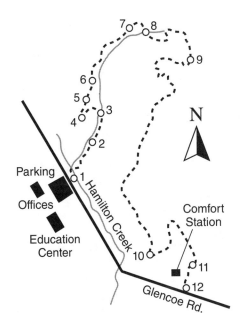

1. Start
2. Stone wall
3. Stream crossing
4. Right turn
5. Bench
6. Old railroad bed
7. Right turn
8. Suspension bridge
9. Bench
10. Overlook
11. Old railroad rail
12. Road crossing

Rock Quarry Trail

 Distance Round-Trip: 2.25 miles
Estimated Hiking Time: 1.25 hours

It's a rough-and-tumble landscape, partly because of the rugged natural terrain and partly because of the major alterations people made for 70 years. It's also a rich and diverse landscape, flourishing despite (and sometimes because of) our human modifications.

Caution: To avoid potentially hazardous areas, stay on designated trails only.

Trail Directions: Park in the parking area for the education center. The trail begins near the maintenance buildings, at a sign for the trail. An interpretive booklet about the common trees of Rockwoods is designed especially for the Rock Quarry Trail, although the booklet can be used anywhere in the area. The tree booklet may be available at the trailhead or at the education center.

The trail begins **[1]** on some switchbacks up a wooded slope. Soon, a valley plunges on your left, and scenic rock outcrops dot the steep slope on your right. The rocks get bigger and blockier until you reach some rock faces at .15 mi. **[2]**. People shaped some of these rock surfaces, as quarry workers drilled and blasted the limestone into fragments that could be hauled to the kilns. Nature is doing some shaping here, too, as the forces of erosion carve these outcrops into wild shapes, with overhangs, undercuts, and lots of shelves.

Signs of past quarrying are more evident at .22 mi. **[3]**, where piles of discarded rocks lie at the base of vertical rock faces. Although these rock piles are a by-product of quarrying, they mimic the natural sloughing off of rocks from natural cliffs (talus) and serve as homes for many plants and animals including insects, centipedes, lizards, snakes, salamanders, chipmunks, and other small mammals.

Another example of how nature can take advantage of human activity can be seen just ahead, just after the trail swings to the right. Notice the beautiful assembly of pincushion moss and reindeer lichen at .51 mi. **[4]** that has covered nearly every inch of soil that was disturbed when this trail was constructed. Soon, you hike on top of the ridge in a mature, open forest with Ozark-like vistas of distant wooded ridges in a 360-degree view. Go straight at .67 mi. **[5]**, at the intersection with the connector that would take you back to the education center. Hike among a rich diversity of trees here, including white oak, persimmon, post oak, cherry, red oak, sassafras, ash, black oak, shagbark hickory, and hackberry.

At 1.33 mi. **[6]**, you descend some wooden stairs and hike along an intermittent stream. Notice the tall, vertical rock faces that appear on your left at 1.57 mi. **[7]**. According to the education staff, vertical-face quarrying techniques were used until the overburden of undesirable rock became too thick to manage. At that point, horizontal excavations began, producing the shallow "caves" that you see at the base of these faces. Notice the long ridges that are remnants of the narrow-gauge railroad used to haul limestone to the kilns. The raised bed acts as a dam, creating an ephemeral pond that benefits woodland amphibians and other wildlife.

As you continue, you see stone building foundations on your left. Cross the stream at 1.73 mi. **[8]** over a small wooden bridge and turn right on the other side. Turn right at the fork in the trail at 1.82 mi. **[9]**. You cross two more small wooden bridges as you hike next to Glencoe Road. Notice the small spring on your right at 2.07 mi. **[10]**, just before you reach the offices and return to the parking lot.

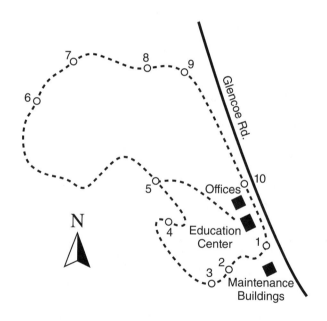

1. Start
2. Rock faces
3. Rock piles
4. Moss mania
5. Go straight
6. Wooden stairs
7. Tall rock faces
8. Wooden bridge
9. Right turn
10. Spring

- Discover spicebush, an aromatic shrub that you can smell when you brush against it on the trail. A tea made from its bark or fruit has been used to treat everything from colds to dysentery to intestinal worms!

- Observe an ant metropolis next to the trail.

- Hike through a grove of pawpaw, the only food plant for caterpillars of a distinctive woodland butterfly, the zebra swallowtail.

- Find at least three official state species on one trail.

Area Information

Dr. Edmund A. Babler Memorial State Park is named after Edmund A. Babler, a renowned and beloved St. Louis physician. After Babler died suddenly from pneumonia at age 54 in 1930, his two brothers, Jacob and Henry, gave the park to the state as a living memorial.

The park, only a 20-minute drive from downtown St. Louis, is an interesting blend of urban and rural characteristics. Manicured lawns and trees surround the full-length bronze statue of Dr. Babler, and the wide-entry avenue with its impressive stone gateway is reminiscent of a metropolitan plaza. Yet Babler is home to unusually tall and rich forests of oak, basswood, sugar maple, and walnut, a quality owing to its geographic location.

Situated in a transition area between the rugged Ozarks to the south and the expansive glacial plains to the north, Babler State Park has both highly dissected ridges and rich soil. Located only about 2 miles from the Missouri River floodplain, the rugged landscape of the park was covered with deep deposits of windblown glacial dust—a fertile soil called loess. These loess deposits and deep sheltered valleys have nurtured Babler's rich forest communities.

An area near the campground is a designated state natural area, featuring an old-growth white oak and sugar maple forest that has remained relatively undisturbed since presettlement times. When dedicated in 1938, Babler was a long drive into the country from St. Louis. Now it is a much-needed green oasis amid an ever-growing suburban landscape.

Directions: Babler State Park is in west St. Louis County. From the intersection of Highways 100 and 109 in Wildwood, drive north on Highway 109 for 3.7 miles. Turn left into the entrance gates.

Hours Open: The park gates open daily at 7:00 a.m. The gates close at 6:00 p.m. from November through March, and at 9:00 p.m. from April through October. The visitor center is open from 8:30 a.m. to 4:00 p.m. daily except for Christmas Day, New Year's Day, and Thanksgiving.

Facilities: The park offers a campground, picnic areas, horse trails, bicycle trails, a tennis court, a visitor center with exhibits, and an amphitheater.

Permits and Rules: Hikers are permitted on hiking, bicycle, and horse trails, but bicycles are permitted only on paved trails and roads. Horses are permitted only on equestrian trails. Pets must always be leashed.

For Further Information: Dr. Edmund A. Babler Memorial State Park, 800 Guy Park Drive, Wildwood, MO 63005-6134; 636-458-3813.

Park Trails

Dogwood Trail (🥾🥾🥾, 2 miles). This trail gives a good sampling of the park's upland forests, ravines, and moist forests. Two sections are united with a horse trail. It shares a trailhead with the Woodbine Trail.

Woodbine Trail (🥾🥾🥾, 1.75 mile). Hike next to a stand of towering sweet gum trees, past a CCC-era stone building, and through some lush, wooded ravines. Bicyclists share a portion of the trail. The trailhead is at the Nature Trail parking area, off Guy Park Drive.

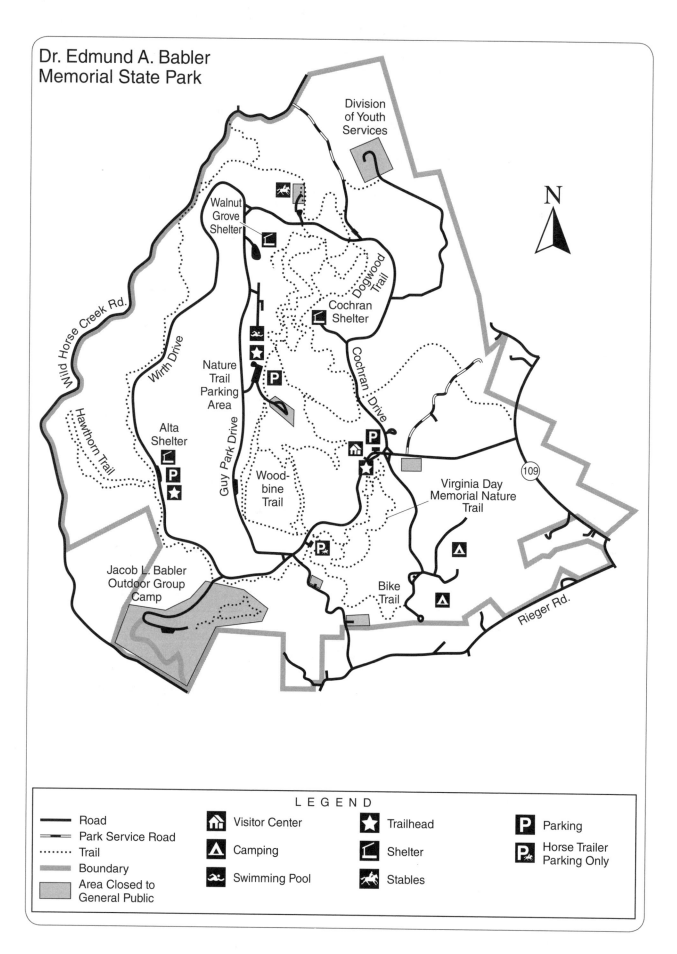

Dr. Edmund A. Babler
Memorial State Park

Division of Youth Services

N

Walnut Grove Shelter

Dogwood Trail

Cochran Shelter

Wild Horse Creek Rd.

Wirth Drive

Cochran Drive

Hawthorn Trail

Nature Trail Parking Area

Guy Park Drive

Alta Shelter

Virginia Day Memorial Nature Trail

109

Wood-bine Trail

Jacob L. Babler Outdoor Group Camp

Bike Trail

Rieger Rd.

LEGEND

Road	Visitor Center	Trailhead	P Parking
Park Service Road	Camping	Shelter	P Horse Trailer Parking Only
Trail	Swimming Pool	Stables	
Boundary			
Area Closed to General Public			

Virginia Day Memorial Nature Trail

 Distance Round-Trip: 1.5 miles
Estimated Hiking Time: 45 minutes

Trace is an old word for trail. People traversing new territory followed the tracks, bent grasses, or other barely perceptible traces of those who had gone before them. Consequently, traces evolved into trails, literally and semantically.

Caution: The trail is hard packed, moist, shaded, and slippery in places. Also, watch out for land snails on the trail to avoid stepping on them; they are abundant here.

Trail Directions: Park at the visitor center and find the trailhead across the road, off a paved loop **[1]**. What little sunlight makes it through the tall canopies of white oak, red oak, and sugar maple is usually blocked by shorter basswood, dogwood, and redbud. Right away, the trail introduces you to one of the most outstanding natural features of the park—dense shade.

Turn right at the three-way intersection at .13 mi. **[2]** and again at .17 mi. **[3]**. If you are here in spring you will be treated to a wildflower display 10 to 20 feet tall in the form of blooming dogwood and redbud. Look for the umbrellas of mayapples here, adding their shade to the rich forest floor. Turn right at the intersection at .31 mi. **[4]**. The patch of shrubs growing on both sides of the trail at .46 mi. **[5]** looks like poison ivy, but it isn't—it's fragrant sumac. Although both plants have "leaves of three," the middle leaflet of poison ivy has a longer stem than the others. The middle leaflet stem of fragrant sumac is either very short or absent.

As you descend into a shaded valley notice how the Christmas ferns increase. Pawpaws are more numerous here too; their giant, unlobed leaves provide a pleasant contrast to the lacy fern leaves below. Turn left at the spur intersection at .66 mi. **[6]**. In the low areas, especially at the big bend at .88 mi. **[7]**, look

for spicebush that tends to encroach on the trail. This aromatic shrub produces shiny green fruit in May that turns bright red by October. The fruit was used during the Revolutionary War as a substitute for allspice, and the leaves were used as a tea during the Civil War. Listen for the trills of tree frogs here and watch out for land snails, feeding on the thin layers of algae and moss on the shaded trail.

Cross a wooden bridge over an intermittent stream at 1.30 mi. **[8]**. When you return to the intersection at **[2]**, turn right to complete your hike.

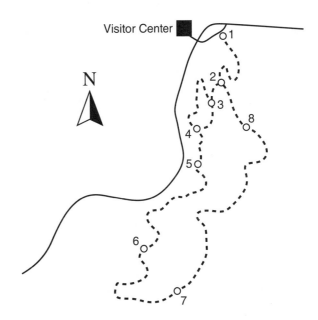

1. Start
2. Right turn
3. Right turn
4. Right turn
5. Fragrant sumac
6. Left turn
7. Spicebush
8. Wooden bridge

Hawthorn Trail

Distance Round-Trip: 1.15 miles
Estimated Hiking Time: 45 minutes

You'll find at least one kind of hawthorn here (of the state's 79 hawthorn species), representative of Missouri's state flower. You'll also find the state tree (flowering dogwood) and the state fossil (crinoid). You may even find the state insect (honeybee) on the glade and the state bird (bluebird) near the trailhead. Chances of spotting Missouri's state aquatic animal (paddlefish), however, are low.

Caution: Check for ticks after passing through the glade.

Trail Directions: Park at the Alta picnic shelter, located on Wirth Drive, on the west side of the park. Begin the trail at the signboard [1] across the road from the south end of the parking lot.

You cross a horse trail near the trailhead and continue on a dry, wooded ridgetop. White oaks and sugar maples are plentiful, as well as flowering dogwood and redbud. Look for sassafras, with three types of leaves on the same tree. Some leaves have no lobes (football shaped), some have one lobe (mitten shaped), and others have two lobes (trident shaped).

Turn left at the intersection at .10 mi. [2]. At around .25 mi. [3], start looking next to the trail on the right side for low mounds of granular soil, dotted with small holes. These are the tops of underground colonies of ants. The main "city" is about 6 feet wide and 75 feet long. The hundreds of thousands of ants that live here are important members of the forest community. Small reptiles and amphibians often feed on ants, as do birds and other insects. If you are here on a warm day you will probably see a steady stream of worker ants (all females) emerge from a hole, drop a load of soil, and return to the tunnel.

A post oak with limbs hanging over the trail marks a rocky, sunny opening in the forest—a limestone glade remnant [4] (.54 mi.). Notice all the bluestem grass here, interrupted by patches of yellow wingstem sunflowers and spiderwort. Bright red fruit of the fragrant sumac adds its color, too. To the left, next to the forest, are several hawthorn trees. Close

observation of the exposed slabs of limestone bedrock on the trail reveals fossils of crinoids and other sea creatures. At the north end of the glade is the former state champion gum bumelia. Normally a glade tree of small, stunted stature, the girth of this one is over 3 feet!

After you reenter the forest, some boulders on your left at .65 mi. [5] provide glimpses of the outlying rugged ridges through the trees. Small patches of ferns appear on your right, and big patches of mayapples cascade down the slope on your left. Watch for the metallic green six-spotted tiger beetle, running and flying ahead of you on the trail. If you've seen zebra swallowtails (medium-sized black-and-white striped butterflies) in the park, credit the abundance of pawpaws, a small, tropical-looking tree of moist woods. The pawpaw is the only food plant for zebra swallowtail caterpillars. At .90 mi. [6] is a grove of pawpaws on both sides of the trail. Check the leaves for caterpillar holes. Turn left at [2] to return to the trailhead.

1. Start
2. Left turn
3. Ant metropolis
4. Limestone glade remnant
5. Overlook
6. Pawpaw grove

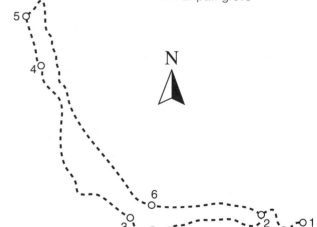

- What was 9 feet high at the shoulder, weighed 5 tons, and had 8-foot-long tusks? (Big hint: A full-sized replica of this animal's skeleton is at Mastodon State Historic Site.)
- Visit the archaeological site that yielded the first solid evidence that humans coexisted with mastodons 12,000 years ago.
- Hike on top of an ancient ocean bed on a natural sidewalk in the forest.
- Stroll quietly on a trail above a gravel-bottomed stream to spy on stonerollers, hornyhead chubs, and northern hog suckers.

Area Information

In the early 1800s, bones of many now-extinct animals were found just south of St. Louis, in what is now known as the Kimmswick Bone Bed. An early discoverer, Albert C. Koch, assembled a colossal collage of animal bones and named his creation the Missouri Leviathan. Describing his creature as "swift as the descending eagle and terrible as the angel of the night," Koch toured the spectacle across the United States, sometimes with a three-piece band playing in its rib cage. Koch's leviathan turned out to be an American mastodon, an elephant-like beast that browsed on trees and roamed what is now Missouri during the Ice Age that occurred from 35,000 to 10,000 years ago.

Over the span of a century, the bones from more than 60 mastodons were reportedly taken from the Kimmswick Bone Bed, which became known as one of the most extensive Pleistocene bone beds in the country. In 1970 four local women led a movement to preserve the bone bed, enabling the state to buy the site in 1976. Archaeological history was made at the site in 1979 when a large stone spear point was found with the bones of American mastodons, providing the first undisputed evidence of the association of human being and mastodon in North America. For the first time, evidence suggested that early humans' contact with mastodons and other large mammals at the end of the Ice Age may have contributed to their extinction.

As you enter the museum at Mastodon State Historic Site, a sign invites you to "Please—touch this tooth," and on top of the display is a genuine young adult mastodon molar. As you run your fingers over the tooth's six mountainlike ridges, you are reenacting a human–mastodon contact that was proved to have taken place on this spot 12,000 years ago.

Directions: At the south edge of St. Louis, take exit 186 (Imperial/Main Street) off Highway 55. Turn north on West Outer Road, and go .9 mile to the museum on Charles J. Becker Drive.

Hours Open: The picnic area is open from 8:00 a.m. to dusk year-round. The museum is open from 9:00 a.m. to 4:30 p.m. Monday through Saturday and from noon to 4:30 p.m. on Sunday from March through November. Call for winter hours in December through February. The museum is closed on Easter, Thanksgiving, Christmas Day, and New Year's Day.

Facilities: The site features a museum with animal and human artifacts, interpretive exhibits, and an audiovisual area. A small fee is collected for entrance to the museum. Excavations have been closed to protect the bone bed, but an interpretive kiosk at the Kimmswick Bone Bed explains the site's past excavations. Picnic tables are available at the museum and the picnic area. The museum annex, operated by volunteers, supplements the museum's exhibits and interpretation. The annex is open intermittently, mostly in the summer.

Permits and Rules: Wading is allowed in Rock Creek at the picnic area. Alcoholic beverages are prohibited on the parking lots and creek beaches. Camping is permitted only by special groups with permission of the site administrator. Pets must be leashed. Collection of plants, wildlife, fossils, or artifacts is prohibited. Hikers may not leave marked trails.

Further Information: Mastodon State Historic Site, 1050 Charles J. Becker Drive, Imperial, MO 63052; 636-464-2976.

Other Areas of Interest

Just southwest of Mastodon, off Highway 21, **Sandy Creek Covered Bridge State Historic Site** features a bridge built in 1872 and rebuilt in 1887—one of only four covered bridges remaining in the state. The site includes a picnic area and an interpretive shelter about covered bridges. For more information, call Mastodon State Historic Site.

Site Trails

Wildflower Trail (👣👣👣, .5 mile). This trail takes you down several flights of steps, across an old limestone quarry, and down to the base of the limestone bluff where the famous human artifacts and mastodon bones were discovered. An interpretive kiosk is at the site. The trail begins behind the museum.

Mastodon State Historic Site

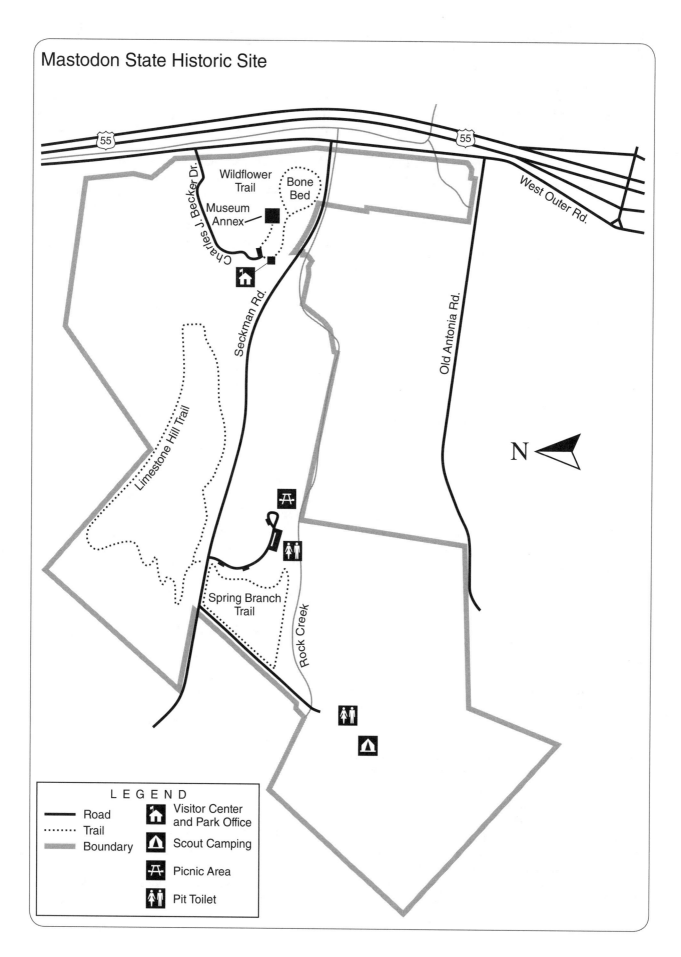

LEGEND

—— Road	Visitor Center and Park Office
···· Trail	Scout Camping
—— Boundary	Picnic Area
	Pit Toilet

Limestone Hill Trail

Distance Round-Trip:
2.25 miles
Estimated Hiking Time:
1.25 hours

I liked the rough limestone boulders that protruded from the ravined slopes, just before the long bluff walk. Tiny orange and red mushrooms shaped like little funnels poked through the dark green moss on the boulders and were as brilliant as any spring wildflower.

Caution: Use caution when crossing Seckman Road; vehicles can be fast and numerous. Also, the trail is sometimes slippery because of small, loose rocks on hills and algae-covered bedrock.

Trail Directions: The Limestone Hill Trail and the Spring Branch Trail share a trailhead, located in the picnic area just west of the visitor center. From the entrance to the visitor center, turn south on West Outer Road and go .2 mi. Turn west on Seckman Road and travel .9 mi. Turn left at the sign for the picnic area. The trailhead is at the corner of the first parking lot on your right.

Begin at the sign for the trailhead [1] and turn right at the intersection at .01 mi. [2]. At .02 mi. [3] are the remnants of the Bollefer family springhouse. Turn right at the fork in the trail, just past the springhouse, and cross Seckman Road at .05 mi. [4]. Turn left at the intersection at .06 mi. [5]. Notice the thorns up and down the trunks of the honey locust trees on your right. New, bright green thorns are mixed in clusters with older brown ones. Many of the vines climbing the sugar maple trees are trumpet creeper, which produces orange-red, trumpet-shaped blossoms in July and August.

Hike onto a natural sidewalk at .10 mi. [6], made of limestone bedrock. Composed of layers of sediment from the bottom of ancient oceans, limestone often reveals its layers as it erodes. Notice the limestone bluffs on your right. Enough soil has accumulated in their eroded cracks to support ebony spleenwort and other ferns. Sometimes you can see the layers in perfectly parallel, horizontal lines. Soon you begin to switchback up a steep, rocky hill through an aged cedar forest, with a few white oaks mixed in. A resting bench provides a good place to stop and notice the knobby and distorted trunks of many of the old cedars, reminiscent of the coniferous forests that were here when mastodons roamed the area.

The trail ascends a good exercise hill under some big ash trees, and the drainage valleys on each side of the trail become more evident. Take the spur on your right at .46 mi. [7] and enjoy the bench and overlook. Turn right at the intersection at .48 mi. [8]. Bear left at

the wide, rocky fork in the trail at .59 mi. [9]. Several red mulberry trees grow on this ridgetop. Box turtles are quick to find their fallen fruit, which resembles a blackberry, in early summer. Pass a resting bench on your left and ignore the spur on your right at .82 mi. [10]. Now it's an easy downhill hike.

Notice the fierce competition for space by shrubs and young trees under the power line at 1.21 mi. [11]. Follow the yellow arrows and turn right at the intersection at 1.34 mi. [12]. The trail passes through a beautiful, shaded forest with deep ravines and rough, protruding boulders. An intermittent stream trickles at the bottom on your left. Just after the trail swings to the right, a scenic limestone bluff appears at 1.40 mi. [13]. Smooth cliff brake and alum root adorn its weathered sides, and wild grape and trumpet creeper vines connect it to the tree canopy. At one point, the trail puts you in a squeeze between the bluff and a hackberry trunk.

The bluff continues at your right shoulder for quite a distance. Look for delicate columbine and an assortment of ferns. Wild hydrangea sprouts where water trickles from small cracks. A small stream crossing the trail marks the end of your bluff walk. You find a spur to the entrance of the picnic area on your left at 2.15 mi. [14]. Turn left at this spur or at the intersection [5] to finish your hike.

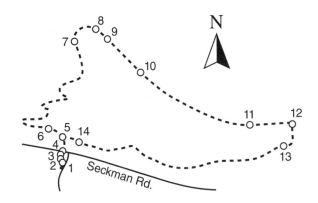

1. Start
2. Right turn
3. Springhouse remnants
4. Road crossing
5. Left turn
6. Natural sidewalk
7. Overlook
8. Right turn
9. Bear left
10. Go straight
11. Power line
12. Right turn
13. Limestone bluff
14. Spur to picnic area

Spring Branch Trail

  Distance Round-Trip: .75 mile
  Estimated Hiking Time: 30 minutes

I walked around the old springhouse, feeling its stone walls. I imagined the sturdy door that must have been in place once, keeping raccoons out of precious milk, hand-churned butter, and Mason jars filled with green beans, dill pickles, and gooseberries.

Caution: The area is prone to occasional flooding because of Rock Creek and the spring branch.

Trail Directions: The Limestone Hill Trail and the Spring Branch Trail share a trailhead, located in the picnic area just west of the visitor center. From the entrance to the visitor center, turn south on West Outer Road for .2 mi. Turn west on Seckman Road for .9 mi. and turn left at the sign for the picnic area. The trailhead is at the corner of the first parking lot on your right.

Begin at the sign for the trailhead **[1]**. Turn left at the intersection at .01 mi. **[2]** and cross the small, wooden bridge over the spring branch of Bollefer Spring, named for a family that once lived in the area. Bushy, green mats of plants in the stream are watercress, an indicator of spring water and a highly favored wild edible. A traditional wilted salad recipe calls for watercress, hot bacon grease, vinegar, and sugar. Across the bridge, follow the trail to the left along the spring branch. Enormous cottonwood and sycamore tree trunks make the stream look smaller than it really is.

At .07 mi. **[3]** is a four-way intersection. Take the second trail from the left, which takes you behind the picnic shelter. Look for box elder trees here, which have leaves that resemble poison ivy and often have small, green sprouts growing from the trunk. Box elder trees can grow in many habitats but are not good choices for landscaping around homes because of inevitable periodic infestations of red and black box elder bugs. Soon you pass another picnic area on your left. Turn right at .20 mi. **[4]** at the wooden bridge and you'll see Rock Creek, a tributary to the Mississippi River, riffling and churning on your left. Several spurs off the trail down to gravel washes and sandbars give testimony to visitors' use of the creek as a summertime wading and splashing hole.

As you walk the trail parallel to the creek, look into the water and notice a variety of fish. Look for stonerollers, 4- or 5-inch-long fish that push small stones around on the creek bottom, grazing on algae

underneath. These curious fish have the odd habit of occasionally flipping vertically out of the water on warm days in late fall. Northern hog suckers live here, too. They resemble small, motionless sharks when seen from above. As you continue, a sprawling catalpa tree looms over the creek near a stand of horsetail, a slender and ancient water-loving plant.

At .42 mi. **[5]**, just before reaching some private homes on the right, turn right on the wide, mowed path. Here the trail winds through a young forest of box elder and hackberry trees near the park boundary on your left. Listen for the mewing calls of the gray catbird, which, like the mockingbird, is often associated with residential areas.

Turn right at the intersection at .58 mi. **[6]** and cross a small, wooden bridge over the Bollefer Spring Branch. The limestone remnants of the Bollefer family springhouse come into view at .70 mi. **[7]**. Taking advantage of the cool year-round temperature of spring water (around 56 to 58 degrees in Missouri), families built springhouses, usually of stone, over springs or spring branches to cool perishable foods like milk and butter in the days before indoor refrigeration. In a few steps you return to an intersection **[2]**, where you turn left to complete your hike.

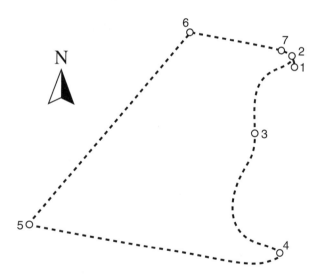

1. Start
2. Left turn
3. Four-way intersection
4. Right turn
5. Right turn
6. Right turn
7. Springhouse remnants

- Examine the largest group of petroglyphs in the state—thunderbirds, snakes, and human figures—carved in limestone bedrock between AD 1000 and 1600.

- Hike on a rich talus slope noted statewide for its luxuriant and diverse spring wildflowers.

- Catch sight of the eastern collared lizard doing push-ups on a rock or running away on its hind legs like a miniature dinosaur.

- Find hematite pieces on the trail near old prospecting sites.

Area Information

The cultural, historical, and natural features of Washington State Park fuse beautifully in many ways. Prehistorically, the area was a significant ceremonial site for villagers of the Middle Mississippian culture, evidenced today by three major groups of petroglyphs. Birds, turkey tracks, arrows, and many other symbols carved in flat limestone sheets may have been part of initiation ceremonies for secret societies. The petroglyphs may have been memory aids for the initiates, who perhaps were required to perform complex sequences of songs and ritualistic rites.

Later, after the petroglyphs became protected as part of Washington State Park, the African-American stonemasons of Company 1743 of the CCC were influenced by the work of these ancient rock carvers, as well as by the natural outcroppings of rock in the park. Between 1934 and 1939, these master craftsmen artfully laid the stone steps of the 1,000 Steps Trail and built Thunderbird Lodge, rental cabins, an octagonal lookout shelter, and a trail shelter that resembles a natural stone outcrop. All their work in the park is listed on the National Register of Historic Places.

Even without its cultural and historical legacy, Washington State Park is remarkable for its natural features and beauty. Expansive limestone glades, rippling with prairie grasses, are home to such uncommon species as Fremont's leather flower and the eastern collared lizard. The hiking trails and lookout shelters offer outstanding views of the Big River Valley. A 68-acre portion of the park's rich hardwood forests is a designated state natural area. In spring, the north-facing slope of the 1,000 Steps Trail is resplendent with the park system's showiest display of woodland wildflowers.

Directions: The park is located 8 miles south of DeSoto on Highway 21.

Hours Open: The site is open year-round, and the park office is open from 8:00 a.m. to 4:30 p.m. Monday through Friday.

Facilities: A campground, picnic areas, and swimming pool are available. The Big River provides opportunities for fishing and canoeing. Kitchen-equipped cabins may be rented, and a park store operates at Thunderbird Lodge.

Permits and Rules: Please stay on designated boardwalks near the petroglyphs to avoid damaging them. Bicycles and horses are not permitted on the trails, nor are cutting implements such as saws and hatchets. Campfires are prohibited. Camping is permitted by backpackers only on the portion of Rockywood Trail that lies west of the campground and swimming pool.

For Further Information: Washington State Park, 13041 Highway 104, DeSoto, MO 63020; 636-586-2995.

Park Trails

Rockywood Trail (🥾🥾🥾🥾, 10 miles). This trail features rugged forested terrain, numerous blufftop overlooks, and open, rocky, scenic limestone glades. The trail begins on the northwest side of Thunderbird Lodge parking lot and is marked with orange arrows in a counterclockwise direction.

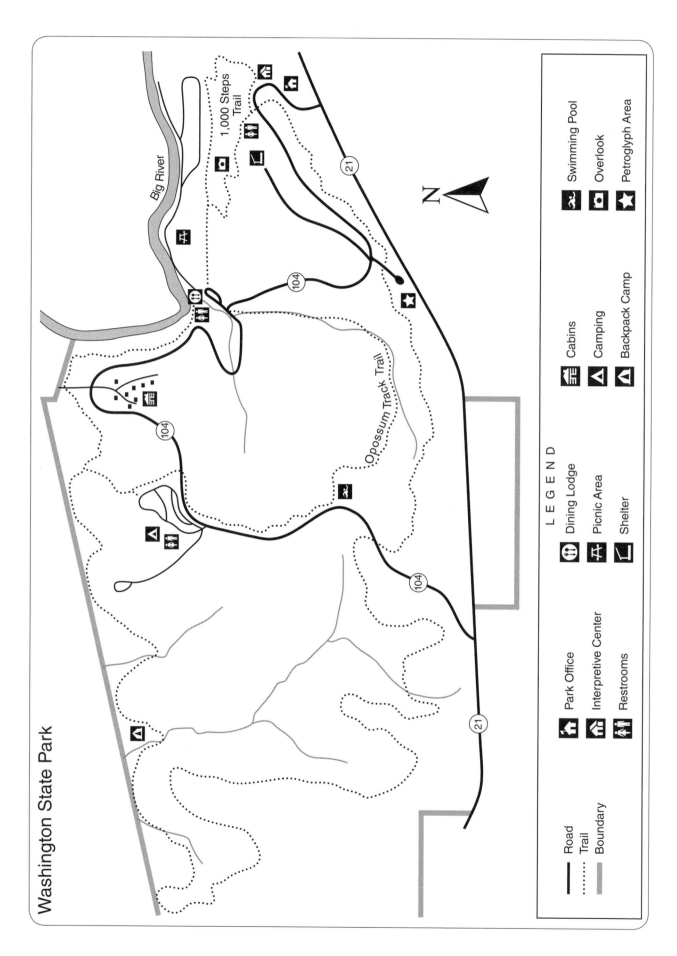

Washington State Park

Big River

1,000 Steps Trail

Opossum Track Trail

21

104

104

104

21

N

LEGEND

	Park Office		Cabins		Swimming Pool
	Interpretive Center		Camping		Overlook
	Restrooms		Backpack Camp		Petroglyph Area
	Dining Lodge				
	Picnic Area				
	Shelter				

——— Road
········· Trail
——— Boundary

1,000 Steps Trail

 Distance Round-Trip: 1.5 miles
Estimated Hiking Time: 1 hour

I was too busy noticing the abundant celandine poppies, wet-weather waterfalls, and sweeping blufftop vistas to count the stone steps laid by the ambitious CCC stonemasons of the mid-1930s. Are there really 1,000?

Caution: The trail at the bottom will be muddy after a hard rain.

Trail Directions: Park at Thunderbird Lodge and begin the trail behind the picnic area at the northeast end of the parking lot **[1]**. You hike on the edge of a rich floodplain of the Big River, which is just to your left. On your right is a mature hardwood forest that has developed on broken-down talus—rock fragments eroded from the dolomite bluff on top. The soil is rich here and kept cool and moist on the north-facing slope, which allows vigorous and diverse growth. Many of the trees here are over 100 feet tall and more than 150 years old.

Also abundant here are wet-weather waterfalls, the first at .04 mi. **[2]**. Before reaching the main intersection of the trail, you'll find three or four more trickling down from the forest slope. Stream water falls down layers of stair-stepped dolomite, covered in mosses and walking fern, and carpets of bluebells, Dutchman's-breeches, and blue-eyed marys adorn the banks.

At the intersection at .15 mi. **[3]**, the stone steps invite you upward. Painstakingly laid over 60 years ago, these steps of native stone now blend beautifully into the forested hillside. Turn right here and again at the top of the steps at the base of the dolomite bluff. At .17 mi. **[4]**, the trail takes you left on top of the bluff—the parent rock for the talus. Soon you find a scenic overlook of the Big River Valley **[5]** (.22 mi.). At .28 mi. **[6]** is a native-stone shelter built into the hillside, offering another inspiring view.

Walk behind the overlook and away from the river to continue the trail. Turn left at .32 mi. **[7]**, where you see a bent tree on your left. You pass a restroom at .45 mi. At .57 mi. is the interpretive center **[8]**, where you can stop in to see exhibits about the petroglyphs in the park. A park office building is here, too, where you can find park information.

Turn left behind the interpretive center to continue. You descend more stone steps under some giant bur oaks, sugar maples, and Kentucky coffee trees. Turn left at .90 mi. **[9]**, just before you reach the picnic shelter. Notice the variety of wildflowers and mushrooms here, growing among the big logs in all stages of decay. At 1.26 mi., go straight at **[3]** and enjoy the wet-weather waterfalls again on your way back to the trailhead.

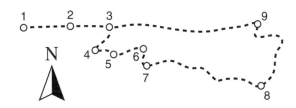

1. Start
2. Wet-weather waterfalls
3. Right turn
4. Left turn
5. Overlook
6. Stone shelter overlook
7. Left turn
8. Interpretive center
9. Left turn

Opossum Track Trail

Distance Round-Trip: 3 miles
Estimated Hiking Time: 1.5 hours

I'm glad someone named something after the ubiquitous and humble opossum. They are quick to "grin" at those who might disturb them, flashing more pretty teeth per mouth than any other mammal in North America. No other animal's footprint more closely resembles a human hand.

Caution: Watch for traffic when crossing the main park road. Use caution near bluff edges.

Trail Directions: The trailhead [1] is across the road from Thunderbird Lodge, just southwest of the parking lot. Turn right at .02 mi. [2], and soon you are hiking next to a shallow forest stream [3], its bed a pleasant jumble of flat sedimentary rocks. Wet areas near the stream are good places to look for the trail's namesake. You cross the stream at .23 mi. [4] and then hike up and down its woodland drainages as the trail parallels it. Cross the stream again at .52 mi.

Soon you reach a good exercise hill, where some beautiful dolomite shelves make good company for the trees. Here, among the loose stones of the trail, is a good place to look for hematite, or iron ore. These rocks are dark brown or rust colored and are heavy. Iron and barite were two minerals mined in the area before it became a state park. At .81 mi. [5] are several old prospecting pits, now nearly filled in. Turn right at .88 mi. [6], just before you get to the parking lot for the swimming pool. Cross a gravel road at .91 mi. and turn right at the intersection at 1.03 mi. [7]. The water tower looks bald, foreign, and sterile, sticking above the tree canopy. Walk toward the water tower and go straight when you pass under it.

The trail parallels the main park road for a while and crosses it at 1.51 mi. [8]. At 1.68 mi. [9], turn right. Turn right again where the trail meets the Rockywood Trail at 1.82 mi. [10]. The trail goes through some switchbacks, around boulders, across a stream, and up into a glade remnant at 1.94 mi. [11]. Note the twisted branches of the chinquapin oaks and the high density of cedars, choking the glade. Glades sometimes look ragged when restoration practices are first applied, but we must be patient—they respond quickly to cutting and burning of the cedars. Seeds of glade plants may lie dormant for many years before they suddenly explode into bloom in unison when the cedars are removed.

Cross a dirt road at 2.17 mi. and turn right at 2.25 mi. [12]. You are suddenly treated to magnificent blufftop views of the Big River Valley and outlying wooded hills. The trail hugs the bluff edge and offers a series of overlooks [13] (2.32 mi.). At 2.42 mi. [14] is an octagonal stone trail shelter built by the CCC. As you descend the bluff, notice the natural tabletops of weathered dolomite, broken off the face of the bluff. Turn left at the intersection at 2.70 mi. [15] and hike directly behind the lodge. Take the wooden bridge over the stream to return to the parking lot.

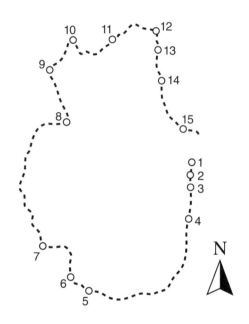

1. Start
2. Right turn
3. Forest stream
4. Stream crossing
5. Prospecting pits
6. Right turn
7. Right turn
8. Road crossing
9. Right turn
10. Right turn
11. Glade remnant
12. Right turn
13. Overlooks
14. Octagonal trail shelter
15. Left turn

- Explore the Pike Run Hills, a rough, rugged, and remote section of the Ozarks that became the favorite refuge for one of Missouri's most notorious Civil War guerrillas.
- Stroll through Mooner's Hollow, named for the moonshine stills that flourished in the 1920s in the isolated hills, rich with cold, clear spring water.
- Hike next to Coonville Creek, a premier Ozark headwater stream that is a designated outstanding state water resource and a state natural area, and is buffered by a state-designated wild area.

Area Information

Like most places, St. François State Park includes a rock in its history. Soft, porous dolomite composes most of the area's bedrock, which has been whittled and carved for eons by water draining to the Big River. Left behind is a rugged landscape of deeply dissected forests, steep bluffs, caves, and numerous streams. South-facing upper slopes are dry, thin-soiled glades and savannas, whereas narrow, shaded valleys are kept cool and moist by spring-fed seepages.

Like most places, too, the park has had its physical characteristics influenced by its ecological and cultural history. Long ago, as the last glacier receded to northern climes, taking a cooler climate with it, a few plants were left behind. These have since been protected in their unusually cool and moist environments. These rare northern plants, such as bog coneflower, swamp wood betony, and queen-of-the-prairie, depend on coldwater seeps and fens for their fragile existence.

People, too, have found refuge in these steep ridges known as the Pike Run Hills. Sam Hildebrand, a deadly Civil War rebel bushwhacker bent on revenging the deaths of his three brothers, reputedly hid out in a small cave, now concealed in the park. Later, the isolated and deep coves of the hills hid the small, primitive stills of Ozark moonshiners, who found one of their product's main ingredients, clear spring water, in abundance. Today, St. François State Park offers the beauty and renewal of an unspoiled, natural setting. For these qualities, it remains a beautiful refuge.

Directions: From the intersection of Highways 47 and 67 in Bonne Terre, turn north on Highway 67 and go 4.3 miles. Turn right at the sign for the park.

Hours Open: The park is open year-round from 7:00 a.m. to 10:00 p.m. from April through October and from 8:00 a.m. to 6:00 p.m. from November through March.

Facilities: A campground is available, as well as picnic areas, a park office, and an amphitheater. Swimming, fishing, and boating are available on the Big River, which forms the southern boundary of the park. Boat access points (carry-on only) are located near both picnic areas. Horse riding is permitted on the Pike Run Trail but discouraged during wet periods.

Permits and Rules: Pets must always be leashed. Bicycles are prohibited on all trails. Camping is permitted only by backpackers on Pike Run Trail, but campfires are prohibited there.

For Further Information: St. François State Park, 8920 U.S. Highway 67 North, Bonne Terre, MO 63628; 573-358-2173.

Other Areas of Interest

St. Joe State Park, Missouri's second largest, features 1,800 acres for off-road-vehicle use. Also available are a 23-mile equestrian trail, an 11-mile paved bicycle and hiking trail, and swimming, fishing, boating, and picnicking. The park is in Park Hills, just south of St. François State Park. For more information, call 573-431-1069.

Missouri Mines State Historic Site, also in Park Hills, includes a museum that interprets the Old Lead Belt of Missouri. Guided tours are available for a fee. For more information, call 573-431-6226.

Park Trails

Pike Run Trail (👣👣👣, 11 miles). Divided into a 6.7-mile south loop and a 4.3-mile north loop, this trail explores much of the scenic 2,101-acre Coonville Creek Wild Area. The trail is open to hikers, backpackers, and equestrians and begins .1 mile north of the campground entrance.

Missouri Trail (👣👣, .5 mile). This linear trail begins at the east end of the campground loop, behind campsite #30, and ends at the west end. It passes through a diversity of plant habitats.

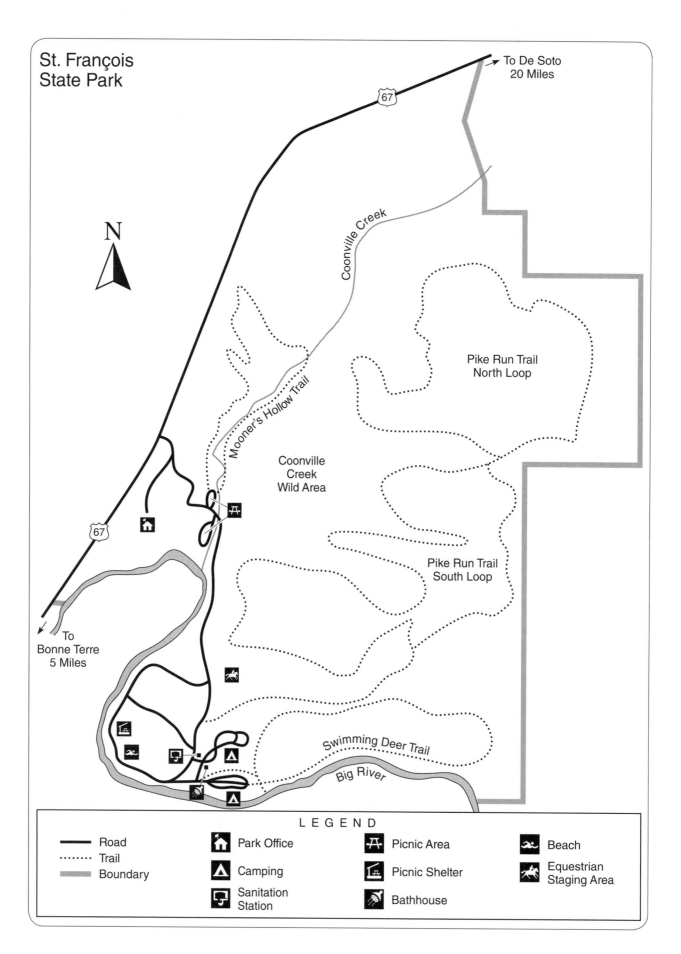

St. François
State Park

To De Soto
20 Miles

N

67

Coonville Creek

Pike Run Trail
North Loop

Mooner's Hollow Trail

Coonville
Creek
Wild Area

Pike Run Trail
South Loop

67

To
Bonne Terre
5 Miles

Swimming Deer Trail

Big River

L E G E N D

Road
Trail
Boundary

Park Office
Camping
Sanitation
Station

Picnic Area
Picnic Shelter
Bathhouse

Beach
Equestrian
Staging Area

Mooner's Hollow Trail

Distance Round-Trip:
3 miles
Estimated Hiking Time:
1.75 hours

A typical moonshine recipe called for cornmeal, rye, and homemade malt, in more or less exact proportions. Most mooners made their own stills from copper sheet and tubing, and a product with a decent reputation would bring $1 per gallon.

Caution: Smooth bedrock on the trail is sometimes slippery because of moist algae and mosses.

Trail Directions: The trail begins near picnic shelter #1, located in the first picnic area in the park, just past the park office. Coonville Creek is fed by numerous seeps and small springs, as you will soon see for yourself, and its cherty, gravel bottom is easy to see beneath the crystal-clear waters of the stream. As you cross Coonville Creek on a wooden bridge [1], you hear the soothing music of its small riffles below—a refreshing sound anyway, but especially if you've just come away from the anxious scurry of Highway 67.

Just across the bridge, a sign welcomes you to Coonville Creek Wild Area, a 2,101-acre area of forested ridges, hollows, glades, and stream valleys protected for its qualities of wilderness and unconfined solitude. Turn left just behind the wild-area sign. Coonville Creek now accompanies you on the left for the first mile, offering many chances to scan its slower, deeper pools for some of the 18 kinds of fish that live there. Breeding males of the orange-throat darter and southern redbelly dace are among the most beautiful fish anywhere, splashing brown creek gravel in spring with brilliant orange, crimson red, and lemon yellow.

After you pass several small gladelike openings on the right, you hike over dolomite boulders blanketed with liverleaf, smooth cliff brake, and mosses. Cross the first of many intermittent tributaries to Coonville Creek at .26 mi. [2]. Ignore the spur on the left at .27 mi. [3] and go straight. A picturesque aquatic scene appears at .34 mi. [4] next to the trail. Robust clumps of heart-leaved plantain emerge from rolling riffles. Tufts of sedges and slender boughs of willow arch gracefully over the water.

Some wooden steps soon lift you to a glade. Keep going and hike out onto flat bedrock at .55 mi. [5], where a panoramic vista of three ridges of the Pike Run Hills greets you. A glorious glade awaits behind you, with pale purple coneflowers, prairie dock, and rose gentian. Pinch the stems of the grasses at the base; little bluestem grass has flat stems, whereas big bluestem grass has oval stems.

Just after crossing a moss- and fern-cloaked tributary, the trail crosses Coonville Creek at .94 mi. [6]. Midstream, find a stable stepping-stone and stop. Look upstream to see magnificent cascades of water, flowing down layer upon layer of stair-stepped bedrock. Look downstream to see half-submerged blocks of rock, gravel bars, and miniature islands with umbrella-like tufts of sedges. Hike beneath some musclewood trees, growing just on the other side of the creek, and pass several small seeps, or wet meadows. Formed by cool, upwelling groundwater, these small wetlands support rare queen-of-the-prairie and grass pink orchids.

After climbing a good exercise hill, the trail swings to the left and follows a ridgetop. Ignore the spur to the left at 1.94 mi. [7] and turn right. You hike into a savanna at 1.97 mi. [8], a grassland with interspersed trees. Several expansive views of wooded ridges appear through large openings in the chinquapin oaks. Just after the trail cuts sharply to the left, you see an intermittent spring outlet on your right at 2.12 mi. [9]. After you cross several more small glades and tributaries, Coonville Creek reappears on your left. As you near the end of the trail, watch out for a wire cable across the trail at 2.90 mi. [10], installed to keep vehicles out of the creek valley. Turn left on the pavement of the picnic loop to finish your hike.

1. Start
2. Tributary crossing
3. Go straight
4. Aquatic scene
5. Glade overlook
6. Coonville Creek crossing
7. Right turn
8. Savanna
9. Intermittent spring
10. Wire cable

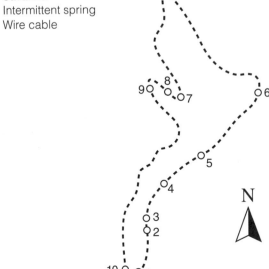

Swimming Deer Trail

Distance Round-Trip: 3 miles
Estimated Hiking Time: 1.75 hours

"They look like the fragments of a broken up world piled together in dread confusion . . ." —reported description by Sam Hildebrand in 1870 of the Pike Run Hills, his Civil War hideout

Caution: Be careful at the steep bluff overlooks, where ivy sometimes obscures the bluff edges. Also, smooth rocks on the trail may be slippery because of moist algae and moss.

Trail Directions: The trail begins at the south end of the park, at the east end of the campground loop. The trailhead is marked by a signboard **[1]** behind campsite #30. Follow green arrows on this trail. Start in a lush and shaded bottom of the Big River, which is just to the right. Along with pawpaw are Ohio buckeye, small trees with palm-shaped leaves and leathery, spiny capsules containing three shiny brown seeds. The leaves emerge in early spring, before the leaves of any other tree, and some people carry the seeds in their pockets to prevent rheumatism. Go straight at .04 mi. **[2]** and turn right at the fork in the trail at .08 mi. **[3]**. Layered dolomite outcrops protrude from the slope on your left. Trees grow so tall in the rich, moist soil that their leaves are difficult to see, but the telltale bark of their trunks reveals that they are black walnut, hackberry, and sycamore.

Appearing soon on your right is a slough, which may be dry. As the trail approaches the Big River, the dolomite outcrops on the left turn into bluffs, scenic in their weathered and eroded condition. Listen for the rattle of kingfishers as you near the river and look for startled ducks and herons. Scan the gravel bars and logs for sunning aquatic turtles and snakes, and search the pools for floating gar and carp. At .32 mi. **[4]**, turn left, toward a wet-weather waterfall that flows over layered blocks of weathered dolomite. The trail ascends these blocks and continues on the right, climbing a bluff. Stop at .36 mi. **[5]** and enjoy some of the fruits of your labors, as the first of several Big River overlooks comes into view on your right. Look down on sycamore tops next to the ambling river and view the remote hills that hid Civil War guerrillas and moonshiners alike.

The trail winds along the blufftop, offering several overlooks as you go, sometimes at the end of short spurs off the main trail. As you descend to river level, spicebush and white crownbeard crowd the trail.

Cross two wooden bridges at .95 mi. **[6]**. The trail widens again as you climb another bluff. Take the small spurs on your right at 1.10 mi. **[7]** through small glades to the highest and best overlooks of all. Sheer cliffs drop to the water, far below, and twisted trunks of ancient cedars cling precariously to the rock face.

The trail and river turn away from each other as the trail curves to the left. On this bend, look for the flattened, long leaves of the blackberry lily, an old homesteader's exotic flower that produces a brilliant orange and blood-red blossom in July. At 1.71 mi. **[8]**, look for a small cabin in the woods on your right, now taken over by creepers and critters. After crossing two rocky, intermittent streams, you pass some curious trenches in the forest floor at 2.19 mi. **[9]**. Miners dug these pits in the 1700s to recover lead. After crossing another stream, you enter an open forest with crisscrossing ravines and a playground of craggy, moss-covered dolomite boulders—perhaps fragments of Sam Hildebrand's "broken up world."

The old, open lead-mining shaft at 2.62 mi. **[10]** is fenced to keep forest wanderers from tumbling in. Some natural sinkholes appear along the trail, too, many of which have filled in with leaves and soil. You pass through a final, small glade at 2.89 mi. **[11]**. Turn right at the fork that you passed earlier **[3]** to finish your Pike Run Hills hike.

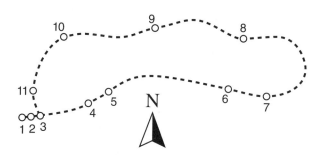

1. Start
2. Go straight
3. Right turn
4. Left turn
5. Big River overlook
6. Wooden bridges
7. Big River overlooks
8. Small cabin
9. Lead-mining trenches
10. Fenced shaft
11. Small glade

- Although you'll be on a trail, you may get the feeling that you are the first person to enter this rugged and unusually scenic pocket of wilderness.

- Hike in a beautiful landscape of sandstone bluffs, outcrops, shelter caves, and steep-walled box canyons.

- Stand at the base of impressive 100-foot-deep canyons, formed from the oldest sedimentary rock in Missouri.

Area Information

Hickory Canyons is named for vertical faces of bedrock that were formed into V shapes by the cutting action of streams over thousands of years. Few places in Missouri have sandstone as the bedrock and parent material for soils, but Hickory Canyons is one of them. At least 500 million years old, LaMotte sandstone is the oldest sedimentary rock in Missouri. It erodes into unusual and dramatic shapes. Besides the distinctive box canyons, some of which are over 100 feet deep, Hickory Canyons Natural Area preserves sandstone cliffs, outcrops, seep springs, wet-weather waterfalls, and shelter caves. Interesting erosional patterns in the sandstone walls include small columns and pillars, spongelike surfaces, and countless shelves and overhangs.

Mixed forests of pine, oak, and hickory cover the thin soils of the upper slopes and ridgetops. Deeper soils and the cool, moist climate of the canyon floors are home to plants that were common during the Ice Age but have since disappeared from most of Missouri. Ice Age relicts still flourishing in the microenvironment of these canyon bottoms are hay-scented fern, shining club moss, and winterberry. A rich array of other rare plants includes rattlesnake orchid, azalea, and northern white violet. Canyon ledges and bluff overhangs hide uncommon liverworts, ferns, and mosses.

Hickory Canyons Natural Area is owned by the L-A-D Foundation, a private, not-for-profit foundation established in 1962 to protect special outdoor areas in Missouri. The area is leased to the Missouri Department of Conservation for management "to assure the preservation of the land's evident natural beauty and resources." Because of the area's unusual sandstone geologic features, natural communities, and rare plants, Hickory Canyons has been designated a state natural area. Coordinated by a committee of representatives from several agencies, the Missouri Natural Area System identifies the best remaining examples of the state's natural communities. By conserving the biological diversity of Missouri, natural areas help protect our rich natural heritage.

Directions: From the intersection of Highways 32 and 144 near Hawn State Park, take Highway 32 east toward Ste. Genevieve and go 2.6 miles. Turn left on Route C and go 3.3 miles. Turn left on Sprott Road and go 1.3 miles. Park on the left side of the road at a pull-out lined with boulders.

Hours Open: The site is open daily from 4:00 a.m. to 10:00 p.m. year-round.

Facilities: The site has no facilities.

Permits and Rules: Destruction or removal of plants or rocks is prohibited. Hunting, bicycles, horses, ATVs, fires, fireworks, and rock climbing are also prohibited.

For Further Information: Resource Forester, Missouri Department of Conservation, 812 Progress Drive, Farmington, MO 63640; 573-756-6488. For more information about Missouri natural areas, contact the Natural Areas Coordinator, Missouri Department of Conservation, P.O. Box 180, Jefferson City, MO 65102; 573-751-4115.

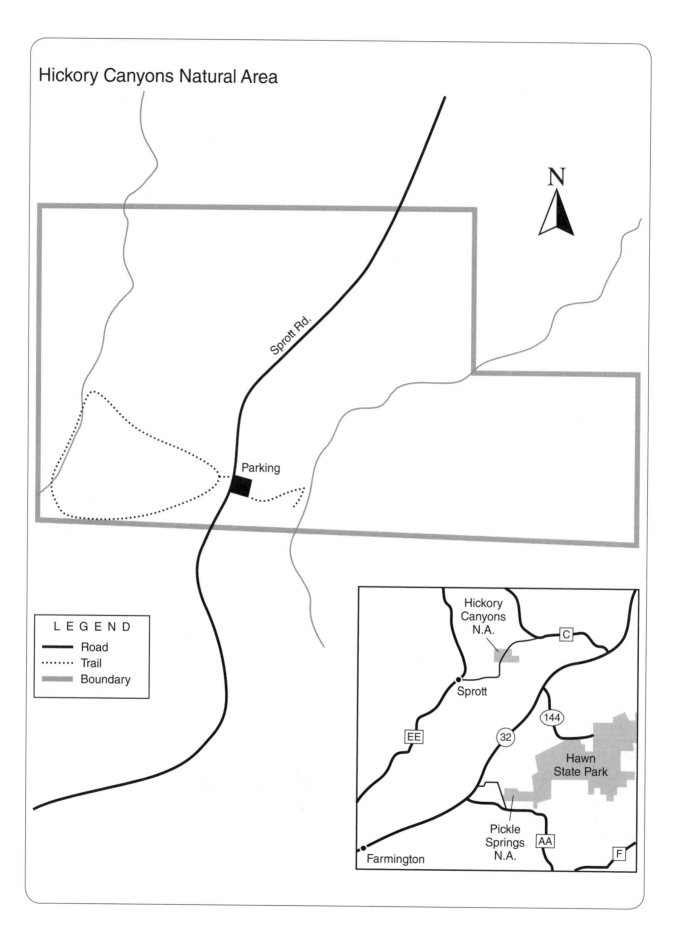

Hickory Canyons Natural Area

Sprott Rd.

Parking

LEGEND
— Road
.... Trail
▬ Boundary

Hickory Canyons N.A.
C
Sprott
EE
144
32
Hawn State Park
Pickle Springs N.A.
AA
F
Farmington

East Trail

 Distance Round-Trip: .5 mile
Estimated Hiking Time: 30 minutes

As you descend into a valley lined with impressive walls of sandstone, you realize that this isn't just a short stroll into the woods. You've entered a fantastic natural feature, a creation of rock, water, and time, 500 million years in the making.

Caution: Please stay on the trail to avoid steep, slippery canyon walls and sheer bluff edges.

Trail Directions: Park in the pull-off for the area on Sprott Road. This is a short linear trail, but a longer loop trail begins just across the road. Start the East Trail on the same side of the road as the pull-off [1] and head into the woods. In a few steps, you reach the trailhead sign, where a brochure on the area may be available. Take a few more steps, and the trees give way to the rocks, which dominate the scene.

Just after the trail swings to the right, you get to meet the celebrity of the area, LaMotte sandstone, which is responsible for the rugged topography, scenic beauty, and unusual plants of the area. Hike right next to an eroded sandstone outcrop at .12 mi. [2] that has layer upon carved layer, each shelf undercut to form an overhang. Look for partridge berry, an uncommon glacial relict plant that thrives on these moist, sandy shelves. Long vines hold small, dark green leaves and red berries, and sometimes drape off shelf tops like streams of dripping water. The rock layers become larger and begin to loom over the trail until you find yourself beneath a shelter bluff at .13 mi. [3]. Look for the remnants of seeds, acorns, and nesting material in the far reaches of crevices. Mice and wood rats use these sheltered ledges for their homes. The long tubes of mud on the ceiling are made by mud dauber wasps, which lay their eggs in these mud nests and provision them with spiders that are paralyzed by the female's sting. When the eggs hatch, the wasp larvae feed on the spiders until they develop enough to chew their way out of the hardened mud case.

As you hike deeper into the canyon, you find a sandstone bluff and a pristine wet-weather waterfall with a small pool at its base at .19 mi. [4]. Depending on the time of the year that you are here and the level of recent precipitation, you may find a pleasant trickle, a splashing flow, or a 35-foot-tall frozen cascade. The trail swings to the left here as you hike on the opposite side of the valley. A tall bluff towers on your right, and a small woodland stream gurgles on your left. The trail swings to the right at .23 mi. [5] as you enter a second, smaller box canyon. You reach the end of the canyon at .25 mi. [6], a good place to sit and listen to the water trickling over the mossy sandstone ledges all around. Retrace your steps to return to the trailhead.

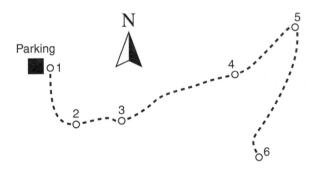

1. Start
2. Sandstone outcrop
3. Shelter bluff
4. Wet-weather waterfall
5. Right turn
6. Box canyon

West Trail

Distance Round-Trip:
1 mile
Estimated Hiking Time:
1 hour

It's hard to believe that a canyon could sneak up and surprise you. But it will. Even if you know it's coming, you'll gasp at its size, its interesting features, and its rugged, natural beauty.

Caution: Stay on the trail to avoid steep, slippery canyon walls and sheer bluff edges.

Trail Directions: Park in the pull-off for the area on Sprott Road. This is a loop trail, and a shorter linear trail begins just across the road. Start the West Trail on the opposite side of the road as the pull-off [1] and head into the woods. In a few steps, you reach the trailhead sign, where a brochure on the area may be available. Turn left at this intersection [2] to hike clockwise on the trail.

Because the trail begins on this ridgetop, the terrain, plants, and trees give no clues about anything out of the ordinary. Oaks, hickories, cedars, and pines manage to survive in the thin, rocky soils. The topography is gently rolling. But the wooden steps at .30 mi. [3] lead you downhill into a different landscape. Suddenly, you are standing on the rim of a surprisingly deep amphitheater of stone, the vertical walls composed of countless shelves, overhangs, and tiny caves carved by water, ice, and other forces of erosion. At the bottom of the steps, turn left to take the short spur to the small shelter bluff to get a close-up view of these canyon features. Explore miniature grottoes, perfectly formed shelves, arches, and keyholes—just inches from your nose. You'll also find partridge berry, ferns, and a variety of lichens and mosses adorning the carved rocks. Return to the bottom of the steps and go straight. The bluff overlook gives you a zoomed-out perspective of this massive yet hidden box canyon at .37 mi. [4]. Hike along the bluff edges for view after

view. The trail meanders along the top before zigzagging down the left side.

Cross Hickory Creek at .47 mi. [5]. Another beautiful canyon, on private property, opens on your left. The trail swings to the right and parallels the creek for a while among boulders, big trees downed by the wind, and patches of Christmas ferns. You cross the creek twice more before crossing it a fourth time at .69 mi. [6]. From here, you start your ascent. Sculpted boulders and scenic sandstone outcrops keep you company as you climb. You encounter several hoodoos (oddly shaped sandstone boulders) along the way, including a friendly and passive rhinoceros on the left side of the trail at .86 mi. [7]. Pick your way over a rocky trail until you return to the trailhead sign at [2], where you turn left to return to Sprott Road.

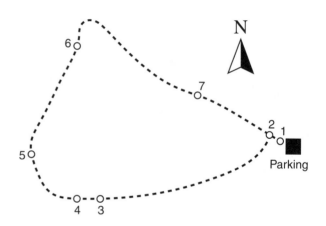

1. Start
2. Left turn
3. Wooden steps
4. Box canyon
5. Creek crossing
6. Creek crossing
7. Rhinoceros hoodoo

25. Hawn State Park

- See, hear, and smell lofty pine trees and feel their needles cushioning the trail.
- Spend some peaceful time in a botanically and geologically rich state park that contains four designated state natural areas and a wild area.
- Find one of Missouri's showiest flowering shrubs, the wild azalea, in abundance on the park's sandstone ledges.
- Hike within the state's finest concentration of distinctive Lamotte sandstone features—sculpted outcrops, terraced cliffs, overhanging shelves, shattered blocks, bedrock slabs, and oddly shaped boulders (called hoodoos).
- See the narrow canyons and overhangs that provide cool refuge for some of Missouri's rarest and most restricted plants, including glacial relicts like Canadian white violet, partridge berry, and hay-scented fern.

Area Information

Located in the LaMotte sandstone basin, Hawn State Park is a superb example of the eastern Ozark sandstone country. LaMotte, a very old, coarse-grained sandstone, lends its distinctive character to the park. Because of the unique ability of the sandstone to hold groundwater moisture and to produce acidic, sandy soils, the park is home to many unusual and rare plants, some of which are found nowhere else in Missouri.

Sandy-bottomed and tea-colored Pickle Creek, with its diverse life and beauty, is the primary feature of Pickle Creek Natural Area. Its narrow shut-ins are some of the few places in Missouri where sandstone and igneous rocks come into contact at the surface. The steep valleys of the stream are lined with sandstone cliffs, undercut ledges, and shaded ravines. Three other natural areas within the park feature 17 species of ferns, rare orchids, sandstone glades, and some of the finest native shortleaf pine forests in the state.

Directions: The park is about halfway between Ste. Genevieve and Farmington. From the intersection of Highways 67 and 32 in Farmington, take Highway 32 east for 12.5 miles. Turn right on Highway 144 and go 3.1 miles. At the T, turn right into the parking lot for the White Oaks trailhead, or turn left to go to the park office and campground.

Hours Open: The park gate is open from 7:30 a.m. to 9:00 p.m. year-round. The park office is open Thursday through Sunday from noon to 4:00 p.m. from April through November.

Facilities: A campground and picnic areas are available, as well as a playground and amphitheater.

Permits and Rules: Much of the flora of the park is unusual and fragile. Stay on the trails and refrain from climbing on rocks and ledges. Entry into Orchid Valley Natural Area is by permit only. Pets must always be leashed. Backpack camping is allowed on the Whispering Pine Trail, but campfires are prohibited there. All trail users must register at the trailhead.

For Further Information: Hawn State Park, 12096 Park Drive, Ste. Genevieve, MO 63670; 573-883-3603. For a free directory of Missouri natural areas, contact the Natural Areas Coordinator, Missouri Department of Conservation, P.O. Box 180, Jefferson City, MO 65102; 573-751-4115; www.mdc.mo.gov.

Other Areas of Interest

Sainte Genevieve, northeast of the park, is the oldest incorporated community in Missouri, founded sometime between 1723 and 1735. Originally settled by French explorers who traveled up the Mississippi River, the town became an important river port. Guided tours are available for a fee at the **Felix Valle House State Historic Site**, which preserves the home of Felix Valle and the headquarters for his company that dealt in furs and American Indian trade goods in Missouri and Arkansas. For more information, call 573-883-7102.

Hawn State Park

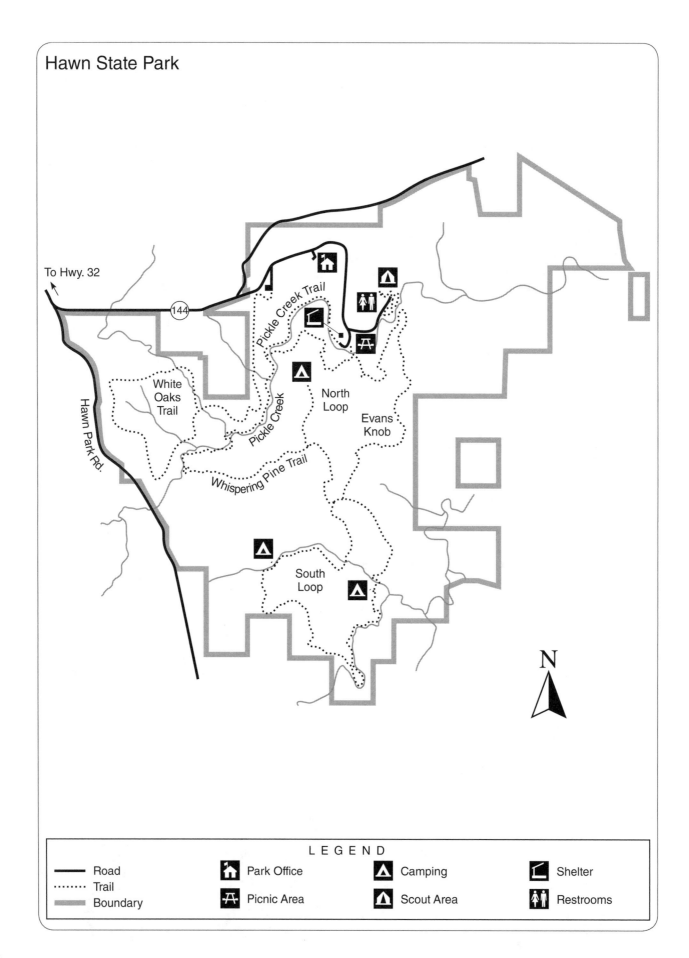

To Hwy. 32

144

Hawn Park Rd.

Pickle Creek Trail

White Oaks Trail

Pickle Creek

North Loop

Evans Knob

Whispering Pine Trail

South Loop

N

LEGEND

—— Road
······ Trail
▬▬ Boundary

🏠 Park Office
⛙ Picnic Area

⛺ Camping
⛺ Scout Area

🏠 Shelter
🚻 Restrooms

Pickle Creek Trail

Distance Round-Trip:
1.5 miles
Estimated Hiking Time:
1 hour

Pickle Creek flows with life. Black-winged damselflies with alarmingly blue bodies flit near the banks. A northern water snake slowly eases down a natural rock waterslide. Tiny black tadpoles dot the bottom of shallow pools, while whirligig beetles nervously scurry on the surface.

Caution: Watch your step as the trail takes you over jumbles of rocks of all different shapes and sizes.

Trail Directions: This trail follows Pickle Creek for the first half and then crosses the creek and uses a section of the Whispering Pine Trail for the return route. Park near the picnic shelter between the park office and campground. The trailhead [1] is just west of the Whispering Pine trailhead, near the picnic shelter. You begin the hike in a natural community that was familiar to Missouri settlers but is rare today—a pine savanna [2]. The large pines here are widely spaced, allowing sunlight to reach the ground where native grasses and wildflowers thrive instead of underbrush and thickets. As with other types of savannas, prescribed fires maintain the open parklike appearance of the area.

You are soon hiking with riffling Pickle Creek on your left and a steep, rocky slope on your right [3] (.16 mi.). Because of its natural beauty, interesting geology, unusual plants, and diverse aquatic life, this section of Pickle Creek has been designated both a state natural area and an outstanding state water resource. Notice the sand on the trail and on tiny beaches along the creek. This sand eroded from the sandstone bedrock and boulders on the slopes above. Sometimes pine needles build up on sandy patches on the trail, making a cushiony layer for hiking feet. Look for the flattened stems of winged elm, a common small tree here. A talus slope of pink granite rocks is located at .26 mi. [4].

Pickle Creek carved through the sandstone and became entrenched between some igneous boulders at .35 mi. [5], creating a shut-in. You may be hesitant to walk out onto the bedrock glade at .56 mi. [6], which looks like a sheet of flowing lava. While you're looking at the interesting textures and colors of this once-molten igneous rock, look for lichen grasshop-

pers, which camouflage themselves as lichens and remain unseen until they jump. Brown fence lizards may make an appearance, too.

At the intersection at .66 mi. [7], turn left and cross Pickle Creek. After you cross, turn left on the Whispering Pine Trail, signed with red arrows and markers. A blood-pumping hill takes you to a blufftop overlook at .89 mi. [8], where the scenery is rich, both near and far. Massive sandstone boulders have fractured and tilted, jamming against those farther downhill. Some of the boulders wear frilly hats of ferns and blueberry bushes, whereas others dress more moderately in mosses and lichens. Pine-clad ridges and knobs fill all distant views.

Turn right at 1.18 mi. [9] and go straight at the fork in the trail at 1.44 mi. [10]. Just after descending a steep hill on a sandy trail with many rocks and roots, turn left at 1.5 mi. [11] and go over two wooden bridges. You are now at the trailhead for the Whispering Pine Trail. Turn left to return to the picnic shelter.

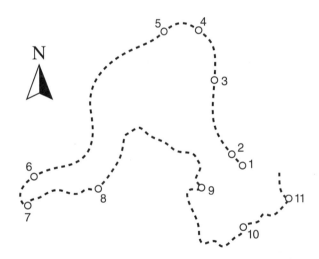

1. Start
2. Pine savanna
3. Pickle Creek
4. Talus slope
5. Shut-in
6. Bedrock glade
7. Creek crossing
8. Blufftop overlook
9. Right turn
10. Go straight
11. Left turn

Whispering Pine Trail

Distance Round-Trip:
10 miles
Estimated Hiking Time:
7 hours

A pine forest is a glorious place to hike. The stately pines are beautiful to see, and their fallen needles soften hard and rocky trails. Whether moistened in new rain or warmed in the sun, their waving boughs fan their unforgettable fragrance. All the while, the slightest breeze plays their timeless music.

Caution: Some trail sections are rife with rocks. Follow trail markers closely to keep your orientation.

Trail Directions: Park in the picnic area between the park office and campground. A signboard marks the trailhead. The trail consists of two loops; the north loop is 6 mi. long (marked with red arrows), and the south loop covers 4 mi. (blue arrows). Fill out a registration card at the trailhead before your hike.

Begin by crossing two wooden bridges [1] and turn right at the intersection at .04 mi. [2]. A rocky and rooty climb will lift you to several overlooks among sandstone boulders, blueberry bushes, and many ferns. As you descend, listen for the shut-ins of Pickle Creek below. Cross the creek at .85 mi. [3] and turn left on the trail on the other side. The cool, clear water splashing around the smooth igneous boulders of the shut-in at .94 mi. [4] will invite you in for a dip. As you continue, the character of the creek changes dramatically. No longer forced around resistant igneous rock, the creek becomes wide and shallow over a sandy bottom, revealing its clear, tea-colored water.

Make a couple of stream crossings and complete a switchback over a sandstone bluff at 2.09 mi. [5]. You pass a white spur to a backpack camp at 3 mi. Climb a steep dome at 3.25 mi. [6], ignoring several paths on the way, and enjoy the views from the top. Turn right at 3.50 mi. [7] to begin the south loop. Pass a white spur to a camp at 4.44 mi. At 4.52 mi. [8], notice a patch of cinnamon ferns on your right.

Many of the Lamotte sandstone boulders at 5.36 mi. [9] exhibit cross-bedding, showing that layers of sand were cemented together at different times. Just after passing under a power line, you meet the River Aux Vases [10] (5.77 mi.) as it meanders at the base of a steep bluff. Cool, shaded, and moist, this terraced rock face is a living fern garden. The stream has undercut the bluff in places, creating mysterious overhangs.

The trail parallels the stream for a while, and several more overhanging shelves appear next to the water, creating terrarium-like gardens. Everywhere, the water is alive with chubs, sunfish, and schools of minnows. When a boulder next to the stream appears to be blocking the trail at 5.90 mi. [11], you can either scamper over the boulder to continue or go around it, up the hill. If you go around, don't climb too far up the hill. Return to the stream to continue.

Pass a white spur to a camp at 6.61 mi. You are soon hiking under a nearly pure stand of shortleaf pines. Turn right at 7.45 mi. [12] to return to the north loop. When your heart rate speeds up again, you are probably climbing Evans Knob [13] (8.10 mi.). After the sharp bend in the trail near the campground, you will enjoy some final overlooks of the Pickle Creek Valley at 9.15 mi. [14]. Turn right when you return to an intersection [2] to finish your hike.

1. Start
2. Right turn
3. Creek crossing
4. Shut-in
5. Switchback
6. Dome overlook
7. Right turn
8. Cinnamon ferns
9. Sandstone boulders
10. River Aux Vases
11. Boulder block
12. Right turn
13. Evans Knob
14. Final overlooks

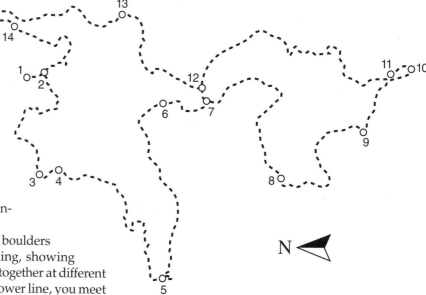

White Oaks Trail

 Distance Round-Trip: 4 miles
Estimated Hiking Time: 2 hours

If you bring a little stress with you to your hike, you'll feel it slip away in the rhythm of your feet on the trail, the whispering of the pines overhead, and the solitude of the open woods all around.

Caution: Tighten up the laces on your hiking boots; some trail sections have embedded rocks of different sizes. Streams may be difficult to cross after heavy rains.

Trail Directions: Park in the lot for the trailhead, where there are restrooms, an information sign, and a registration box. The trail begins [1] in a scenic, open woods of pines and oaks. Boulders and bedrock outcrops are splashed with green lichens and mosses, adding scenery with their interesting shapes. You make the first of several crossings over picturesque woodland streams at .16 mi. [2]. Many of the trees have character, sporting burls, gnarly limbs, and contorted shapes. Some have been worked over by woodpeckers. Our largest woodpecker, the pileated, makes oval or rectangular holes up to 3 inches wide and 5 inches tall. Sometimes these holes are low on the trunk if the bird has found a colony of carpenter ants inside. Our smallest woodpecker, the downy, makes rounder, smaller holes. Hollow trees are sometimes remodeled into squirrel and owl condos.

Cross another intermittent stream and a small tributary at .52 mi. [3]. Just after crossing a larger stream, turn right at the intersection at 1.10 mi. [4] to begin the loop. As you hike alongside this pretty stream for a while, look for fish darting in the deeper pools. Christmas ferns cascade from the banks. Accumulated sand provides the material for miniature sandbars, peninsulas, and deltas.

Just after the trail makes a 90-degree turn to the left, take a close look at the boulders that you'll cross in the middle of the trail at 1.65 mi. [5]. Larger pebbles are cemented together with the normally fine-grained sand of this sandstone. Geologists call this type of rock with varied grain sizes conglomerate. Enjoy the parklike appearance of these open, scenic woods. You cross an intermittent stream at 1.73 mi. [6]. Just before the trail swings to the left, notice a knob on your left, capped with boulders, at 2.17 mi. [7]. As the trail bends around this monument-like feature, the boulders take on a more carved look. Intermingled craggy trees add to the intriguing scene. Look down the slope on your right to view eroded layers of sandstone sliced by the stream on its way to making the steep little valley below. You cross another beautiful woodland stream over sandstone bedrock at 2.46 mi. [8].

Another scenic outcrop of boulders appears on your left at 2.53 mi. [9]—similar to the last knob but on a smaller scale. Yes, this is the White Oaks Trail, but a monstrous black oak next to the trail welcomes you at 2.76 mi. [10]. Go straight at the intersection [4] to cross the stream and return to the trailhead.

1. Start
2. Stream crossing
3. Stream crossing
4. Right turn
5. Boulders
6. Stream crossing
7. Boulder-capped knob
8. Stream crossing
9. Boulder-capped knob
10. Black oak

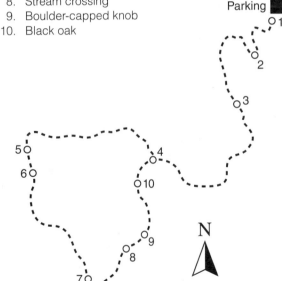

26. Pickle Springs Natural Area

- Visit an area so geologically and botanically rich and unusual that it is designated both a state natural area and a national natural landmark.

- See rocks do magic tricks as they erode into cliffs, tunnels, arches, and strange boulders called hoodoos.

- Hike where mammoths once strolled, munching on lush vegetation pushed south by glaciers.

- Say something in Spirit Canyon to try out the acoustics.

- Bring your camera with lots of memory cards.

Area Information

Pickle Springs tells many stories. Ripple marks seen in the sandstone tell of the rivers that made them 500 million years ago. Oddly shaped rock pillars called hoodoos look like mushrooms, animals, or people, and tell of the ice, rain, and wind that have shaped them. Over 20 glacial relict plants tell of their southward push by the glaciers 2 million years ago. They survive here today because of the acidic soils and the deep, moist, cool canyons that retain the climatic characteristics of an earlier age. There is the story of the mammoths, which grazed here on the northern plants like cinnamon fern, partridge berry, club mosses, northern white violet, and orchids—all plants living at Pickle Springs today. There is the area's namesake, William Pickles, a settler from Illinois who owned the land in the 1850s and who was supposedly shot by the infamous Sam Hildebrand. Then there are the neighbors, who reported the rumbling, thunderous sounds of a great rock collapse in one of the box canyons in the spring of 1959.

Because of these stories, and because of this unique concentration of rare plants and geologic features, Pickle Springs has been designated a Missouri natural area and a national natural landmark. Missouri natural areas are natural communities or geologic features that represent the natural charac-

ter, diversity, and ecological processes of the state's native landscapes. Similarly, the National Natural Landmarks Program of the National Park Service recognizes these natural sites of national significance. Come to see and hear these fantastic stories being told and retold. You may find yourself making some stories of your own.

Directions: From the junction of Highway 32 and Highway 67 in Farmington, travel east on Highway 32 for 7.2 miles. Go east on Route AA for 1.7 miles to Dorlac Road. Turn left and drive .4 mile to the parking lot on the right.

Hours Open: The area is open daily from 4:00 a.m. to 10:00 p.m.

Facilities: There is a picnic table in the parking lot.

Permits and Rules: Hunting, camping, rock climbing, bicycling, fires, horses, motorized vehicles, and littering are prohibited. Pets must always be leashed. Please do not disturb animals, plants, or rock formations.

For Further Information: Missouri Department of Conservation, Southeast Regional Office, 2302 County Park Drive, Cape Girardeau, MO 63701; 573-290-5730. For more information on Missouri natural areas, contact the Natural Areas Coordinator, Missouri Department of Conservation, P.O. Box 180, Jefferson City, MO 65102; 573-751-4115.

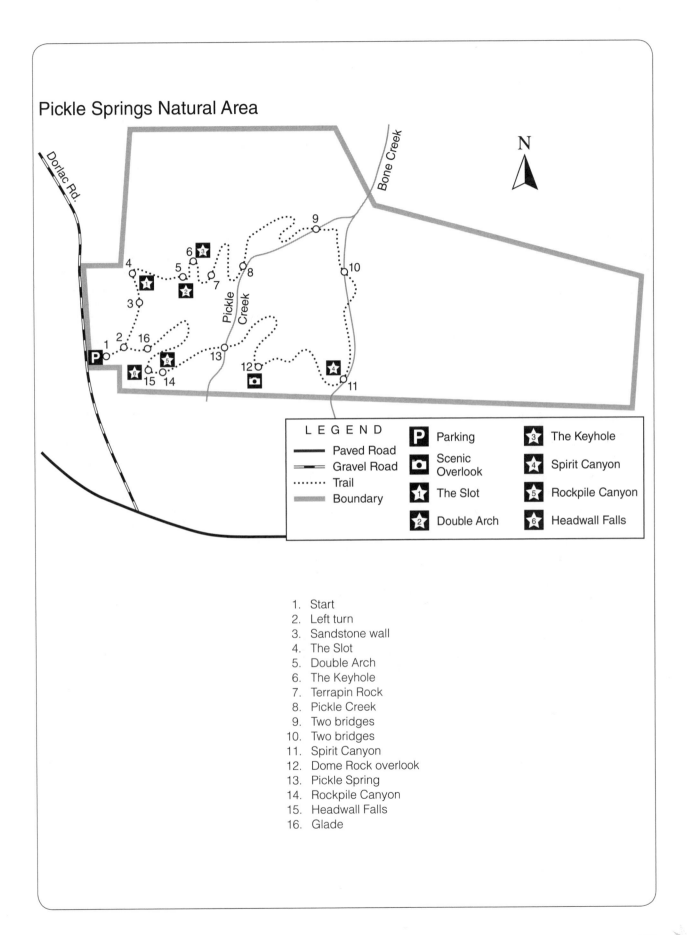

Pickle Springs Natural Area

LEGEND

— Paved Road
╪ Gravel Road
··· Trail
— Boundary

P Parking

▣ Scenic Overlook

★1 The Slot

★2 Double Arch

★3 The Keyhole

★4 Spirit Canyon

★5 Rockpile Canyon

★6 Headwall Falls

1. Start
2. Left turn
3. Sandstone wall
4. The Slot
5. Double Arch
6. The Keyhole
7. Terrapin Rock
8. Pickle Creek
9. Two bridges
10. Two bridges
11. Spirit Canyon
12. Dome Rock overlook
13. Pickle Spring
14. Rockpile Canyon
15. Headwall Falls
16. Glade

Trail Through Time

Distance Round-Trip:
2 miles
Estimated Hiking Time:
1.75 hours

Allow yourself more time than you normally would for a trail of this length. Whether you're into geology, scenery, botany, vistas, exercise, natural communities, imagining, or photography, you'll find something (or many things) to amaze you on this trail.

Caution: Be careful on the high, steep bluff of Dome Rock overlook.

Trail Directions: Park in the lot for the area, just off Dorlac Road, and start the trail at the east end of the lot **[1]**. At .03 mi. **[2]** is the trailhead, where a brochure about the features of the area may be available. Turn left here. Right away, you are introduced to the main feature of the area, sandstone, because the trail begins on sandstone bedrock. If you are here on a sunny day, you may notice the sparkle of individual grains of sand, which were deposited by ancient rivers. Although sand grains are extremely hard, the minerals that cemented them together are usually soft, allowing forces of erosion to sculpt and carve away the rock into beautiful and fantastic shapes. Notice the lichens, mosses, and other plants growing on the sandstone wall next to the trail at .08 mi. **[3]**.

Soon, the trail seems to disappear as you swing to the right into a slit in the earth known as the Slot at .16 mi. **[4]**. The Slot was formed as water moved through a vertical crack in the sandstone, leaching away the minerals that held the sand grains together. The loose sand was eventually broken apart and removed by the action of wind, plants, freezing and thawing, and water—a process that continues to this minute.

Just after descending some wooden steps, you meet the Double Arch at .45 mi. **[5]**—two elegantly sculptured pillars holding up a huge rock shelf. How could such an odd arrangement happen? After looking up, down, and all around, go through the larger arch to continue the trail. At .49 mi. **[6]**, the trail passes through the Keyhole, another type of arch formed by massive boulders leaning against each other. Let your imagination go wild among this playland of boulders called hoodoos. The hoodoo on your left at .55 mi. **[7]**, just as you hike over a wooden bridge, is known as the Terrapin Rock.

From here, you descend into a beautiful valley and cross Pickle Creek at a bridge at .64 mi. **[8]**. You cross two small bridges at .80 mi. **[9]** and two more bridges over Bone Creek at 1 mi. **[10]**. The upcoming feature will be too big to get into your camera, or even your eyes, all at once. The giant wall of Spirit Canyon appears at 1.14 mi. **[11]**. Forming a tall and graceful bluff shelter, Spirit Canyon gives you the impression of being in a cathedral. Rare plants thrive in the cool, acidic soil of this canyon, where the sun never penetrates and where water drips even on the hottest, driest summer days.

Not long after crossing a wooden bridge, you feel a breeze on your face as you approach Dome Rock overlook at 1.42 mi. **[12]**. Hike out among the hoodoos and pine trees for splendid views of distant wooded ridges and rock outcrops. To continue, turn into the woods and descend some wooden steps. You cross a wooden bridge near Pickle Spring at 1.72 mi. **[13]**. Cross another bridge before reaching a large jumble of rocks on your left known as Rockpile Canyon at 1.82 mi. **[14]**. Notice the sharper, more angular edges on these rocks, which erosion has not yet worn smooth. Local residents told of the thunderous sounds these rocks made when they fell from the wall in the spring of 1959.

At 1.84 mi. **[15]**, you reach an overlook of a small box canyon known as Headwall Falls, where layers of eroded shelves cascade with trickling water and hay-scented ferns. Backtrack slightly from the overlook and turn left, uphill, just behind the bench. At 1.97 mi. **[16]**, notice the small glade on your left. Lichens are at work, breaking down the bedrock. Notice the curly leaves of poverty grass, growing in the shallow pockets of soil. Turn left at **[2]** to finish your trail through time.

27. Rock Pile Mountain Wilderness

- See the ancient circle of granite stones believed to be of human origin, at the crest of Rock Pile Mountain.
- Hike in the uncommon solitude of a 4,000-acre federally designated wilderness.
- Hike across a broken ridge from one mountain to another.
- On Rock Pile Mountain, find stark bedrock glades that look like a landscape on another planet.
- Watch for the harmless hognose snake, which may puff up with air, flare like a cobra, or just roll over and play possum.

Area Information

The St. François Mountains began as molten rock around 1.5 billion years ago, when volcanoes dominated the southeast region of Missouri. Magma cooled slowly and hardened into solid masses of igneous rock. After millions of years of inundation by warm seas, which deposited hundreds of feet of sedimentary rock on top of the igneous rock, uplift and erosion uncovered the ancient granites, andesites, and rhyolites, among others. Contrasted with the porous, highly erodible sedimentary rock, these igneous rocks—gray to dark blue or purple, dark red, or pink—are among the hardest and oldest on the continent.

Rock Pile Mountain Wilderness was designated by an act of Congress on December 22, 1980, to be managed under the provisions of the Wilderness Act of 1964. One of seven wildernesses in Missouri on the Mark Twain National Forest, it is managed by the U.S. Forest Service. Located in the St. François Mountains region of the Ozarks, the 4,131-acre wilderness is characterized by steep, rocky slopes, deep ravines, igneous outcrops and glades, and dense forests of oak, hickory, and pine.

Rock Pile's namesake is an ancient circle (or remnants of several circles) of granite stones, piled at the crest of the mountain. Around the turn of the century early white settlers noted the structure to be about 4 feet high, but human disturbance has reduced it to its present level. Although we know few details of the site, the stones may be remnants of Native American burial cairns or ceremonial structures.

Directions: From Fredericktown, take Highway 67 south 5.9 miles to County Road C, where you turn right. Take Highway C 5.1 miles to County Road 406, where you turn right. Go 2.5 miles to Forest Road 2124, where you turn left. The road ends after 1 mile at the parking lot for the trailhead.

Hours Open: The wilderness is always open.

Facilities: There are no facilities.

Permits and Rules: Wilderness regulations are designed to reduce human impact that could damage or destroy the wilderness resource. Prohibited activities include littering, leaving a fire without completely extinguishing it, cutting live or dead standing trees, using bicycles or motorized equipment, and building rock fire rings or other structures. Camping is permitted, but fires must be kept low and small. Hunting is permitted but not near the trail. Avoid using trail ribbons and tread lightly so that nature can endure and replenish. Strict laws prohibit the disturbance of archaeological sites and artifacts on federal property.

Further Information: Potosi–Fredericktown Ranger District, Highway 8 West, Potosi, MO 63664; 573-438-5427; www.fs.fed.us/r9/forests/marktwain.

Area Trails

Rock Pile Mountain Wilderness and adjacent Forest Service property contain numerous old roads and trails open to the public. The trail heading west from [7] on the featured trail leads to shut-ins on Cave Branch Creek, caves and bluffs along the St. Francis River, and Chimney Rock Bluff, a variety of fractured and weathered features in sedimentary rock. A compass and topo map are recommended.

Rock Pile Mountain Trail

Distance Round-Trip: 7 miles
Estimated Hiking Time: 3.5 hours

After staring from several different angles at the old stones that formed the curious, misshapen circle, my mind was in high gear. Was this a burial place? A ceremonial structure? Who? When? Why?

Caution: Loose and protruding rocks cover several steep sections. Refrain from climbing on the rock cairns or disturbing them in any way. Bring a compass and topo map if you choose to extend this hike or do some cross-country exploring.

Trail Directions: Park in the lot for the trailhead on top of Little Grass Mountain and walk to the north end of the lot. The trail begins to the left (west) of a granite boulder with "ROCK PILE MTN. WILDERNESS" engraved in it [1]. As the trail begins a C-shaped curve, you find a registration box at .06 mi. [2]. Register before you continue.

You now descend a rocky hill where granite and rhyolite boulders are dark red, gray, or dark purple and speckled with different-sized mineral crystals (porphyritic). You pass through a scenic, open forest of oaks, hickories, and occasional pines, where tumbled-down boulders fill steep ravines and igneous outcrops protrude from the forest floor. At .53 mi. [3], the trail bends right, and you begin hiking across a series of ridgetops to Rock Pile Mountain.

As you hike, listen for a variety of woodpecker calls and drummings. Woodpeckers hammer on hollow trees, not only to search for food and to hollow out nesting cavities but also to communicate with other woodpeckers. The flat terrain and the mature trees here have allowed a buildup of soil, and the trail is now relatively free of rocks. The trail then goes uphill and becomes rocky again. You find a series of igneous glades at 1.60 mi. [4], with tall big bluestem grass and large, rounded boulders.

At 2.20 mi. [5], you pass a small pond on your right, with bur reed and dozens of frogs, many of which are southern leopard frogs. Leopard frogs are easy to identify at night in March and April because their breeding call is a distinctive quacklike chuckle. As you hike on an old road, watch for round ant lion pits, iridescent turkey breast feathers, and long, barred turkey wing feathers. Go straight at the four-way intersection at 2.62 mi. [6] and turn left at the three-way intersection at 3.09 mi. [7].

After turning right at the intersection at 3.16 mi. [8], you are back in the company of rocks. A big outcrop on your right invites you to climb on it. As you begin your ascent to Rock Pile Mountain, you find a different rock on the trail—ashy gray on the outside and black inside—still with a porphyritic structure. After a final ascent, you reach the peak and find the ancient circle of stones on your right that gave the mountain its name [9] (3.52 mi.). With the rock pile on your right, turn left to discover another strange (though not human-made) structure. Climb on huge, billowing rocks that look as if they flowed from the earth like lava. A little exploration reveals that this lunarlike landscape caps much of the mountaintop. After examining Rock Pile's rocky curiosities, retrace your steps to finish your hike.

1. Start
2. Registration box
3. Bear right
4. Igneous glades
5. Small pond
6. Go straight
7. Left turn
8. Right turn
9. Circle of stones

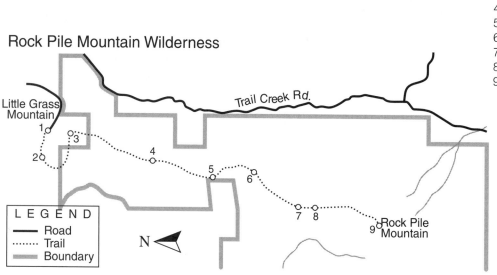

Rock Pile Mountain Wilderness

Trail Creek Rd.

Little Grass Mountain

LEGEND
— Road
...... Trail
▬ Boundary

N

Rock Pile Mountain

- From the convenience and safety of a board-walk, hike through a swamp that survived 40 years of attempts to drain it.

- Hike out onto an observation tower in a vast marsh and look for egrets, herons, and ducks while listening for the splashes of turtles, fish, muskrats, and beavers.

- Bring your binoculars to help you see the colorful but often tiny songbirds that frequent the canopies of towering bottomland trees.

- Bring your tree guide to help you identify and learn more about the unusual trees that live in the swamp.

Area Information

Mingo National Wildlife Refuge is part of a system of refuges administered by the U.S. Fish and Wildlife Service and dedicated to the preservation of wildlife. Situated among marshes and hardwood swamps on the Mississippi Flyway, Mingo is an important refuge for migrating waterfowl. The refuge is managed to provide open water, protection, and ample food for ducks, geese, swans, and other wildlife.

Mingo was formed in an abandoned channel of the Mississippi River when the river shifted east about 18,000 years ago. Then, like now, the swamp was a refuge for wildlife of many kinds. Native Americans lived nearby and hunted the swamp, but legends regarded the swamp as a spooky place. *Mingo*, in fact, means "treacherous" or "unreliable" in local Native American language.

Settlers of the late 1800s quickly exploited the swamp for its centuries-old cypress and tupelo logs, and then set out to drain the swamp for farming. Drainage attempts continued through the Great Depression but with only limited success. The result was economic and ecological bankruptcy. In 1945 Mingo got a new start as a national wildlife refuge, and much of the natural productivity of the swamp has been restored. Today, careful management practices provide an important refuge for wildlife and excellent wildlife viewing opportunities for the public.

Directions: From the intersection of Highways 67 and 60 in Poplar Bluff, turn east on Highway 60 and go 14.8 miles. Turn north on Highway 51 and drive 14.1 miles. Turn left at the sign for the visitor center.

Hours Open: The refuge is open daily. From March 15 through September 30, it is open a half hour before sunrise to a half hour after sunset. During the remainder of the year, visitors should check with regulations provided at the visitor center. The visitor center is open from 8:00 a.m. to 4:00 p.m. Monday through Friday year-round. In spring and fall, it is open from 9:00 a.m. to 4:00 p.m. on Saturdays and from noon to 4:00 p.m. on Sundays.

Facilities: The refuge offers a visitor center with exhibits, displays, and audiovisual programs, five wildlife observation platforms, a 25-mile auto tour route, picnic areas, and boat ramps. Canoeing, fishing, and limited hunting are also available.

Permits and Rules: The visitor center and hiking trails are free, but a $3 daily entrance fee is required for each vehicle from March 15 through November 30. The use or possession of gas-powered boat motors is prohibited on all refuge waters. Electric trolling motors are permitted, but only outside the wilderness area. Fishing is possible year-round, and certain types of hunting are allowed in season on designated portions. Consult the refuge manager for current regulations.

For Further Information: Mingo National Wildlife Refuge, 24279 State Highway 51, Puxico, MO 63960; 573-222-3589.

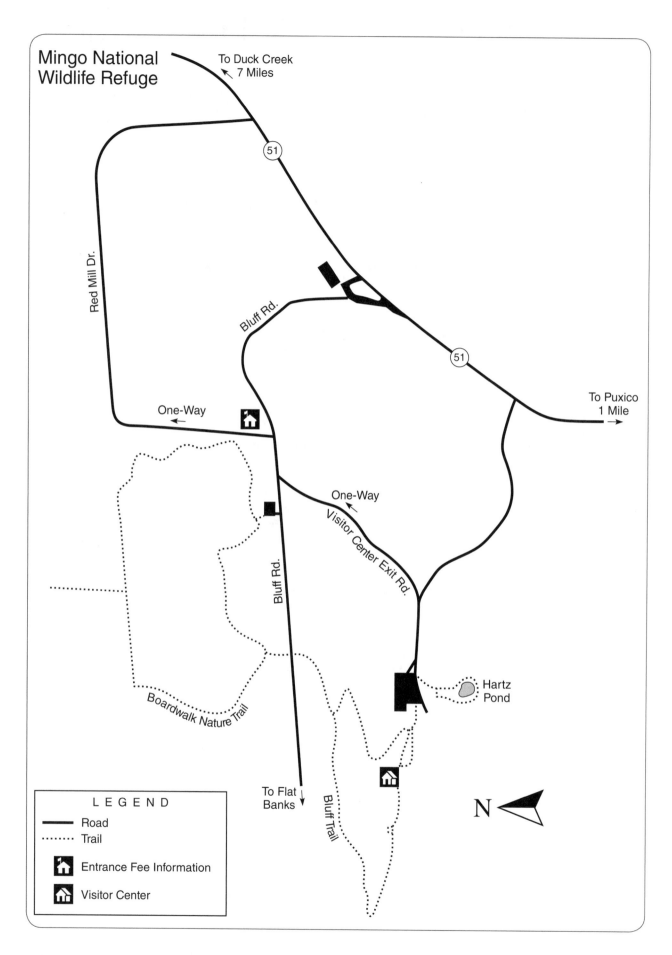

Mingo National Wildlife Refuge

To Duck Creek
7 Miles

51

Red Mill Dr.

Bluff Rd.

51

To Puxico
1 Mile

One-Way

Bluff Rd.

One-Way

Visitor Center Exit Rd.

Boardwalk Nature Trail

Hartz Pond

To Flat Banks

Bluff Trail

LEGEND

——— Road

·········· Trail

Entrance Fee Information

Visitor Center

N

Hartz Pond and Bluff Trail

    Distance Round-Trip: .75 mile
Estimated Hiking Time: 45 minutes

Don't be alarmed if an occasional dragonfly zips and hovers near your head, crinkling and rattling its cellophane wings. It is chasing your enemy, the mosquito, which it catches and eats on the wing.

Caution: Although not as numerous here as in the swamp, mosquitoes will still be present.

Trail Directions: Park in the lot for the visitor center and find the trailhead at the southeast corner of the lot. Begin at the signboard **[1]** and hike beneath the small, compound leaves of black walnut. Look for the smooth, knobby bark of persimmon and the bumpy, corky bark of hackberry. Hike quietly to increase your chances of spotting wildlife at Hartz Pond, which comes into view at .08 mi. **[2]**. Look for ducks or muskrats bobbing or swimming on the surface. Watch for the high, arching leaps of bullfrogs jumping into the water and scan the surface for their bulging, bubblelike eyes. Don't forget to check logs and the pond banks for sunning turtles.

Turn left to make your way clockwise around the pond. Two moisture-loving trees are on the pond bank—look for the star-shaped leaves of sweet gum and the feathery, fernlike leaves of bald cypress. The cypress has adapted to living in standing water, and you can see many of them in Mingo's swamps and marshes. You pass patches of several kinds of ferns before crossing a wooden bridge. When you return to **[2]**, turn left to return to the signboard **[1]**.

Back in the parking lot, turn left and walk on the paved walkway to the visitor center. Notice the beautiful kaleidoscope of varied leaves overhead. Yellow-green, pumpkin-shaped leaves of basswood contrast with the small leaves of black walnut and the wavy-edged leaves of swamp chestnut oak. At .31 mi. **[3]**, arrive at the visitor center, which offers exhibits and a slide show about the refuge. Find the signboard for the Bluff Trail at the west end of the building and begin the trail next to a rock wall.

You reach the Rockhouse overlook at .37 mi. **[4]** for fabulous vistas of Rockhouse Marsh. Here, at the north boundary of the Mississippi Lowlands, a contrast between two landscapes becomes evident. Looking over the flat marsh in the foreground, the ridges and domes of the Ozark foothills form the horizon in the distant north. Bear right at the fork in the trail at .41 mi. **[5]**. Just after the trail makes a sharp right, you hike next to limestone boulders covered with wild hydrangea, ebony spleenwort, and other ferns. As the trail turns more rugged and rocky and a steep slope dips on your left, you may think that you're in the Ozarks and forget all about Mingo, a marsh and swamp refuge.

At .53 mi. **[6]**, the limestone boulders turn into big bluffs at your right shoulder, and the swamp comes into view below you on the left. Wild ginger, ferns, and several colors of mushrooms decorate the forest floor. Passing beneath immense bottomland trees, you can look down on the tropical leaves of pawpaw on your left. At .64 mi. **[7]**, turn right at the spur to the Boardwalk Nature Trail. The trail zigzags up a good exercise hill before taking you to the intersection at .73 mi. **[8]**, where you turn left to return to the parking lot.

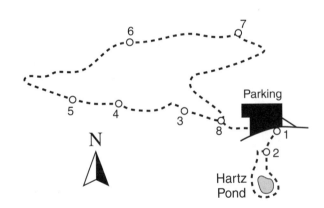

1. Start
2. Hartz Pond
3. Visitor center
4. Rockhouse overlook
5. Bear right
6. Swamp
7. Right turn
8. Left turn

Boardwalk Nature Trail

Distance Round-Trip: 1 mile
Estimated Hiking Time: 45 minutes

There is something primeval about a swamp. . . . We know their facts, yet their legends persist. We are attracted to them, yet uneasiness hangs like the sultry air in their shadows.

Caution: Unless you are here in winter, do not even attempt to hike this trail without mosquito repellent.

Trail Directions: Exit the visitor center parking lot and make the first left. Turn left at the stop sign and turn right into the parking lot for the Boardwalk Nature Trail. Interpretive brochures are available at the trailhead for this self-guiding trail. Numbered stations along the trail do not correspond to numbered features in this book.

Before you begin, notice the trees with long, thin leaves shading the parking lot. These are willow oaks, moisture-loving trees restricted to swampy habitats. Start at the trailhead [1] in the northwest corner of the lot and turn right at the first intersection at .01 mi. [2]. The trail begins in a swamp, although you may not see standing water here right now. Water levels in swamps fluctuate naturally, according to the seasons and rainfall. Flooding water may persist for months. The trees and plants that thrive here are specially adapted to this wetland habitat.

As the boardwalk makes a pleasant drumming sound underfoot, listen above for the drumming of woodpeckers. At .20 mi. [3], a sturdy bench makes a good spot to listen for the songs of warblers and many other songbirds that find refuge at Mingo. Turn left on the paved walkway at .24 mi. [4]. The standing water on your right is one of the ditches dug in the 1920s in an unsuccessful attempt to drain the swamp for farming. At .38 mi. [5], turn right on the arched bridge over the drainage ditch. Notice the bald cypress trees near the bridge. These wetland trees often have an enlarged, or buttressed, trunk that is thought to give the tree greater stability in saturated, soft soils. Notice the knobby stumps all around the trees; these are cypress knees, extensions of the tree that are thought to carry oxygen to its waterlogged roots.

Go over the bridge and continue to the observation tower. As you exit the swamp and enter the marsh, look near the boardwalk for buttonbush, an aquatic shrub with white, globe-shaped flowers about the size of Ping-Pong balls. As the trail goes over the remnants of a beaver lodge at .47 mi. [6], notice that aluminum sheeting has been installed on the upright posts of the boardwalk in attempts to beaver-proof them. At .56 mi. [7] is the observation tower, complete with a shaded bench and a free viewing scope. Although the greatest number of ducks, geese, swans, and eagles frequent this marsh from November to March, various birds and wildlife can be seen from the tower all year long. Spend some time gazing at the wide, open marsh, dotted with monstrous cypress trees. Return to [5] and turn right.

Just after passing a bench on the left, turn left on the boardwalk at .83 mi. [8] to enter a darker section of the swamp. Half-submerged twisted tree limbs arch out of the water like sea serpents. Look for water snakes gliding over the surface and listen for unexplained splashes just under the boardwalk. Turn left at the spur to the Bluff Trail at .88 mi. [9]. Two more swamp trees grow close to the boardwalk. A water tupelo is on the left at .92 mi. [10]. Notice that it has a flared trunk like the bald cypress. Look for the spines on the trunk of the water locust at .93 mi. [11]. It resembles the honey locust, a close relative. Turn right at the intersection [2] to finish your swamp hike.

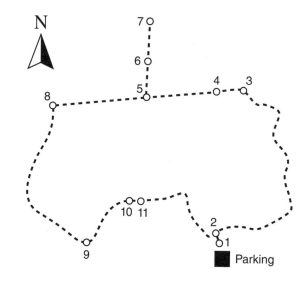

1. Start
2. Right turn
3. Wooden bench
4. Left turn
5. Arched bridge
6. Beaver lodge
7. Observation tower
8. Left turn
9. Left turn
10. Water tupelo
11. Water locust

29. Morris State Park

- Experience a unique geologic formation left over from the Ice Age—a phenomenon known as Crowley's Ridge.

- Hike beneath tulip poplar, sweet gum, and massive beech trees, species more typical of eastern, Appalachian forests.

- See trees and plants restricted to the southeastern part of Missouri, including red buckeye, willow oak, and devil's walking stick.

Area Information

When Crowley's Ridge was born, Missouri's Bootheel was a different world. The Gulf of Mexico lapped at the foothills of the Ozark Mountains. Pleistocene ice ages produced rivers of glacial meltwater, which washed layers of gravel and sand down from the Ozarks. When the ocean receded, a long thin ridge of high ground was left behind. Summer flooding washed away the land on either side of the ridge. Winter winds whipped clouds of fine glacial dust into the air, where they were carried until they reached the obstruction that would become Crowley's Ridge. Windblown soil drifted behind the ridge, much like sand or snow drifts behind a fence. As much as 50 feet of windblown soil settled on top of the ridge of gravel and sand, forming a gradual slope on the western, windward side and steep drop-offs on the eastern, leeward side.

The resulting high ground is 100 to 250 feet high, .5 to 5 miles wide, and about 150 miles long, stretching into parts of Arkansas and Tennessee. Juxtaposed with the flatter-than-a-pancake Mississippi River delta floodplain that it rests on, Crowley's Ridge is a distinctive phenomenon that is obvious when viewed from several miles away.

In 1999 Jim D. Morris, a Springfield businessman who grew up on his family's nearby cotton farm, donated 161 acres of this area to the Missouri Department of Natural Resources so that a portion of this unique natural feature could be protected. Many plants exist within the park and region that cannot be found anywhere else in the state. Rare natural communities include a sand forest, acid seeps, and remnants of a prairie that had formed at the base of the ridge. Over 300 different plants and 100 species of birds are found here. Because of the unique geologic formation, unusual soil types, and rare plant species, Morris State Park preserves a unique part of Missouri's natural heritage for future generations to experience and enjoy.

Directions: From Dexter, take Highway 25 south to Malden. Take Route J west from Malden for 4.5 miles. Take Route WW south for 1 mile and turn left at a sign for the park.

Hours Open: The park is open year-round from 6:00 a.m. to 10:00 p.m.

Facilities: The park offers an accessible walkway and overlook, a restroom, a parking area, water, and interpretive signs.

Permits and Rules: Bicycles and ATVs are prohibited on the area. Please stay on the trail to minimize damage to the area. Soils of Crowley's Ridge are delicate and unusually susceptible to erosion.

For Further Information: Morris State Park, c/o Hunter-Dawson State Historic Site, P.O. Box 308, New Madrid, MO 63869; 573-748-5340; www.mostateparks.com.

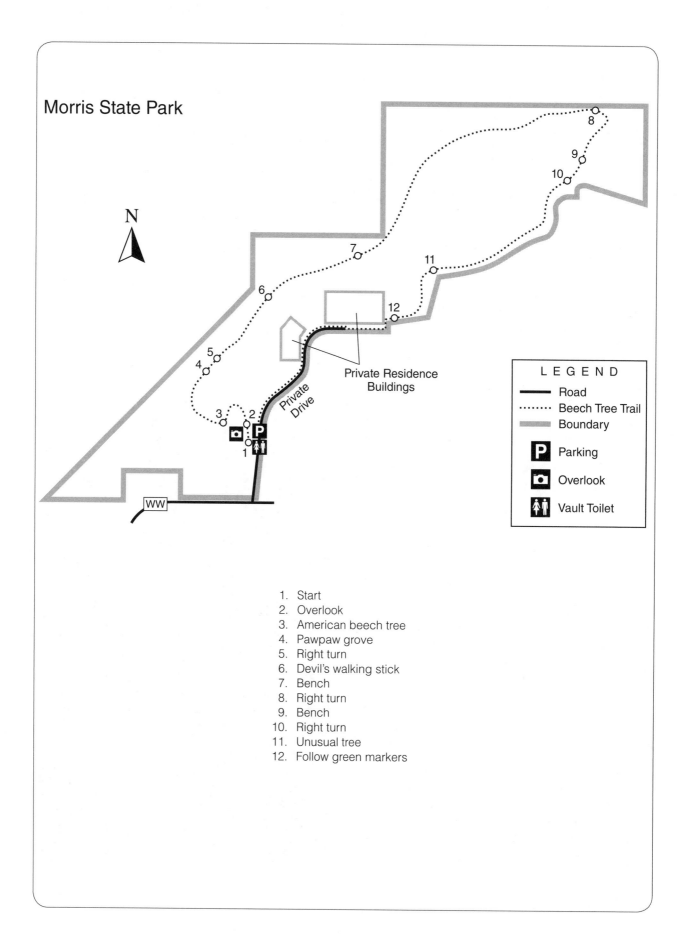

Morris State Park

N

LEGEND
— Road
⋯⋯ Beech Tree Trail
▬ Boundary

P Parking

📷 Overlook

🚻 Vault Toilet

Private Residence
Buildings

Private Drive

WW

1. Start
2. Overlook
3. American beech tree
4. Pawpaw grove
5. Right turn
6. Devil's walking stick
7. Bench
8. Right turn
9. Bench
10. Right turn
11. Unusual tree
12. Follow green markers

Beech Tree Trail

 Distance Round-Trip: 2.35 miles
Estimated Hiking Time: 1.5 hours

As you hike on the ridgetop, look on the trail for the occasional pebble. Unlike the jagged-edged chert and limestone rocks found in the rest of the Ozarks, these rounded stones have been carried and worn smooth by ancient meltwater streams.

Caution: Please stay on the trail to minimize damage to the area. Soils of Crowley's Ridge are delicate and unusually susceptible to erosion.

Trail Directions: Park in the lot for the area and begin the trail **[1]** on a paved walkway. An interpretive brochure may be available at the restroom. Several interpretive signs explain the unusual formation and natural communities of the area. In just a few steps, you see how these woods are different from most others, including the hilly forests of the Ozarks. You are looking at the eastern side of Crowley's Ridge, which is the leeward, steeply dropping side. Add the fact that the soils are windblown loess, extremely fine, and easily eroded, and you have a rich woods with some serious vertical depth. Step out onto the overlook at .05 mi. **[2]** to appreciate the wildly dissected forest around you.

As you continue, some large trees testify to one of the qualities of the loess soil—its fertility. Extremely deep, fertile soil and abundant moisture allow trees to grow quickly here. Very large trees are usually not as old as you might think. Old or not, the American beech tree at .16 mi. **[3]** is an impressive sight, with its giant, smooth trunk and massive limbs. The exposed roots demonstrate another quality of the loess soil— its susceptibility to erosion. Restricted in Missouri to the Crowley's Ridge area, beech trees produce sweet, edible nuts and can live up to 400 years.

At .23 mi. **[4]**, you find a small grove of pawpaw trees around an intermittent stream lined with Christmas ferns. The pawpaw is a member of a tropical family, and pawpaw extract has been used experimentally in cancer therapy. Turn right at the intersection at .25 mi. **[5]**. Here in the bottomland, watch for river birch, sycamore, sweet gum, and willow oak trees. Another plant restricted to the Bootheel region appears at .40 mi. **[6]**. Known as the devil's walking stick or Hercules club, this small tree is named for the stout, sharp prickles that line its thin trunk. Devil's walking stick often forms colonies by sending up new shoots from underground runners. After hiking next to several patches of blackberry bushes, you reach a bench and a small wooden bridge at .65 mi. **[7]**.

As the trail approaches the park boundary, you'll see the vast expanse of crop fields just on the other side of the fence. What a sharp contrast in landscapes! The trail swings right at 1.22 mi. **[8]** and starts zigzagging up the ridge. You reach a well-placed bench at 1.42 mi. **[9]**. Turn right at the intersection at 1.47 mi. **[10]**. The path on your left would take you into a private peach orchard. Apparently, the gently sloping western slope of Crowley's Ridge is perfect for growing peaches; nearby Campbell, Missouri, is famous for this fruit crop. Hike along the spine of the ridge here, with hundreds of peach trees on your left and the steep drop-off of the ridge on your right. You pass an unusual tree growing right next to the trail at 1.91 mi. **[11]**. At 2.03 mi. **[12]**, step out into the open field and follow the green trail markers in front of the private residence. Just past the house, hike on the gravel road to return to the parking lot.

- Wait until the leaves have fallen and bring your binoculars to scan the sycamore trees near the lake—not for birds, but for plants! Wappapello is one of the few places in Missouri where you can find wild mistletoe.

- Come in winter to look for eagles, ospreys, and a variety of ducks in the arm of the lake by Asher Creek, a designated winter waterfowl refuge.

- Imagine what the devil's walking stick might look like and then find this unusual, slender tree growing next to the trail.

Area Information

The peninsula on which Lake Wappapello State Park is now situated was once part of the rich southeastern Ozark foothills used as hunting grounds by various Native American tribes. The St. Francis River flowed freely through the pine-clad ridges then, before dropping into the Mississippi Lowlands farther south.

Pioneers arrived in the early 1800s and began lumbering and farming. Named after a Shawnee chief who had hunted in the area, the town of Wappapello was established as a Frisco railway station. In 1941 the U.S. Army Corps of Engineers completed a dam on the St. Francis River, the first of many large dams built by the corps in Missouri, and 8,400-acre Wappapello Lake was the result. Lake Wappapello State Park and Table Rock State Park are the oldest of the corps' reservoir parks in the system.

The hills surrounding the lake are steep and covered in a diverse mix of trees and plants. Typical Ozark flora of white oak, hickories, and shortleaf pine is joined by species of the Mississippi Lowlands like sweet gum and devil's walking stick. American beech, tulip tree, and mistletoe add their unusual flavor to the park's environment. The Wappapello landscape is much different today from what it was in the time of the Shawnee chief or even the pioneers. A resilient and diverse area, it still has much to offer.

Directions: From the intersection of Highways 60 and 67 in Poplar Bluff, take Highway 67 north for 13.3 miles. Follow Highway 172 east for 8.3 miles to the park office.

Hours Open: Day-use areas of the park are open from 8:00 a.m. to dusk. From April through October, the park office is open from 8:00 a.m. to 4:00 p.m. Sunday through Thursday, from 8:00 a.m. to 6:00 p.m. on Friday, and from 8:00 a.m. to 5:00 p.m. on Saturday. From November through March, the park office is open from 8:00 a.m. to 4:00 p.m. Monday through Saturday.

Facilities: The park offers picnic areas, an amphitheater, rental cabins, and campgrounds that feature many campsites next to the lake. A sand swimming beach and boat ramp are available, and fishing, boating, and water skiing are available on the lake.

Permits and Rules: Bicycles and horses are allowed on the Lake Wappapello Trail but are prohibited on all other trails. Camping is permitted by backpackers only along portions of the Lake Wappapello Trail. Campfires and cutting implements are prohibited on all trails. Pets must always be on leashes 10 feet long or shorter.

For Further Information: Lake Wappapello State Park, HC2 Box 102, Williamsville, MO 63967; 573-297-3232 (park office) or 877-422-6766 (cabin or camping reservations).

Other Areas of Interest

The **U.S. Army Corps of Engineers** operates 12 recreation areas and landings on Lake Wappapello that primarily feature water recreation and camping. The corps' visitor center, located on Highway T near the dam, offers nature walks and tours of the gatehouse. For more information, call the visitor center at 573-222-8562.

A Civil War battle was fought at the old town of **Greenville**, located 20 miles north of Wappapello on Highway 67. Pioneer history is brought to life here in special events including Old Greenville Black Powder Rendezvous and Old Greenville Days. For more information, call 573-222-8562.

Park Trails

Lake Wappapello Trail (🐾🐾🐾🐾, 15 miles). This loop trail, designed for hiking, backpacking, bicycle, and equestrian use, extends beyond the park boundaries over varied and rugged terrain. Sections of the trail, identified on a park trail map, are closed to camping. The trailhead is .3 mile west of the park office on Highway 172.

Lake View Trail (🐾🐾, .5 mile). Open to hikers only, this trail offers excellent views of the lake from the south shore of Allison Peninsula. It begins in the day-use area west of the cabins.

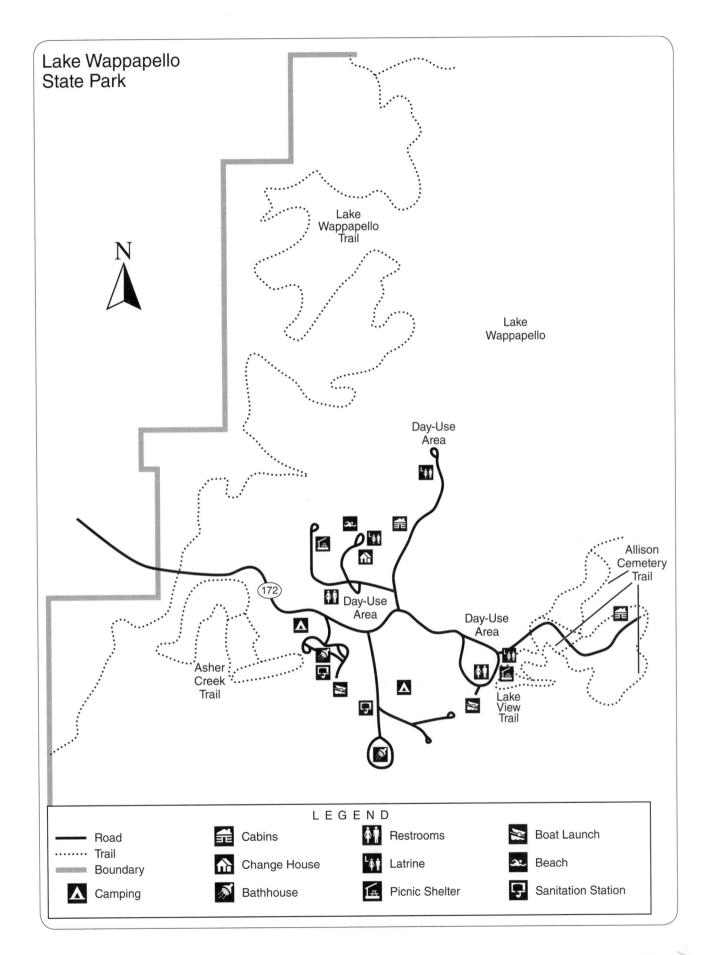

Lake Wappapello
State Park

N

Lake Wappapello
Trail

Lake
Wappapello

Day-Use
Area

172

Asher
Creek
Trail

Day-Use
Area

Day-Use
Area

Allison
Cemetery
Trail

Lake
View
Trail

L E G E N D

—— Road		Cabins		Restrooms		Boat Launch
···· Trail		Change House		Latrine		Beach
Boundary		Bathhouse		Picnic Shelter		Sanitation Station
Camping						

Asher Creek Trail

Distance Round-Trip: 2 miles
Estimated Hiking Time: 1.25 hours

It was in the middle of a warm afternoon, and I had already spooked three deer from the trail by the lake's edge. Later, a fourth one ran up the slope above me, stopping to stamp its front leg on the ground and issue a few explosive, bull-like snorts.

Caution: Stay on the trail to avoid several large patches of poison ivy.

Trail Directions: Pull into the driveway marked with a campground sign, located .3 mi. southeast of the park office. Turn right at every opportunity until you reach the lake. The trailhead is next to the lake, behind campsite #57.

Begin at the signboard **[1]** and follow red arrows and markers clockwise on this trail. The trail follows the lake shoreline here on the side of a dry, rocky slope. Beside Ozark hickories and oaks are sweet gum trees, more common in the Mississippi Lowlands. The trees with papery, flaky bark growing at the edge of the water are river birch. If you are here in fall or winter, watch the nearby skies and water for ducks and geese that stop at Wappapello on their migration routes. The cove in front of you is a designated winter waterfowl refuge.

At .25 mi. **[2]** is an intersection with a connector link; go straight as the trail swings to the right. Reach a second connector at .47 mi. **[3]**; go straight here also. The trail swings to the left just after it crosses a wooden bridge over a small stream. Note the diversity of trees here and see whether you can distinguish them by their bark alone. White oaks have light bark with loose scales that rub off on your hands. Dark brown, fissured bark of sweet gum might be confused with that of southern red oak or cherrybark oak. The bark of shagbark hickory and river birch is a giveaway!

Note the large, tulip-shaped leaves of the tree on your left at .61 mi. **[4]**. This is a tulip tree, a species more common in the Appalachian region of the United States. If you find a tree with corky wings on its twigs, you have discovered either a winged elm or a sweet gum tree. Winged elms have small leaves with serrated edges. Sweet gum leaves are star-shaped and have five lobes.

Soon the trail veers to the right, opening more views of the lake and the surrounding steep hills and knobs. Look for the hornbeam tree, also called musclewood, named for its smooth trunk, which has fluted, muscle-like ridges. Just after the trail veers right again, away from the lake, turn right at .86 mi. **[5]** and climb a hill into the woods. Blueberries, fragrant sumac, and wild grapes grow in this drier, rockier habitat. Look for bright yellow-orange chanterelle mushrooms, which come up in profusion the summer after a prescribed fire. Go straight at the intersection with the connector link at 1.4 mi. **[6]**. Turn left at the intersection at 1.72 mi. **[7]** to return to the trailhead.

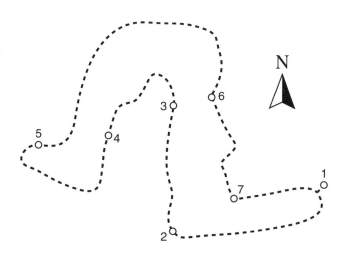

1. Start
2. Go straight
3. Go straight
4. Tulip tree
5. Right turn
6. Go straight
7. Left turn

Allison Cemetery Trail

 Distance Round-Trip: 3.5 miles
Estimated Hiking Time: 1.75 hours

After hearing so much about the devil's walking stick in the park, I was on a mission to find it. What would it look like? Where would it be? Why would he leave it? Would he want it back?

Caution: Watch for traffic when you cross the main park road.

Trail Directions: Drive to the end of the main park road and park at the end of the cabin area, located 1.7 mi. east of the park office. Begin at the signboard **[1]** and walk downhill toward the lake. Near the bottom of the hill, turn right at the intersection at .06 mi. **[2]** and follow green arrows in a clockwise direction from here on.

The trail takes you between the lake and a wooded slope on your right, shaded by a tall canopy of tulip, white oak, and sugar maple leaves. As you descend into a cooler, protected draw, you pass through a grove of pawpaws and patches of Christmas ferns. After the trail swings to the right at .48 mi., look for a shrub near the trail whose five shiny, dark green leaflets look like an outspread hand. This is the red buckeye **[3]**, a shrub restricted to southeast Missouri and noted for its red flowers and its shiny, dark brown seeds. Some Ozark old-timers carry buckeye seeds in their pockets for good luck.

The patch of strange-looking, flat-topped small trees at .61 mi. **[4]** is devil's walking stick, or Hercules club—the evil reference, no doubt, deriving from the myriad of sharp spines protruding from the trunk of the tree. Listen for the blows and snorts of white-tailed deer as they discover your whereabouts just moments before you discover theirs. An overlook of the lake opens at .67 mi. **[5]** as the trail veers to the right. Just after hiking around a small cove, you find several glade remnants at 1 mi. **[6]**, complete with little bluestem grass, leadplant, and black-eyed susans. Go straight at the connector link option at 1.11 mi. **[7]**.

After traversing several rocky draws, turn right at 1.39 mi. **[8]**, at the intersection with the Lake View Trail. At 1.42 mi. **[9]**, hike to the right of the picnic shelter and reenter the forest on the trail behind the restrooms. Turn left at the bottom of the wooden steps. Cross the main park road at 1.68 mi. **[10]** and turn left at the intersection with the connector link at 1.81 mi. **[11]**. The 1,854 acres that make up the state park were owned by the Allison family from after the Civil War until the early 20th century. Now known as Allison Peninsula, the area became surrounded by water after the creation of Lake Wappapello in 1941. You are now

hiking on an old roadbed that leads to the Allison family cemetery, at the tip of the peninsula.

Go straight at the intersection at 2.31 mi. **[12]** if you choose to take the spur to the cemetery. Pass a smooth-barked tree at 2.37 mi. **[13]**, an American beech. A clearing in the trees on your right reveals old gravestones at 2.40 mi. **[14]**. A bench overlooks the lake just ahead, a site known for its remarkable sunset views. Return to **[12]** and turn left. Just after passing a musclewood tree on your right, you reach two connector intersections at 3.10 mi. Go straight at **[15]** and turn left at **[16]**. As the trail joins an old roadbed, continue on the left. Turn left when you approach the sewage lagoon at 3.14 mi. **[17]** and reenter the forest at the trail sign. Turn right when you return to an intersection **[2]**. Your vehicle is at the top of the hill.

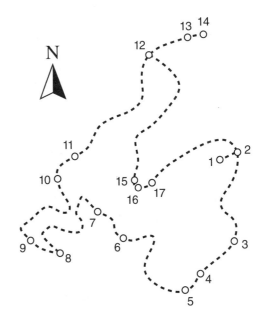

1. Start
2. Right turn
3. Red buckeye
4. Devil's walking stick
5. Lake overlook
6. Glade remnants
7. Go straight
8. Right turn
9. Picnic shelter
10. Road crossing
11. Left turn
12. Spur to cemetery
13. American beech
14. Allison cemetery
15. Go straight
16. Left turn
17. Left turn

31. Sam A. Baker State Park

- Climb to 1,313 feet above sea level at the top of Mudlick Mountain, an exposed igneous dome in one of the oldest mountain regions in North America—the St. François Mountains.

- Challenge your hiking skills on difficult, though interesting, terrain—talus fields, also known as rock glaciers.

- Hike on a national recreation trail through one of the most significant undisturbed natural landscapes in Missouri, the 4,420-acre Mudlick Mountain Wild Area.

- In spring look for the uncommon yellowwood tree, whose large, fragrant blossom clusters often overhang small streams.

- Visit the only park whose entire area is a historic district.

- See gnarled, knobby, 200-year-old oak trees that illustrate the effects of ice storms, violent winds, and repeated lightning strikes on their mountaintop home.

Area Information

Named in honor of a Missouri governor and well-known educator, Sam A. Baker State Park is one of the state's first-generation parks, having the first portion of its 5,164 acres acquired in 1926. At the southern edge of the scenic St. François Mountains, the park features Mudlick Mountain, one of the highest and most distinctive igneous domes in the region.

Mudlick Mountain originated some 1.5 billion years ago, when volcanoes dominated the landscape of southeast Missouri and created some of the oldest and hardest exposed rock on the continent. After warm oceans completely buried the ancient mountains under hundreds of feet of sedimentary rock, down-cutting streams, wind, and rain gradually began to expose the resistant, igneous knobs. These conical, domelike hills remain, some over 1,000 feet high, covered with mixed hardwood and pine forests and surrounded by boulder-strewn slopes and narrow, winding valleys.

Big Creek is a clear, rocky Ozark stream that forms most of the eastern boundary of the park. Its valley is one of Missouri's largest and deepest canyonlike gorges, with shut-ins, glades, and sheer rock bluffs. Big Creek flows into the St. Francis River at the southeast end of the park. Both streams offer park visitors recreation opportunities as well as beauty.

Directions: The park is in southeast Missouri, 4 miles north of Patterson on Highway 143.

Hours Open: The site is open year-round. The nature center is open from 10:00 a.m. to 8:00 p.m. Monday through Saturday and from 10:00 a.m. to 5:00 p.m. on Sunday from mid-May through Labor Day. Call for nature center hours during the off-season.

Facilities: The park offers a campground, an equestrian camp, a nature center, rental cabins, a dining lodge, a general store, canoe rentals, an amphitheater, picnic areas, a paved bicycle trail, and a boat ramp. Swimming, fishing, and boating are available on Big Creek and the St. Francis River.

Permits and Rules: Horses are allowed on most of the Mudlick Trail. Camping is permitted on the Mudlick Trail, but only by backpackers. Three hiking shelters are open for overnight use from October 1 to May 15 on a first-come, first-served basis. Except in the shelters, campfires are prohibited. Bicycles are allowed only on the paved bicycle trail or park roads. All pets must be kept on leashes.

For Further Information: Sam A. Baker State Park, Route 1, Box 113, Patterson, MO 63956; 573-856-4411 (park office) or 573-856-4223 (cabin reservations).

Park Trails

Mudlick Trail—West Section (🐾🐾🐾🐾🐾, 7.75 miles). From the hiking shelters, this segment delves into Mudlick Hollow, ascends Green Mountain, traverses the park's west border, descends into Logan Creek Valley, and climbs the southern edge of Mudlick Mountain. There are no trailheads on this section. The west section and the east loop together compose the entire Mudlick Trail (12 miles).

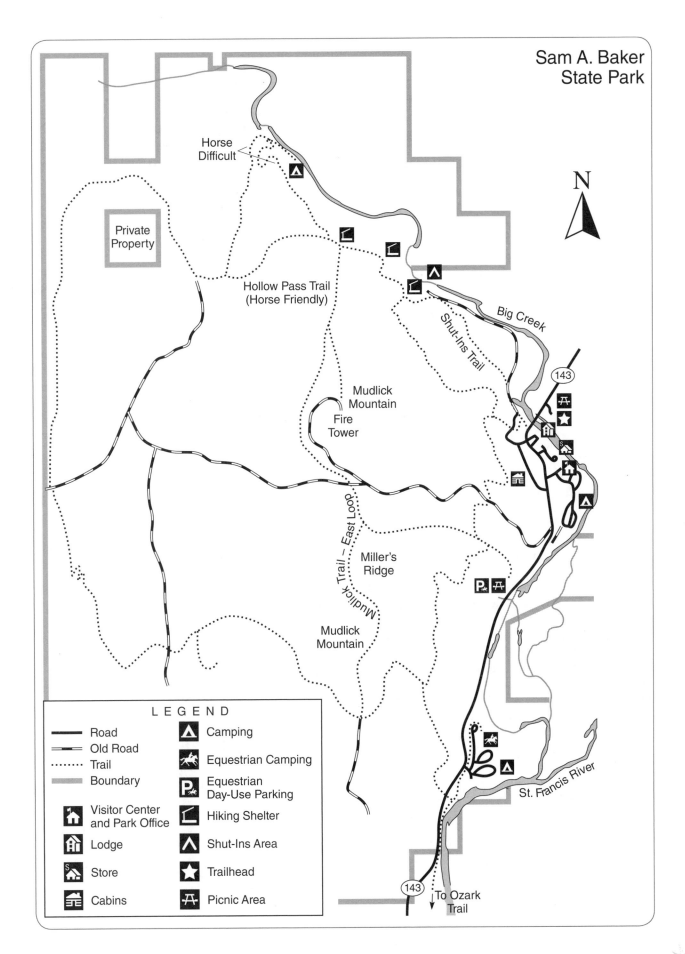

Sam A. Baker
State Park

N

Horse
Difficult

Private
Property

Hollow Pass Trail
(Horse Friendly)

Big Creek

Shut-Ins Trail

143

Mudlick
Mountain
Fire
Tower

Mudlick Trail – East Loop

Miller's
Ridge

Mudlick
Mountain

St. Francis River

LEGEND

— Road
—‖— Old Road
········· Trail
Boundary

Camping

Equestrian Camping

Equestrian
Day-Use Parking

Hiking Shelter

Shut-Ins Area

Trailhead

Picnic Area

Visitor Center
and Park Office

Lodge

Store

Cabins

143

To Ozark
Trail

Mudlick Trail–East Loop

Distance Round-Trip:
7.15 miles
Estimated Hiking Time:
3.75 hours

Precambrian volcanoes, inundating oceans, tectonic compression . . . beneath the serenity of this wilderness lie the products of nature's most cataclysmic events.

Caution: Talus is difficult terrain to hike; wear sturdy boots and keep the laces tight to help prevent a twisted ankle.

Trail Directions: Park in the lot for the trailhead [1], across the highway from the dining lodge and slightly toward the Big Creek bridge. Fill out a registration card before you begin. Follow yellow arrows and markers on this trail.

If you're here on a warm day, you'll feel the temperature drop as you descend into the floodplain of Big Creek. Just after crossing a wooden bridge over a clear, small stream, turn left at the intersection at .09 mi. [2]. At .18 mi. [3], cross an old road. Turn right at the three-way intersection at .32 mi. [4], where an oak-hickory forest dotted with sugar maples replaces floodplain trees. At .63 mi. [5] is the first of many stream crossings through deep-cut ravines. Like most other rock in the St. François Mountain region, this extremely hard and old rock began as molten lava.

As you continue on the wide, rocky trail, look for ebony spleenwort, a fern whose fronds stand nearly straight up. At 1.20 mi. [6], a small stone cabin, hiking shelter #1, appears through the trees. Built of local dellenite, this is one of three shelters on this trail built by the CCC in the early 1930s. Take the spur to the rock ledge in front of the cabin for an outstanding view of Big Creek's canyon. Turn right after returning to the main trail and ascend a sweat-er hill. (You probably won't reach the top without sweating.) Pass shelter #2 and turn left at the intersection at 1.73 mi. [7], at shelter #3.

Turn left at 2.20 mi. [8] on the spur to the mountain summit and fire tower. Turn left on the limestone gravel road to climb to the mountain-top at 2.45 mi. [9]. The CCC-era fire tower is not open to the public, but this is a good place to relax. Many old oaks with missing limbs and twisted, scarred trunks tell their tales of 200 years of tornadoes, snow, ice, and lightning.

Return to [8] and turn left. When the trail turns into a jumble of rocks of all sizes, you have entered a talus field [10] (2.90 mi.). Talus is rock that has broken off from bluffs or bedrock above and tumbled down the slope.

Cross an old road at 3.48 mi. [11] and arrive at a connector link at 3.71 mi. [12]. Going straight will shorten the hike by 2.35 mi. Turn right to continue. Go up and over Miller's Ridge while your feet get some relief on this wide, grassy, old roadbed that is free of talus. Find an old field at 3.99 mi. [13], now grown up in persimmon groves and blackberry briars. Go up and over the south end of Mudlick Mountain. Turn left at the intersection at 4.62 mi. [14] and hit the rocky trail again. You pass several glade openings at 4.94 mi. [15]. Turn left at the spur to the equestrian camp at 5.11 mi. [16]. You soon enter another talus field. Cross several streams that splash around some of these boulders. Turn left at 6.02 mi. [17] and turn right at 6.08 mi. [18]. Cross the fire-tower road at 6.30 mi. [19] and pass under a power line. Turn right when you return to [4] to finish your hike.

1. Start
2. Left turn
3. Road crossing
4. Right turn
5. Stream crossing
6. Hiking shelter #1
7. Left turn
8. Spur to summit
9. Peak of Mudlick Mountain
10. Talus field
11. Road crossing
12. Right turn
13. Old field
14. Left turn
15. Glade openings
16. Left turn
17. Left turn
18. Right turn
19. Road crossing

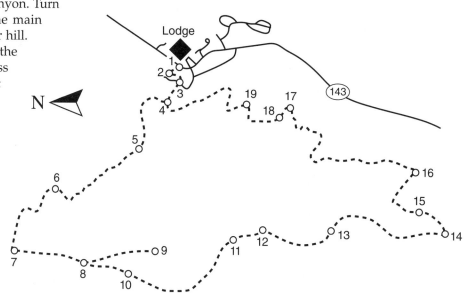

Shut-Ins Trail

Distance Round-Trip:
3 miles
Estimated Hiking Time:
2 hours

Pass through a junglelike creek bottom (complete with bamboo) next to wet-weather waterfalls that splash their way down boulders, creating little open terrariums of mosses and ferns. Listen for the deep "Chug . . . chug, chug" of green frogs in the pools of the stream as you hike to the overlook.

Caution: The trail to the overlook is steep and covered with small, loose rocks.

Trail Directions: Park at the dining lodge; the trailhead is just behind it. Begin at the signboard **[1]**. If you're here on a warm day, you'll probably hear shouts of joy and exhilaration from children and adults alike as they swim and play in Big Creek, a clear-water, rock-bottom stream that forms most of the eastern boundary of the park. The trail follows Big Creek a short distance near the trailhead. Follow blue arrows on this trail.

Descend some wooden steps and follow the trail under the Big Creek bridge. At the intersection at .09 mi. **[2]**, turn left. Pawpaw, slippery elm, and massive sugar maple trees of the Big Creek floodplain cover the trail with dense shade. Cross a wooden bridge at .14 mi. **[3]** over a small stream and notice the washboard appearance of the weathering bedrock on the stream bank. Go straight at the following trail intersection and at the old road crossing at .17 mi. **[4]**. Descend some switchbacks and turn left at the bottom.

Dellenite boulders protrude from the steep slope on the left, and giant grapevines hang from tall black walnut and hackberry trees. Thick vegetation and calm, humid air contribute to the junglelike atmosphere. The trail passes through a stand of 12-foot-tall canes of native bamboo at .25 mi. **[5]**. Now uncommon, this member of the grass family was abundant in Missouri's presettlement wetland and riverine habitats. At .40 mi. **[6]**, take the spur to the left to find massive boulders and talus tumbled into a gorgelike ravine, crisscrossed by several wet-weather waterfalls. The towering tree here with star-shaped leaves is a sweet gum. You might have seen its seed balls on the trail. These "gum balls" have a long, cherrylike stem and prickly spikes.

Turn left after returning to the main trail. After a flood or heavy rain you may come across a slough that covers part of the trail. In various places, the trail's surface is gravel, silt, or sand—materials deposited by the flooding creek. If it's dry enough, walk up the streambed on your left at 1.02 mi. **[7]** to see another wet-weather waterfall tumbling down mossy boulders. At medium flow, its water falls into a small pool and disappears! Return to the main trail and turn left.

At 1.15 mi. **[8]**, turn left just after crossing a small stream. Follow the sound of running water and ascend some steps to begin the trail's grand finale—a blood-pumper hill to an overlook of the Big Creek canyon. Look for brown fence lizards scurrying on this talus slope. You find several glade remnants along the way. Bear left at the fork in the trail at 1.36 mi. **[9]**. When you reach the stone cabin (hiking shelter #1), walk toward the rock ledge in front of the shelter for a vista of the forested, mountainous landscape **[10]** (1.5 mi.). From here, you have the option of descending the Mudlick Trail (yellow arrows) or retracing your steps to return to the dining lodge.

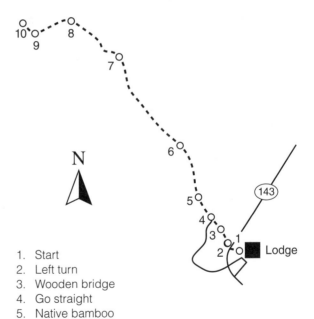

1. Start
2. Left turn
3. Wooden bridge
4. Go straight
5. Native bamboo
6. Spur to ravine
7. Spur to disappearing waterfall
8. Left turn
9. Bear left
10. Overlook

- Hike alongside a mile-long stretch of shut-ins in one of the state's most scenic rivers, the St. Francis.

- Discover potholes—not in the asphalt road but in the ancient, sculpted, igneous boulders of the streambed.

- Hike on pine-covered bluffs next to massive granite boulders and on top of billowing out-crops of pink bedrock.

- Sit in the "air conditioner," a trailside log structure left over from an old silver mine where the temperature stays about 60 degrees year-round.

- See a curved dam across the St. Francis River, built of granite blocks in 1879.

- Find a pack rat's lair.

Area Information

Silver Mines Recreation Area is located on the St. Francis River at the site of a historic mining operation, where the Einstein Mining Company began recovering lead and silver from the area's granite bluffs in 1877. Two years later, the company constructed a dam across the river to divert water to power machinery for mining operations. The town of Silver Mountain sprang up on the ridge just above the mine and included a post office, school, blacksmith shop, several stores, and around 850 citizens. Granite, one of the hardest rocks known, did not yield its treasures easily, however, and the mine soon shut down, with total production recorded at 50 tons of lead and 3,000 ounces of silver.

The St. François Mountains, which surround the recreation area, are sometimes referred to as the geologic core of the Ozarks. Igneous rock exposures, some of the oldest on the continent, are dated at well over a billion years old. Granite and felsite masses contain extensive veins of minerals. Besides silver, lead, and tungsten ores found in quartz veins, more than 20 minerals have been identified in the area.

The narrow, deep valley of the St. Francis River with its 200-foot bluffs reveals the erosive action that the water has carried on for millennia. Constricted in a series of rocky narrows locally known as shut-ins, the river has created a natural playground of sculpted and polished rocks, with small waterfalls, waterslides, and calm pools. The St. Francis River is the only river in Missouri classified as white water, and the high water of spring attracts kayakers from around the nation for Olympic trials as well as annual and regional races.

Silver Mines Recreation Area, in the Potosi–Fredericktown District of the Mark Twain National Forest, is managed by the U.S. Forest Service. With its unique blend of history, geology, scenery, and recreation, Silver Mines is a sure bet for outdoor fun.

Directions: From the south end of Ironton, take Highway 72 east 14.3 miles to the second intersection with Highway D. (Pass the first intersection at 2.4 miles.) Go southwest on Highway D for 3 miles and turn right at the sign for the area. Go straight until the road dead-ends in a parking lot for the footbridge over the St. Francis River.

Hours Open: The site is open year-round. The campground is open from 6:00 a.m. to 10:00 p.m.

Facilities: The site offers three campgrounds, a group camp, and three picnic areas. Water and restrooms are available in the campgrounds, but there are no showers. Fishing, wading, and carry-on canoeing are available on the St. Francis River.

Permits and Rules: A $2 fee is required per day per vehicle. The Forest Service advises against climbing on the dam or hiking across it. Hunting is prohibited within the recreation area, and all pets must be leashed.

For Further Information: District Ranger, U.S. Forest Service, Potosi–Fredericktown District, Highway 8 West, Potosi, MO 63664; 573-438-5427; www.fs.fed.us/r9/forests/marktwain.

Other Areas of Interest

Just upstream from Silver Mines, **Millstream Gardens Conservation Area** features more shut-ins of the St. Francis River and includes a state natural area. The area also offers a 1-mile asphalt hiking trail (wheelchair accessible), picnic areas, demonstration sites, an archery range, and a hand-launch boat ramp on the river. The site, 8 miles west of Fredericktown on Highway 72, is managed by the Missouri Department of Conservation. For more information, call 573-290-5730.

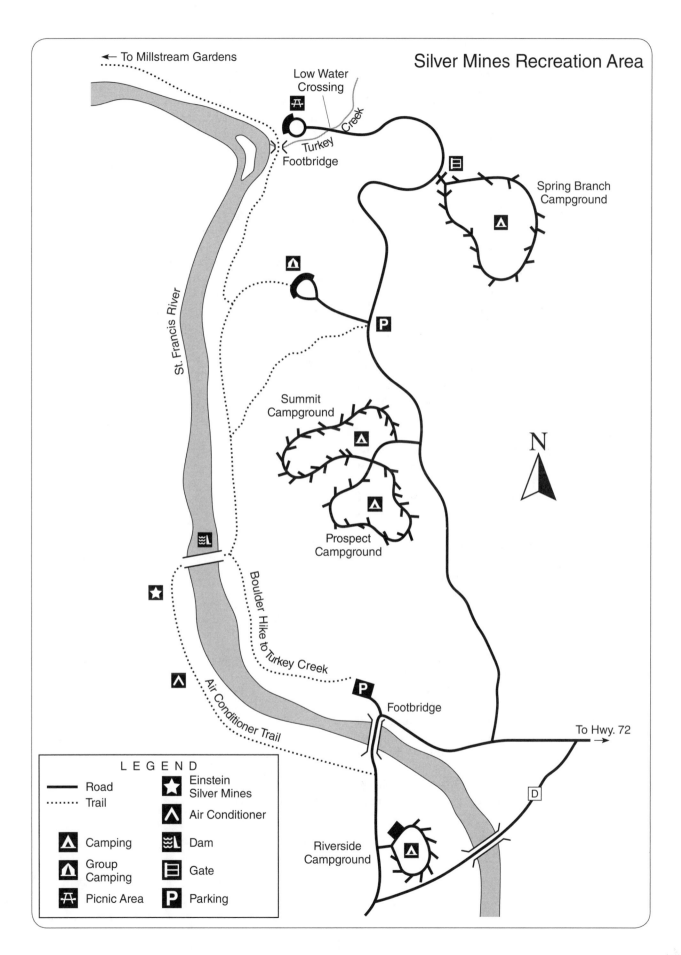

To Millstream Gardens →

Silver Mines Recreation Area

Low Water Crossing

Turkey Creek

Footbridge

Spring Branch Campground

St. Francis River

Summit Campground

N

Prospect Campground

Boulder Hike to Turkey Creek

Einstein Silver Mines

Air Conditioner Trail

To Hwy. 72

Footbridge

D

Riverside Campground

LEGEND

— Road

······ Trail

▲ Camping

▲ Group Camping

🎪 Picnic Area

★ Einstein Silver Mines

◣ Air Conditioner

〰 Dam

🚪 Gate

P Parking

Air Conditioner Trail

Distance Round-Trip:
1.4 miles
Estimated Hiking Time:
1 hour

Hike this trail on a muggy summer day and be rewarded with a walk-in air conditioner, complete with wooden benches and shade, compliments of the Einstein Mining Company.

Caution: Several steep slopes, especially near the dam, have loose rocks.

Trail Directions: Park in the lot for the concrete footbridge over the St. Francis River, at the south end of the area. Begin the trail by starting across the footbridge **[1]**. Halfway across, at .03 mi. **[2]**, this bridge offers an in-the-river view of unusually beautiful shut-ins, where the swirling waters of the St. Francis churn around, over, and around huge igneous boulders, smoothing and sculpting them into abstract forms. Water rushes down natural waterslides, cascading into white, bubbly pools below. When the river is low, shallow pools form in depressions in the bedrock, creating little aquariums full of life. Look for small longear sunfish, chubs, and crayfish in these ephemeral pools.

Across the bridge, pass a picnic area on your left and turn right on the trail, into the woods at .10 mi. **[3]**. You hike uphill among outcrops of igneous boulders, splashed green with lichens. Higher on the hill, rounded outcrops of bedrock like the backs of elephants or rhinos bulge through the forest floor between columnlike trunks of shortleaf pine. Take the spur on your right at .35 mi. **[4]** past a ravine filled with boulders to an overlook of the river. From this view of the river bend, far below, look upstream to see the stone block dam built by the Einstein Mining Company in 1879 to divert the river to a turbine that powered machinery for hoisting and crushing ore. Downstream, the river continues its ceaseless journey over and around Precambrian granite and felsite boulders, some of the hardest and oldest rocks on the continent. Turn right after returning to the main trail.

The trail continues through gardens of boulders, where sensitive ferns and mosses emerge from vertical cracks. The rocks themselves look like living, growing things because of their ever-present green lichen coats. The rocks and the abundance of hickory nuts in fall, collecting on the trail faster than the squirrels can carry them away, may complicate trail navigation. After turning right at the fork in the trail at .54 mi. **[5]**, you soon reach the air conditioner at .60 mi. **[6]**, a roofed log structure over a gated mine shaft. Sit on one of the benches and feel the cool air billowing out of the shaft, which extends into the ridge behind.

Follow the small stream emerging from the shaft, past some cattails and willows. Hike downhill on some loose rocks, toward the river, and arrive at the base of the concave side of the stone dam at .70 mi. **[7]**. Look for aquatic snakes, sunning themselves on the dam blocks near the water. Watch for suckers coasting across the bottom of this large pool and look for turtles and smallmouth bass near the surface. A large section of the steep valley wall across from you is solid rock, displaying dramatic diagonal fractures and several colors of its igneous composition. Retrace your steps to return to the trailhead.

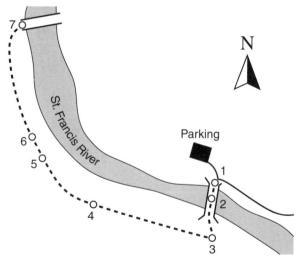

1. Start
2. Shut-ins
3. Right turn
4. Spur to river overlook
5. Right turn
6. Air conditioner
7. Stone dam

Boulder Hike to Turkey Creek

 Distance Round-Trip: 1.65 miles
Estimated Hiking Time: 1 hour

While hiking, I kept thinking of the miners, just across the river, and their search for silver and lead long ago. Today, people come searching for fun, relaxation, and the beauty of the shut-ins.

Caution: Several steep slopes, especially near the dam, have loose rocks.

Trail Directions: Park in the lot for the concrete footbridge over the St. Francis River, at the south end of the area. The trail follows the east bank of the river and overlooks almost the entire 1 mi. stretch of shut-ins. Begin the trail near the restrooms **[1]**.

Like the Air Conditioner Trail, this trail traverses igneous boulders in various shades of pink, gray, and gray-purple. The sound of small waterfalls and cascades of the shut-ins rise up the steep valley wall on your left, while rounded boulders decorated with green lichens growing in circular, targetlike patterns protrude from the slope on your right. Take the spur on your left at .18 mi. **[2]** on a giant slab of contoured, pink bedrock that slopes downhill toward the river.

At the end of the bedrock, with the splashing and churning waters of the shut-ins in front of you, look on your right, in the bedrock of the streambed, for a round hole about the size of a washtub. This is a good example of a pothole, created when river sediment scoured a depression in the bedrock. As larger stones settled in the depression and tumbled in the currents, they gradually enlarged the depression, carving it rounder and deeper. Look for smaller potholes and remnants of potholes that have eroded out of shape. Turn left after returning to the main trail.

1. Start
2. Spur to shut-ins overlook
3. Spur to dam
4. Wood rat nests
5. Go straight
6. Go straight
7. Go straight
8. Arched bridge

As you gain elevation, pine trees become more common and the boulders more imposing, sometimes perched like small houses next to the trail. Take the steep and rocky spur at .38 mi. **[3]** to the stone dam. If you are here in spring or fall, watch for ospreys (fish hawks) perched in trees near the water, and listen for their call—a series of loud, clear whistles. In winter, look for bald eagles. Any time, you might see great blue herons, little green herons, and kingfishers. The smooth, sculpted bedrock makes a good place to relax in the sun or listen to the stereo sound of multiple riffles of the shut-ins. Turn left after returning to the main trail.

Soon, the large boulders near the trail turn into rock walls. Take a close look into some of the cracks and small ledges of the rocks at .45 mi. **[4]** and you'll likely see messy nests of twigs, leaves, nutshells, and bones, made by eastern wood rats. Nicknamed pack rats for their habit of collecting shiny objects like foil candy wrappers, pull tabs, and bottle caps, these nocturnal rodents sometimes use the same disorderly nest their entire life, constructing multiple levels and including underground passages. Ignore the spur at .47 mi. **[5]** and go straight. After passing two more spurs at .55 mi. **[6]**, you pass an interesting spheroidal boulder on the trail.

As you climb even higher on this bluff, several rock ledges allow you to step to the edge and view the shut-ins through gaps in the trees. The sound is a hushed roar now, far below, and blends with the whispers in the pine trees around you. Ignore the spur on your right at .73 mi. **[7]** and go straight. You hike next to another assortment of huge granite boulders and rock walls that line the trail and march off onto the slope above you. Sensitive ferns, mosses, and several kinds of lichens adorn these rocks. After a descent, you find an arched bridge over Turkey Creek, which joins the St. Francis here at .83 mi. **[8]**. A pleasant picnic area just across the bridge makes a good place to relax before you retrace your steps to the trailhead.

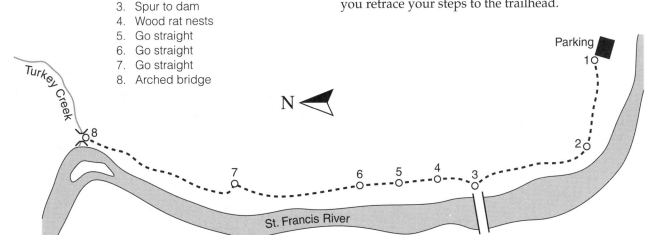

- See a rare geological formation known locally as the Devil's Honeycomb.

- Explore willy-nilly at the mountain summit—it's one big, open, lunarlike landscape.

- Feeling a little old? The rocks on Hughes Mountain will make you feel young—they are around 1.5 *billion* years old!

- Not into rocks? Come for the views. The top of the mountain offers a 360-degree panorama.

Area Information

Hughes Mountain is an igneous knob capped by expansive glades, unusual geology, and a variety of forest types. The rocks on Hughes Mountain are Precambrian rhyolite, which is a type of igneous rock. Formed between 1.4 and 1.5 billion years ago, the rocks are among the oldest exposed rocks on the continent.

Although the big glades provide an unusual opportunity to hike on an expansive, lunarlike landscape, and although the sweeping vistas are some of the best that you'll find anywhere in the state, the real phenomenon of the area is rhyolitic rock formed into vertical columns by a geological process known as polygonal jointing. According to *Geologic Wonders and Curiosities of Missouri* by Thomas R. Beveridge, other world-famous examples of this formation are the Devils Tower National Monument in Wyoming, Devils Postpile National Monument in California, and the Giant's Causeway in Ireland. Once-molten rock cools, contracts, and cracks vertically, resulting in columns. On Hughes Mountain, the columns have four to six sides, are up to 10 inches in diameter, and are 3 to 4 feet tall. The feature is known locally as the Devil's Honeycomb.

The 462-acre area is named for John Hughes, the first European settler in the area. He arrived about 1810 and operated a gristmill on a creek near the mountain. In 1982 the property was designated a Missouri natural area to protect its geology and natural communities. The mountain's relatively undisturbed glades are one of the largest igneous rhyolite glade complexes in the state's natural area system. The Missouri Department of Conservation owns and manages the area.

Directions: From Potosi, take Highway 21 south for 10 miles. Turn east on Route M and go 3.6 miles to the parking lot on the right.

Hours Open: The site is open daily from 4:00 a.m. to 10:00 p.m. year-round.

Facilities: The site has no facilities.

Permits and Rules: Horses, ATVs, and bicycles are not permitted on the area. Camping is not allowed.

For Further Information: District Forester, Missouri Department of Conservation, 2360 Highway D, St. Charles, MO 63304; 636-441-4554; www.mdc.mo.gov.

Devil's Honeycomb Trail

Distance Round-Trip:
1.75 miles
Estimated Hiking Time:
1.75 hours

Bring lots of memory for your camera. The beauty of this stark landscape will surprise you. You'll find something (or lots of things) that will intrigue you on top of the mountain.

Caution: Be careful when navigating the Honeycomb. Some of the rocks are sharp, and some are loose.

Trail Directions: Park in the lot for the area and begin the trail at the south end of the lot **[1]** on a mowed path through an old field. Soon, you enter the woods and wind your way uphill. As you look ahead, you see boulders looming through the trees, covered with mosses and lichens and blending in with the tree-covered sloping terrain. As you hike next to these ancient boulders, look closely at them. The rock is rhyolite porphyry—once-molten rock with varied crystal sizes.

Just before you walk out onto the first rocky opening at .23 mi. **[2]**, look around next to the trail for prickly pear cactus plants. You are about to enter a glade landscape, and prickly pear, Missouri's only native cactus, is well suited for this dry environment. Follow the trail markers to continue uphill.

As you climb, notice the trees. Most are small, gnarly, and stunted—testimony to their harsh life on this rocky, windswept landscape. The larger trees, often damaged, are older than they look. Some of the white oaks and post oaks are well over 100 years old. At .33 mi. **[3]**, follow the markers as the trail makes a 90-degree turn to the left. At .43 mi. **[4]**, turn to the left and follow an intermittent stream, which may be dry. At .59 mi. **[5]**, you step out of the woods onto a lunarlike landscape. Notice the metal post here, which will help you find the trail on your way back.

From here, make your own trail. Explore the huge sheets of bedrock. Find vertical columns of rhyolite exhibiting polygonal jointing. If rain has fallen recently, you may find tiny ponds known as *tinajitas* atop the bedrock. The views keep getting better as you hit the high points. Eventually, make your way to the summit at .85 mi. **[6]**, where you have a 360-degree view of surrounding wooded ridges and knobs. You'll find the best example of stair-stepped honeycomb structure, the Devil's Honeycomb, on the west side of the peak. When you're finished exploring, return to the metal post, where the trail takes you back to the trailhead.

Hughes Mountain Natural Area

1. Start
2. Cactus
3. Left turn
4. Left turn
5. Open landscape
6. Summit

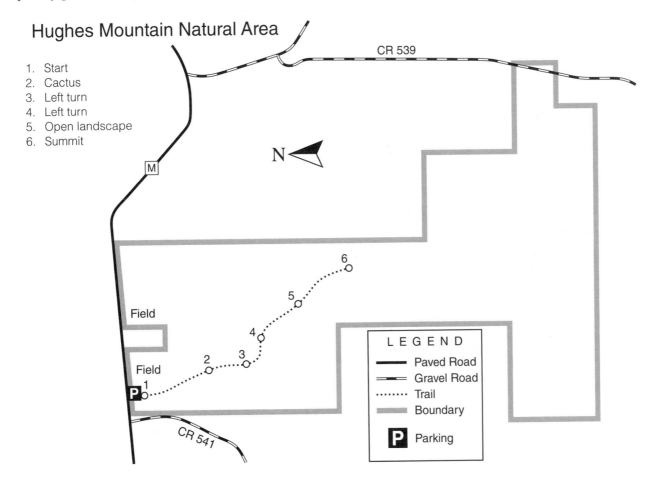

- See and touch the pink elephants, some of the most curious geological wonders in Missouri and among the oldest rocks on the earth's surface.

- Hike on the first trail in the state designed especially for people with visual and physical disabilities.

- Find a wealth of life in the short-lived pools of the *tinajitas*.

- Learn how the elephants were formed 1.3 billion years ago, how quarry workers split them in the late 1800s, and how weather is eroding them today.

- Hike among the Precambrian elephants and let your imagination go wild.

Area Information

Although these titanic, spheroidal granite boulders currently dominate the summit of a bedrock dome, they began as a solid mass deep beneath the earth's surface. Originating as molten rock, magma was pushed up toward the surface, where it cooled slowly, forming solid granite. Cracks developed in the granite, producing stacks of huge, oblong blocks. Through a combination of mountain-forming uplift and hundreds of millions of years of erosion, the blocks were eventually brought to the surface, where they began to face, as they still do, the effects of weather. Rainwater, freezing, thawing, wind, and sun all play their parts to break down the rocks. Even plants and trees growing in cracks help break them apart. As these agents wear at the corners and edges of the rocks, the rounded shapes of the elephants begin to appear.

The economic value of granite, one of the hardest rocks known, was quickly recognized. Several quarries are located within the park, and just outside the park is the oldest granite quarry in the state, which opened in 1869. These quarries supplied granite for paving stones for some of St. Louis's streets, for massive blocks for the piers of the Eads Bridge at St. Louis, and for the state capitols of Iowa and Illinois. Fortunately, the legacy of these ancient rocks is preserved today. They are tangible parts of the geological core of the Ozarks. Come hike among the elephants, an old and peaceful herd.

Directions: The park is at the northwest edge of Graniteville on Highway 21. The entrance is 1.2 miles north of the intersection of Highway 21 and Highway N.

Hours Open: The site is open year-round from sunrise to sunset.

Facilities: Picnic areas, restrooms, a small fishing lake, and drinking water are available.

Permits and Rules: No bicycles, in-line skates, or rock-climbing equipment is allowed in the park. Rock collecting and camping are prohibited. No disposable containers are allowed on the trail. Hikers must stay on the trail. Pets must always be leashed.

For Further Information: Elephant Rocks State Park, P.O. Box 509, Pilot Knob, MO 63663; 573-546-3454 (Fort Davidson State Historic Site).

Other Areas of Interest

Earthwork remnants of a Civil War fort occupied by Union forces are still visible at **Fort Davidson State Historic Site**. A visitor center interprets the historic September 27, 1864, battle, and the site includes a picnic area and playgrounds. The fort is on Highway V in Pilot Knob, just north of Ironton. For more information, call 573-546-3454.

Elephant Rocks Braille Trail

Distance Round-Trip: 1 mile
Estimated Hiking Time: 1 hour

Rock, animal, vegetable . . . they're all mixed up at Elephant Rocks State Park. You never know what will loom up through the trees next. Is that a nose? Is that a mouth? Watch out! That is most certainly a pachyderm!

Caution: Take insect repellent for summer evening hikes among the elephants; *tinajitas* can produce mosquitoes.

Trail Directions: Begin the trail **[1]** at the large interpretive signs at the north end of the parking lot. The paved trail is ideal for park visitors who are disabled or elderly. The signs here, as well as those along the hike, describe the origin of the massive spheroidal granite boulders and explain why they look the way they do. Some of the oldest and hardest rocks on the earth, these elephants have a long and interesting history.

As you begin, the rounded contours of the first elephants loom through the trees. Turn right at the intersection at .05 mi. **[2]**. Because of its outstanding geologic value, the seven-acre site encircled by this trail is a designated state natural area. Although it is tempting to explore the area, please stay on the trail to avoid broadening unauthorized paths. Later, a boardwalk will take you to the top of the mountain, where you can roam at will among the elephants.

Along the way there are plenty of low, smooth boulders (baby elephants) that make great natural benches. At .29 mi. **[3]** is a circular bench made from red granite blocks. Take the overlook spur to your left at .37 mi. **[4]** to view an interesting jumble of sprawling white oaks and piles of red granite left from quarry work. On the horizon are the forested igneous domes of the St. François Mountains. Continue on your left after returning to the main trail.

Turn left at the spur at .50 mi. **[5]** to walk among the elephants. At this summit you can see the names of early quarry workers engraved in some of the boulders. The workers often carved their names on the date that they became master stonecutters. At the feet of the elephants look for *tinajitas*—natural depressions in the rock sometimes filled with temporary pools of water. Grasses and mosses find homes here, and frogs, toads, and insects often lay their eggs in the water. Turn left after returning to the main trail. Turn left again at .59 mi. **[6]** to pass through Fat Man's Squeeze, a natural fracture between two boulders.

Turn right at .62 mi. **[7]** to walk beside some piles of granite blocks, some of which still bear holes drilled by quarry workers. Turn right at **[6]** to pass again through Fat Man's Squeeze.

At .73 mi. **[8]** is an overlook of a water-filled quarry, where granite blocks were extracted to pave streets in St. Louis and other U.S. cities. An iron wedge used to split the granite still remains in a stone at .77 mi. **[9]**. Turn left at the fork at .82 mi. **[10]** and turn right at the intersection **[2]** to finish the trail.

Elephant Rocks State Park

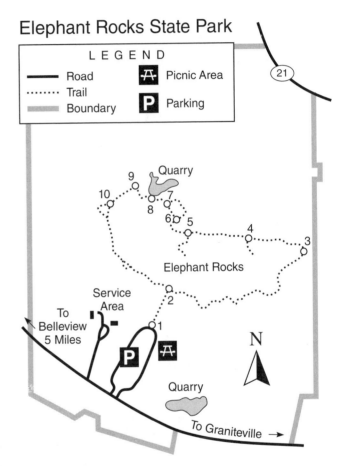

1. Start
2. Right turn
3. Red granite bench
4. Overlook spur
5. Spur to elephants
6. Left turn
7. Right turn
8. Quarry overlook
9. Iron wedge
10. Left turn

Southeast

35. Taum Sauk Mountain State Park

- Stand at the summit of Taum Sauk Mountain, the highest point in Missouri.
- Hike next to the 132-foot cascades of Mina Sauk Falls, the tallest waterfall in the state.
- If you dare, gain admittance through Devil's Toll Gate, a narrow gap in a ridge of rock 50 feet long and 30 feet high, located in the state's deepest valley.
- Hike in the state's largest designated natural area, the 7,028-acre St. François Mountains Natural Area.
- Emerge from the forest onto rocky glades with tremendous views of the seemingly endless layers of the forested Ozark Highlands.

Area Information

The 5,000-square-mile St. François Mountains include 30 forested peaks and constitute the great geologic dome of the Ozark interior. At the apex of this dome is Taum Sauk Mountain, the state's highest point, at 1,772 feet above sea level. Rock exposures give evidence of the geologic origins of the area, which can be traced to volcanic activity around 1.5 billion years ago.

The character of the area can best be described as wilderness. Probably no other place in the state is home to as many plants, animals, and geologic features in their unspoiled state. Rich forests of oak, hickory, and shortleaf pine are interspersed with extensive glades, allowing unobstructed views of the rugged, expansive landscape. Prairie blazing star and rattlesnake master contribute their color to the red rocks of the glades, and fire pink, wild crocus, and ferns adorn the woodlands.

Zigzagging its way through the steep terrain is a portion of the Ozark Trail, which will be 500 miles long when complete. The trail begins in St. Louis, follows a scenic route through the Ozarks of southern Missouri, and will join the Ozark Highlands Trail of Arkansas.

Directions: From Ironton, go 6.5 miles south on Highway 21. Turn west on Highway CC, which dead-ends in 4 miles at Taum Sauk Mountain State Park.

Hours Open: The park is open year-round.

Facilities: The site offers an overlook, camping, picnic areas, and restrooms. Water is available from April through October. A fire tower, maintained by the Missouri Department of Conservation, is located on Highway CC 1 mile from the campground and is open to the public for climbing during daylight hours.

Permits and Rules: The Mina Sauk Falls Trail and the Taum Sauk Section of the Ozark Trail are open to foot traffic only. Standard wilderness ethics apply, which include staying on the trail, leaving plants, animals, and rocks undisturbed, and carrying out everything you brought in.

For Further Information: Taum Sauk Mountain State Park, c/o Johnson's Shut-Ins State Park, HC Route 1, Box 126, Middlebrook, MO 63656; 573-546-2450. For more information on the Ozark Trail, call the Missouri Department of Natural Resources trail coordinator at 573-751-5359.

Park Trails

Taum Sauk Section—Ozark Trail (, 12.8 miles). Although the entire Taum Sauk Section is 33 miles long, the segment from Taum Sauk Mountain to Johnson's Shut-Ins State Park is only 12.8 miles long and offers ambitious day hikers an unforgettable hike. Approximately 3 miles of this trail closest to the shut-ins had to be rerouted due to the Taum Sauk reservoir breach of 2005. As of this printing, this section wasn't finalized. Check www.mostateparks.com or call the park office for details.

Mina Sauk Falls Trail and Ozark Trail to Devil's Toll Gate

Distance Round-Trip:
5 miles
Estimated Hiking Time:
3.25 hours

Hike Missouri's trail of superlatives. This 5-mile hike includes the state's highest mountain, deepest valley, tallest waterfall, oldest rocks, and a portion of its longest trail (when completed), all within Missouri's largest designated natural area.

Caution: Rocks are numerous on this trail. Some are sharp, and many are loose.

Trail Directions: Begin the hike **[1]** near the signs at the edge of the parking lot at Taum Sauk Mountain. The trail begins as a sidewalk to the state's highest point. From there (obviously) it's a steady decline to the bottom. At .16 mi. **[2]**, turn left on the spur to the peak of Taum Sauk, marked with a red granite monument stating that you are now 1,772.68 feet above mean sea level. Return to the main trail and turn left. Turn right at the intersection at .24 mi. **[3]**.

The first of many glades opens at .47 mi. **[4]**. Blue and green lichens add their colors to the red volcanic rock. This rock, rhyolite, is well over a billion years old. Prescribed fires set by park staff have allowed native plants, including rattlesnake master, to thrive in abundance here. Back in the forest, fire invigorates wildflowers like the brilliant fire pink and the deep blue wild crocus, found along the entire trail. Another glade starts at .70 mi., and the views of outlying forested domes keep getting better until .94 mi. **[5]**, where the best view of all will stop you in your tracks. Mountain after mountain is layered in uninterrupted succession, the farther ones increasingly shrouded in blue-gray haze.

Go straight at 1.36 mi. **[6]** at the trail sign, which directs you to the top of the main cascade of Mina Sauk Falls. A wet-season waterfall, Mina Sauk flows most often during spring and fall. In all, the falls drop 132 feet in a series of cascades, splashing down one volcanic rock ledge after another. For a better view of Mina Sauk near the bottom, return to the trail sign and turn left on the Ozark Trail, toward Devil's Toll Gate. At 1.46 mi. **[7]**, you reach the base of the falls, where you can feel the mist on your face and become engulfed in the water's timeless roar. Cross the rocky stream here and turn right at the fork at 1.61 mi. **[8]**.

The trail soon parallels Taum Sauk Creek. Although not in its lowest point, you are now in Missouri's deepest valley **[9]** (1.87 mi.), measuring 1,000 feet from top to bottom. Turn left at the intersection at 2.19 mi. **[10]**, just after crossing a rocky stream. Suddenly, an igneous rock ridge rises through the trees, leaving only an 8-foot gap through which the trail passes. Return to Mina Sauk Falls after experiencing Devil's Toll Gate **[11]** (2.32).

Turn right at **[6]** and pass several more cascades of Mina Sauk Falls. The trail treats you to the music of the stream as you pass several glades on your left, including some with remarkable vistas of the Ozark landscape. Turn left at the intersection at 4.49 mi. **[12]**. Turn right when you return to the intersection **[3]** to finish your hike.

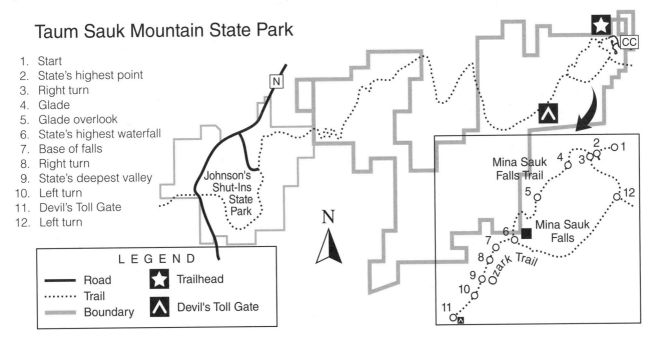

Taum Sauk Mountain State Park

1. Start
2. State's highest point
3. Right turn
4. Glade
5. Glade overlook
6. State's highest waterfall
7. Base of falls
8. Right turn
9. State's deepest valley
10. Left turn
11. Devil's Toll Gate
12. Left turn

LEGEND
— Road
···· Trail
— Boundary
★ Trailhead
Λ Devil's Toll Gate

- Stand on huge, rounded boulders on open, igneous glades and take in panoramic views of placid Crane Lake and rocky glades on distant ridges.
- On the glades, keep an eye out for basking reptiles, including six-lined racerunners and eastern collared lizards.
- Hear the music making of a myriad of orthopterans (grasshoppers, crickets, and katydids) in the tall vegetation of an old field.
- In the fall, find a big patch of strongly fragrant ladies' tresses orchids.
- Hike across the pillowlike, sculpted igneous boulders of the shut-ins on Crane Pond Creek.

Area Information

Crane Lake is nestled between several ridges of the St. François Mountains, a 5,000-square-mile landscape that is one of the oldest mountain ranges in North America. Often considered the geologic core of the Ozarks, the St. François Mountains originated around 1.5 billion years ago as molten rock, which cooled and hardened into the ancient igneous rocks that typify this region.

Besides igneous rock exposures, Crane Lake has other features characteristic of the area, including ridgetop glades and shut-ins, which are gorgelike streambeds filled with bedrock and boulders, created when a stream forced its way through resistant outcrops of igneous rock. The site also boasts scenic ridgetop overlooks, a variety of Ozark habitats, and a picturesque and peaceful lake.

Crane Lake was originally created by an earthen dam constructed across the shut-ins of Crane Pond Creek. After the original dam failed in 1968, a concrete dam was installed in 1971–72 to impound about 100 acres of water. The U.S. Forest Service bought the lake and surrounding area in 1973. Crane Lake Trail is one of only five national recreation trails in the state. This special designation identifies the trail as an outstanding recreation resource and qualifies it for public recognition through U.S. Department of the Interior publications and news releases.

Directions: From Ironton, take Highway 21 south 15.1 miles to Chloride, where you turn east on Iron County Road #124 (just past Doe Run iron smelter).

Go 3.8 miles and turn right at the sign for the area. Go 2.1 miles to a fork in the road, where you turn left into the parking lot for the boat ramp.

Hours Open: The area is always open.

Facilities: A boat ramp is available, making 100-acre Crane Lake accessible for fishing, canoeing, and boating. Picnic tables are provided, as well as grills and a toilet. Crane Lake Trail is open to hiking and biking, and a portion of the trail is open to equestrian use. The area can also be used to access the Marble Creek Section of the Ozark Trail.

Permits and Rules: No camping is allowed. Horses are allowed only on the southwest half of the trail and along the west shore of the lake. Motorized vehicles are prohibited on the trail. Boat motors are restricted to electric trolling motors. Pets must be leashed.

For Further Information: District Ranger, U.S. Forest Service, Potosi–Fredericktown District, Highway 8 West, Potosi, MO 63664; 573-438-5427; www.fs.fed.us/r9/forests/marktwain. For more information on the Ozark Trail, contact the Missouri Department of Natural Resources, Ozark Trail Coordinator, P.O. Box 176, Jefferson City, MO 65102-0176; 800-334-6946.

Other Areas of Interest

Marble Creek Recreation Area, also managed by the U.S. Forest Service, offers camping, picnicking, and wading and fishing in Marble Creek. The remains of a gristmill dam and building foundation are visible. The area is named for deposits of attractively colored dolomite that were mined and used in the building trade as "Taum Sauk Marble." The area is a trailhead for the Ozark Trail. The site is 9 miles northeast of Crane Lake, just off County Highway E. For more information, call the Potosi–Fredericktown Ranger District at 573-438-5427.

Area Trails

Marble Creek Section—Ozark Trail (🥾🥾🥾, 8 miles). Although the entire 21-mile section is not complete, the 8-mile portion that connects Crane Lake with Marble Creek Recreation Area is finished and is open to the public. The trail traverses Reader Hollow, glades, bottoms, and ridges, and offers views of Kelly and Patterson mountains before finishing at Marble Creek's parking area.

Crane Lake Trail

Distance Round-Trip:
5 miles
Estimated Hiking Time:
2.75 hours

"It's kind of a booger to get to . . . kinda outa the way. But it's a mighty purty place." —resident of Chloride, describing Crane Lake

Caution: Vegetation crowds the trail in the creek bottom, so consider wearing long pants.

Trail Directions: Park in the lot for the picnic area and boat ramp. The trail begins between two chert boulders at the edge of the parking lot **[1]**. After passing through the picnic area, the trail takes you along the shore for fantastic views of the tranquil lake. Fingers of pine-clad ridges reach down to touch the water, and the sun plays with ripples near the edge like so many sparkling jewels.

At .72 mi. **[2]**, you cross a small stream that feeds the east bay of the lake. As the trail bends right at 1.15 mi. **[3]**, white and tan sedimentary rocks are replaced by dark gray and purple igneous rocks, which form an interesting contrast with the patterns of green lichens that grow on them. The forest suddenly gives way to open glades at 1.30 mi. **[4]** with huge, rounded, igneous boulders. A fabulous vista of the lake soon opens over your right shoulder. Watch for eastern collared lizards sunning on the rocks.

As you descend into the valley of Crane Pond Creek, you pass several walls of pink boulders next to the trail. After crossing a few intermittent streams, you emerge into a large, old field at 1.86 mi. **[5]**. Watch

for soaring birds of prey here and listen for their clear, whistlelike calls. Turn right at the intersection with the Ozark Trail at 2.04 mi. **[6]**. The streambed at 2.11 mi. **[7]** is an eclectic rock collection, with specimens of varied colors, textures, and formation. Blue lobelia and brown-eyed susans bloom next to the stream.

At 2.20 mi. **[8]**, cross two streambeds of Crane Pond Creek. Turn right at 2.24 mi. **[9]**, just across the second streambed, which may be flowing with spring water. In a weedy bottom, turn left at the intersection at 2.35 mi. **[10]**, away from the creek. Next, you hike along an old farm field on an old road, lined with white oaks and shagbark hickories. Just after turning right at the fork in the trail at 2.49 mi. **[11]**, look for blooming ladies' tresses orchid (August through November), a strongly fragrant orchid with small, white flowers spiraled on a stem about a foot tall. After passing through rocky woods, you find more igneous glades and overlooks at 2.87 mi. **[12]**, with views across the chasmlike valley of Crane Pond Creek, far below.

Turn right at 3.06 mi. **[13]** and again at the dam at 3.10 mi. **[14]**. This spur leads to the shut-ins of Crane Pond Creek. Explore the billowing, sculpted rocks of the shut-ins at 3.14 mi. **[15]**. After returning to the dam, follow the shoreline to continue. After crossing a small stream that feeds the south bay, turn right at the intersection with an old road at 3.55 mi. **[16]**. The trail now hugs the shoreline. After crossing a concrete bridge at 4.82 mi. **[17]**, go straight on the gravel road. Turn right at the intersection with the county road at 4.90 mi. **[18]** to return to the trailhead.

1. Start
2. Stream crossing
3. Igneous rocks
4. Glades and overlook
5. Old field
6. Right turn
7. Rocky streambed
8. Creek crossing
9. Right turn
10. Left turn
11. Right turn
12. Glades and overlooks
13. Right turn
14. Spur to shut-ins
15. Shut-ins
16. Right turn
17. Concrete bridge
18. Right turn

Crane Lake Recreation Area

L E G E N D
— Road
···· Trail
🏕 Picnic Area
🚤 Boat Launch
〰 Springs
🌊 Dam
🅿 Parking

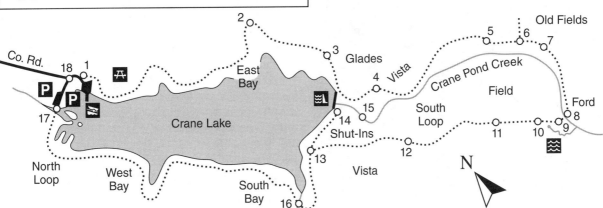

- Hike next to a spring stream, a wet meadow, a glade, a pirated stream, two sections of ancient collapsed cave passage, and three cave entrances—all on one trail!
- Feel the cool air emerging from Mushroom Cave, where mushrooms were farmed commercially in the early 1900s.
- Look for your favorite wild edibles on the Natural Wonders Trail—82 different ones have been found there so far.

Area Information

Meramec State Park is 6,896 acres of forests, savannas, caves, and bluffs along one of Missouri's most beautiful rivers—the Meramec. Its natural communities are diverse, ranging from moist, towering forests to dry, rocky glades. Lush vegetation and a great diversity of trees thrive in the lower elevations, and impressive displays of wildflowers adorn the highest savannas and glades, dotted with twisted and gnarled chinquapin oaks.

The Meramec River almost became Meramec Lake. The U.S. Army Corps of Engineers had already begun construction of a dam on the Meramec River when a public vote in 1978 resulted in deauthorization of the project. Today, the Meramec still flows freely, and several miles of the scenic river and its wooded banks are preserved in the park, providing a haven for abundant wildlife. The Meramec contains the greatest variety of aquatic life in Missouri. Exhibits in the visitor center interpret this healthy and diverse habitat.

Missouri has over 6,000 caves, and 47 of these are hidden within Meramec's expansive forests—more than in any other park in the state. Naturalist-led tours of the largest and most spectacular cave in the park, Fisher Cave, offer the park visitor adventure, outstanding cave scenery, and insight into how caves and calcite deposits are formed. The 90-minute tours are given four times daily during the summer for a small fee.

Directions: From Sullivan, travel 3.2 miles south on Highway 185 to the park entrance.

Hours Open: The park is open year-round. The front gate is open from 7:00 a.m. to 10:00 p.m. daily from April through October and from 7:00 a.m. to 9:00 p.m. daily from November through March. The visitor center is closed on Thanksgiving, Christmas Day, and New Year's Day.

Facilities: The park offers a visitor center that includes a 3,500-gallon aquarium, a large campground, an outdoor amphitheater for interpretive programs, cabins, a motel, a convention center, a grill, a boat ramp, picnic areas and shelters, play areas, a store, and canoe and raft rentals.

Permits and Rules: Do not enter any cave without first contacting the visitor center. Some caves require a permit to enter. Pets must always be leashed. Some campsites are reservable, although others are not.

For Further Information: Meramec State Park, 115 Meramec Park Drive, Sullivan, MO 63080; 573-468-6072 (visitor center) or 573-468-6519 (cabin and canoe rental).

Park Trails

Deer Hollow Trail (👣👣, 1.8 miles). This linear trail, which connects the dining lodge to Fisher Cave, is a good trail to see blooming dogwood trees in late April, fall colors in early October, and white-tailed deer all year long.

Walking Fern Trail (👣👣👣👣, .5 mile). This trail takes you next to Indian Cave, through a lush forest, next to a boulder covered with walking ferns, and up onto a dry upland forest. The trail begins and ends at Fisher Cave.

River Trail (👣👣, .8 mile). This loop trail begins at the southern end of the campground and winds along a slough of the Meramec River.

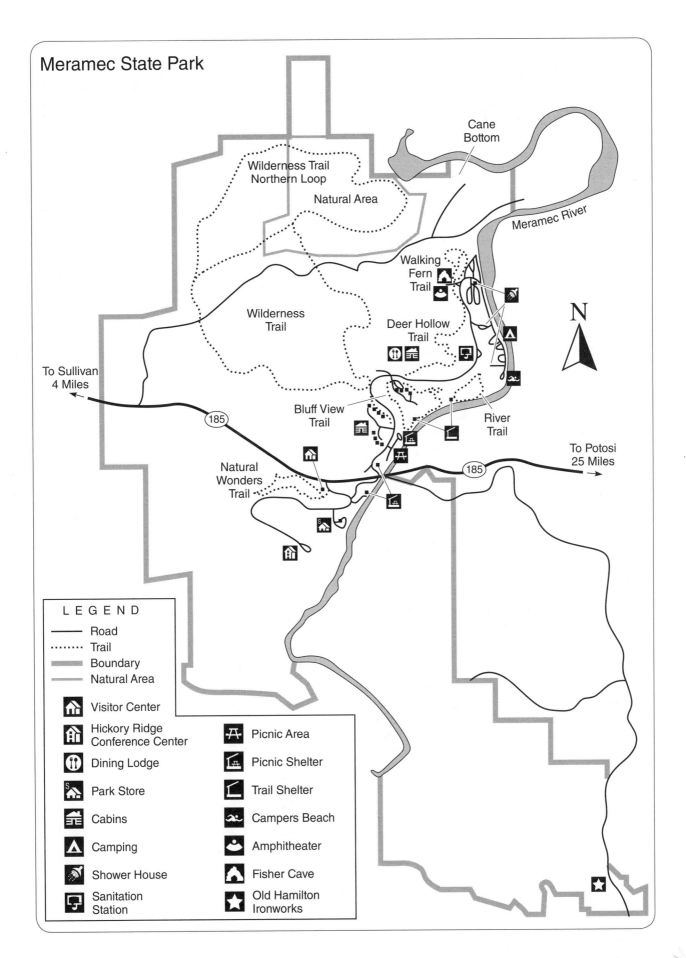

Meramec State Park

Wilderness Trail
Northern Loop

Natural Area

Cane
Bottom

Meramec River

Wilderness
Trail

Walking
Fern
Trail

Deer Hollow
Trail

To Sullivan
4 Miles

185

Bluff View
Trail

River
Trail

N

To Potosi
25 Miles

185

Natural
Wonders
Trail

LEGEND
—— Road
.... Trail
▬▬ Boundary
▬▬ Natural Area

🏠 Visitor Center

🏠 Hickory Ridge
Conference Center

🍴 Dining Lodge

🏠 Park Store

🏫 Cabins

⛺ Camping

🚿 Shower House

Sanitation
Station

🛖 Picnic Area

🏕 Picnic Shelter

Trail Shelter

Campers Beach

Amphitheater

Fisher Cave

⭐ Old Hamilton
Ironworks

Natural Wonders Trail

Distance Round-Trip: 1.3 miles
Estimated Hiking Time: 45 minutes

I had been sitting on a large rock on the glade for about 15 minutes before I noticed a rather large, coiled eastern coachwhip snake about 6 feet away. I admired its braided brown and tan coloring before I crept slowly away, leaving the snake to its morning reptilian business.

Caution: Do not enter any cave without contacting the visitor center for a review of cave regulations and a check for the possibility of a flash flood.

Trail Directions: Before or after your hike, be sure to see the exhibits and the park slide show in the visitor center. Park in the lot for the visitor center and begin the trail at the trailhead **[1]** at the southeast end of the lot. Turn right at the intersection at .08 mi. **[2]**, and soon you are hiking under the whispering branches of a shortleaf pine grove. Ignore the spur to the right at .13 mi. **[3]** and go straight, looking for signs of beaver on nearby trees. Elm Spring Creek riffles along the trail at .17 mi. **[4]**. Look for beaver here, as well as at the Beaver Pond behind the visitor center. October is the best time to watch for beaver, when their preparations for winter make the nocturnal rodents more active during the day.

Just after you cross a small drainage at .22 mi. **[5]**, you find a wet meadow on your left. The stream flowing out of Mushroom Cave (passed later on the trail) keeps this area eternally moist, providing a good habitat for burrowing devil crayfish. You may see their mud chimneys near the trail here. Stop by the stream pool at .27 mi. **[6]** and look for camouflaged sculpin fish lying on the bottom and agile water striders skating across the top. You also find watercress here and a good patch of spearmint.

Just before you cross a wooden bridge at .44 mi., you'll see an entrance to Camp Cave **[7]**. More accurately, this is an exit to Camp Cave because the water flowing out of it comes from another opening to the cave (encountered later), which acts as a surface stream drain. This situation is known as stream piracy. Cross the bridge to continue. Climb the hill and find

the continuity of the forest broken by a beautiful glade **[8]** (.53 mi.). Layers of the sedimentary dolomite created three levels of the glade, making a three-tiered minidesert, resplendent with prairie dock, shooting star, Indian paintbrush, and purple coneflower.

At .67 mi. **[9]**, stand at the top of the wooden switchbacks and look down the ravine. This is part of a collapsed cave passage. At the bottom of the switchbacks is the inlet entrance to Camp Cave. Hike under the canopy of black walnut, white oak, pawpaw, and dogwood trees on your way to yet another cave opening. Find the yawning maw of Mushroom Cave at 1.05 mi. **[10]**, the site of several commercial mushroom farming operations in the early 1900s. Today, wild hydrangea flourish near the cave's outflowing stream, which is always cool enough to refresh hot feet—even in the middle of summer. The minicanyon just across the trail is another section of an ancient, collapsed passageway. On your way back, go straight at the intersection at **[2]** to return to the trailhead.

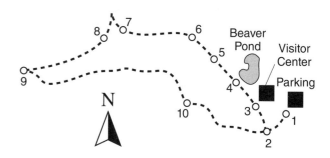

1. Start
2. Right turn
3. Go straight
4. Elm Spring Creek
5. Wet meadow
6. Stream pool
7. Camp Cave outlet
8. Glade
9. Camp Cave inlet
10. Mushroom Cave

Bluff View Trail

 Distance Round-Trip: 1.5 miles
Estimated Hiking Time: 1 hour

Meramec means "big catfish" in the Algonquin language, which says something about the productivity of its rippling, spring-fed waters. With over 100 species of fish and 40 species of mussels, the Meramec River is one of the most diverse aquatic habitats in the United States.

Caution: Sections of the trail contain large rocks and tree roots. Also, be careful near the bluff edges.

Trail Directions: Park in one of the parking areas at the store and grill. This is also the lodging rental office (formerly known as the dining lodge). Find the trailhead **[1]** by the west entrance to the store, about 50 yards from the main park road. If you are here on a cold day, look for frost flowers—fragile white ribbons of ice that sometimes flow from the stems of certain plants. Dittany, a mint with small, teardrop-shaped leaves, is one of only three plants in Missouri that can produce frost flowers. Dittany is common on this trail, especially around the twin black oaks at .03 mi.

Turn left at .30 mi. **[2]**, ignoring the small trail on the right. Soon you discover a plot of native bluestem grasses taking advantage of the opening in the forest canopy that a power line provides. In summer, this spot is a colorful jumble of orange butterfly weed, purple prairie clover, and yellow black-eyed susans.

At .53 mi. **[3]**, you find an unusual octagonal stone building. Built in 1935 by the CCC, this trail shelter was used as a model for shelters built in national and state parks in other parts of the nation. Today, it's a good place to stop for a moment, catch your first glimpse of the sparkling Meramec River below, and hear the music of its riffles.

The path to the right goes to the picnic area and picnic shelter #3. Continue the trail to the left and follow the blufftop along the river. At .62 mi., stop at the overlook **[4]** to enjoy the view. In summer, look for brown softshell "pancake" turtles floating near the surface over deep pools of the river. Swallows elegantly dive and swoop for flying insects over the water by day. Bats replace them as afternoon eases into evening.

Descend to river level and discover a patch of spanglegrass, or wild oats, near the bottom. Notice how wide the seeds are. But look closer . . . they are as flat as paper. At .71 mi. **[5]**, follow the trail to the left over a wooden bridge, hike through a stand of wild

rye (which looks like wheat except that the seed grains are farther apart), and go up again to the blufftop. Take the short spur on your right to the overlook at .77 mi. **[6]** and again at .84 mi. **[7]**, where dried, twisted trunks of ancient cedars still cling to the bluff face and brilliant black-eyed susans contrast with the dark craggy dolomite rocks found on top.

At 1.03 mi. is another stone trail shelter **[8]**, and the trail meets the River Trail. Go straight to continue the Bluff View Trail. After a few steps, look for bottlebrush grass on both sides of the trail. Bottlebrush grass looks like wild rye having a bad hair day.

Cross an intermittent stream at 1.11 mi. **[9]**, take a few steps, and turn right. Go uphill a short distance and bear right at the intersection at 1.13 mi. **[10]**. Continue uphill and turn left at the next intersection at 1.14 mi. **[11]**. Ignore the path on the left at 1.25 mi. **[12]** and continue straight to complete the switchback and finish the trail.

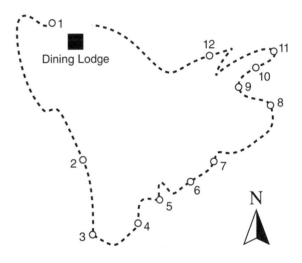

1. Start
2. Left turn
3. Octagonal trail shelter
4. Overlook
5. Wooden bridge
6. Overlook
7. Overlook
8. Trail shelter
9. Stream crossing
10. Bear right
11. Left turn
12. Go straight

Wilderness Trail

Distance Round-Trip:
9 miles
Estimated Hiking Time:
4.75 hours

Hike in the most remote area of the park on a trail that has it all—open woods, grand trees, a diverse natural area, streams, glades, vistas, and one of the crown jewels of the park, beautiful Copper Hollow Spring.

Caution: You may want to call ahead to make sure that the trail isn't closed for prescribed burns or special hunts. Also, if you plan to use one of the eight backpacking camps along the trail, register at the registration box at .23 mi. The camps are first come, first served.

Trail Directions: From the visitor center, travel into the park .2 mi. and turn left at the stop sign. Go another .7 mi. and turn left into a small parking lot near cabins 1 through 4. Park in this lot and start the trail at the sign for the trailhead **[1]**. This trail has a 6 mi. southern loop and a 4 mi. northern loop. Both loops include a 1 mi. white connector. To hike the perimeter trail, follow red arrows going clockwise.

As the trail winds behind the rental cabins, look for pocket glades on your right—small, rocky openings where native grasses and wildflowers flourish. Turn left at the intersection at .39 mi. **[2]**. At .67 mi. **[3]**, you pass a spur on your right that leads to the first backpacking camp. Cross an intermittent stream and pass a spur to camp #2 on your left at .76 mi. **[4]**. As you enter Campbell Hollow, the trees become much larger and more widely spaced. The trail flattens as it meanders back and forth across the intermittent stream. Enjoy passing through several pawpaw groves and scenic, open woods dotted with boulders and minibluffs.

The trail meets Highway 185 Spur at 2.09 mi. **[5]** and continues on the other side, slightly to the right. Before long, big shortleaf pines enter the scene. On a warm day, your nose may detect that famous evergreen odor. The CCC planted these pines in the mid-1930s. Turn left at the intersection with the shortcut connector at 2.46 mi. **[6]** to begin the northern loop. At 2.59 mi. **[7]**, you pass a spur to a backpacking camp on your left. Within a few steps, cross an abandoned fire road and pass a spur on your left to another camp **[8]**. Then it's down you go, back into the land of ferns and pawpaws. Aromatic spicebush lines both sides of the trail here as you enter Copper Hollow. You cross an intermittent stream several times while passing three more backpacking camps on your left at 3.41 mi. **[9]**, 3.48 mi. **[10]**, and 3.71 mi. **[11]**. You are now entering Meramec Upland Forest Natural Area, the largest undisturbed Ozark chert forest in the state. Look for the different-shaped leaves of sassafras, mulberry, and basswood. If you're here on a warm day, you may feel cooler air as you approach Copper Hollow Spring, which erupts from the base of the bluff at 4.32 mi. **[12]**. Please note that the cave at the base of the bluff is restricted; entrance requires a permit and specialized equipment. The trail soon crosses the spring branch, lush with watercress, liverworts, and ferns. Just after crossing the spring branch a second time, turn right at 4.37 mi. **[13]**. You now begin an ascent that gives you a view of the Meramec River, especially if the leaves have fallen. As the trail turns away from the river, you emerge from the forest and reach the first of several glades at 4.98 mi. **[14]**. For the next mile, views of the forested ridge on your left expand, and the glades become more extensive. The stunted and craggy trees here are chinquapin oaks, one of the few trees that can tolerate the harsh, desertlike conditions of these rocky openings. Watch for lizards scurrying among the rocks and wildflowers like prairie dock, black-eyed susan, and rattlesnake master. After you reenter the forest, you reach the intersection with the shortcut connector at 6.32 mi. **[15]**. Turn left here to stay on the main trail. Climb uphill onto the ridge that you've been admiring while on the glades. You hike beneath more pines before reaching the intersection with Highway 185 Spur at 6.90 mi. **[16]**. The trail continues directly on the other side. You pass the spur to the last backpacking camp on your left at 7.70 mi. **[17]**. Go straight at the intersection with the gravel road at 8.05 mi. **[18]**. At the intersection at 8.60 mi. **[2]**, turn left to return to the trailhead.

1. Start
2. Left turn
3. Camp #1
4. Camp #2
5. Highway 185 Spur
6. Left turn
7. Camp #3
8. Camp #4
9. Camp #5
10. Camp #6
11. Camp #7
12. Copper Hollow Spring
13. Right turn
14. First glade
15. Left turn
16. Highway 185 Spur
17. Camp #8
18. Go straight

38. Bell Mountain Wilderness

- Hike in the uncommon solitude of a U.S. Forest Service wilderness area.

- Find so many huckleberry bushes that you won't have to venture off the trail to find ripe fruit (June through August).

- Hike on igneous glades—natural communities under extreme drought stress that turn into minideserts in the summer.

- Climb a mountain with panoramic views from the top without a house, barn, or road in sight.

Area Information

The expression "as old as the hills" has geologic meaning in the Ozarks, which have been an exposed land mass for over 250 million years. Bell Mountain Wilderness is 9,027 acres in the St. François Mountains, one of the oldest landforms in North America—at least 1.3 billion years old. Like the other six wilderness areas in Mark Twain National Forest, Bell Mountain required an act of Congress to be designated. Generally, a U.S. Forest Service wilderness must be at least 5,000 acres, basically roadless, and show little evidence of human works. A wilderness is a natural area affected primarily by the forces of nature. Some wilderness areas are classified as airsheds and are protected by laws to prevent their deterioration.

Most of Bell Mountain is rugged, dry, rocky, and forested by a variety of oaks and hickories, with interspersed shortleaf pines. Species of mature forests such as pileated woodpeckers, woodthrush, and ovenbirds thrive here. Igneous glades and rock outcrops are common and add to the diversity of wildlife habitat and scenery. Blackjack oak, winged elm, and native grasses live on the glades, which are havens for snakes, lizards, and plants specially adapted to the hot, dry conditions. Although Bell Mountain's big rocks are fun to hike around and the uninterrupted views from the mountaintop are stupendous, its best feature is its peacefulness.

Directions: From Potosi take Highway 21 south to Highway 32. Turn west on Highway 32 and drive 7 miles to Highway A. Turn south on Highway A and go 5.6 miles. The parking lot for trailhead #2 is on the right. To get to trailhead #1, go south on Highway A for .5 mile, turn left on Farm Road #2228 (gravel), and drive 1.9 miles. The parking lot is on the right.

Hours Open: The wilderness is always open.
Facilities: There are no facilities.
Permits and Rules: Hunting is allowed but not within 150 yards of the trail. Horses are allowed, but ATVs are prohibited. Camping is allowed, but users must observe regulations designed to protect the wilderness beauty. Choose a campsite away from the trail and avoid constructing a fire ring. Cut no standing trees (live or dead) and extinguish all campfires, scattering their evidence before leaving. Leave no litter, trail-marking ribbons, or other evidence of your presence.
For Further Information: District Ranger, U.S. Forest Service, Potosi–Fredericktown District, Highway 8 West, Potosi, MO 63664; 573-438-5427; www.fs.fed.us/r9/forests/marktwain/ranger_districts/potosi.

Other Areas of Interest

Council Bluff Lake, a 440-acre impoundment of the Big River, offers boating, canoeing, fishing, camping, picnicking, and swimming. From Bell Mountain, return to Highway 32 and turn west. Go north on Highway DD 3.2 miles and turn right. For more information, call 573-438-5427.

Area Trails

Lindsey Mountain Trail (🥾🥾🥾, 4.3 miles). Just east of the Bell Mountain Trail, this trail offers two good exercise climbs and the opportunity to hike up another mountain (1,600 feet) in wilderness solitude. Large boulders are scattered on the mountain, and the trail is difficult to follow near the end. To reach the trailhead, continue on Farm Road #2228 for 2.7 miles past trailhead #1. Turn right on Farm Road #2359, which dead-ends in 2 miles at the Lindsey Mountain trailhead.

Taum Sauk Section—Ozark Trail (🥾🥾🥾🥾, 33 miles). This is one of the most scenic and rugged sections of the entire Ozark Trail. The western access connects with the Bell Mountain Trail at point #4. Hiking south, the trail crosses Goggins Mountain and enters the shut-ins area of Johnson's Shut-Ins State Park. The trail may be closed east of Highway N while trail rerouting and construction continues as a result of the Taum Sauk reservoir breach of 2005. As of this printing, the section wasn't finalized. Check www.mostateparks.com or call the park office for details.

Bell Mountain Trail

Distance Round-Trip: 10 miles
Estimated Hiking Time: 5 hours

"What would the world be, once bereft of wet and of wildness? Let them be left, oh let them be left, wildness and wet, long live the weeds and the wilderness yet." —Gerard Manley Hopkins

Caution: Rocks are found on most parts of the trail. Hunting is allowed in national forests. Bring a compass and topo map if you choose to extend this hike or explore off the trail.

Trail Directions: Park in the lot for trailhead #2, which is directly off Highway A. The northern trailhead for the Taum Sauk section of the Ozark Trail is also here, and the first 1.92 mi. of the Bell Mountain Trail is a portion of this Ozark Trail section. This linear hike can be extended; the trailheads are about 9 mi. apart. A 3 mi. loop section in the middle down to Joe's Creek adds options.

Begin by taking the trail directly north out of the parking lot **[1]**. The trail parallels Highway A for a short distance. Turn right at .03 mi. **[2]** and cross Highway A. The trail gains a little elevation here, so you might huff and puff a bit. For compensation, you have trailside scenery of lichen-covered igneous boulders and bountiful wildflowers. Larger rhyolite outcroppings shade small seeps and damp areas, and

provide habitat for mosses, ferns, and water-loving sedges. The several switchbacks here up the side of the mountain are the most difficult part of the trail.

Near the end of the first mile, the trail finally levels off at the top of the ridge. For the next mile, vistas of neighboring Ozark mountains appear through rocky openings in the forest. One of several igneous glades appears on your right at 1.20 mi. **[3]**. The jumble of huge boulders and rock fragments makes natural overlook decks. Notice the stunted trees and shrubs here—this exposed bedrock becomes a solar oven in summer.

At 1.92 mi. **[4]** is the intersection with the Ozark Trail. Turn left (north) to continue the Bell Mountain Trail. At 2.91 mi. **[5]**, go straight. Soon you see evidence of early settlers of Bell Mountain—a farm pond and an old pasture, now thick with blackberries, sumac, and buckbrush. Turn left at the intersection at 3.29 mi. **[6]**. Your feet will enjoy the temporary lack of rocks on the trail. A gradual ascent takes you to the peak of Bell Mountain at 4.35 mi. **[7]**. Take the short spur behind the campsite to find a superb spot to snack, relax, and take in views of the world from 1,702 feet up.

After you return to the trail, visit the post oaks **[8]** on the glade at 4.63 mi. Their twisted trunks and contorted branches bespeak their hard lives on this thin, dry, rocky soil. Hike through several more glade openings before turning around at the entrance gate to the forest—some oversized boulders at the outer edge of the last glade **[9]** (4.95 mi.).

Bell Mountain Wilderness

LEGEND
—— Road
········ Trail
▬▬▬ Boundary
P Parking
★ Trailhead

1. Start
2. Right turn
3. Igneous glade
4. Left turn
5. Go straight
6. Left turn
7. Peak of Bell Mountain
8. Post oaks
9. Boulders

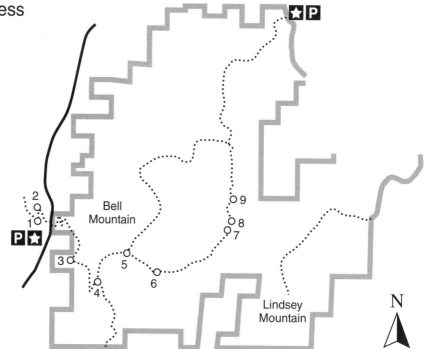

- Sit in a natural, river-carved whirlpool and let the cool, clear waters of the Black River splash and bubble all around you.
- Learn about shut-ins, yet another Ozark geologic curiosity.
- Explore the diversity of 8,646-acre Johnson's Shut-Ins State Park, home of East Fork Wild Area, Goggins Mountain Wild Area, and three state-designated natural areas.
- Hike in one of Missouri's most botanically rich areas; over 900 species of trees, shrubs, grasses, wildflowers, and ferns have been identified here so far.
- See recovery efforts—both natural and human-made—after the disastrous Taum Sauk reservoir breach of 2005.

Area Information

Locally called shut-ins, this canyonlike gorge was formed when the swift water of the Black River was forced to pass through a valley of rhyolite, a volcanic rock that is extremely hard and erosion resistant. For eons the river churned and swirled over the ancient igneous rock, slowly scouring potholes, chutes, and spectacular cascades. Although the state has other shut-ins, Johnson's Shut-Ins are Missouri's most outstanding example.

Also remarkable is the park's wild and diverse character. State-designated wild areas and natural areas within the park are home to bottomland woods, upland ridges, bluffs, wet meadows, fens, and igneous glades with outstanding vistas.

On December 14, 2005, Johnson's Shut-Ins State Park changed instantaneously when the upper reservoir of the Taum Sauk hydroelectric plant breached, sending 1.3 billion gallons of water crashing down the mountain and through the park. The flood destroyed most of the main-use area of the park, washing away buildings, trees, and trails. Sand and clay covered roads and campsites, sometimes more than 8 feet deep. Approximately 15,000 truckloads of sand and ground-up trees were hauled out of the park in the first five months of cleanup.

As of this printing, restoration and construction still continue. Plans include a new campground, a new visitor center, and reconstructed hiking trails at Goggins Mountain, the Shut-Ins Trail, and the Ozark Trail. Portions of the park will be closed during construction, so check the park's Web site or call before you visit.

Directions: The park is 8 miles north of Lesterville on Highway N.

Hours Open: The main-use area and the shut-ins are open for day-use only.

Facilities: The park offers a campground, a visitor center, a park store, picnic areas, and fishing and swimming in the East Fork of the Black River.

Permits and Rules: Food, drinks, and pets are prohibited in the shut-ins area and on the trail. In all other areas, pets must be attended at all times and kept on leashes 10 feet in length or shorter. Diving and jumping from rocks in the shut-ins area are prohibited. Canoes, kayaks, and other boats are not allowed on the river within the park.

Further Information: Park Superintendent, Johnson's Shut-Ins State Park, HC Route 1, Box 126, Middlebrook, MO 63656; 573-546-2450; www.mostateparks.com.

Park Trails

Goggins Mountain Equestrian Trail (👟👟👟👟, approximately 10 miles). This trail traverses an oak-hickory forest in the Goggins Mountain Wild Area. A section of this equestrian and hiking trail is scheduled to be rerouted to accommodate a new campground. The trailhead is on Highway MM, approximately 1 mile north of the park entrance.

Taum Sauk Section—Ozark Trail (👟👟👟👟👟, 33 miles). This section passes about midway through Johnson's Shut-Ins State Park. Bell Mountain Wilderness, to the northwest of the park, and Taum Sauk Mountain State Park, to the east, are each about 12.5 mi. away. A new trailhead and parking lot are proposed off Highway N, north of the shut-ins. A section of the trail just east of the shut-ins had to be rerouted due to the reservoir breach of 2005. As of this printing, this section wasn't finalized. Check www.mostateparks.com or call the park office for details.

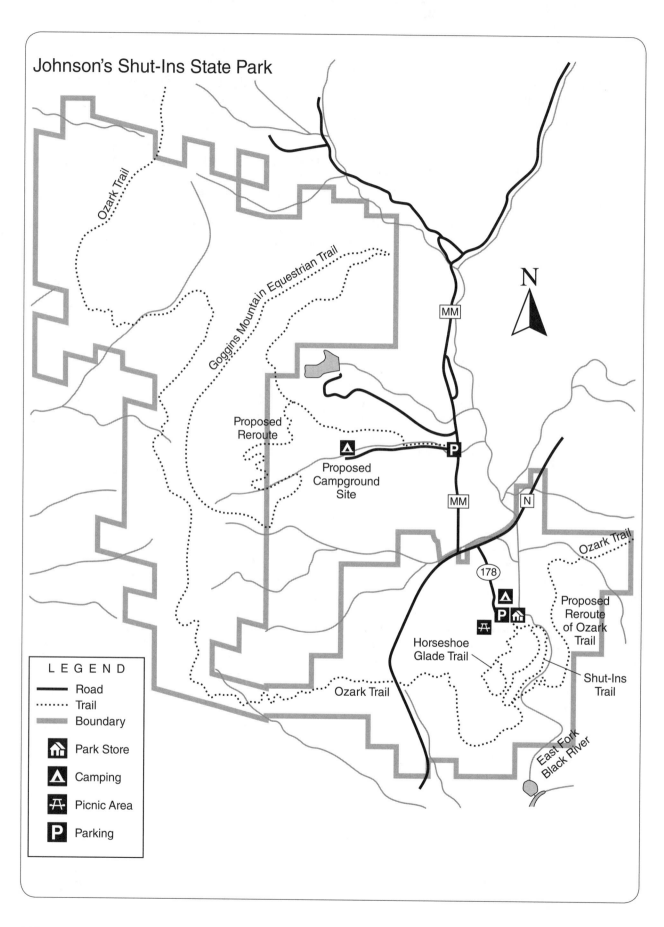

Johnson's Shut-Ins State Park

LEGEND

— Road
···· Trail
▬ Boundary
🏠 Park Store
⛺ Camping
🏕 Picnic Area
🅿 Parking

Ozark Trail

Goggins Mountain Equestrian Trail

MM

N

Proposed
Reroute

Proposed
Campground
Site

🅿

MM

N

Ozark Trail

178

Proposed
Reroute
of Ozark
Trail

Horseshoe
Glade Trail

Shut-Ins
Trail

Ozark Trail

East Fork
Black River

Shut-Ins Trail

Distance Round-Trip:
3.1 miles
Estimated Hiking Time:
2.25 hours

As you sit in the shut-ins, with the water bouncing and gurgling all around you, it's easy to imagine you are one of the many igneous boulders getting the same treatment. The main difference is that you've been here for only an hour or so, while the boulders have been here about 1.3 billion years!

Caution: The rocks in the shut-ins are slippery, even when dry. Wear shoes if you choose to wade in. Avoid white water and do not jump or dive from rocks.

Trail Directions: Park in the main lot at the south end of the park near the store. Begin at the store **[1]** and take the paved trail east as it heads behind the store and toward the shut-ins. Pass the trailhead for the Horseshoe Glade Trail on your right at .08 mi. **[2]** and continue on a wide, paved path. The sturdy benches on your left at .17 mi. **[3]** are made from recycled materials from the park. The stones are from the thousands of tons of rock washed into the park from the Taum Sauk reservoir breach of 2005; the cedar logs are from Goggins Mountain, where the new park campground will be built.

Soon, you'll be on the boardwalk, with splendid views of the East Fork of the Black River. While interpretive signs explain the geology of the constricted, or "shut-in," stream, the best way to experience the shut-ins is to get wet! You'll find steps leading down to the stream at .32 mi. **[4]**. As you continue on the boardwalk, more signs explain features of the shut-ins, including potholes, plunge pools, and chutes (natural waterslides). After you ascend some steps, you'll reach the bluff hole overlook at .5 mi. **[5]**, so named for the deep pool at the base of the tall wall of rock you are standing on. The blue, gray, pink, and purple hues of rhyolite turn red as the rocks get wet.

At this point, you'll leave the boardwalk and ascend a hill on a rocky trail. Turn left at the intersection with the connector link at .58 mi. **[6]** and follow blue trail markers to continue. Just after following a zigzag in the trail, you'll see what looks like an avalanche. This is a talus slope. All these rocks broke off the bluff above and rolled down the hill, perhaps thousands of years ago. The trail parallels the river for a while on a sandy path among cup plant, river oats, buttonbush,

witch hazel, and a variety of other interesting plants. If the river is low, explore the streambed to find a stunning array of colorful rocks. Notice that many of the boulders have chipped edges—telltale signs of their recent trip down the mountain in the floodwaters of the reservoir breach. Some of these rocks may have bounced here from nearly 2 mi. away.

Just after the trail turns away from the stream, turn left at a trail intersection at 1.38 mi. **[7]**. You'll soon cross an intermittent tributary and continue to hike parallel with the stream. Notice the musclewood trees in the bed of another intermittent tributary, which you'll cross at 1.59 mi. **[8]**. Turn right at the intersection with the Ozark Trail at 1.67 mi. **[9]**. From here, you'll hike uphill and away from the stream. After you pass some mini-shut-ins on your right, the trail climbs the bed of a wet-weather waterfall. Turn right after passing a second wet-weather waterfall at 1.85 mi. **[10]**. You'll pass through several glades, and the one at 2.03 mi. **[11]** offers a scenic view of the shut-ins as well as the surrounding mountains. Turn left at the intersection at 2.62 mi. **[12]** and go straight at the intersection with the connector at 2.81 mi. **[13]**. Turn left onto the pavement at 3.04 mi. **[14]** and you'll soon be back at the park store.

1. Start
2. Horseshoe Glade Trail
3. Benches
4. Steps to stream
5. Bluff hole overlook
6. Left turn
7. Left turn
8. Tributary crossing
9. Right turn
10. Right turn
11. Glade overlook
12. Left turn
13. Go straight
14. Left turn

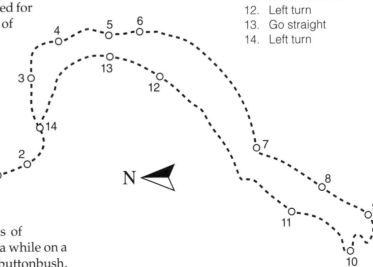

Horseshoe Glade Trail

Distance Round-Trip: 2.2 miles
Estimated Hiking Time: 1.5 hours

"In the end, our society will be defined not only by what we create, but by what we refuse to destroy." —*John C. Sawhill*

Caution: Glades are sensitive habitats. If you venture out on the glade, please take care not to disturb rocks, plants, or the beautiful but extremely slow-growing lichens.

Trail Directions: Park in the main lot at the south end of the park near the store. Begin at the store **[1]** and take the paved trail east as it heads behind the store and toward the shut-ins. At .08 mi. **[2]** you'll find the trailhead and interpretive sign for the Horseshoe Glade Trail on your right. Turn right to begin the trail.

You'll hike on a big zigzag up a moderate slope in a mixed forest of oak and hickory. Chunks of rhyolite, an igneous rock, lie around in sizes varying from toasters to big suitcases. Look for disturbed leaf litter or soil in places along the trail. Turkeys often scratch in dead leaves, looking for acorns and bugs, though they usually don't disturb much soil. Armadillos often leave long, crooked lines or small trenches, but feral hogs can do significant damage. Feral hogs, which have been a problem in the park, can root up large patches of soil, overturning rocks and logs in the process of looking for food. They eat plants, roots, mushrooms, acorns, insects, reptiles, amphibians, bird eggs, small mammals, and even deer fawns. Feral hogs sometimes create mud wallows in creek bottoms and can damage sensitive natural communities such as fens and glades.

At .6 mi. **[3]** you'll reach the intersection with the loop portion, where you'll turn right to hike the loop counterclockwise. After a little more moderate climbing, you'll approach the top of the peak, where the trail

levels off and shortleaf pines become more prevalent. You'll get your first views of Horseshoe Glade on your right at .91 mi. **[4]**. Take the small spur on your right at 1.07 mi. **[5]** to step out onto some red rhyolite bedrock for some awesome views of the expansive glade and several distant forested mountains. A small drainage bisects the glade, making a pretty glade even more dimensional and scenic and creating two lobes of the horseshoe. Look for lichen grasshoppers here, which blend in so perfectly with the lichens that it's nearly impossible to spy them unless they suddenly fly from their resting spots. After exploring the glade and soaking in the vistas, return to the main trail and turn right to continue. After the trail makes a gentle bend to the left, you'll see a second, smaller glade on your right at 1.25 mi. **[6]**. On the opposite side of the valley is a long, wooded ridge of Proffit Mountain. Far below, the East Fork seems to sprawl wider after being shut in upstream. After crossing an intermittent creek at 1.42 mi. **[7]**, you'll return to **[3]**, where you turn right to return to the trailhead.

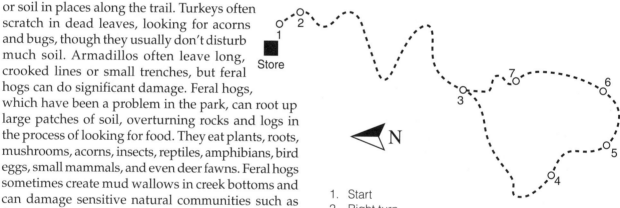

1. Start
2. Right turn
3. Right turn
4. First views
5. Spur to glade
6. Small glade
7. Creek crossing

- Hike along the banks of one of the Ozarks' premier streams, the Current.

- Be mesmerized by the sapphire waters of Missouri's deepest and bluest spring.

- Listen for the rattle of the kingfisher, the whining cry of the red-shouldered hawk, and the ascending buzz of the parula warbler.

- Find interesting plants next to the river like bamboo, musclewood, and a jackpot of woodland wildflowers.

- Look for the secretive Louisiana waterthrush ducking among roots and brush along the banks, constantly bobbing its tail.

Area Information

The trailhead for this hike is at the Powder Mill river access, which is managed by the National Park Service as part of the Ozark National Scenic Riverways. National riverways are natural streams that have recreational, natural, and cultural resources of national significance. The Ozark National Scenic Riverways was created by an act of Congress in 1964 to protect 134 miles of the Current and Jacks Fork rivers. Both the Current and Jacks Fork are clean, diverse, scenic rivers, and offer endless possibilities for floating, fishing, swimming, and tubing. Most of the rivers' flow comes from 58 springs. The area is known for its karst features and scenic beauty as well as its diversity of plants and animals.

Blue Spring is the signature feature of the Blue Spring Natural Area, a 17-acre part of the Current River Conservation Area, which is owned and managed by the Missouri Department of Conservation. Named "Spring of the Summer Sky" by the Osage Indians, Blue Spring absorbs and reflects wavelengths of light, giving it a sky blue hue. The depth of the water must have something to do with its color—Blue Spring is over 300 feet deep, making it Missouri's deepest spring. With an average daily flow of 87 million gallons, it is the state's eighth largest.

Directions: From Eminence, take Highway 106 east 13.7 miles. Turn right at a sign for the area on Shannon County Road 106-535. The road ends at .9 mile at the area. Although the Blue Spring Trail and picnic area can be accessed by a gravel road 1.8 miles east of Powder Mill off Highway 106, the road is steep and rough. Better access to the trailhead is provided by the Powder Mill area.

Hours Open: The park is open year-round. The Ozark National Scenic Riverways headquarters and visitor information office in Van Buren is open weekdays from 8:00 a.m. to 4:30 p.m.

Facilities: Powder Mill offers boating access to the Current River, parking, campsites, restrooms, drinking water, and picnic tables.

Permits and Rules: No wading, fishing, swimming, boating, or tubing is allowed in the spring or spring branch, but all these activities are allowed in the Current River.

For Further Information: Missouri Department of Conservation, Ellington Field Office, Route 2, Box 187, Ellington, MO 63638; 573-663-7130; www.mdc.mo.gov/areas/natareas; Ozark National Scenic Riverways, P.O. Box 490, Van Buren, MO 63965; 573-323-4236; www.nps.gov/ozar; Ozark Trail Association, 406 W. High Street, Potosi, MO 63664; 573-436-0540; www.ozarktrail.com; Pioneer Forest, P.O. Box 497, Salem, MO 65560; 573-729-4641; www.pioneerforest.com.

Area Trails

Just across the river from the Blue Spring Trail is the Current River Section of the **Ozark Trail**. The Ozark Trail extends from St. Louis into Arkansas and will be 500 miles long when all portions are completed. The Current River Section begins at the bridge on Highway 106 and extends 30 miles to Highway 60 in Carter County.

Just north of Powder Mill is **Roger Pryor Pioneer Backcountry**, a 61,000-acre part of Pioneer Forest, which is owned by the L-A-D Foundation and is leased to the Missouri state park system for public use. The backcountry offers 27 miles of trail, including nearly 15 miles of frontage on the Current River.

Blue Spring Trail

Distance Round-Trip: 3 miles
Estimated Hiking Time: 1.75 hours

Although Blue Spring is always beautiful, its 300-foot-deep water has different qualities depending on the light, shadows, angle of the sun, time of day, and perspective of the viewer.

Caution: The area is prone to flash flooding. Call for conditions after heavy rains. Protect fragile plants by staying on the designated trail.

Trail Directions: Park in the area for the Current River access. The trail begins [1] at a small sign at the end of the road loop, just downstream from the parking area. The trail follows the banks of the Current River, which accompanies you for your entire hike. Begin among box elder and maple trees as you hike away from the river. When you reach the bluff, turn right. The trail parallels a slough of the river. Look for the willowlike leaves and cornlike woody stems of cane, which is a native bamboo plant. A member of the grass family, cane grows along rivers in the Ozarks and can reach over 15 feet tall. If water is in the slough, watch for stalking herons, swimming wood ducks, and sunning turtles.

Where the slough joins the river at .14 mi. [2], look around for a musclewood tree next to the trail. A fairly small tree, musclewood has smooth bark. Long ridges under the bark look like muscles and veins beneath skin. Musclewood is one of the hardest and strongest woods in North America. You are soon treated to splendid views of the Current River as you hike next to some rock outcrops, carved into interesting shapes by the water. You cross a small wooden bridge over a tributary at .25 mi. [3].

As you hike, watch for congregations of woodland butterflies along the trail. Look for the black-and-white striped zebra swallowtail, the tiny eastern tailed blue, and the red-spotted purple, which is black and iridescent blue. You reach a small spring erupting at .46 mi. [4] amid a colony of scouring rush. Take advantage of the bench at .57 mi. [5] to absorb the sights and sounds all around you. At 1.08 mi. and 1.17 mi. [6], you reach an intersection with a trail on your left, which leads to the Blue Spring picnic area, where you find picnic tables and restrooms. Go straight at both intersections to continue to the spring.

You hear Blue Spring before you see it. It's hard to miss the sound of 87 million gallons of water per day! At 1.23 mi. [7], take the stone steps down on your right to see where the spring branch enters the river. Back on the main trail, turn right. Just after crossing a couple of tributaries, you find gemlike Blue Spring erupting from the base of a bluff at 1.4 mi. [8]. Take the walkway behind the spring to ascend the bluff. You find an overlook at the top, which gives you a different perspective of this tranquil scene. Retrace your steps to return to the trailhead.

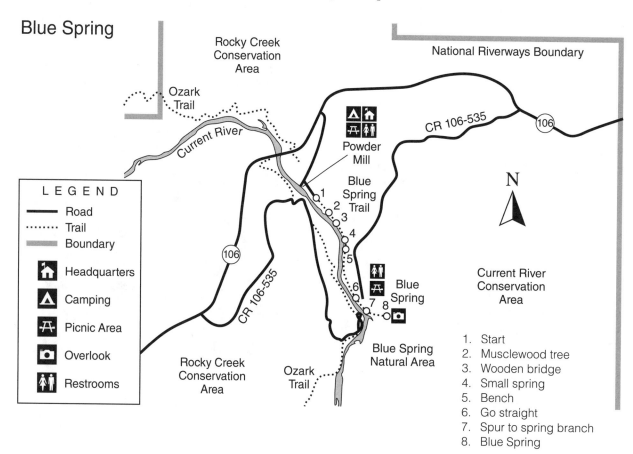

Blue Spring

LEGEND
— Road
···· Trail
▬ Boundary
🏠 Headquarters
⛺ Camping
🎋 Picnic Area
📷 Overlook
🚻 Restrooms

1. Start
2. Musclewood tree
3. Wooden bridge
4. Small spring
5. Bench
6. Go straight
7. Spur to spring branch
8. Blue Spring

- Witness the beauty and power of Big Spring, the largest single-outlet spring in the nation.
- Look and listen in the slough for the loud, rising whistles of the wood duck, one of North America's most beautiful (and quackless) ducks.
- Stand under 12-foot-high native bamboo canes (in the grass family) and imagine what it's like to be an insect in your lawn.
- Hike onto blufftop overlooks with vistas of the Big Spring Branch, the Current River, and the rugged horizon of forested Ozark highlands.

Area Information

Big Spring roars from the mouth of a cave at the base of a towering dolomite bluff. Daily flow records kept at Big Spring since 1921 show an average of 284 million gallons per day. The lowest daily reading, 152 million gallons, was during a dry period in 1956. Maximum flow is estimated to be 840 million gallons per day. Although other spring systems have more total volume, Big Spring is the nation's largest single-outlet spring and among the 10 largest springs in the world. Archaeological excavations in the park give evidence that Big Spring has been a gathering place for people for at least 10,000 years.

Formerly Big Spring State Park, Big Spring is now part of Ozark National Scenic Riverways, managed by the National Park Service. National riverways are natural streams that have recreational, natural, and cultural resources of national significance. Ozark National Scenic Riverways is composed of two rivers—the Current River and the Jacks Fork (a total of 134 river miles). Both rivers are famous for their scenic beauty and offer excellent opportunities for floating, fishing, and sightseeing. Big Spring flows into the Current River at the CCC Historic District in the park.

About 80,000 acres of riverways land border the rivers and are preserved to help protect the rivers' outstanding health and natural beauty. This riverways corridor includes many springs and caves, historic mills, campgrounds, and hiking and equestrian trails. The riverways also includes 13 natural areas, which are biological communities or geological sites chosen by a panel of experts as the best areas of natural integrity remaining in Missouri.

Directions: From Van Buren, take Highway 103 south for 4 miles to the park entrance.

Hours Open: The park is open year-round. The Ozark National Scenic Riverways headquarters and visitor information office in Van Buren is open weekdays from 8:00 a.m. to 4:30 p.m.

Facilities: The park offers camping, fishing and boating access, picnic areas, and shelters. The CCC Historic District features a dining lodge and rustic cabins that may be reserved. Cultural demonstrations at the Depression Farm include quilting, johnboat building, and storytelling on weekends from May to September. Canoe and tube rentals are available in Van Buren.

Permits and Rules: Because springs are fragile ecosystems, wading, fishing, swimming, tubing, and boating are not allowed in any spring. All these activities are allowed in the Current and Jacks Fork rivers. Glass containers are prohibited on the rivers and trails.

For Further Information: Ozark National Scenic Riverways, P.O. Box 490, Van Buren, MO 63965; 573-323-4236; www.nps.gov/ozar. Free copies of the *Directory of Missouri Natural Areas* are available by contacting the Natural Areas Coordinator, Missouri Department of Conservation, P.O. Box 180, Jefferson City, MO 65102; 573-751-4115.

Other Areas of Interest

Skyline Drive is a 4-mile loop road that offers at least a dozen scenic vistas of the surrounding Ozark hills. The drive is in the Mark Twain National Forest and is managed by the U.S. Forest Service. Skyline Drive is off Highway 103 and is labeled FR 3280; one access is 1 mile northwest of the Big Spring park entrance, and another is closer to Van Buren State Park. For more information, call 573-996-2153.

Located 13 miles north of Eminence, **Round Spring** features a tranquil spring pool set in a natural amphitheater of dolomite rock. A great variety of wildflowers decorates the area in spring and summer. Round Spring also offers a cave, a year-round campground, boat access, a picnic area, and a playground. Cave tours are offered from May until September for a small fee. For more information, call 573-323-4236.

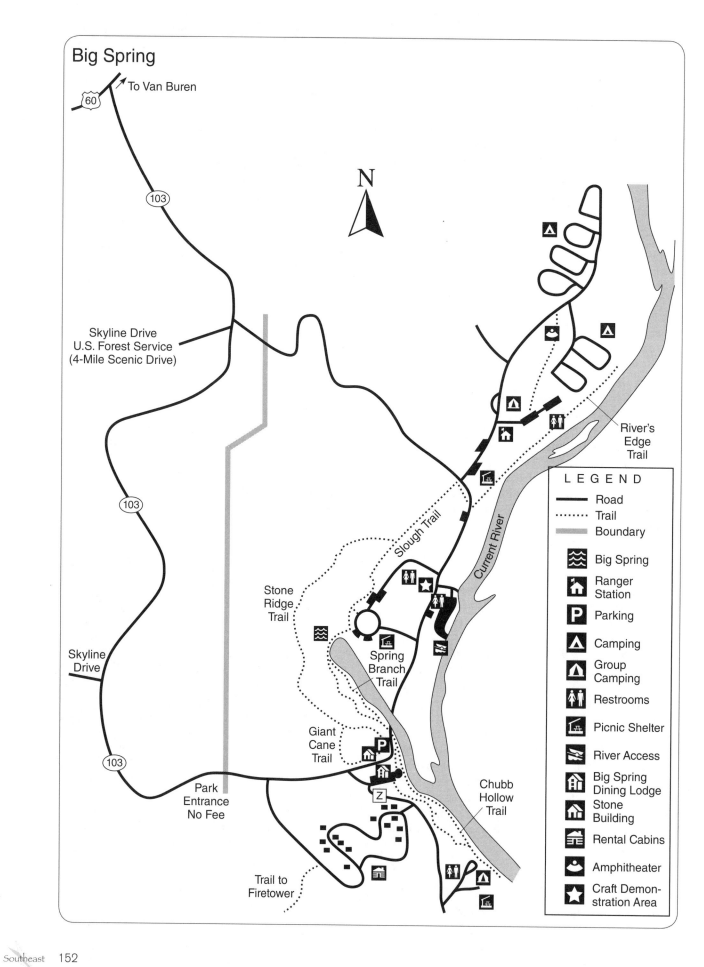

Big Spring

To Van Buren

60

103

Skyline Drive
U.S. Forest Service
(4-Mile Scenic Drive)

103

N

Skyline
Drive

103

Park
Entrance
No Fee

Stone
Ridge
Trail

Spring
Branch
Trail

Giant
Cane
Trail

Slough Trail

Current River

River's
Edge
Trail

Chubb
Hollow
Trail

Trail to
Firetower

LEGEND

— Road
⋯⋯ Trail
▬ Boundary

Big Spring
Ranger Station
P Parking
Camping
Group Camping
Restrooms
Picnic Shelter
River Access
Big Spring Dining Lodge
Stone Building
Rental Cabins
Amphitheater
Craft Demonstration Area

Stone Ridge Trail

Distance Round-Trip: 2.5 miles
Estimated Hiking Time: 1.5 hours

We are familiar with rivers, or sections of them at least. We usually see only a short piece of them, or occasionally a confluence. But to witness a river's birth . . . to see it erupt from a hole in the earth is magical. In a way, it seems sheer nonsense.

Caution: The area behind the spring may be closed; weathering action on the bluff above the spring occasionally causes rocks to fall onto the trail there.

Trail Directions: As you enter the park, you find a CCC-era stone building on the left side of the road, .5 mi. from the park entrance. Park at this building and begin the trail **[1]** on the sandstone steps directly in front of the parking area. Two big sycamore trees, flanking the steps, welcome you to the trailhead. Notice how the 20 steps are skillfully placed between the jumble of boulders on this hill. These steps were crafted by CCC laborers, some of whom became master stone carvers during their tenure.

You are soon treated to overlooks at .05 and .07 mi. **[2]**. The stream closest to you, with unusual aquamarine water and vivid, bright green aquatic plants is the Big Spring Branch. On a calm day, you can hear the rush of the cool water flowing by—at the rate of 284 million gallons per day! Just a few yards beyond, across the narrow ribbon of trees, is the Current River. On the foggy blue horizon are layers of the ancient and worn peaks of the Ozark Mountains.

As you ascend, you learn why this trail was given its name. Moss-covered dolomite boulders are replaced by lichen-covered chert boulders of all shapes and sizes. Twisted red cedars cling to steep bluff faces on the right, and shortleaf pines and massive white oaks tower on the left. Go straight at the intersection with the Giant Cane Trail at .16 mi. **[3]**. Enjoy the warm feeling in your legs as you continue climbing—you're only halfway to the peak! Views keep getting better as you near the top, amidst a symphony of boulders and trunks of huge trees. You finally begin the descent at .64 mi. **[4]**.

The trail makes a few switchbacks just before it intersects the Slough Trail at 1.25 mi. **[5]**. From here, you have several options. Turn left to continue the Slough Trail, which connects with the River's Edge Trail that goes to the campground. Turn around and retrace your steps to the trailhead, or turn right on the Slough Trail, which will take you to Big Spring. The Slough Trail follows an abandoned channel of the Current River, and interpretive signs along the way explain the history, prehistory, and natural habitat of the area.

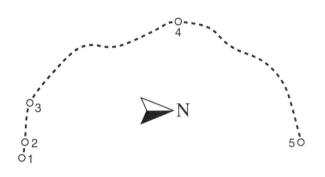

1. Start
2. Overlooks
3. Go straight
4. Ridge peak
5. Slough Trail intersection

Chubb Hollow Trail

Distance Round-Trip:
4 miles
Estimated Hiking Time:
2.25 hours

Jillikens n: *backwoods. "Them folks live away back in the jillikens; don't come to town but twice a year." —from* Down in the Holler, A Gallery of Ozark Folk Speech, *by Vance Randolph*

Caution: Watch for traffic when crossing the paved roads.

Trail Directions: Park in the lot for the Big Spring dining lodge in the historic district. The trail begins **[1]** at a small sign behind the dining lodge and takes you to the top of the wooded ridge for remarkable views of one of the Ozarks' premier rivers, the Current. From the overlook at .10 mi. **[2]**, you get a hawk's-eye view of the spot where 280 million gallons of water per day flow into the Current River. The stream on your left is Big Spring's spring branch, and the stream on your right is the Current.

Just after crossing a small wooden bridge, you reach the delightful position of being between a rock wall on your right, draped in lichens and mosses, and the scenic river just below you on your left. At .19 mi. **[3]**, you find another river overlook. Look across the river, slightly downstream, to see a stand of Missouri's largest species of native grass—giant cane. From the trailhead sign at .27 mi. **[4]**, you may take the lower trail upstream, along the riverbank, which takes you back to the dining lodge. Otherwise, continue the trail over a wooden bridge.

Turn right at the intersection at .31 mi. **[5]** and hike toward the picnic shelter. The trail resumes at a small sign at the end of the shelter. Soon, you begin a steady climb. At the ridgetop, notice that many of the big trees have suffered damage from lightning, ice, and wind. Life is tough at the top! Cross a gravel road at .97 mi. **[6]** and cross Highway Z at 1.08 mi. **[7]**. After passing under a metal gate, you follow a wide gravel road where you can stretch out your hiking legs and stride. Views of distant wooded ridges soon appear on both sides of the trail. The valley on your right, Chubb Hollow, is home to one of the highest-quality pine-oak forests in the Ozarks and has been designated the Big Spring Pines State Natural Area. At 2.15 mi. **[8]**, take the short spur to the left to the Big Spring lookout tower, which was once part of a regional wildfire protection system. Although it is scheduled to be refurbished, the tower may be closed for climbing. Look around the tower for the long wing feathers of turkey vultures, which often roost on high points such as this. Return to **[8]** and turn left to continue.

Turn right at 2.5 mi. **[9]**, at the intersection with the Kinnard Hollow Trail. Enjoy more distant views here as you hike among boulders and some giant shortleaf pine trees. Prescribed fires maintain this pine-oak forest, and you may see tree trunks blackened at the base. Take a close look at the layered, platelike bark of the pines, which makes them fire resistant. After passing a green water tower on your right, turn left on a gravel road at 3.75 mi. **[10]**. In just a few steps, the trail continues on the right at a small trail sign. Cross a paved road at 3.88 mi. **[11]** near the rental cabins, built in the early 1930s by the CCC. Turn left on Highway Z at 3.98 mi. **[12]**. In a few steps, turn right into the parking lot for the dining lodge.

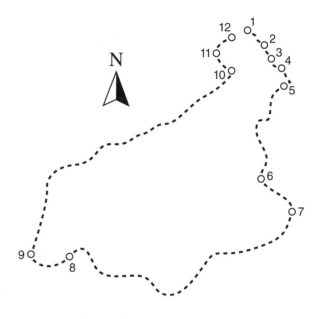

1. Start
2. Confluence overlook
3. River overlook
4. Trailhead
5. Right turn
6. Gravel road crossing
7. Highway Z crossing
8. Spur to lookout tower
9. Right turn
10. Left turn
11. Paved road crossing
12. Left turn

42. Peck Ranch Conservation Area

- Climb a 1,300-foot mountain on rocks of all shapes and sizes.
- If the steep climb up the rocky side of Stegall Mountain doesn't leave you gasping for breath, the overwhelming views from the top might.
- Hike quietly in spring or summer to increase your chances of spotting a black bear.

Area Information

George Peck, a Chicago businessman, bought 19,000 acres along Mill and Rogers creeks in the early 1900s and established the Mid-Continent Iron Company there. One hundred cords of wood were cut from the rich oak forests each day to fuel the blast furnaces of the smelter. But the iron ore was low grade, and the company soon folded. By 1945 the wild turkey was nearly exterminated in the state, and the Missouri Department of Conservation bought Peck Ranch for wild turkey management. This and other acquisitions restored wild turkeys throughout the state.

Peck Ranch consists of 23,048 acres of rugged hills, hollows, limestone and rhyolite glades, and oak-hickory forests mixed with pine. The area contains 119 ponds, 7 caves, and 31 springs. The wilderness-like area supports turkey, deer, bobcat, and an occasional black bear. Eastern collared lizards survive on the largest igneous glade complex in the lower Ozarks. Four state-designated natural areas on Peck Ranch protect a sinkhole pond, a pirated stream, bottomland forests, glades, and scenic waterfalls.

The Ozark Trail, a long-distance trail designed primarily for hikers and backpackers, begins in St. Louis, traverses the rugged and scenic Ozarks, and joins the Ozark Highland Trail of Arkansas. When complete, the trail will be 500 miles long. A 9.5-mile segment of the Current River Section of the Ozark Trail passes through Peck Ranch and features shut-ins, clear streams, scenic forests, and mountaintop panoramas.

Directions: From Winona, take Highway H east 5.4 miles to a sign for the area. Take the gravel road (Peck Ranch Road) east another 5.8 miles to a parking lot for the Ozark Trail, on the left. Both featured trails begin from this parking lot.

Hours Open: The public hunting area is open daily from 4:00 a.m. to 10:00 p.m.

Facilities: Area headquarters is .9 mile south of the Ozark Trail parking lot and offers camping (no hook-ups), restrooms, drinking water, picnic tables, a short nature trail, a firearms shooting range, and a walk-through archery course. The Stegall Mountain lookout tower is open to the public for climbing, although the cab at the top is locked. The tower can be reached from the Ozark Trail or from a driveway 3.7 miles east of Highway H off Peck Ranch Road. (The driveway to the tower is gated near the top.)

Permits and Rules: Bikes and horses are not allowed on the Current River Section of the Ozark Trail. Elsewhere, horses are restricted to vehicle roads. ATVs and free-running pets are prohibited. Hunting and primitive camping are allowed in designated areas. Special regulations apply in the special management area. Contact the area office for details.

For Further Information: Peck Ranch Conservation Area, Route 1, Box 1395, Winona, MO 65588; 573-323-4249; www.mdc.mo.gov. For more information on the Ozark Trail, call 573-751-5359.

Other Areas of Interest

Rocky Falls, one of the most beautiful waterfalls in the state, is a 40-foot series of cascades over a wide outcrop of pink and purple igneous rocks. The site is in the Stegall Mountain Natural Area and is managed by Ozark National Scenic Riverways, National Park Service. Although no camping is allowed, the site offers picnic tables, grills, restrooms, and wading. To reach Rocky Falls, return to the intersection of Highway H and Peck Ranch Road. Turn north on H and go 3.4 miles to Highway NN, where you turn right. Go 2.1 miles and turn right at a sign for the area. Go .3 mile and turn left at another sign. This road ends at the parking lot. For more information, call 573-323-4236.

Area Trails

Current River Section—Ozark Trail (🐾🐾🐾🐾, 30 miles). This section begins at Owls Bend on the Current River and ends on Highway 60, west of Van Buren. The 9.5-mile section that goes through Peck Ranch connects portions to the north, maintained by the Ozark National Scenic Riverways, with the segment to the south, maintained by the Mark Twain National Forest.

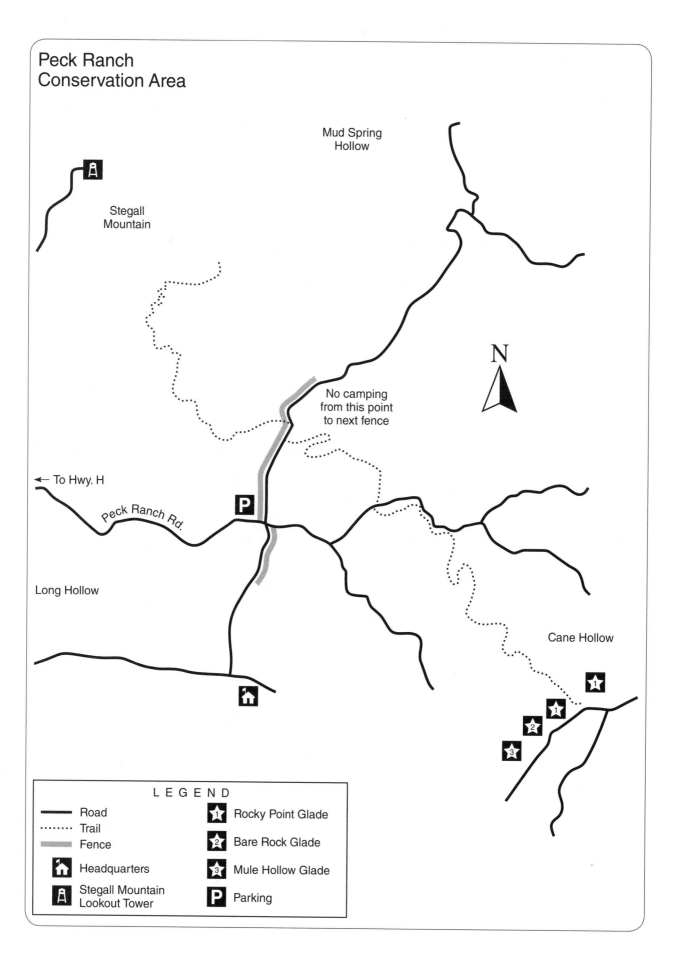

Peck Ranch
Conservation Area

Mud Spring
Hollow

Stegall
Mountain

No camping
from this point
to next fence

N

← To Hwy. H

Peck Ranch Rd.

P

Long Hollow

Cane Hollow

1

1

2

3

LEGEND

—— Road

········ Trail

Fence

Headquarters

Stegall Mountain
Lookout Tower

1 Rocky Point Glade

2 Bare Rock Glade

3 Mule Hollow Glade

P Parking

Ozark Trail to Stegall Mountain

Distance Round-Trip:
4 miles
Estimated Hiking Time:
2.25 hours

Don't be fooled by the common scenes at the beginning of the trail. Stegall Mountain packs a punch, with views from the top that will knock your hiking socks off!

Caution: You will traverse some steep sections with loose rocks. From October through January, special hunts may take place in the area; call ahead to make sure that the trail is open. Bring a compass and topo map if you want to extend this hike to the lookout tower.

Trail Directions: Park in the lot for the Ozark Trail trailhead and climb the steps over the fence in the northeast corner of the lot [1]. Turn left on the gravel road, which is a spur to the Ozark Trail. The gravel road is mostly downhill and lined with several kinds of oaks, hickories, and shortleaf pines. Go straight at the sign for the Ozark Trail on your right at .38 mi. [2], which is the trail to Rocky Point Glade. Soon after crossing a small creek with cardinal flower on its banks, you find another sign for the Ozark Trail on your left at .48 mi. [3]. Turn left here.

The trail is well marked with Ozark Trail markers, which are green and white or brown and white "OT" signs on trees. Trail markers may tilt to indicate a bend in the trail ahead, and double markers indicate a sharp bend. Although vegetation may crowd the trail near the road, you soon enter a clear, rolling forest. Go straight at the intersection with an old road at .51 mi. [4]. The old field on your left at .71 mi. [5] is growing back in native grasses. By early fall, this field will be ablaze with bright orange and red sumac and brilliant yellow goldenrod, set against bronze and golden grasses. Watch for turkey, deer, and other wildlife moving between the oak and hickory forest and the brushy, grassy old field. Deer use old fields to browse on shrubs and grass, and turkeys feed there on grasshoppers and other insects.

As the trail ascends a few rocky hills, shortleaf pine replaces oak and hickory. Highbush and low-bush blueberry shrubs indicate the acidic soil here. Although lowbush blueberry shrubs (huckleberry) are only a quarter as tall as the highbush shrubs, their fruits are much tastier. Cross a gravel road at 1.32 mi. [6] and continue on the other side. At 1.57 mi. [7], rocks of all shapes and sizes in hues of red, pink, and dark purple suddenly inundate the trail. From huge boulders to tiny pebbles, red granite and rhyolite of the core of Stegall Mountain poke through the forest floor at the mountain's base.

You now begin a series of switchbacks up the rocky side of Stegall, and the trail becomes more difficult. Massive outcrops of red granite, blanketed with green lichen, erupt from the slope amidst grassy glades with leadplant and black-eyed susans. The trail skirts the base of one red boulder the size of a small house. At 1.82 mi. [8], climb on top of this pink granite outcrop and be treated to an unusually expansive view of your surroundings. As remarkable as this vista is, it's only a hint of what is to come.

Continue uphill to a vast glade landscape with billowing, smooth igneous bedrock on the surface. If you can resist, wait until you get to the very top of the mountain before taking a look around. At 2 mi. [9], among several rock cairns marking the peak of Stegall Mountain, stop to survey your world. This point commands a stupendous view in a 180-degree sweep. Lesser mountains line up and fall away from Stegall like dominoes, and the blue haze of water vapor melts distant ridges into one another all across the horizon.

If you have leftover hiking energy or if the view has energized you, follow the peak of Stegall Mountain northwest about .75 mi. to the lookout tower, which you can climb for more tremendous views of the Ozark landscape. Otherwise, retrace your steps to complete your mountain hike.

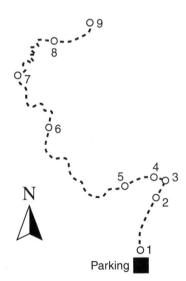

1. Start
2. Go straight
3. Left turn
4. Go straight
5. Old field
6. Gravel road crosssing
7. Stegall's red rocks
8. Glade overlook
9. Mountain peak

Ozark Trail to Rocky Point Glade

  Distance Round-Trip: 6.4 miles
Estimated Hiking Time: 3 hours

Hike this trail in spring or summer to find a jubilee of wildflowers on the glades contrasting with the dark gray dolomite boulders and the fine, arching stems of prairie dropseed grass.

Caution: You will traverse some steep sections with loose rocks. From October through January, special hunts may take place in the area; call ahead to make sure that the trail is open.

Trail Directions: Park in the lot for the Ozark Trail trailhead and climb the steps over the fence in the northeast corner of the lot **[1]**. Turn left on the gravel road, which is a spur to the Ozark Trail. The gravel road, mostly downhill, is lined with several kinds of oaks, hickories, and shortleaf pines. Turn right at the sign for the Ozark Trail at .38 mi. **[2]**. The trail is well marked with Ozark Trail markers, which are green and white or brown and white "OT" signs on trees. Trail markers may tilt to indicate a bend in the trail ahead, and double markers indicate a sharp bend.

The trail takes you uphill in a beautiful, open forest with black oaks, sugar maples, and tall pines. Flowering dogwood, the state tree, decorates the forest in April and May with snow white blossoms. Maidenhair ferns turn brown and collapse into the leaf litter by October, whereas ebony spleenwort and Christmas ferns stay green all year long. After you reach the top of this ridge, you pass an odd, solitary sandstone boulder on your right at .58 mi. **[3]**, covered with small, delicate ferns.

If you're hiking in fall, you will probably become acquainted with beggar's lice (tick trefoil), which leaves triangle-shaped seedpods sticking to your clothing as you go along. If you collect these stickers and pull them off elsewhere, you are a seed dispersal agent for the plant. These seeds are edible when they are green and puffy (after removing the sticky case) and taste like peanuts. Continue on the chert and sandstone gravel trail, with huckleberries and pussytoes (indicators of acid soil), until you cross a gravel road at 1.06 mi. **[4]**. Continue on the other side. The trail follows the gravel road for a while and is lined with reindeer lichen, dittany, and baby pine trees. With a grassy field on your right, cross an old road at 1.79 mi. **[5]**.

At 2 mi. **[6]**, the trail takes you down into a ravine, where you hike between two slopes. Look for tracks and signs of deer and other wildlife that use this natural corridor of the forest. You pass a talus slope (a collection of rocks that broke off from bluffs or bedrock above and tumbled down) on your left at 2.11 mi. **[7]**. The next slopes that you climb are so covered in chert and sandstone gravel that the trees seem not to be anchored in any soil at all. After a prescribed fire, sassafras sprouts light up the forest in fall with bright yellow, orange, and red leaves, splashed against the white gravel.

At 2.71 mi. **[8]**, you are on a narrow, gravelly ridge occupied by black oak and hickory. Grassy slopes appear on your right, as well as views of distant wooded ridges. At 3.21 mi. **[9]**, you reach Rocky Point Glade, where craggy, dark gray dolomite boulders stick out from the slope in ledges. Spring, summer, and early fall (depending on the rainfall) will find these glades awash in color, from lemon yellow Missouri evening primrose to deep purple blazing star. Seven-foot nodding yellow blooms of prairie dock are taller than some of the woolly buckthorn trees, gnarled and stunted in this dry, desertlike environment. To explore two more glades nearby, descend the slope and turn right (west) on the gravel road. The next slope on your right is Bare Rock Glade, and the one beyond that is Mule Hollow Glade, a state natural area. Retrace your steps to return to the trailhead.

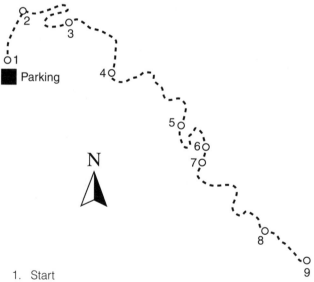

1. Start
2. Right turn
3. Solitary boulder
4. Road crossing
5. Old road crossing
6. Ravine
7. Talus slope
8. Gravelly ridge
9. Rocky Point Glade

- See the blue-green waters of Onondaga Spring, the only natural entrance to Onondaga Cave.
- Hike next to an oxbow lake—a channel that the Meramec River abandoned.
- See how the red-eared slider got its name.
- Feel reindeer lichens to check the humidity.

Area Information

Onondaga's human history is every bit as colorful as its speleothems (calcite deposits). Around the turn of the century, several of the cave's early owners intended to remove and sell its splendid calcite, or "cave onyx," but several factors, including a glutted market, prevented these operations. A break came in 1904 when the World's Fair came to St. Louis. Visitors were brought from St. Louis to Leasburg by the Frisco Railroad and then transported by buggies to the cave. For an extra 25¢, visitors could rent clothes to wear on their adventurous cave tour.

Several owners of Onondaga managed the cave as a public attraction, but none was as successful or memorable as Les Dill, who took partial ownership of the cave in 1949. Dill, famous for fabricating tall tales about his show caves, had both a P.T. Barnum-style showmanship and a genuine interest in the cave's natural integrity—a combination that elevated Onondaga to become a nationally known show cave.

If a visitor had to choose only one cave in Missouri to explore, Onondaga should probably be it. Recognized as one of America's most spectacular caves because of the great abundance and quality of its speleothems, Onondaga has been designated a national natural landmark, joining the roll of the country's outstanding natural features kept by the U.S. Department of the Interior's National Park Service.

Missouri celebrated 1990 as the Year of the Cave, when it officially recorded its 5,000th cave. Governor John Ashcroft proclaimed Missouri "the Cave State" and encouraged people to become aware of the state's underground mysteries and natural beauty. About this time, the state dedicated the new visitor center at Onondaga Cave State Park, which illustrates and interprets the state's fantastic subterranean world.

Directions: From the I-44 Leasburg exit (214), take Highway H southeast for 7 miles.

Hours Open: The park is open year-round, and the gates to the campground are open from 7:00 a.m. to 10:00 p.m. The visitor center is open from 9:00 a.m. to 5:00 p.m. daily, March through October, with shortened hours during the other months. The visitor center is closed on Thanksgiving, Christmas Day, and New Year's Day.

Facilities: The park offers a visitor center, a campground, an amphitheater, picnic areas, and boating, swimming, and fishing on the Meramec River. Onondaga Cave tours are given daily, March through October, for a fee. Cathedral Cave tours are given on weekends from Memorial Day to Labor Day.

Permits and Rules: Pets must always be leashed. Boats without motors are allowed to be carried onto the oxbow lake, where fishing is allowed. Horses and bicycles are not allowed on the hiking trails.

For Further Information: Onondaga Cave State Park, 7556 Highway H, Leasburg, MO 65535; 573-245-6576.

Park Trails

Oak Ridge Trail (👣👣👣, 3 miles). This trail takes you across several wet-weather streams, through an upland forest, and up into some glades that are responding well to restoration and management practices. The trail also passes a number of wet-weather waterfalls and a pirated stream. The trailhead is in the campground, next to the playground.

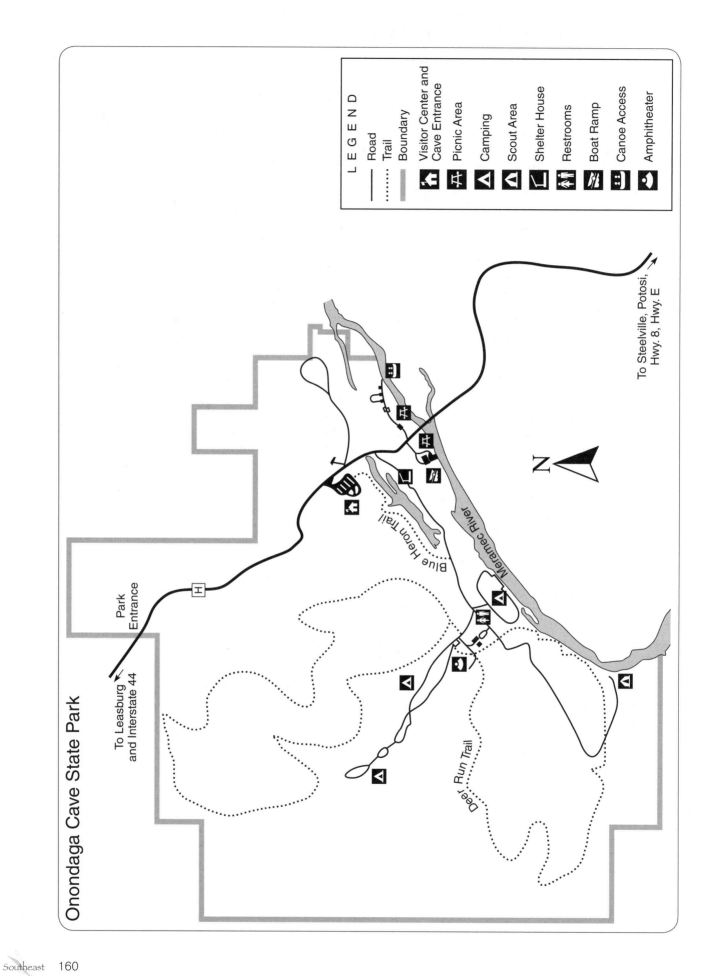

Onondaga Cave State Park

To Leasburg
and Interstate 44

Park
Entrance

H

Blue Heron Trail

Deer Run Trail

Meramec River

To Steelville, Potosi,
Hwy. 8, Hwy. E

N

L E G E N D

Road
Trail
Boundary

Visitor Center and
Cave Entrance

Picnic Area

Camping

Scout Area

Shelter House

Restrooms

Boat Ramp

Canoe Access

Amphitheater

Blue Heron Trail

  Distance Round-Trip: 1 mile
  Estimated Hiking Time: 30 minutes

While hiking, I kept thinking of the early explorers of Onondaga Cave swimming through the spring and sinking johnboats under the bluff to get in. Today, over 100 years later, the cave's beauty is still intact, and the tour route is wheelchair accessible!

Trail Directions: This is a good trail to explore while waiting for a cave tour to begin. The trail begins near the visitor center, in the south end of the parking lot [1]. Soon you see an old river channel on your left. A breeze blowing across the surface may fool you; this channel is no longer flowing. This oxbow lake [2] (.05 mi.) was left when the Meramec River cut a new channel and began flowing along a different course. Oxbow lakes, often horseshoe shaped, are most easily identified from aerial photographs.

The trail parallels the lake for most of its length, giving you time to watch for aquatic turtles basking in the sun near the water. Look closely for the red-eared slider, a medium-sized turtle with a patch of red on each side of its head and a propensity for sliding gracefully into the water when disturbed. At .14 mi. [3] is Onondaga Spring, the site of several mills during the latter half of the 19th century. Damming of the spring in the 1880s forced early explorers to enter Onondaga Cave by johnboat through the spring—the only natural entrance to the cave. The first artificial entrance is beneath the small concrete roof, just to the left of the spring.

As you continue, look in the forest edge for blooming wildflowers, including toothwort, dogtooth violet, and spring beauty, which sometimes blooms in February. The limestone bluffs and rocky slopes on the right are also home to the graceful columbine, which blooms through July. On the left, the oxbow lake

becomes shallower until it tapers off into a slough. This place is apparently a favorite nighttime feeding spot for beaver [4] (.35 mi.), judging by the number of chewed-off trees and sprouts. Here is a good spot to look for the trail's namesake, blue heron, fishing in the shallows.

At .38 mi. is a rather authoritative boulder of layered, weathered dolomite [5]. A form of limestone that contains magnesium, dolomite is relatively soft and easily eroded. At .45 mi. [6], where the trail meets the blacktop road to the campground, turn around and hike back to the trailhead.

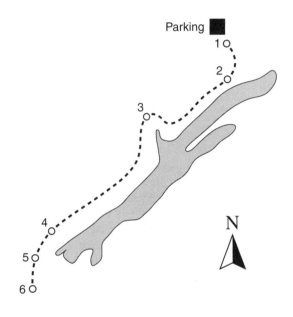

1. Start
2. Oxbow lake
3. Onondaga Spring
4. Beaver feeding area
5. Dolomite boulder
6. Turn around

Deer Run Trail

Distance Round-Trip: 2.5 miles
Estimated Hiking Time: 1.5 hours

You may find yourself on your belly, as I did, examining the multitude of delicate mosses and lichens up close. You will find green meadows and hummocks, swales, and handsome forests only millimeters high—just inches from your nose.

Caution: Crossing the stream bottom may be difficult after a rainy period. Use caution near the blufftop overlook edges.

Trail Directions: The trailhead **[1]** for the Deer Run Trail is in the campground, between the amphitheater and shower house. Parking is available near the playground equipment. Hike toward the amphitheater and then turn left at the intersection at .04 mi. **[2]**. At the intersection at .09 mi. **[3]**, turn right, toward the forest.

The structure at .40 mi. **[4]** is the locked entrance to Cathedral Cave, the other show cave in the park besides Onondaga. Tours of Cathedral Cave are given by handheld lanterns and reveal rooms filled with cave coral, white flowstone, and delicate soda straws. Entire fossilized algae blooms (stromatolites) nearly the size of Volkswagens hang from the ceiling. Walking underneath them makes you feel like a mole, tunneling under the bulbous roots of plants in a garden.

The interesting thing about the old paved road at .60 mi. **[5]** is that you can hardly see it. Leaves have fallen on it, building soil. Plants are growing in the ever-widening cracks. Trees have closed the gap overhead, and shrubs continually crowd in from the sides. Nature is taking it back. Continue the trail across the road and then hike next to some small hills covered with mosses and airy puffs of reindeer lichen **[6]** (.65 mi.). The lichen is lighter green than the mosses, has antlerlike tips, and, like all lichens, is made up of a fungus and an algae. Reindeer lichen is soft and rubbery in high humidity and wiry and brittle in dry times.

Notice all the cedar trees at .91 mi. **[7]**, announcing the presence of an upcoming glade. Native grasses dominate where breaks occur in the thick cedar cover.

The regular hardwood forest canopy resumes as you exit the glade at 1.15 mi. Descend the hill to the stream bottom, cross the wooden bridge at 1.61 mi. **[8]**, and walk under a bent tree at 1.64 mi. **[9]**. Cross a gravel road at 1.72 mi., hike through a cedar-choked glade remnant, and go straight at the intersection at 1.84 mi. **[10]**.

As you climb the hill, you approach the bluff edge, and soon the Meramec River comes into view below you. You pass several overlooks here. One of the best is at 1.94 mi. **[11]**, complete with gnarly, ancient cedars and views of the forested hills and winding river. At 2.12 mi. **[12]**, cross a footbridge before taking a final view of the river from a grassy knoll. Turn left at the intersection at 2.25 mi. **[13]**, cross a gravel road at 2.29 mi., and turn right at the intersection at 2.33 mi. **[3]**. Soon you are back at the trailhead.

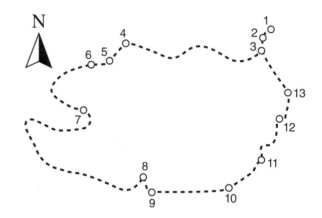

1. Start
2. Left turn
3. Right turn
4. Cathedral Cave
5. Old paved road
6. Reindeer lichen
7. Glade
8. Wooden bridge
9. Bent tree
10. Go straight
11. Overlook
12. Footbridge
13. Left turn

South Central

The south central region of Missouri is the area south of Highway 70, west of Highway 19, and east of Highway 65.

Topography

Topographically, this region can be divided into two areas—the Ozarks and Ozark border. The Ozark Highlands, which cover almost the lower half of Missouri (40 percent of the state), compose the lower 80 percent of the south-central region of Missouri. The Ozarks are an unglaciated area of greater relief and elevation than surrounding areas. The area is characterized by steep topography, thin, rocky, residual soils, deep erosion by streams, and extensive forests. While glaciers, seas, or floods repeatedly covered the surrounding areas, the Ozarks have been an exposed land mass for 250 million years. Distinctive topographic features in the southwest corner of this region are conical peaks, or knobs, of sedimentary bedrock.

The Ozark border is a transition zone between the Ozarks and the big rivers. In the south central region of Missouri, this area lies just south of the Missouri River and covers the upper 20 percent of the region. The Ozark border contains rugged hills that resemble the Ozark landscape but also includes more gentle hills and rolling plains. Soils, composed of loess and alluvium, are much deeper and more productive than in the lower Ozarks.

Major Rivers and Lakes

The Missouri River forms the north boundary of this region. The Osage River, the state's third largest, flows from Kansas and joins the Missouri River just east of Jefferson City. The Union Electric Company of St. Louis dammed the Osage in 1931, forming Lake of the Ozarks, an impoundment of 55,342 surface acres and 1,150 miles of shoreline—the Midwest's largest hydroelectric reservoir. Lake of the Ozarks State

Park, Missouri's largest at 17,441 acres, highlights the area's rich natural resources, while the lake area itself has become a highly developed commercial playground.

The White River used to meander back and forth between Missouri and Arkansas but has been dammed to create five reservoirs—three of which lie, at least partially, at the southern end of this region. Powersite Dam, built in 1912, created Lake Taneycomo. Bull Shoals Lake is split nearly in its middle by the state line, and Norfork Lake's northern end lies just east of Gainesville.

Other rivers in this region include the Osage Fork of the Gasconade, Gasconade, Maries, and Big Piney. The James, Current, Jacks Fork, and Eleven Point rivers also have their headwaters here.

Common Plant Life

The great age and physiographic variety of the Ozarks make it the area of greatest species diversity in Missouri. Deciduous, pine-oak, and pine forests were the main vegetation in presettlement times, and still dominate today. Glade, woodland, savanna, fen, and bottomland communities also exist. Dry-mesic chert forests, characterized by white oak, red oak, shortleaf pine, various hickories, and flowering dogwood, are common in this region. Common plants are Virginia creeper, tick trefoil, black cohosh, bedstraw, and Christmas fern.

Although most glade communities in the Ozarks are threatened by aggressive growth of cedar trees because of fire suppression, thousands of these rocky, sunny openings still occur in the forest landscape. Dolomite glades are a characteristic of the Ozarks, and the glades of the White River area are the most notable examples.

Grasses dominate, interspersed with stunted trees and shrubs. Wildflowers are numerous and often showy. These include Missouri evening primrose, compass plant, blazing star, prairie dock, black-eyed susan, silky aster, and yellow coneflower.

Although upland deciduous forest was the main presettlement vegetation in the Ozark border, glades, woodlands, savannas, marshes, bottomland forests, and even prairie communities existed. Much of the Ozark border has been converted to pastures and crop fields, but fragmented forests and forested bottomlands still persist. Mesic forests are rich, well-developed upland forests where trees reach 90 to 140 feet and the canopy is dense. Deep soils support rich growths of mixed herbs, ferns, and mushrooms. Sugar maple, red oak, white oak, and basswood are distinctive trees in mesic forests; understory species include pawpaw, spicebush, flowering dogwood, and musclewood. Some of the many wildflowers are blue-eyed mary, spring beauty, Dutchman's-breeches, toothwort, mayapple, wild ginger, purple trillium, and celandine poppy.

Common Birds and Animals

Birds prevalent in upland forests of the Ozarks include wild turkey, turkey vulture, screech owl, crow, various woodpeckers, summer tanager, ovenbird, parula warbler, black-and-white warbler, red-eyed vireo, and white-breasted nuthatch. Other animals include white-tailed deer, bobcat, gray fox, raccoon, armadillo, wood rat, gray squirrel, chipmunk, black rat snake, and various bats.

While on some of the expansive woodlands and savannas of the region, watch for the great crested flycatcher, eastern bluebird, prairie warbler, indigo bunting, goldfinch, and kestrel. You may also see the coyote, red fox, ornate box turtle, six-lined racerunner, glass lizard, speckled kingsnake, and yellowbelly racer.

Mesic forests are home to barred owl, whippoorwill, eastern wood pewee, blue-gray gnatcatcher, wood thrush, Kentucky warbler, and Carolina wren. Other animals include white-tailed deer, opossum, three-toed box turtle, spring peeper, pickerel frog, leopard frog, gray tree frog, redbelly snake, and five-lined skink.

Climate

The south central region's temperatures average 57 degrees F in spring, 78 degrees F in summer, 57 degrees F in fall, and 31 degrees F in winter. Mean annual precipitation varies from 40 inches at the top of this region to 46 inches at the bottom.

Best Features

- Rolling, expansive woodlands, resplendent with wildflowers
- Desertlike glades with craggy boulders, panoramic views, and 6-foot-tall wildflowers
- Large and fabulously decorated caves
- Splendid karst features—springs, caves, natural bridges, pirated streams, sinkholes, and canyonlike collapsed caverns
- Burial mounds and mysterious prehistoric earthworks at Van Meter State Park
- Rich, moist, tall forests of white oak, sugar maple, and basswood
- Rock-bottomed, spring-fed, clear, scenic streams
- Blufftop vistas of endless, densely wooded ridges

- Find the odd sandstone Blossom Rock in the forest and make your guess about how it got there.

- Hike on ridgetop glades with magnificent views of the scenic Little Piney Creek Valley.

- See the unusual outlet of Lane Spring, where each day 11 million gallons of water percolate from a loose, sandy bottom, creating strange, circular "boils" of sand.

- Get the feeling of beach hiking, as your boots sink into the soft sand of the trail next to Little Piney Creek.

Area Information

Lane Spring Recreation Area features a campground, picnic area, and spring on the banks of Little Piney Creek, and is one of six recreation sites managed by the U.S. Forest Service in the Houston–Rolla–Cedar Creek District of the Mark Twain National Forest. Encompassing nearly 200,000 acres in the south central region of the state, the district provides facilities for camping, picnicking, hiking, horseback riding, fishing, floating, and hunting. Hikers can discover a variety of landscapes—forests with interspersed pines, streams, springs, caves, bluffs, and glades in hilly, rolling terrain.

Unlike many springs that have an obvious outlet or two, the fishhook-shaped spring branch of Lane Spring is an accumulation of dozens of small outlets. These outlets, evidenced by underwater "boils" in the loose sand, range in size from dinner plates to coins. Lane Spring joins Little Piney Creek a short distance downstream from the picnic area. The Missouri Department of Conservation stocks the area with rainbow trout, providing visitors a special fishing opportunity.

The namesake of Lane Spring's Blossom Rock Trail is an unusual mass of sandstone that abruptly juts from the forest floor and has a way of surprising hikers with its sudden presence. The origin of the rock is uncertain. One theory is that the sandstone was deposited in a dolomite cave and, because it was more resistant, remained as the blossom after the walls and roof of the cave weathered away. Another theory is that the sandstone is a remnant filling of an ancient sinkhole—a suggestion substantiated by the roughly circular shape of the blossom. Blossom Rock is only one of Lane Spring's wonders—come and explore them all!

Directions: From the intersection of I-44 and Highway 63 in Rolla, take Highway 63 south 13.2 miles. Turn right at the sign for the area and go 1.3 miles to the parking lot.

Hours Open: The site is open daily from 6:00 a.m. to 10:00 p.m. The picnic areas are open from 6:00 a.m. to 9:00 p.m. only.

Facilities: The area offers two campground loops, picnic areas with shelters and grills, restrooms (but no showers), a playground, and fishing for rainbow trout and other fish in Little Piney Creek.

Permits and Rules: A $2 parking fee is required for each vehicle per day. (Single campsites are $8.) ATVs and horses are prohibited on the trails. An annual state trout permit is required for possession of trout, and special regulations apply. Statewide seasons and regulations apply to all other fish species. All pets must be leashed.

For Further Information: District Ranger, U.S. Forest Service, Houston–Rolla–Cedar Creek Ranger District, 108 South Sam Houston Boulevard, Houston, MO 65483; 417-967-4194. For pavilion reservations, call 877-444-6777; www.fs.fed.us/r9/forests/marktwain.

Other Areas of Interest

Dillard Mill State Historic Site features a picturesque red mill perched on a bluff that overlooks the clear, spring-fed Huzzah Creek. A small waterfall next to the mill cascades to the millpond below. Dillard Mill was built around 1900 and continued to grind grain until the 1960s. Restored to operational order, it is one of Missouri's best-preserved examples of a water-powered gristmill. Guided tours of the mill are available for a small fee. The site includes picnic areas. The mill is 25 miles southeast of Steelville, off Highway 49. For more information, call 573-244-3120.

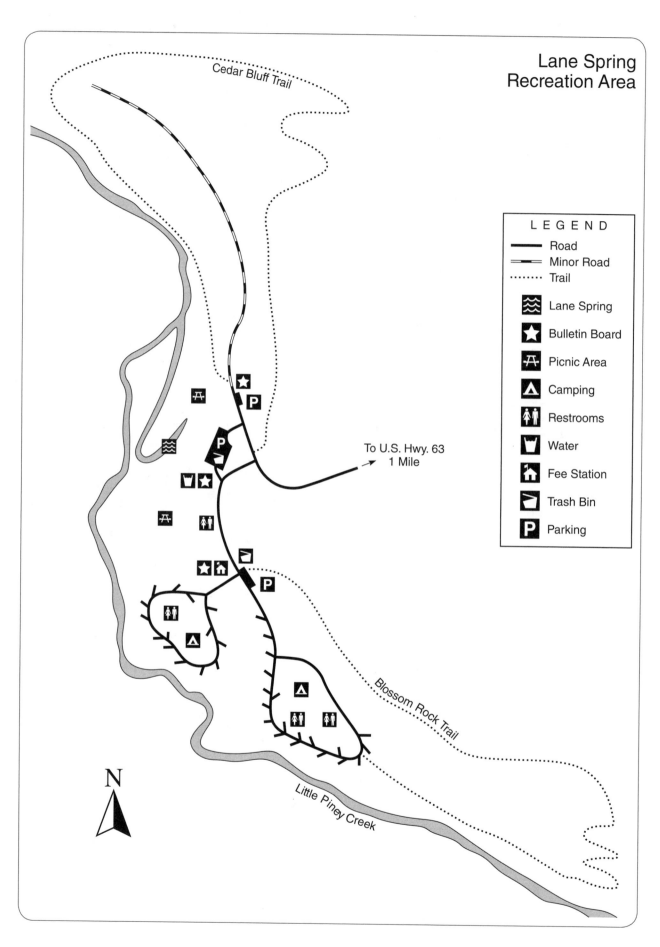

Lane Spring
Recreation Area

Cedar Bluff Trail

LEGEND
Road
Minor Road
Trail
Lane Spring
Bulletin Board
Picnic Area
Camping
Restrooms
Water
Fee Station
Trash Bin
Parking

To U.S. Hwy. 63
1 Mile

Blossom Rock Trail

Little Piney Creek

N

Blossom Rock Trail

Distance Round-Trip:
1 mile
Estimated Hiking Time:
45 minutes

Was the Blossom Rock still here? What is a blossom rock, anyway? Signs in the parking lot didn't mention it. The first part of the trail yielded no clues. I had written the thing off as an obscure fragment of sketchy local history, when suddenly I was standing before it, and all my questions were answered. So that's a blossom rock!

Caution: Stay on the trail to avoid stinging nettles in the creek bottom.

Trail Directions: Park in one of several lots between the picnic area and campground loops. The trailhead is across the road from the campground host site.

Begin the trail on a wide, mowed path through a mixed forest on the Little Piney Creek floodplain **[1]**. Two of the dominant plants here have winged stems— wing-stem sunflowers and white crownbeard, both of which may be 7 feet tall by summer's end. White crownbeard is one of only a few plants in Missouri that can produce frost flowers—white, delicate ribbons of frost that extrude from the plant's stem near the base. Look for frost flowers after hard freezes, especially early in winter. Among the slippery elm and black walnut trees are sweet gum, which have five-lobed, star-shaped leaves and prickly "gum ball" seed cases.

A small slough, which may be dry, soon appears on your right. Tall hackberry trees block most of the sun, and a subcanopy of pawpaws finishes the job. Cross an intermittent stream at .12 mi. **[2]** and find three musclewood trees just on the other side. Musclewood has some of the hardest wood of any American tree. Its other name, hornbeam, comes from *horn*, meaning hard, and *beam*, an old-world word for tree. Ignore the spur on your right at .15 mi. **[3]**. Look for thin strips of bark that peel off sycamore limbs, fall onto the trail, and crunch like eggshells under your feet. Just after crossing another intermittent stream, turn left at the intersection at .27 mi. **[4]** and go up a rocky hill. Dittany, goldenrod, and aster bloom next to the trail, and a steep ravine plunges on your left. As you climb higher, flowering dogwoods replace pawpaws, and white oaks replace hackberry trees.

The Blossom Rock appears without announcement at .42 mi. **[5]**. Although this 50-foot-high pinnacled mass of sandstone may have been named because it erupts from an underlying bed of dolomite, what is more striking is that it "blossoms" from the forest floor without another rock mass or boulder in sight. Explore the blossom, looking for sunning brown fence lizards and spectacular green blooms of spreading lichens. Turn left after returning to the trail.

The trail passes through a dry forest with occasional slabs of sandstone. You find some glade remnants on the switchbacks at .45 mi. **[6]**, with blazing star, black-eyed susans, and wild onions, which produce clusters of six-pointed, star-shaped lavender flowers in late summer. As you complete the last switchback, you see sparkling Little Piney Creek below you at .50 mi. **[7]**. Hike on a side slope, with protruding sandstone and dolomite ledges, and turn left at the bottom of the hill, at .65 mi. **[8]**.

After crossing a small, wooden bridge over a sandy tributary, follow the trail to the right and hike along the creek, with great views of the stream's clear water and a variety of lush aquatic plants. Look in the deep sand on the trail for small, round depressions, made by carnivorous doodlebugs (antlion larvae), who make their living by trapping ants and other small insects in tiny pitfall traps. Turn right at .75 mi. **[9]** onto the pavement of the campground loop. Bear right at all intersections of the loop to return to the trailhead.

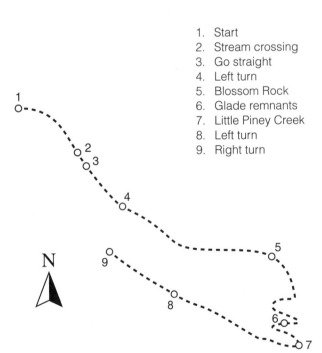

1. Start
2. Stream crossing
3. Go straight
4. Left turn
5. Blossom Rock
6. Glade remnants
7. Little Piney Creek
8. Left turn
9. Right turn

N

Cedar Bluff Trail

Distance Round-Trip:
1 mile
Estimated Hiking Time:
45 minutes

Hike next to a spring-fed river, past a moist rock garden, and up onto cliff overlooks, where congregations of blooming black-eyed susans, goldenrod, and asters stand all around you and a rugged and forested world opens in front of you.

Caution: Stay on the trail to avoid stinging nettles and poison ivy in the creek bottom.

Trail Directions: Park in the small lot for the trailhead, which is at the end of the paved road, north of the picnic areas. Begin the trail just to the left of the locked gate at the north end of the lot **[1]** and hike on a wide, mowed path through the dense vegetation of the Little Piney Creek floodplain. The trail is shaded by numerous sweet gum trees, whose brilliant yellow and red star-shaped leaves in fall compete with maples in their beauty. The ruffled leaves at the top of the tallest sycamores find breeze, even on balmy days.

At .07 mi. **[2]**, you hike next to Little Piney Creek and feel the cool air from its spring-fed waters. Lane Spring contributes its 11-million-gallon-per-day output into the creek just a few yards upstream from here. Notice that the streambed is composed of different substrates—sometimes rock, sometimes gravel, and sometimes sand—providing a variety of habitats for riverine plants and shrubs. As the trail follows the creek, numerous spurs lead to the water's edge, providing opportunities to watch for mink, raccoons, herons, kingfishers, and other wildlife using the stream. Breezes reveal the silvery white undersides of the leaves of the silver maple, the fastest growing of all maples.

Go straight at the intersection at .35 mi. **[3]**. After crossing a small spring emerging from a rocky ravine, the trail swings to the right, going uphill. At .44 mi. **[4]** is a natural rock garden, where blooming hydrangea adorns the top of some of the craggy boulders and maidenhair ferns arise from moist crevices. As you climb, the soil becomes thinner, drier, and rockier, and river-bottom species like box elder and silver maple are replaced by white oak, post oak, and cedar. The trail soon becomes a matrix of roots and rocks.

At .46 mi. **[5]**, a glade remnant welcomes you to the top of the bluff. Among the silvery blue prairie

grasses are goat's rue and the surprisingly large leaves of prairie dock. As you hike along the blufftop, several overlooks open on your right, the best of which is at .48 mi. **[6]**. From sandstone ledges, with chinquapin oaks and ancient cedars all around, a tremendous vista of the Little Piney Creek Valley opens before you in a 180-degree sweep. Look for rattlesnake master and other glade plants near the trail as you continue.

At .61 mi. **[7]**, you begin some zigzags down the hill. After crossing a seep (where groundwater flows over bedrock, beneath a thin layer of soil) at .73 mi. **[8]**, you find an abundance of Christmas ferns, gracefully arching their fronds over the side of the trail. Look in these moist areas for persimmon trees and blue lobelia, a tall wildflower whose blossoms have a two-parted upper lip and three-parted lower lip. Near the bottom of the hill, the ravine on your right becomes a slough, which may hold standing water (watch out for mosquitoes). After crossing a small, wooden bridge, you reach the pavement of the picnic area at .98 mi. **[9]**, where you turn right to finish your bluff hike.

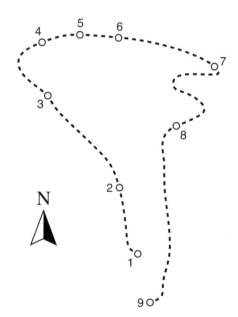

1. Start
2. Little Piney Creek
3. Go straight
4. Rock garden
5. Glade remnant
6. Blufftop overlook
7. Descent
8. Small seep
9. Right turn

- See the humble beginnings of the Ozarks' premier float stream—the Current River.

- Look for all seven of the spring outlets, which were born from a single mother spring after it was filled by gravel and debris from a torrential downpour in 1892.

- Try your hand at tricking a *Salmo gairdneri*, a rainbow trout, onto your dinner plate.

- Hike in a mature, scenic oak-pine woods in the Montauk Upland Forest Natural Area.

Area Information

Named by the first pioneers of the area, who were from Montauk Point, Long Island, New York, the village of Montauk sprang up in the early 1800s next to Montauk Spring. With a flow of over 40 million gallons of water per day, Montauk Spring powered at least four sawmills and gristmills, the last of which, built in 1896, is still standing as the last remnant of the village of Montauk.

Montauk Spring was once a single big spring outlet. In 1892 extremely heavy rains washed sand, gravel, and debris into the spring, dividing it into the seven springs that we see today. From these springs is born one of the most scenic and popular canoeing rivers in the Midwest—the Current. The Current and the nearby Jacks Fork rivers make up the Ozark National Scenic Riverways, managed by the National Park Service.

Since its purchase by the state in 1926, Montauk State Park has remained a popular recreation spot. Nestled in a scenic Ozark valley, the natural resources in the area offer the same features that attracted settlers in the early 1800s. With its long, cold spring branches, Montauk is probably best known for its trout fishing. One of Missouri's four "trout parks," Montauk features a 3.5-mile section of stream stocked with rainbow trout. The Missouri Department of Conservation operates a trout hatchery in the park. Trout season is from March 1 to October 31, and catch-and-release fishing is available on weekends during winter.

Directions: The park is about halfway between Licking and Salem. From the intersection of Highways 63 and 32 in Licking, take Highway 32 east for 11.2 miles. Turn south on Highway 119 and go 10.2 miles into the park.

Hours Open: The site is open year-round. The park office is open from 8:00 a.m. to 4:30 p.m. Monday through Sunday during trout season, and from Monday through Friday during the off-season.

Facilities: The park offers a campground, cabins, a motel, a dining lodge, a store, a fish hatchery, and picnic areas. Tours of Montauk Mill are available from the naturalist's office.

Permits and Rules: A state fishing license and daily permit required for trout fishing are available from the park store. Fish feeding is allowed in the hatchery's rearing pools, but only food bought on site may be used. Pets must always be leashed.

For Further Information: Montauk State Park, R.R. 5, Box 279, Salem, MO 65560; 573-548-2201 (park office), 573-548-2434 (cabins and motel), 573-548-2225 (naturalist's office), 877-422-6766 (camping reservations); www.mostateparks.com.

Other Areas of Interest

Roger Pryor Pioneer Backcountry, in Shannon County, is a 61,000-acre portion of Pioneer Forest, the state's largest privately owned forest. Leased to Missouri's state parks for public use and enjoyment, the area is dedicated to primitive outdoor recreation and includes 15 miles of Current River frontage and 27 miles of trails. For more information, call Johnson's Shut-Ins State Park at 573-546-2450.

Park Trails

Montauk Lake Hike (👣, .75 mile). This trail begins at the naturalist's office and takes you to the trout-rearing pools and the wetlands around Montauk Lake. Watch for tiny spring outlets "boiling" up through the sand at the bottom of the lake.

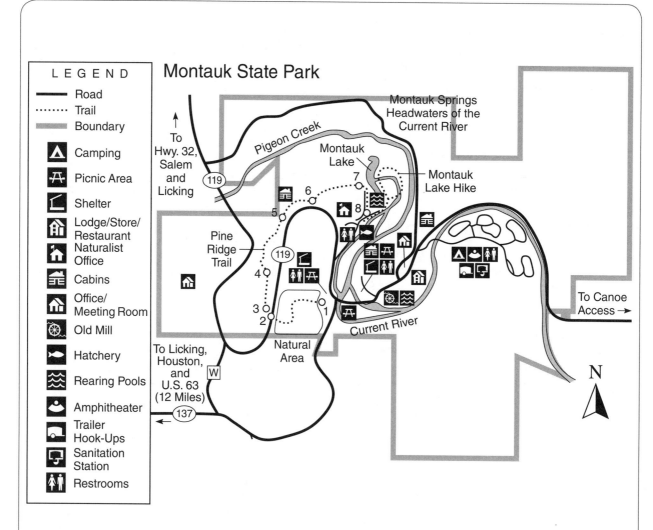

Montauk State Park

LEGEND
- ▬ Road
- ⋯ Trail
- ▬ Boundary

- 🔺 Camping
- 🏕 Picnic Area
- 🏕 Shelter
- 🏠 Lodge/Store/Restaurant Naturalist Office
- 🏠 Naturalist Office
- ⚏ Cabins
- 🏠 Office/Meeting Room
- ⚙ Old Mill
- 🐟 Hatchery
- 〰 Rearing Pools
- 🎭 Amphitheater
- 🚐 Trailer Hook-Ups
- 🚻 Sanitation Station
- 🚹🚺 Restrooms

To Hwy. 32, Salem and Licking

Pigeon Creek

Montauk Springs Headwaters of the Current River

Montauk Lake

Montauk Lake Hike

Pine Ridge Trail

119

Current River

Natural Area

To Licking, Houston, and U.S. 63 (12 Miles)

W

137

To Canoe Access →

N

1. Start
2. Highway crossing
3. Grand shortleaf pine tree
4. Dead pine tree
5. Right turn
6. Wooden bridge
7. Veer right
8. Naturalist's office

Pine Ridge Trail

 Distance Round-Trip:
2 miles
Estimated Hiking Time:
1.25 hours

Shortleaf pines can live for centuries and can keep a record of the frequency of fires that have passed around them in their lifetime. Inspection of annual rings of ancient pines in Missouri has revealed that in presettlement times, fires swept through many places in the Ozarks every three to five years.

Caution: Be careful crossing Highway 119 and when hiking on the park road to return to the trailhead.

Trail Directions: Park in the lot for the old rock picnic shelter, found in the southwest corner of the park. The trail begins [1] behind the shelter. Cross a slough over a bridge made from slabs of bedrock and turn right just past the bridge. You are soon immersed in a beautiful scene. A small stream accompanies you as you hike between moss-covered rock outcrops on both sides of the trail. You are entering the Montauk Upland Forest Natural Area, which is managed and protected as one of the state's best examples of an Ozark oak-pine forest. Mature shortleaf pines cap the ridgetops and blufftops, and steep ravines lend a dramatic effect to the landscape.

Soon, you cross the small stream and begin to climb the ridge on the other side. If you are here in spring, look for blooming violets, bloodroot, toothwort, jack-in-the-pulpit, trillium, bellwort, spring beauty, and buttercups. Nearly anytime, you find a scattering of Christmas and rattlesnake ferns. Scan the open woods. When you find a tree trunk with large, flat plates of bark, you've found a shortleaf pine tree. Pines become more numerous as you reach the top of the ridge.

Cross Highway 119 at .32 mi. [2] and continue on the other side. You meet a grand, old shortleaf pine tree next to the trail at .36 mi. [3]. Pines are your constant hiking companion now as you hike along this ridgetop. Once a common natural community in the Ozarks, old-growth pine woodlands were extensively logged from 1890 to 1920.

Notice the assortment of uses creatures have found for the big dead pine tree at .56 mi. [4]. Many insects have found shelter under the bark, and beetle larvae and other insects eat the wood itself. Woodpeckers excavate holes to find insects and to make nests. Later, flying squirrels and owls may use renovated woodpecker cavities for their own shelter. Nature recycles! A huge valley soon opens on your left, revealing splendid views of wooded ridges on the horizon.

At .81 mi. [5], make a 90-degree turn to the right at a significant rock in the middle of the trail. In a few steps, you cross a gravel road that leads to Reed's Cabins. Continue the trail on the other side. After passing beneath a power line, you hike downhill to reach a small stream. Look for various plants and wildflowers here like liverleaf and wild geranium. Cross a small, wooden bridge at 1.10 mi. [6] and start to climb the next slope. As the trail veers to the right at 1.45 mi. [7], you have views of Montauk Lake and rectangular concrete boxes where thousands of rainbow trout are raised before being released into the spring branch to tempt anglers. You reach the naturalist's office at 1.50 mi. [8], where you can stop in to get answers to your nature questions. Turn right to hike on the park road just in front of the fish hatchery office. After passing a cemetery on your right, you hike along the spring branch for a while before you return to the old rock picnic shelter.

- See the huge, blue eye of Alley Spring, framed by a natural amphitheater of sheer, smooth bluffs.

- Imagine 81 million one-gallon milk jugs full of water . . . how many bathtubs is that? How many swimming pools is that? It's an average day's flow from Alley Spring.

- Take a tour of the red, three-story Alley Mill—once the center of a turn-of-the-century community and now one of the most photographed buildings in the state.

- Hike next to the chilly waters of the spring branch, beneath overhanging rock ledges, and up to a rocky overlook with a soaring vulture's view of the entire spring valley.

- Bring a mushroom identification book; many mushrooms are so brilliantly colored that they compete with the wildflowers.

Area Information

The story of Alley begins with its spring, which is Missouri's seventh largest—a round, blue pool about 60 feet across and 30 feet deep, with a 150-foot-deep chasm below it. Every day, Alley gushes forth around 81 million gallons of water at a temperature of about 57 degrees year-round. Surrounding the spring pool are tall walls of smooth dolomite, the parent rock from which is carved most caves and springs in the Ozarks. The spring branch flows for a half mile before entering the Jacks Fork, about a quarter mile down North River Road.

Constructed in 1894, the Alley roller mill harnessed part of the spring's power to grind flour for local farmers. Farmers sometimes had to wait for days for their turn at the mill, which became a center for storytelling, news exchange, and checker playing. By 1900 a community was flourishing around the mill, including a blacksmith shop, general store, post office, school, and baseball diamond. The mill was expanded to saw lumber and generate electricity. On Sundays and holidays, festivities around the spring included target shooting, amusements, dancing, speeches, horseshoes, and the ever-popular picnics.

Alley Spring, managed by the National Park Service, is part of the Ozark National Scenic Riverways, which includes over 134 miles of the Current and Jacks Fork rivers. National riverways are natural streams that have recreational, natural, and cultural resources of national significance. Both the Current and Jacks Fork are clean, diverse, scenic rivers, and offer endless possibilities for floating, fishing, and exploring the Ozarks.

Directions: From Eminence, take Highway 106 west 5.9 miles to the Alley Spring picnic area, on the right. The campground and river access are .4 mile east of Alley Spring on Highway 106.

Hours Open: The spring area, trails, picnic area, and campground are open year-round. Alley Mill is open every day from Memorial Day through Labor Day. Storys Creek School is open on Friday, Saturday, and Sunday from Memorial Day through Labor Day.

Facilities: The site offers free admission and tours of Alley Roller Mill, which serves as an interpretive center. Picnicking is available near the spring; horseback and bicycle riding are available on North River Road; and camping, boating, fishing, floating, and swimming are all available at the campground. Check bulletin boards for scheduled events and programs.

Permits and Rules: No wading, fishing, swimming, boating, or tubing is allowed in the spring, but all these activities are allowed in Jacks Fork River. No horses or bikes are allowed on the trails, but both may be ridden on North River Road. The Alley Spring area is closed to all hunting or shooting.

For Further Information: Ozark National Scenic Riverways, P.O. Box 490, Van Buren, MO 63965; 573-323-4236; www.nps.gov/ozar.

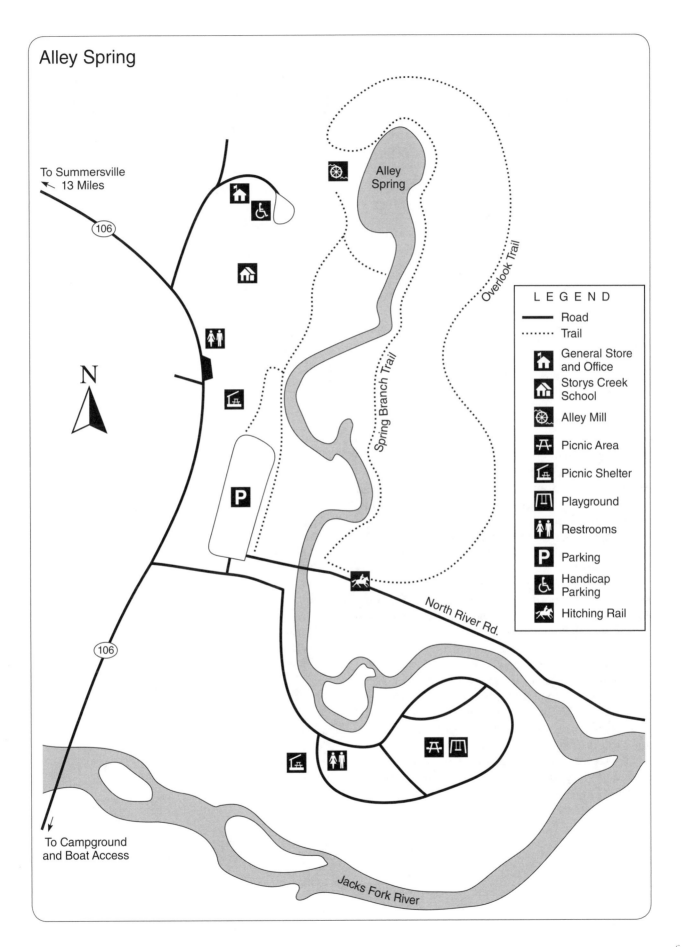

Alley Spring

To Summersville
← 13 Miles

106

N

Alley
Spring

Overlook Trail

Spring Branch Trail

P

North River Rd.

LEGEND
— Road
······ Trail

General Store
and Office

Storys Creek
School

Alley Mill

Picnic Area

Picnic Shelter

Playground

Restrooms

Parking

Handicap
Parking

Hitching Rail

106

To Campground
and Boat Access

Jacks Fork River

Spring Branch Trail

Distance Round-Trip: .75 mile
Estimated Hiking Time: 45 minutes

There is something about spring water . . . it often has vapor rising from it, and whether it's boiling from a 30-foot-deep pool or rolling along a 2-foot-deep spring branch, its beautiful, almost eerie, blue-green hue is unmistakable.

Caution: Some of the flat rocks on the trail may be slippery because of rainwater and seeps.

Trail Directions: Park in the lot for the Alley Mill. The trail begins on North River Road, which is just across the wooden bridge over the spring branch, near the southeast corner of the parking lot. Cross the bridge at the sign that reads "Local Traffic Only," and begin the trail just across the bridge **[1]**, on your left.

Aside from the mill and the historical significance and attractions of the area, the spring and spring branch have a beauty all their own. You probably already noticed the sound of this cool water, pushed along by the millions of gallons emerging from its source, just ahead. The watercress is surprisingly green, and the blue-tinged water obscures its depth. At a bend in the stream at .04 mi. **[2]**, look near the water for a patch of tall, pencil-thin plants that have no obvious leaves. These are horsetails, which represent a family of nonflowering plants that flourished some 400 million years ago, before flowering plants evolved. Just across the trail is a Carolina buckthorn tree, whose smooth, shiny leaves turn yellow in the fall. Its sweet, edible fruit gives the tree its other name, Indian cherry.

Another interesting tree appears at .07 mi. **[3]**, just to the right of a boulder on your left. This is a musclewood tree, so named for the unusual, musclelike ridges beneath its smooth bark. One of the hardest and strongest woods in North America, musclewood has been used for tool handles, wedges, and golf clubs. Like giant eyebrows of the steep slope on your right, dolomite ledges soon protrude from the hill and hang over the trail. Hydrangea sprouts where water seeps or drips. Alum root and columbine grow up the bluffs, and Virginia creeper trails from the top. You pass some small caves in the bluffs at .12 mi. **[4]**, and both the caves and the bluffs continue nearly to the mill. Notice the island at .16 mi. **[5]**, covered with jewelweed.

After climbing some stone steps, go straight at the intersection at .25 mi. **[6]** and go up some more steps. The water becomes louder as it rushes around boulders and islands. The red mill comes into view on the left as the big, blue eye of Alley Spring **[7]** (.32 mi.) appears in front of you. Bur reeds wave in the calmer shallows, a fog persists over the boiling center, and smooth, sheer dolomite bluffs frame the whole scene. Continue around the spring. When you arrive at the mill at .42 mi. **[8]**, turn left and follow a sandstone walkway. Turn right at .45 mi. **[9]** and go over a wooden bridge. Just across the bridge, turn left and take the spur on your right at .48 mi. **[10]** to the small, white schoolhouse and peek inside.

Turn right after returning to the sidewalk, and you'll find an interpretive display at the corner of the parking lot at .67 mi. **[11]**, with photos and information on the community that developed around Alley Spring during the late 1800s. Continue on the sidewalk until you reach the "Local Traffic Only" sign at .74 mi. **[12]**, where you turn left to finish your spring hike. The Overlook Trail also begins here, which gives you a different view of Alley Spring.

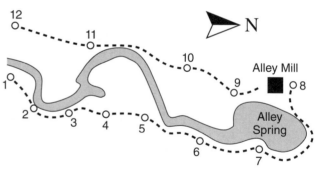

1. Start
2. Horsetails
3. Musclewood
4. Small caves
5. Jewelweed island
6. Go straight
7. Alley Spring
8. Alley Mill
9. Right turn
10. Spur to schoolhouse
11. Interpretive display
12. Left turn

Overlook Trail

Distance Round-Trip:
1.5 miles
Estimated Hiking Time:
45 minutes

From the overlook, it's easy to imagine the busy general store, the loud blacksmith shop, and the rest of the little town that once flourished far below. What remains are the soft red mill and the blue dot of the spring that started it all.

Caution: Small, loose rocks cover the trail on some of the inclines.

Trail Directions: Park in the lot for the Alley Mill. This trail shares a trailhead with the Spring Branch Trail. Cross the bridge at the sign that reads "Local Traffic Only" and begin the trail just across the bridge **[1]**.

Go straight on North River Road and pass a few hitching rails for horses and some picnic tables. At .05 mi. **[2]**, ascend the stone steps on your left that lead uphill into the woods. Ignore the spurs on your right and continue on the main trail as it zigzags up the hill. The sudden abundance of little bluestem grass and the opening in the tree canopy signal a glade remnant at .16 mi. **[3]**. As on prairies, flowers bloom on glades from early spring through fall. Wildflowers that bloom in spring are usually short, but later-blooming species grow taller, when they have to compete with the tall prairie grasses. By fall, the yellow flowers of prairie dock, sunflowers, and compass plant may be 6 to 8 feet high!

Unless you visit in winter, you are likely to find mushrooms here in all sizes and shapes, especially after a wet period. Look for bright orange miniature chanterelles, poking through dark green moss beds. Large, candy-apple-red mushrooms are here, as well as smaller ones, lemon yellow and dull green. Oyster mushrooms grow snow white and earlike on rotting logs, whereas the king bolete looks like a hamburger bun on a fat stalk. Near the top of the ridge, you hike through an open forest with some grandpa and grandma white oak trees and several stands of large shortleaf pines. Feel the pine bark. You'll discover that it's made of layers of thin plates that can flake off, making the tree resistant to fires.

Listen for the rushing water of Alley Spring; you soon reach a spot on this ridgetop where the sound is funneled up from far below. The vast expanse of the entire spring valley and outlying wooded hills opens in front of you at the overlook at .75 mi. **[4]**. From here, you can see the red mill, which became the center of a thriving community just after the turn of the century. After the overlook, look for coneflowers, blazing star, and rattlesnake master in several more glade remnants on your way downhill. You may also see false foxglove here, a tall plant sometimes so full of yellow flowers that the long branches droop to the ground. The trail makes some switchbacks downhill, and you pass a small, wet-weather waterfall at 1.02 mi. **[5]**.

You reach Alley Mill at 1.18 mi. **[6]**, which you can tour during open hours. Turn left, in front of the mill, and follow the sandstone walkway. Turn right at 1.21 mi. **[7]** and cross the wooden bridge over a small stream. Just across the bridge, turn left, and pass Storys Creek School and a picnic shelter on your right. At the corner of the parking lot at 1.40 mi. **[8]**, you find an interpretive display with photos and information on the turn-of-the-century community that once thrived here and literature on the Ozark National Scenic Riverways. Return to your vehicle here or continue on the sidewalk until you reach the "Local Traffic Only" sign at 1.48 mi. **[9]**, where you turn left to return to the trailhead.

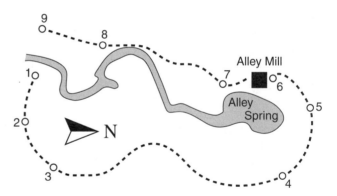

1. Start
2. Stone steps
3. Glade remnant
4. Scenic overlook
5. Wet-weather waterfall
6. Alley Mill
7. Right turn
8. Interpretive display
9. Left turn

- From a 200-foot-high blufftop overlook, view the Boomhole and find out how it got its name in the late 1800s.

- Water, water everywhere! Hike next to a serene forest lake, numerous spring branches, streams, and the Eleven Point River.

- Discover the gum bumelia tree, or woolly buckthorn, which is in the family of trees from which chewing gum chicle comes and looks like a big bonsai tree on the blufftop glades.

- Begin and end your hike next to the enchantingly tranquil Lake McCormack.

Area Information

McCormack Lake Recreation Area is in the Doniphan–Eleven Point District of the Mark Twain National Forest and is managed by the U.S. Forest Service.

Two major features of the area are the Eleven Point River and the Ozark Trail. Although the McCormack-Greer Trail connects the McCormack Recreation Area with the Greer Recreation Area and river landing, most of the trail is also a segment of the Eleven Point River Section of the Ozark Trail. The Ozark Trail follows the most scenic and varied route from the St. Louis metropolitan area southwestward through southern Missouri to the Arkansas border and will be 500 miles long when completed. The Eleven Point River, part of the national wild and scenic river system, is fed by over 30 springs and provides a cool swim or wade even on the hottest summer days. Picnic areas, boat launch ramps, campgrounds, and eight float camps, accessible only by watercraft, are located along the river.

Originally established as a bass-rearing pond in the late 1930s, McCormack Lake is now a peaceful setting for camping, resting, or reconvening from an outdoor trip. At the McCormack Lake area alone, visitors can find excellent places for hiking, backpacking, camping (including riverside camping), picnicking, boating (by canoe, kayak, or johnboat), tube floating, fishing, bird and wildlife watching, photography, berry and mushroom gathering, and horseback riding. Plenty of spots are also available to sit next to a stream and just listen to the forest.

Directions: McCormack Recreation Area is 13.3 miles south of Winona on Highway 19. Or, from the south, it is only 5.5 miles north of the Greer Spring Trail on Highway 19.

Hours Open: The site is open year-round.

Facilities: The area offers developed campsites, restrooms, picnic areas, fishing, boating on Lake McCormack (by carry-on boats only), and drinking water (except during winter months).

Permits and Rules: No firearms may be discharged. No boat motors are allowed. All pets must be leashed. Fires are restricted to fire pits while camping in the developed campground.

For Further Information: Eleven Point Ranger District, #4 Confederate Ridge Road, Doniphan, MO 63935; 573-996-2153; www.fs.fed.us/r9/forests/marktwain. For more information on the Ozark Trail, contact the Missouri Department of Natural Resources, Ozark Trail Coordinator, P.O. Box 176, Jefferson City, MO 65102; 573-751-5359.

Other Areas of Interest

Turner's Mill North Picnic Area was the site of the town of Surprise and has a spring that was used to power Turner Mill. A large waterwheel still sits in the spring branch. The area is on the Eleven Point River and offers easy access. Go 2.1 miles south of McCormack Lake on Highway 19. Turn onto FR 3152 and travel 6 miles. Then take FR 3190 for 3 miles.

Falling Spring Picnic Area, a scenic spot and favorite area of photographers, includes a spring, millpond, old mill, and 100-year-old cabin. Go 3 miles north of McCormack Lake on Highway 19. Turn onto FR 3170 and take FR 3164 to the left for 2 miles. For more information about either area, contact the Eleven Point Ranger District in Doniphan at 573-996-2153.

McCormack-Greer Trail

Distance Round-Trip: 8.5 miles
Estimated Hiking Time: 4.5 hours

Hike next to boulders carpeted with ferns, lichens, and lush mosses while trailside streams provide music along the way.

Caution: You cross many streams on this trail. During high water and floods, stream crossings will be difficult or impossible. Also, take care not to hike onto adjoining sections of the Ozark Trail by mistake—it's 500 miles long!

Trail Directions: Begin the trail at the south end of the parking lot for McCormack Lake **[1]**. Most of this trail is also a portion of the Ozark Trail, which is marked with green and white "OT" trail markers. Hike next to the lake until you get to the spillway at .22 mi. **[2]**, where you turn left.

You can't go far in the Ozarks without coming upon a spring branch or stream, and soon you will find one gurgling and snaking along near the trail. Where the trail crosses a stream at .42 mi. **[3]**, you also find a beaver dam. Cross a dirt road at .48 mi. **[4]** and continue the trail on the other side. You cross two more streams at .55 and .57 mi. **[5]**.

At .62 mi. **[6]**, you walk up to a magnificent boulder. Make your way along the stream until you come to an intersection at 1.11 mi. **[7]**, where you turn left uphill among some moss-covered boulders.

At the top of the mountain you find a glade—a rocky, grassy opening in the forest. At 1.52 mi. **[8]**, you walk out onto the Boomhole overlook. Near the turn of the century, the bluff across the river supported a wooden chute. Lumbermen cut massive logs from virgin shortleaf pine and slid them down the chute, where they plunged into the river below with thunderous booms. The logs floated downriver and were placed on log trains, bound for the mill at Winona.

The trail turns away from the river and passes through the pine-oak forest before treating you to another outstanding overlook at 2.62 mi. **[9]**. From here, descend to river level and cross a stream. At 3.11 mi. **[10]**, turn right at the intersection. At 3.5 mi. **[11]**, the river more than doubles in volume because of the inflow of the Greer Spring Branch. About a mile up this branch is Greer Spring.

At 3.88 mi. **[12]**, turn left, cross a small stream, and follow the trail under the Highway 19 bridge. At 4.02 mi. **[13]** is Greer Recreation Area, where restrooms, water, and camping are available. Hike on the pavement, away from the river, and you'll see the trail markers where the trail reenters the forest. Turn left at the intersection at 4.25 mi. **[14]**. When you reach Highway 19 at 4.43 mi. **[15]**, turn right on the road for about 50 yards and pick up the trail on the other side. You cross a couple rocky, singing streams before returning to the intersection at **[10]**. Turn right here. You get to experience both overlooks and the other sights all over again before returning to the trailhead.

McCormack Recreation Area

LEGEND
— Road
...... Trail
P Parking

1. Start
2. Left turn
3. Beaver dam
4. Go straight
5. Stream crossings
6. Boulder
7. Left turn
8. Boomhole overlook
9. Overlook
10. Right turn
11. Greer Spring Branch
12. Left turn
13. Greer Recreation Area
14. Left turn
15. Right turn

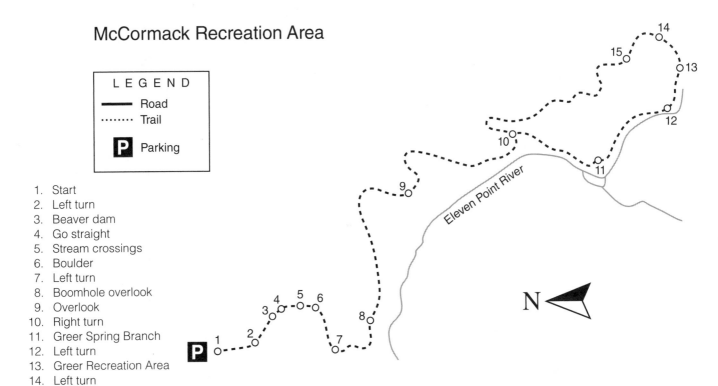

- Hike in a shortleaf pine and hardwood mixed forest and hear the hushed roar of Greer Spring, over half a mile away.

- Find Christmas ferns in their favorite habitat and experience the sight of a Christmas fern mania.

- Stand next to the "boil" and witness the power of the 220-million-gallon-per-day flow of Greer Spring, Missouri's second largest.

- Why did the walking fern cross the rock? Find the answer at the bottom of the Greer Spring Trail.

Area Information

You couldn't tell from looking at it now, but Greer Spring has a long history of milling and timbering operations that included dams, turbine waterwheels, and two mill buildings at the spring site as well as a third on a ridge above it. It all started when Samuel Greer bought the spring in 1859, built a gristmill, and began operating the mill powered by water from the spring. After serving in the Civil War, Greer returned home to find that roaming guerrillas had burned his mill and driven off most of his livestock.

Around 1870 Greer rebuilt the mill, constructed a dam, installed a turbine waterwheel, and expanded operations. Greer's mill now could grind grain, saw timber, gin cotton, and card wool—all from harnessing the spring's tremendous power. Greer expanded again in 1883, rebuilding the dam and starting construction on a new roller mill located on the ridge above the spring. A unique cable system was used for transferring power from the turbine wheel at the spring to the new mill on the ridgetop. The mill continued operating until 1920.

Today, visitors to Greer Spring can experience the area in its natural and nearly undisturbed state. This opportunity is the result of good stewardship of the land since 1920, conscientious management by the U.S. Forest Service, which has owned the area since 1993, and nature's incredible ability to renew itself.

Directions: From Alton, travel north on Highway 19 for 7.5 miles to the small town of Greer. The entrance to the parking lot for the trail, marked by a U.S. Forest Service sign, is .6 mile north of Greer.

Hours Open: The site is intended for day use only and is open year-round from dawn to dusk.

Facilities: Restrooms are available, but water is not.

Permits and Rules: Camping, hiking, and hunting are allowed on the national forest land surrounding Greer Spring, but no hunting or camping is allowed near the spring or trail. Regulations posted near the trailhead also prohibit shooting, littering, picnicking, horses, ATVs, bicycles, swimming, fishing, boating, glass containers, smoking, night use, pets off leash, and audio devices.

For Further Information: Winona Office, Eleven Point Ranger District, Route 1, Box 1908 Highway 19 North, Winona, MO 65588; 573-325-4233.

Other Areas of Interest

The 53-degree water of Greer Spring rolls down a rock-filled canyon for 1 mile before entering the **Eleven Point River**, which it more than doubles. The Eleven Point is a national scenic river, part of the National Wild and Scenic Rivers System, and is protected by the U.S. Forest Service. The Forest Service has picnic areas, campgrounds, and boat and canoe accesses along the river. Several outfitters rent canoes. For more information, call 573-325-4233.

Greer Spring Trail

 Distance Round-Trip: 2 miles
Estimated Hiking Time: 1.5 hours

Although over a billion pounds of water billow from Greer Spring every day, its steep valley walls and omnipresent mist create a terrarium that you can walk in. Here you'll find mats of water-loving mosses and ferns, tiny trickles of spring water emerging from cracks in the rock walls, handsome jack-in-the-pulpit, and the delicate yellow lady-slipper orchid.

Caution: Watch out for poison ivy along the trail.
Trail Directions: The trail begins at the northwest end of the parking lot, near a wooden bench and a regulations sign **[1]**. Before you begin hiking, stop here and listen. The slightest breeze will incite a pleasant "Shh-hhhh . . . shhhhhh" from the shortleaf pines towering above. In this part of the Ozarks, the shortleaf is in its native habitat. Besides two species of juniper, it is Missouri's only native evergreen tree.

As you begin the trail, notice how the pines intermingle with the hardwood oaks and hickories. Pines often dominate the ridgetops in the area because they can tolerate the thin, drier soils there. Find a wooden bench at .19 mi. **[2]** and a wooden bridge at .32 mi. **[3]**. Soon after you cross the bridge, start listening down in the valley for the hushed roar of the 220-million-gallon-per-day flow of Greer Spring, the second largest spring in Missouri after Big Spring on the Current River.

Find another wooden bench at a switchback at .48 mi. **[4]**. From the wooden bridge at .59 mi. **[5]**, you can view a Christmas fern mania. So named because they

are green at Christmastime, Christmas ferns are actually green all year long. These shaded, rocky, wooded slopes with acidic, well-drained soils are their favorite habitat. Cross a final wooden bridge at .64 mi. **[6]**.

Soon you come to an interpretive sign that explains how sedimentation formed the nearby rocks. Layers of resistant sandstone were formed between layers of dolomite, which is softer and quicker to erode. As the layers of dolomite dissolved away, the remaining sandstone broke into unusual cubical shapes. You see many of these curious cubes here along the trail. At .79 mi. **[7]**, you find a natural sandstone bench.

At .87 mi. **[8]**, you can step out onto the stone overlook to hear and see the mighty spring. Greer Spring actually emerges from two openings. One is from Greer Spring Cave, on your far left, and the other is from the big "boil" on your right. To descend to water level, take the steps at the far left of the overlook.

At the bottom at .94 mi. **[9]**, you can feel the water vapor in the air and see the lush vegetation that it supports. Here are several species of aquatic plants, watercress, and carpets of thick mosses and liverworts clinging to boulders in the cold spring water. Look on some of the larger boulders to find heart-shaped leaves with extremely long tips poking through layers of moss. Look carefully at these walking ferns and you'll see tiny plantlets forming at the tips of many of the leaves. These plantlets are what make walking ferns "walk." Aha! Walking ferns cross rocks to reproduce.

Wading or swimming is not allowed, but you can have fun exploring more wonders of nature near the spring and spring branch before hiking back to the trailhead.

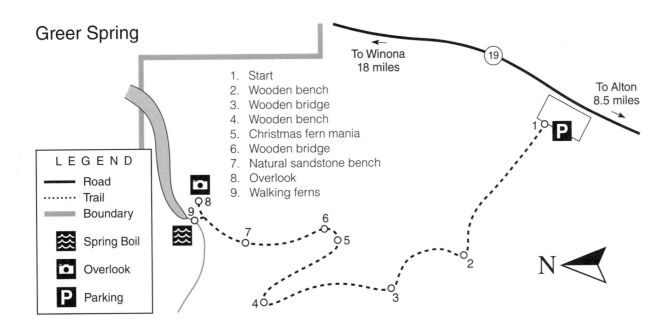

Greer Spring

1. Start
2. Wooden bench
3. Wooden bridge
4. Wooden bench
5. Christmas fern mania
6. Wooden bridge
7. Natural sandstone bench
8. Overlook
9. Walking ferns

LEGEND
— Road
...... Trail
▓ Boundary
≋ Spring Boil
◙ Overlook
P Parking

To Winona
18 miles

To Alton
8.5 miles

49. Grand Gulf State Park

- See the most spectacular collapsed cave system in the Ozarks.

- Discover a collapsed cave passage, a sinkhole, a spring, a pirated stream, a cave, a natural bridge, and wet-weather waterfalls, all on two short hikes.

- From four overlooks, watch a stream splash along, vanish underground, and emerge again in a geological disappearing act called stream piracy.

- See the cave where local Ozark old-timers claimed to have dumped sacks of oats into the draining stream to watch the grains emerge at Mammoth Spring, Arkansas, 9 miles away.

Area Information

The story of Grand Gulf begins in a seemingly unlikely place—the bottom of a warm-water ocean over 450 million years ago. Here, calcium-rich sediments formed dolomite, the dominant rock found in the area. As the land was uplifted, the ocean waters receded, and fresh water began to erode the landscape. Surface streams carved down through the soft rock, creating fissures and channels in the bedrock. Mildly acidic groundwater dissolved passageways underground, which later became air filled, and a cave system developed.

But the water did not stop there. The erosional forces that formed the cave continued, and at Grand Gulf today is a cave system whose roof collapsed thousands of years ago. The result is a vertical-walled canyon about .75 mile long, which is often called the Little Grand Canyon. A bit of remaining roof forms one of the largest natural bridges in Missouri. Grand Gulf is a national natural landmark.

Like many other geological wonders, Grand Gulf has a long history of public attraction, local pride, and folklore. In 1892, using a boat and candles, scientist Luella Agnes Owen set out to explore the cave,

which drains all the water from the gulf. Her account included seeing "small eyeless fish, pure white and perfectly fearless; the first I had ever seen, and little beauties."

Although the sack-of-oats experiment may sound dubious, modern investigators have used dye tracing to confirm that water from Grand Gulf does indeed travel to Mammoth Spring, Arkansas. Today, visitors can still see water winding and eroding its way through the gulf, a testimony to the forces that created it thousands of years before.

Directions: Grand Gulf is in south central Missouri, just a few miles from Arkansas. From Thayer, travel west on Highway W for 5.8 miles to the entrance.

Hours Open: The park is open daily from 8:00 a.m. to sunset year-round. Park gates close at dusk.

Facilities: The park offers picnic areas, boardwalks, and four overlooks. Restrooms are available, but water is not.

Permits and Rules: Grand Gulf is a day-use park only; camping is not allowed. Stay on the boardwalks and trails to prevent erosion, and always keep pets on leashes.

For Further Information: Grand Gulf State Park, Route 3, Box 3554, Thayer, MO 65791; 417-264-7600, or call the park office at Montauk State Park, 573-548-2201.

Other Areas of Interest

After hearing the story of the water at Grand Gulf State Park and seeing the cave where the water enters the earth, why not drive down into Arkansas to **Mammoth Spring** and see where all that water comes out? It's just 9 miles south of Grand Gulf on Highway 63. Billowing 850 million gallons of water per day, Mammoth Spring is one of the largest springs in the nation. The site is an Arkansas state park and includes a picnic area, federal fish hatchery, and aquarium. For more information, call Mammoth Spring State Park at 870-625-7364.

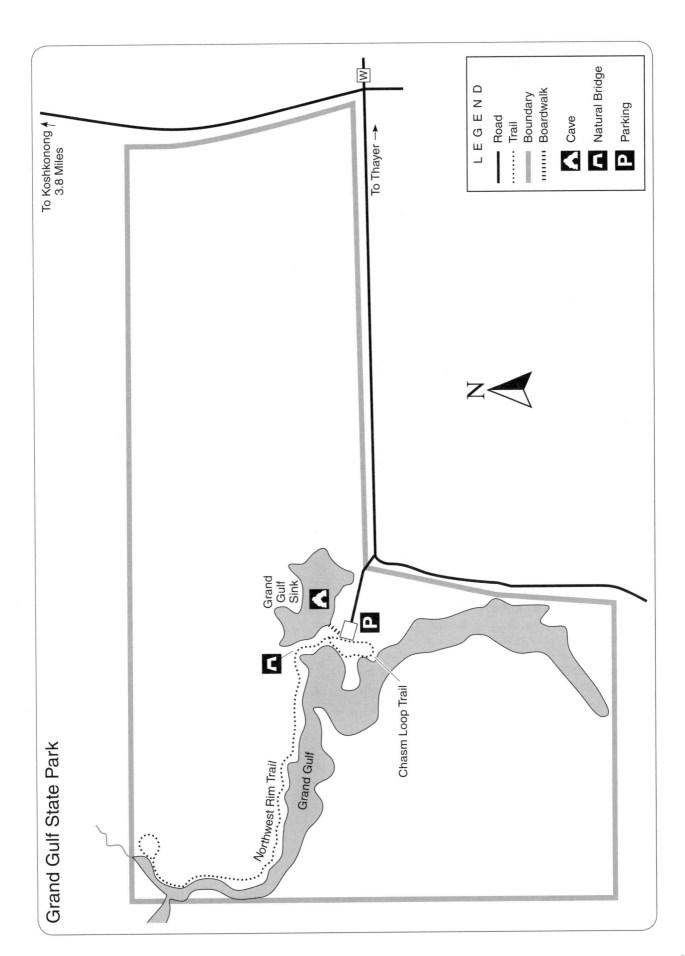

Grand Gulf State Park

To Koshkonong ↑
3.8 Miles

To Thayer →

W

Grand Gulf Sink

Northwest Rim Trail

Grand Gulf

Chasm Loop Trail

N

LEGEND

Road
Trail
Boundary
Boardwalk
Cave
Natural Bridge
Parking

Chasm Loop Trail

 Distance Round-Trip: .25 mile
Estimated Hiking Time: 30 minutes

Look down the gulf and imagine how the cave would have looked while it was still intact, perhaps as recently as 10,000 years ago. The rock faces that you see were here then. So was the water. It was water that dissolved this stone, giving birth to the cave eons ago. And water flows through the chasm today, carving it ever deeper.

Caution: Stay on the boardwalks and trails to avoid the edges of the 130-foot vertical cliffs. Also, keep pets on leashes and children in control.

Trail Directions: Before you begin, you may want to take the boardwalk on your far right to the overlook for views of two of the highlights of the park—the Grand Gulf Sink and the cave that drains the Bussell Branch stream and Shiloh Spring. This water, a combination of surface drainage and spring water, enters the cave and travels 9 mi. underground to reemerge at Mammoth Spring, Arkansas.

Begin the trail at the interpretive signs in the northwest corner of the parking lot **[1]**. At .01 mi. **[2]**, turn left to take the small spur to the Grand Junction overlook. From here you are looking into the main passage of an ancient cave, the roof of which has collapsed. The giant boulder on the left constricts the gulf. This point is called the Needle's Eye. The area at the far end, called the Narrows, is where the cave passage ended. Today, a wet-weather stream joins the sink here in an erosional continuum tens of thousands of years old.

Just after you return to the main trail, turn left at the intersection at .03 mi. **[3]**. At .05 mi. **[4]**, you come to Natural Bridge overlook, so named not because you look over a natural bridge but because you are standing on one! Because of its resistance to erosion or its architectural soundness, this is a portion of the cave roof that didn't collapse. Continue down the wooden steps.

At .09 mi. **[5]**, you come upon the third overlook of the trail. Step out onto the overlook and look to your far left. At the end of the chasm are slabs of bedrock, which form a waterfall after a heavy rain. At the base of the falls is Shiloh Spring, which bubbles up for a few feet before disappearing below the surface. It reappears below the overlook, just to the left, where it gurgles and trickles its way into the mouth of the cave in the Grand Gulf Sink. Turn right at the intersection just past the overlook.

At .15 mi. **[6]** is a wooden deck and an opportunity for you to take the steps to the bottom of the chasm. Choosing this option affords a unique perspective of the gulf and adds another boot or two to the difficulty rating for this trail. Turn right to descend the 119 steps into the chasm or turn left to ascend the steps and complete the trail.

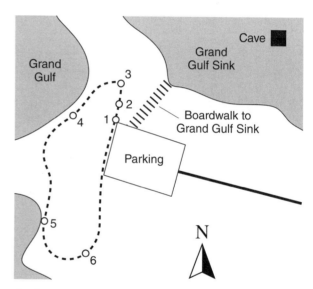

1. Start
2. Grand Junction overlook
3. Left turn
4. Natural Bridge overlook
5. Shiloh Spring overlook
6. Steps to bottom of chasm

Northwest Rim Trail

Distance Round-Trip: 1 mile
Estimated Hiking Time: 45 minutes

Shiloh Spring stream was cheerily gurgling along far below me, and a tufted titmouse was busy with his spring song the day I was here. But oh, what a different sound these canyon walls must have heard one day long, long ago . . . the day the ceiling came tumbling down.

Caution: Stay on the trail to prevent erosion problems and avoid dangerous drop-offs.

Trail Directions: Before you begin, you may want to take the boardwalk to the far right of the interpretive signs for a great view of the Grand Gulf Sink and cave. Also be sure to stop at Grand Junction overlook to get an end view of all the features that you will be hiking alongside. This overlook is on a small spur on your left, just after you begin either trail.

Begin the trail at the interpretive signs at the northwest corner of the parking lot **[1]**. When you come to an intersection at .03 mi. **[2]**, look on your right at the beckoning oak, silently gesturing the way you should go. Go straight here to continue the trail.

At .04 mi. **[3]**, look down in the bottom of the deep sinkhole on your right and see where the sunken passage meets the still-intact cave. At about 200 feet, the cave is in the deepest part of the chasm and acts as a drain for all the water flowing into the gulf. Early explorers of the cave reported finding a large lake inside, as well as blind cavefish, but exploration halted in 1921 when a tremendous storm washed trees and other debris into the gulf, damming the cave a short distance inside the entrance. In the early 1990s, a camera-carrying robot named STEVE was sent into the cave to investigate the blockage. Currently, access to the cave beyond the flood debris is not feasible.

Turn left at the intersection at .06 mi. **[4]**. Take the small spur at .08 mi. **[5]** on the left to enjoy the view of the natural bridge that you were standing on a few minutes ago. With an opening 75 feet high and a span of 250 feet, this natural bridge is one of the largest in the state.

Return to the main trail and turn left. Turn right at each intersection, ignoring all spurs to the left. For most of the way, the chasm has been fairly yawning on your left as you hike, but you soon approach the area known as the Narrows, where the collapsed cave passage ends and an intermittent surface stream begins. At .37 mi. **[6]**, take the small spur on your left to see the gravel pit that pirates (drains) the spring stream at this end of the chasm. During heavy rain, runoff from approximately 20 square miles cascades over the smoothed bedrock above the gravel, making a wet-weather waterfall. Heavy rain sometimes turns the gulf into a skinny lake that reaches a depth of over 100 feet. Most of this water slowly drains through the cave.

At .43 mi., ignore the spur on your left. You reach the end of the trail at .51 mi. **[7]** at a minitrail cul-de-sac. Retrace your steps to make your way back to the trailhead.

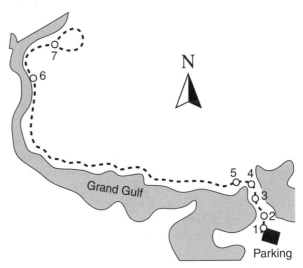

1. Start
2. Beckoning oak
3. Cave in sink
4. Left turn
5. Natural bridge
6. Wet-weather waterfall
7. Cul-de-sac

- Climb a bluff over the Big Piney River. See a pine forest, sparkling sandstone boulders, and magnificent views of ridges, valleys, meadows, and the river below.

- Bring your tree book to help you identify both moisture-loving trees like river birch, persimmon, box elder, and musclewood and dry-habitat trees like post oak, blackjack oak, and woolly buckthorn.

- Entertain yourself endlessly, watching the scenic river and its interactive inhabitants.

Area Information

The Big Piney River begins just north of the Willow Springs District of the Mark Twain National Forest and flows north, through the Houston–Rolla–Cedar Creek District and Fort Leonard Wood U.S. Army base before joining the Gasconade River. The Big Piney is the Gasconade's largest tributary. Numerous good-sized springs give the river a good temperature for swimming all summer long and keep the river floatable all year, except during droughts.

The Big Piney is an excellent fishing stream for smallmouth, goggle-eye, sunfish, and catfish, and its gravelly and sandy streamed makes it ideal for gravel-bar camping. Despite its scenic pine-capped limestone bluffs and overall health and natural beauty, it is often overlooked by river users. Without the hoopla of Missouri's more celebrated rivers, the Big Piney offers floaters a quieter place to be on the river. On weekdays and in fall and winter, canoeists may find that they have the river to themselves.

Slabtown River Access, in the Houston–Rolla–Cedar Creek District of the Mark Twain National Forest, is managed by the U.S. Forest Service. Just east of the popular Paddy Creek Wilderness, with its 17-mile Big Piney Trail and two recreation areas, Slabtown offers the outdoor enthusiast an access and stopover for combination outings of floating, camping, and hiking.

Directions: From Licking, travel 4 miles west on Highway 32. Turn northwest on Highway N for 2.2 miles and west on Highway AF for 5.9 miles. Turn left at the sign for the area.

Hours Open: The site is always open.

Facilities: Besides the boat ramp on the Big Piney, the area offers a small campground with picnic tables, grills, a pit toilet, and campsites for tents.

Permits and Rules: When building campfires near trailheads or developed areas, use existing fire rings. When camping elsewhere in the national forest, select a site away from the trail and use only dead and downed wood for fires. Make sure that the fire is cold and scatter its remains before you leave. The section of the river from Slabtown to Ross Access is designated a special smallmouth bass management area, and regulations are posted at these sites.

For Further Information: Main Office, Houston–Rolla–Cedar Creek Ranger District, 108 South Sam Houston Boulevard, Houston, MO 65483; 417-967-4194. *Missouri Ozark Waterways*, available from the Missouri Department of Conservation (573-751-4115), is a detailed guide to 37 major float streams in the Ozarks. It includes maps and describes features and accesses along the way.

Slabtown Bluff Trail

Distance Round-Trip:
1.75 miles
Estimated Hiking Time:
1 hour

I stopped along the trail to watch the river and found it full of life. A northern water snake lazily glided to shore while a smallmouth bass and a goggle-eye became fish statues, suspended below.

Caution: Vegetation crowds the trail along the river; consider wearing long pants.

Trail Directions: Park in the lot for the river access. The trail begins near the boat ramp **[1]** and follows the east bank of the Big Piney River, heading upstream. At the trailhead, you cross an intermittent tributary that passes through a grove of river birch trees with papery, peeling bark. At .01 mi. **[2]**, turn right at the fork in the trail. As you hike along the river, notice the different types of aquatic plants in the transition zone between water and land.

At .07 mi. **[3]**, a pawpaw grove forms a green awning over the trail, and several stump statues (carved by beaver) line the walkway. Keep an eye on the river, watching and listening for the variety of wildlife that it attracts. In the morning or early evening, watch for mink and raccoon, cruising along the banks. Anytime, listen for the rattling "chir-rrrr" of kingfishers and the startled (and startling) "bwaaaack!" of great blue herons.

After passing through a patch of horsetail, or scouring rush, at .20 mi. **[4]**, you find many moisture-loving trees like persimmon and musclewood. Pick your way over the talus (rocks broken off from the bluff above)

at .32 mi. **[5]** and watch the sun sparkle on a section of riffles in the river. Gaze a while longer at the river—you two will soon part ways. At .80 mi. **[6]**, the river bends right as the trail swings left.

As you climb the hill onto the rocky blufftop, bear right at a couple of places where the trail seems to fork. Large dolomite boulders lie scattered about—some weathered into flat-topped pinnacles. By .91 mi. **[7]**, you should arrive at the top, where views across the valley begin to open on your left. Species that thrive in drier environments, like sassafras, post oak, and chinquapin oak, become more abundant, and glade remnants dot the top and side slopes. Spectacular views across the Big Piney Valley open at 1.02 mi. **[8]**. Just past the river, far below, is a grassy meadow, surrounded by lush forest. On the opposite ridge are sheer, white bluffs, where black mineral stains drape down their sides like curtains. Downstream, river-bluff faces are pocketed with dark caves.

As you continue, dolomite gives way to sandstone, and shortleaf pines dominate the ridgetop. In rocky outcrops, sparkly sandstone peeks through blankets of green lichens. More vistas open intermittently on your left through gnarly limbs of big oaks and pines. At 1.40 mi. **[9]**, you begin your descent. You hike downhill beneath more pawpaws and sugar maples, where Christmas ferns grow next to the trail. The sound of the Big Piney meets you again as you approach the trailhead.

1. Start
2. Right turn
3. Pawpaw grove
4. Horsetail
5. Talus
6. Swing left
7. Blufftop
8. Overlook
9. Descent

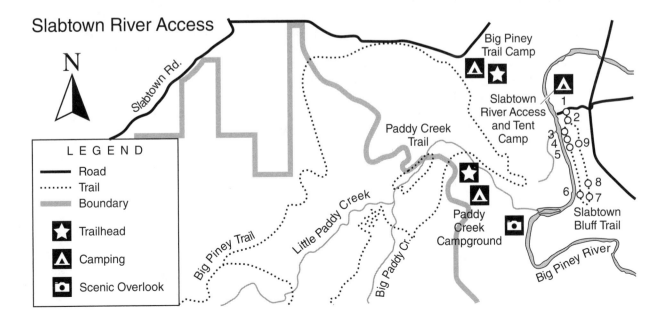

- Hike through a hidden, C-shaped natural tunnel that looks like a cave from either end.

- Discover a wide, shallow spring emerging from the base of a dolomite bluff and riffling into a rocky creek.

- In the middle of a field, find the deep, round, emerald blue eye of Wilkins Spring.

- Stroll on high, breezy ridgetops with sand underfoot and pines overhead.

Area Information

The Mark Twain National Forest, managed by the U.S. Forest Service, includes 1.5 million acres in southern and central Missouri in a diversity of natural communities and habitats. The forest is managed for multiple uses, including recreation, wilderness, timber, watershed, minerals, and fish and wildlife habitats. Fourteen floatable streams—most of them spring fed, gravel bottomed, and amazingly clear—provide infinite possibilities for floating, fishing, swimming, and boating. Sixteen lakes, ranging in size from 3 to 440 acres, add recreational opportunities. Many of the national forest's campgrounds are located near lakes or streams.

The national forest is divided into seven districts within the state, which are visible on many highway maps as green-shaded blocks. The Houston–Rolla–Cedar Creek District, which is just south of Interstate 44 between Rolla and Fort Leonard Wood, includes nearly 200,000 acres and six recreation sites. Mill Creek, within this district, includes a picnic area and the adjacent Kaintuck Hollow, which features a multiuse trail.

Following explorers like Daniel Boone, many pioneers from the Kentucky and Tennessee region settled in the Ozark hill country. Surely the Mill Creek and Little Piney Creek valleys reminded some of these early Missourians of their Kentucky homeland. It is believed that "Kaintuck" is fashioned from the Ozark dialectical trend of dropping a syllable here and there to produce a local variation of "Kentucky." The Kaintuck Trail includes multiple loops, which allow options for shorter or longer hikes, and features a 3-million-gallon-per-day round spring, a 175-foot-long natural tunnel hidden in the forest, and a good serving of the beauty and solitude of the area.

Directions: From Rolla, take I-44 west 7.2 miles to Highway T. Turn left and follow Highway T through Newburg. Turn left on 1st Street and turn right on Water Street. After crossing the railroad tracks and Little Piney Creek, turn right onto Highway P and travel 3 miles to County Road 7550, where you turn left. Travel 2 miles to the Mill Creek picnic area.

Hours Open: The site is open year-round.

Facilities: The Mill Creek area offers picnic tables and an artesian well for drinking water. Fishing and wading are available in Mill Creek. Bikes, horses, and backpack camping are allowed on the Kaintuck Trail. Parking lots are not developed, but horse trailers may be parked in a field .8 mile down the gravel road from the Mill Creek bridge. Picnic tables, primitive campsites, and a pit toilet are available at Wilkins Spring.

Permits and Rules: Fishing in Mill Creek is regulated by wild-trout management restrictions, which are posted. No motor vehicles are permitted on the Kaintuck Trail, but bikes and horses are allowed. Backpack camping is allowed at several campsites along the trail.

For Further Information: U.S. Forest Service, Houston–Rolla–Cedar Creek District, 108 South Sam Houston Boulevard, Houston, MO 65483; 417-967-4194.

Other Areas of Interest

Meramec Spring Park is in Saint James, just east of Rolla on I-44. The park features trout fishing in a stocked stream and includes a campground (two weeks' notice required), Meramec Spring, trout-rearing ponds, and two museums. Trout fishing season is from March 1 through October 31. Residents and nonresidents can buy daily fishing licenses. For more information, call 573-265-7387.

Kaintuck Trail— Northern Loops

Distance Round-Trip:
9 miles
Estimated Hiking Time:
4.75 hours

Around the old springhouse is a medley of aquatic plants, grasses, and wildflowers, attended by swallowtails, pearl crescents, and hummingbird moths.

Caution: Bring a flashlight if you want to explore in the natural tunnel. Bring a compass and topo map if you choose to extend this hike or explore off the trail. Hunting is allowed in national forests, so wear orange clothing during spring turkey season and throughout the fall. Creek crossings may be difficult or impossible after rainy periods.

Trail Directions: From the Mill Creek picnic area, take the first gravel road to the left, just past the picnic area. Cross the Mill Creek bridge and go .4 mi. on the gravel road. Park on the side of the road or in the small pull-off on the right for the trailhead.

Begin at the trailhead [1] and descend into a creek bottom, where weeds and grass may encroach the trail by late summer. When you reach the gravel-bottomed creek at .13 mi. [2], a tributary to Mill Creek, notice the spring at the base of the dolomite bluff just across the stream. The spring emerges from two wide outlets, riffles through a big patch of watercress (a spring indicator), and flows into the creek. Look for pickerel frogs and southern leopard frogs—both medium-sized spotted frogs that are powerful jumpers. Cross the stream here. Ignore the spur on your right to the campground at .21 mi. [3] and follow the trail as it bends to the left.

Ascend a steep hill with loose rocks on the trail and arrive on a ridgetop, where breezes pass between the trunks of oaks, hickories, and shortleaf pines. You find sparkling sandstone here and a buildup of sand on the trail. Where pine needles have accumulated over the sand, your feet will feel some cushioned relief from the otherwise rocky terrain. Go straight at the spur on your left at 1.47 mi. [4] and at the intersection at 1.62 mi. [5].

Go straight at the intersection at 2.61 mi. [6] and turn right at 2.71 mi. [7]. Approach the old farm pond at 2.94 mi. [8] quietly to watch for deer or other wildlife. After passing a glade rem-

nant, complete with a variety of colorful wildflowers, you reach a picnic and primitive camping area. Hike through the picnic area, turn left at the spring pond, and find the round, blue-green eye of Wilkins Spring at 3.87 mi. [9]. Return to the picnic area and resume the trail on your right, beneath a black locust tree with long, curly seedpods. Turn left at 4.01 mi. [10], where the trail splits from an old road. After winding through an old field, you pass another farm pond at 4.18 mi. [11]. Hike on a narrow ridge, covered with pines, and turn left at 5.06 mi. [12]. Turn right at the intersections at [7] and [6]. This section is a rocky and sandy hike downhill.

At 5.88 mi. [13], you stand on top of the Kaintuck Natural Tunnel! Take the small spur to your left. You can enter the cavelike entrance, hike through the C-shaped tunnel, and emerge at a small campsite at the other entrance. If you don't want to go through the tunnel, return to [13] and turn right. Keep bearing right until you arrive at the small campsite near the other tunnel entrance. From the campsite, hike away from the tunnel and ignore the spur on your left. At 6.38 mi. [14], just after crossing two rocky streams, turn left at a small parking area. Turn left on the gravel road at 6.87 mi. [15]. Cross the creek and turn left again, just on the other side, at 6.92 mi. [16]. While hiking up a steep and rocky hill, look behind you for clear views of the steep, wooded ridge on the other side of Kaintuck Hollow. After hiking through a sandy, old hay field with a small pond, turn right at an intersection [5] to finish your hike.

1. Start
2. Spring and creek crossing
3. Bear left
4. Go straight
5. Go straight
6. Go straight
7. Right turn
8. Old farm pond
9. Wilkins Spring
10. Left turn
11. Old farm pond
12. Left turn
13. Kaintuck Natural Tunnel
14. Left turn
15. Left turn
16. Left turn

Mill Creek

LEGEND
— Road
······ Trail
⛺ Picnic Area
🏠 Kaintuck Natural Tunnel
≋ Wilkins Spring

- Enjoy the peace and tranquility of a federally designated wilderness.

- Sit on a rocky ledge at the scenic overlook and look down on an arena of treetops.

- Find a small stream creating a wet-weather waterfall over flat sandstone ledges next to the trail.

- In late summer, nibble on huckleberries found on sandy and piney ridgetops.

- Hike alongside crystal-clear and boulder-strewn Paddy Creek, where longear sunfish, smallmouth bass, and chubs hover in its aquarium-like pools.

Area Information

Paddy Creek Wilderness is within the Houston–Rolla–Cedar Creek District of the Mark Twain National Forest and became a federally designated wilderness when President Reagan signed Public Law 409 on January 3, 1983. The 7,020-acre area is named after Sylvester Paddy, who began the first logging of the area in the early 1800s, floating timber downriver to St. Louis to help supply a growing need for construction lumber. The area was homesteaded and grazed as open range until the 1930s.

The wilderness is characterized by steep ridges with sandstone and dolomite outcrops, and oak and hickory forests with interspersed shortleaf pine. Big Paddy and Little Paddy creeks flow through the area and join the Big Piney River just outside the northeast wilderness boundary. A feature of the area is the Big Piney Trail, a 17-mile hiking and horseback trail that explores a good variety of Ozark terrain and connects two Forest Service recreation areas and a trail camp, located just outside the wilderness boundary.

Roby Lake Recreation Area, at the southwest corner, provides a small lake for fishing and is one of three trailheads for the Big Piney Trail. Big Piney Trail Camp, at the northeast corner, is designed primarily as a campground for equestrians. Paddy Creek Recreation Area, just south of the trail camp, is the most developed area near the wilderness and offers a picnic area and campground with tables and fire rings. At all trailheads, visitors to the wilderness are encouraged to practice no-trace, minimum-impact camping and trail use to protect the solitude and natural beauty.

Directions: To reach **Roby Lake Recreation Area**, take Highway 17 north from Roby for 1 mile. Turn southeast at the sign for the area on Forest Road 274 and go .9 mile to the parking lot for Roby Lake. **Big Piney Trail Camp** is 2 miles north of Roby on Highway 17 and 5.5 miles down County Road 2800. To reach **Paddy Creek Recreation Area**, take Highway 32 west from Licking for 13.4 miles to Paddy Creek Road, where you turn north. Go 6.9 miles and turn right on Campground Drive. The campground loop begins at the end of the picnic area.

Hours Open: The wilderness and its three trailheads are always open. Paddy Creek campground is closed December 1 through March 15, but camping is permitted in the picnic area during that time.

Facilities: Roby Lake Recreation Area offers a five-acre lake for fishing, drinking water, a toilet, and a picnic area. Big Piney Trail Camp includes picnic tables, fire rings, a toilet, hitching posts, and a stock-water pond. Paddy Creek Recreation Area provides a picnic area with grills, a toilet, and 23 camping units with tables and fire rings.

Permits and Rules: Horses are permitted on the Big Piney Trail but are not allowed in Paddy Creek Campground. Bicycles and motorized vehicles are not allowed in the wilderness. Shooting is prohibited in all recreation areas. Boat motors on Roby Lake are restricted to trolling motors. Littering and building "structures" such as rock fire rings or lean-tos in the wilderness are prohibited.

For Further Information: Houston–Rolla–Cedar Creek Ranger District, 108 South Sam Houston Boulevard, Houston, MO 65483; 417-967-4194.

Area Trails

Big Piney Trail (🐾🐾🐾🐾, 17 miles). This hiking, backpacking, and equestrian trail traverses the rugged wilderness landscape and crosses Little Paddy and Big Paddy creeks. With three trailheads and a connecting link in the middle, this trail offers multiple hiking options.

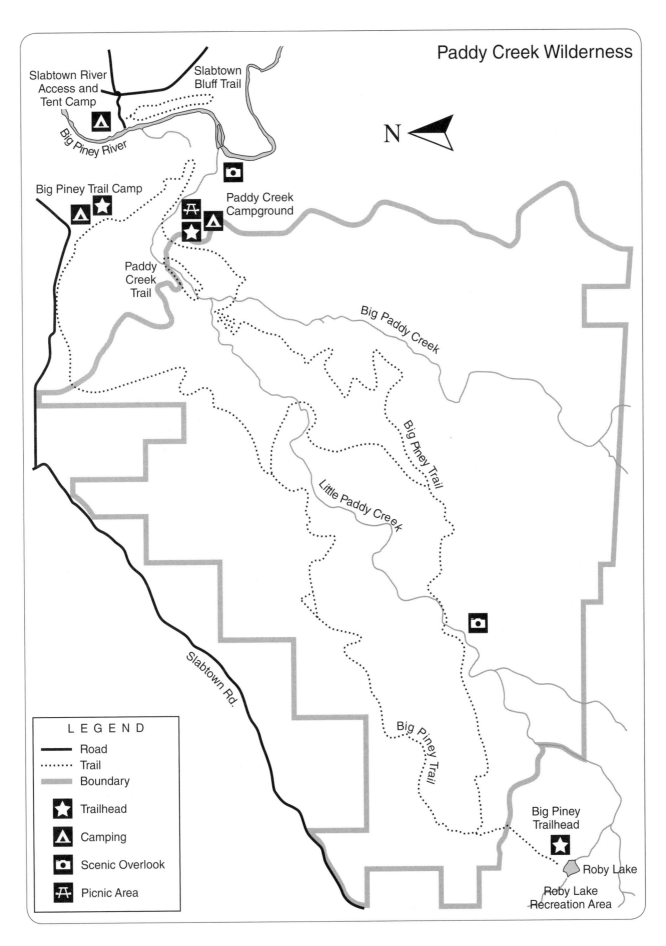

Paddy Creek Wilderness

N

Slabtown River Access and Tent Camp

Slabtown Bluff Trail

Big Piney River

Big Piney Trail Camp

Paddy Creek Campground

Paddy Creek Trail

Big Paddy Creek

Big Piney Trail

Little Paddy Creek

Slabtown Rd.

Big Piney Trail

Big Piney Trailhead

Roby Lake

Roby Lake Recreation Area

LEGEND

— Road
···· Trail
▬ Boundary

★ Trailhead
▲ Camping
◉ Scenic Overlook
🏕 Picnic Area

Big Piney Trail

 Distance Round-Trip: 4.5 miles
Estimated Hiking Time: 2 hours

Even the cadence of your feet on the trail can be numbing to the senses. At the overlook, sit quietly on the sandstone ledge with the plunging valley below you. Listen. You'll hear nothing but the whispers of the pine forest and the animals that live there.

Caution: Depending on the season, the first part of the trail may warrant chigger repellent.

Trail Directions: Park in the lot for Roby Lake Recreation Area. Walk north on the driveway (back the way you came) until you find an iron gate in the fence on your right. This marks the Big Piney trailhead. Go through the gate to begin the trail **[1]**.

To reach the wilderness boundary, just to the northeast, hike through a large, open field of Indian grass, which is up to 7 feet tall. Near the end of the field, sumac, locust, and cedar take over the field, and several white oak and post oak wolf trees stand as living witnesses to earlier, different times. At the four-way intersection at .15 mi. **[2]**, go straight. At .20 mi. **[3]**, you come across two iron gates in a fence. Go through the smaller one on the right, and you soon find the wilderness trail registration box, which marks the wilderness boundary. Register before continuing.

The trail now immerses you in a gently rolling, open woods dominated by oak and hickory. Small drainage streams are relatively frequent and shallow. If you are here in late August or September, look for the first signs of fall in the red-tinged leaves of Virginia creeper and poison ivy. Sassafras is another champion of the fall forest wardrobe, dependably turning bright orange, yellow, and red, while oaks and hickories, still green, wait for favorable weather. At the intersection of the north and south loops of the trail at .73 mi. **[4]**, turn right to begin the south loop. As you hike, look for a variety of woodpeckers attracted to this large, mature forest. When you get a woodpecker in view with binoculars, notice that they use their tails as props when they scale tree trunks and do their hammering. Woodpecker tails, with stiff, strong feathers, are specially adapted for this purpose.

Just after passing a shallow pond on your left, you hike through a young pine grove at .90 mi. **[5]**. Look closely as you pass to see the straight rows of an abandoned pine plantation project. At 1.42 mi. **[6]**, the trail takes you next to a wet-weather waterfall over sheets of sandstone bedrock. A little farther downstream, the creek has cut through blocks of rock, creating a miniature canyon, lined with bluffs. Cross the creek just upstream from the waterfall. You then ascend a dry hill with mounds of reindeer lichen, which always seems to grow together with clumps of pincushion moss. Reindeer lichen (also incorrectly called reindeer moss) not only resembles the branching antlers of reindeer but also is a staple food of reindeer living in tundra regions.

The valleys on each side of this ridge suddenly come surprisingly close to the trail, and at 2 mi. **[7]**, you find yourself on a narrowing tongue of a ridgetop. From here, the show begins. Undercut layers of sandstone hang off the steep sides, which drop straight down and become lost in the treetops far below. You are surrounded by pines, which sigh in the breeze. Hike among huckleberry bushes on a trail blanketed with pine needles to 2.15 mi. **[8]**, where you find a spectacular view. A wide rock ledge makes a perfect overlook deck, where you can enjoy the panorama and listen to the wilderness. Splendid views continue on the trail until 2.25 mi. **[9]**, which is a good spot to turn around and enjoy the views again on your way back to the trailhead.

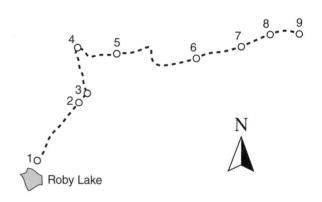

1. Start
2. Go straight
3. Iron gates
4. Right turn
5. Pine grove
6. Wet-weather waterfall
7. Ridgetop
8. Overlook
9. Turn around

Paddy Creek Trail

Distance Round-Trip:
.85 mile
Estimated Hiking Time:
45 minutes

Paddy Creek is a long, stretched-out aquarium. Through its clean, clear water I could see all the vibrant colors of the longear sunfish—bright orange head with iridescent emerald stripes and glowing, red eyes—as beautiful as any angel fish of the coral reef.

Caution: Vegetation crowds the trail along the river; consider wearing long pants. Do not attempt this trail during periods of high water.

Trail Directions: Park in the picnic area and walk back to the low-water bridge over Paddy Creek. The trail begins on the east side of the creek, near the bridge **[1]**.

The gray metal box on your left at .03 mi. **[2]** contains an instrument that monitors the water level of Paddy Creek. Hydrologists from the U.S. Geological Survey use this data for making graphs and models, and for other analysis. As you continue, you hike between the creek and some large sandstone boulders that tumbled down from above, almost making it to the streambed. The ridged texture of the boulders is caused by mineral-filled fracture lines that are slightly more resistant to weathering than the rest of the sandstone. Blocky talus (rocks that broke off from bluffs above) continues on the trail at .05 mi. **[3]**, making for challenging hiking. Marginal shield ferns and hydrangea grow on top and between the rocks, creating green, streamside gardens.

Look in the creek for an assortment of Ozark stream fish. While you stand on the bank, sunfish sometimes rise near the surface, waiting for their chance to slurp terrestrial insects that fall in the water from overhanging bushes. The tan fish with a black vertical bar on its tail is a young smallmouth bass. These fish sometimes follow suckers as they root around on the stream bottom, snapping up uncovered crayfish and aquatic insect larvae.

Hike on top and around boulders, some decorated with delicate ferns and mosses and others covered with what looks like green spaghetti, an appearance caused by numerous "walkers" of walking fern. Continue next to the stream until you reach a large boulder (about the size of a toolshed) that has two flat sides and is tilted on end next to the water **[4]** (.31 mi.). This chunk of sandstone, before it was cemented by

minerals, was sand on the beach. The rippling action of ocean water lapping on the shore created the washboard texture of its flat sides. Remember this rippled boulder; you'll return to it later.

As you begin the spur to the swimming hole, you pass a deep hole filled with water on your left at .34 mi. **[5]**, next to a boulder. Whether an old sinkhole or an abandoned creek channel, the hole has been adopted by several frogs. At .43 mi. **[6]**, you find a gravel beach and a picturesque swimming hole, where the water gradually deepens to a pool at the base of a gray, dolomite bluff. Deep blue blossoms of lobelia and dayflower surround the beach, and ninebark (a streamside shrub in the rose family) emerges from the gravel. After enjoying a dip, or just the scenery, return to the rippled boulder to continue.

Just upstream from the rippled boulder is a good place to cross the stream. On the other side find the trail and turn right at .59 mi. **[7]**. At a small spring stream at .65 mi. **[8]** is a grove of musclewood (American hornbeam) and persimmon, two trees known for their hard, heavy wood. After crossing another small spring stream, you arrive on a gravel road at .77 mi. **[9]**. Turn right here and cross the low-water bridge to return to the picnic area.

1. Start
2. River gauge
3. Blocky talus
4. Rippled boulder
5. Frog pond
6. Swimming hole
7. Right turn
8. Musclewood grove
9. Right turn

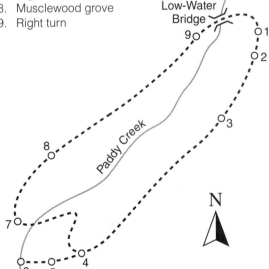

- Hike through remnant stands of shortleaf pine trees—Missouri's only native pine.

- Discover an old-growth forest, flower-filled glades, an ancient cedar tree clinging to a cliff, and remarkable vistas on top of a bluff overlooking the Big Piney River Valley.

- See Stone Mill Spring emerging from the base of a bluff and pouring 18 million gallons of water per day over underwater patches of vibrant green watercress.

- Find a historic petroglyph on the blufftop, made by a landowner in 1921.

Area Information

The Big Piney River, which gets its name from numerous pine-clad ridges and rocky bluffs along its route, begins near Cabool and flows north through Fort Leonard Wood, a U.S. Army base, before joining the Gasconade River. Native Americans lived along the Big Piney and no doubt took advantage of its clear, productive waters. The high quality of its water, its gravelly and sandy streambed, and its scenic beauty make the Big Piney ideal for nature watching, fishing, and camping adventures. Numerous good-sized springs keep it floatable all year long.

Fort Leonard Wood, a 61,411-acre installation of the U.S. Army located in a richly forested area southwest of Rolla, offers many outdoor recreation opportunities to the public. Fishing is available on several small lakes on the base, as well as on Big Piney River and Roubidoux Creek. Canoe access points are also maintained on these streams. Stone Mill Spring is periodically stocked with trout from spring through summer. Visitors can camp for free at Big Piney Camping Area, near the East Gate, and numerous areas of the forests are intermittently open for hunting.

Stone Mill Spring Recreation Area is located on U.S. Forest Service property, although it is best accessed through Fort Leonard Wood. It is part of the Big Piney River Recreational and Interpretive Corridor, which is managed by the Natural Resources Branch of the Public Works Directorate of the base. The corridor features recreational, natural, and cultural resources along several bends of the Big Piney River. All its

facilities are open to the public and are within a short drive, canoe trip, or hike.

Directions: From exit 161A (St. Robert) off I-44, take Missouri Avenue south into Fort Leonard Wood 4.2 miles to 1st Street, where you turn left. Travel 3.8 miles on 1st Street to a sign for Happy Hollow Picnic Ground, where you turn right. Go 3.4 miles and turn left to cross a narrow bridge over the Big Piney River. Go 1.7 miles (you pass a golf course on your left) and turn right at a sign for Stone Mill Spring. Go .7 mile and park in the lot for the spring and trail.

Hours Open: Stone Mill Spring Recreation Area is normally open during daylight hours year-round.

Facilities: Stone Mill Spring offers a picnic area with grills, toilets, and fishing in the spring branch and on the Big Piney River.

Permits and Rules: Although many resources on the military base are open to the public, training missions often involve live ammunition, and most areas are closed to public entry. Visitors who wish to hunt or fish at the base must first obtain a post sportsman's permit from the Outdoor Recreation Center and must check daily listings for area closings. Bikes and horses are prohibited on the trails.

For Further Information: Natural Resources Branch, Environment, Energy, and Natural Resources Division, Directorate of Public Works, Building 2112, Fort Leonard Wood, MO 65473; 573-596-2814. For information on hunting and fishing permits, call the Outdoor Recreation Center at 573-596-4223.

Area Trails

Miller Cave Trail (👣👣👣👣, .2 mile). Miller Cave, one of the largest caves on Fort Wood, offers catacomb-like passages in its entrance and a tremendous view of the Big Piney River Valley. To reach the cave, turn southeast (along the river) from the bridge near the golf course and go 1.2 miles to Road TA 256, where you turn left. Go 1.4 miles and turn right, just before reaching Training Area #61. Go 1 mile and park on the side of the road. The trail begins on your left.

Sandstone Spring Trail (👣👣, .04 mile). This short trail begins across the road from the bridge near the golf course and leads to a picturesque spring that emerges from the base of a bluff.

Stone Mill Spring Trail

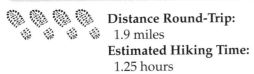

Distance Round-Trip:
1.9 miles
Estimated Hiking Time:
1.25 hours

I scampered up the bluff, counted the wildflowers on the glades, and oohed and aahed at the overlooks, but my favorite was the ancient cedar—growing out of a rock, a twisted veteran and survivor of ice, wind storms, lightning, and untold generations of humans.

Caution: Be careful near bluff edges, especially at the cliff edge near the ancient cedar.

Trail Directions: Park in the lot for Stone Mill Spring and find the trailhead marked with a sign at the southeast corner of the lot [1]. The first part of the trail is more vertical than horizontal, and you quickly gain elevation over the Big Piney River. Climb a trail over dark gray dolomite boulders and cedar tree roots to reach the first of a series of glades at .06 mi. [2]. Look closely on the craggy dolomite rocks and you'll find a different sedimentary rock fused on top. The lighter colored rock is chert, which is extremely resistant to weathering.

Keep climbing among an understory of flowering dogwood and ironwood. Views of the river valley explode in front of you at a glade overlook at .12 mi. [3]. You are parallel with tall, wooded ridges on your left and are about the same height as turkey vultures soaring over the vast valley. Look behind you to find a slope covered with flat, tilted slabs of sandstone.

Hike over the sandstone to continue. Note the ripple marks, left by ocean water lapping on ancient beaches, which make the rocks look like big washboards. You are now beneath a stand of shortleaf

pine that escaped loggers' saws on this rugged bluff. At .14 mi. [4], turn right at the intersection beneath a tall hickory tree to enter a mature forest with grand white and black oaks. Hike across a ridgetop, where chert gravel accumulates on the trail. Take a look at the odd, bubblelike burl erupting from the forest floor on your left at .29 mi. [5].

Just after turning left at the intersection at .37 mi. [6], look for a series of depressions near the trail at .39 mi. [7] that resemble sinkholes. Made by neither caves nor foxes, these foxholes were dug by soldiers in training. A wooden bench at .62 mi. [8] marks another overlook of the Big Piney, far below. With the overlook in front of you, turn right and walk 12 steps. Look on your left for a boulder with carvings on top at .63 mi. [9]. Beneath the lichens you can still make out "Chas. Ramsey 1921." Keep hiking on your right, toward the end of the bluff, to find a bonsai-shaped ancient cedar at .65 mi. [10]. Although the age of this tree is not known, some blufftop cedars in Missouri are over 1,000 years old. With a good view of the river, this is an excellent spot to watch for ospreys in spring and fall and bald eagles in winter. Turn left after returning to the wooden bench.

At the end of another ridge, you find another wooden bench and overlook at .82 mi. [11]. The trail swings right and takes you down to a moist bottom inhabited by pawpaws and Christmas ferns. Turn left at the clearing to find Stone Mill Spring at 1.10 mi. [12]. Turn right, in front of the bridge, and pass two big pecan trees on your left. Turn left at 1.27 mi. [13] over the bridge and hike along the other side. Go straight when you return to the bridge near the spring at 1.41 mi. [14]. Hike on a gravel road between the Big Piney River and the bluff that you just climbed. Go straight at the gravel loop to finish your blufftop hike.

1. Start
2. Glade
3. Glade overlook
4. Right turn
5. Burl
6. Left turn
7. Foxholes
8. Overlook
9. Ramsey petroglyph
10. Ancient cedar
11. Overlook
12. Stone Mill Spring
13. Left turn
14. Go straight

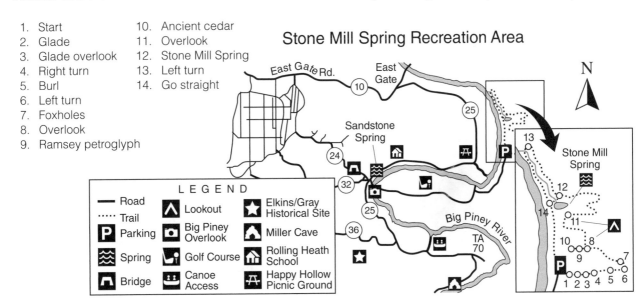

- Come see what a couple of little creeks can do to a wall of stone.

- Hike in a scenic hollow in the state's first designated natural area.

- Find a graceful and handsome natural arch tucked away in the woods.

Area Information

Identified by an interagency committee, Missouri natural areas represent the natural diversity and ecological processes of Missouri's native landscapes. Natural areas are the best remaining examples of the state's natural heritage and are managed to maintain or improve their biological diversity. A 230-acre portion of Clifty Creek Conservation Area, Clifty Creek Natural Area probably looks very much as it did 200 years ago. It was designated the state's first natural area in December 1971.

According to Thomas Beveridge's *Geologic Wonders and Curiosities of Missouri*, *clift* was a synonym for *cliff* before the word fell from common usage. But Ozarkers have a way of holding on to old English and other archaic words, especially if they are usefully descriptive. It's no wonder that someone named this valley Clifty Hollow, because Clifty Creek has carved more than its share of steep-walled bluffs and cliffs along its way.

Although the area includes a rich oak-hickory forest, blufftop glades, cliffs, an Ozarks headwater stream, and a diversity of plants, the real gem of the site is a natural arch in the streambed of Clifty Creek.

The arch spans 40 feet and, according to Beveridge, was formed in a ridge of dolomite by the erosive action of two creeks. Clifty Creek, on the south side, undercut the ridge, making it narrower at the base. Little Clifty Creek, on the north, made its way through a crack in the ridge, eventually carving the crack into an arch opening. Today, Little Clifty Creek flows through the arch and meets Clifty Creek on the other side.

Clifty Creek Natural Area is owned by the L-A-D Foundation, a private, not-for-profit foundation established in 1962 to protect special outdoor areas in Missouri. The area is leased to the Missouri Department of Conservation.

Directions: Just south of Vienna, take Highway 28 west 13.6 miles. Turn left onto Route W at a sign for the area. Go 3.4 miles on pavement. When you reach the gravel road, go straight an additional .7 mile until you reach the small parking lot on the left.

Hours Open: The site is open from 4:00 a.m. to 10:00 p.m. year-round.

Facilities: This site has no facilities.

Permits and Rules: Horses, ATVs, and open fires are not permitted. Bicycles are allowed only on roads open to vehicles. Dogs must be leashed. Primitive camping is allowed within 200 feet of the parking lot.

For Further Information: Missouri Department of Conservation, USDA Service Center, 1315 E. Main, Linn, MO 65051; 573-897-3797; www.mdc.mo.gov. For more information on Missouri's natural areas, contact the Natural Areas Coordinator, Missouri Department of Conservation, P.O. Box 180, Jefferson City, MO 65102; 573-751-4115.

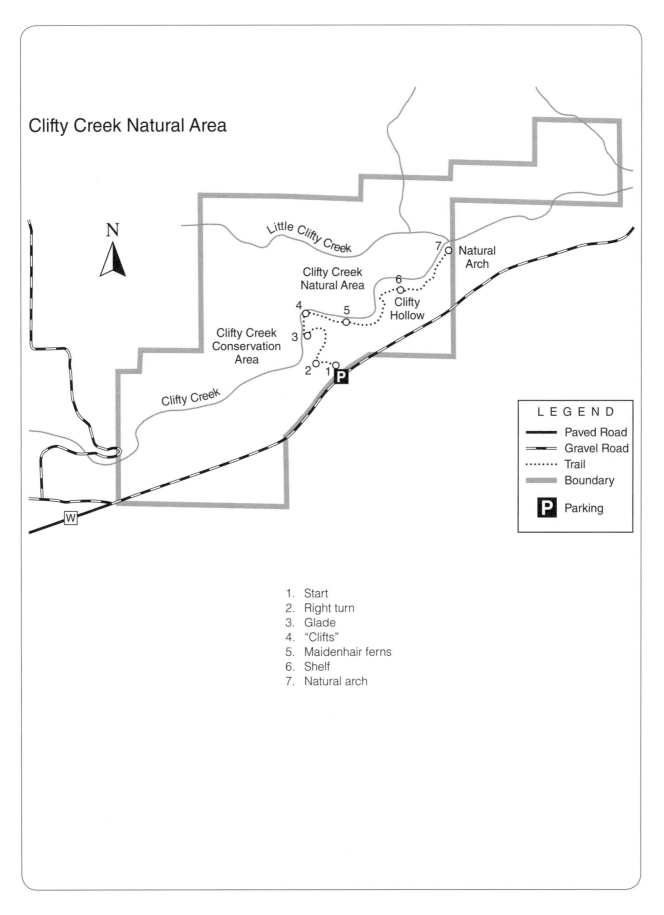

Clifty Creek Natural Area

N

Little Clifty Creek

Clifty Creek
Natural Area

Clifty Creek
Natural Area

Clifty Creek
Conservation
Area

Clifty Creek

7 — Natural Arch

6

5

4

3

2 1 P

W

Clifty Hollow

LEGEND
— Paved Road
‖ Gravel Road
···· Trail
▬ Boundary
P Parking

1. Start
2. Right turn
3. Glade
4. "Clifts"
5. Maidenhair ferns
6. Shelf
7. Natural arch

Natural Arch Trail

Distance Round-Trip:
2.2 miles
Estimated Hiking Time:
1.75 hours

Pack a picnic in your backpack. You'll want to kick off your boots, lean back, and lounge in the beauty and serenity of the natural arch. Stick your hot feet in the cool creek and stay a while!

Caution: The trail approaches sheer drop-offs in several spots.

Note: A loop trail is scheduled to be completed in early 2009. An extension of this linear trail will begin at the arch, take you westward on the north side of the creek, and connect at point [2], creating a loop of approximately 2.5 miles in length. See an updated map for the trail route.

Trail Directions: Park in the lot for the area. The trail begins [1] in the northeast corner of the lot at an information sign and quickly takes you into a mature hardwood forest. Notice the three distinct layers. Tall oaks and hickories form the tallest canopy. Flowering dogwood, serviceberry, and other small trees make up the subcanopy, and wildflowers, ferns, lichens, and other plants form the ground layer.

At .07 mi. [2], where the trail makes a sharp turn to the right, Clifty Hollow opens on your left, with views of several distant wooded ridges. Continue in an open, pleasant woods. Elephant-ear-like leaves of prairie dock and a splash of sunshine welcome you to the first miniglade at .26 mi. [3]. You get your first

views of Clifty Creek here, too. Look for the fine, lacy leaves of prairie clover and the ashy gray-green leaves of leadplant here, along with lots of bluestem grass. You hike through several more of these blufftop pocket glades as you continue.

At .33 mi. [4], you reach the bottom of the hollow and have a fine look at the first of Clifty Creek's many bluffs, or "clifts," on the opposite bank. Cutting 200 feet down through this valley, Clifty Creek seems to have left more bluffs than most streams its size. Notice the cavelike undercuts in the bluff carved by the creek and lots of time. A small riffle is followed by a calm, clear pool as you hike next to a rock outcrop adorned with hydrangea and ferns.

The trail continues in a rocky area as you cross two small drainages and navigate two switchbacks. Notice the maidenhair ferns in the second drainage at .45 mi. [5]. As you go, enjoy the beautiful assembly of leaf shapes and patterns next to the trail. Ladder-like false Solomon's seal climbs out of a carpet of tick trefoil, and palm-shaped leaves of Virginia creeper (below) and pawpaw (at eye level) add their tropical flair. Just after passing through a small glade with a 60-foot drop-off nearby, you hike on a flat shelf at .80 mi. [6]. The creek floodplain is far below on your left, and a row of bluffs is above on your right.

After descending to creek level, you may be surprised when the natural arch pops up in front of you at 1.1 mi. [7]. The beautifully sculpted arch and the remarkably clear water all around create a tranquil scene. Observe the tiny drama of the fish, frogs, tadpoles, and water striders in the calm pool before retracing your steps to the trailhead.

- Enjoy spectacular views of the Osage River Valley from two observation decks.
- Look for cormorants, wood ducks, and other water birds on the river; watch for bald eagles, osprey, and turkey vultures soaring overhead.
- Take an early morning hike in April or May and hear wild turkey gobblers on surrounding ridges.
- Stand next to a living 600-year-old eastern red cedar tree.

Area Information

It would be a good guess that Painted Rock Conservation Area gets its name from the bright green lichens and mosses that "paint" the many chert, sandstone, and dolomite boulders along the trail and in the forest. But the name more likely comes from the pictographs placed high on the bluff above the Osage River by Native Americans ages ago. The pictographs, one of them a bison, were used as landmarks by early traders and river travelers. The river-bluff paintings (not accessible by the trail) probably were made between AD 1200 and 1300, but the lands of Painted Rock show evidence of human occupation as early as 9,000 years ago.

Painted Rock Conservation Area consists of 1,480 acres and is bordered on the west by the Osage River. The area features an oak-hickory forest, vertical river bluffs, a scenic hiking trail, several glades, small fishless ponds (for amphibians and other wildlife), and two overlook decks. A 5-acre fishing lake is located down a gravel road 1.3 miles south on Highway 133 from the scenic trail road. The Missouri Department of Conservation owns the area and manages it for timber harvest, wildlife, outdoor recreation, and natural community restoration. The area supports hiking, primitive camping, horseback riding, bicycling, hunting, fishing, and bird-watching.

Directions: From Jefferson City, take Highway 50 east 10 miles. Take Highway 63 south 3 miles. Turn right on Highway 133 (south) and go 6.7 miles. Turn right on a gravel road at a sign for the area. The road dead-ends at the parking lot for the Osage Bluff Scenic Trail.

Hours Open: The area is open year-round from 4:00 a.m. to 10:00 p.m.

Facilities: Several primitive campsites are accessible from three gravel roads and access trails. There are restrooms at Painted Rock Lake.

Permits and Rules: Primitive camping is allowed on designated sites only. No pets are allowed on the scenic trail.

For Further Information: Missouri Department of Conservation, 1315 E. Main, Linn, MO 65051; 573-897-3797.

Other Areas of Interest

Runge Conservation Nature Center offers five hiking trails through a variety of restored natural communities—prairie, savanna, forest, marsh, and glade. Get a good view of the area from atop a fire tower on the Raccoon Run Trail. Inside is a 3,400-gallon aquarium, a wildlife viewing area, a library, hands-on exhibits, and interpretive programs about the fish, forests, and wildlife of Missouri. The nature center is open seven days a week, and is .25 mile north of Highway 50 on Highway 179 in Jefferson City. For more information, call 573-526-5544.

Binder Park contains 644 acres and has a fishing lake, a boat ramp, three fishing jetties accessible to people in wheelchairs, hiking and biking trails, a campground, a waterfowl viewing blind, several picnic areas, a concession stand, and playgrounds. Take Highway 50 west from Jefferson City and take the Apache Flats exit. Turn right on Binder Road, go .5 mile to Rainbow Drive, and turn left. Go .25 mile. The entrance gate is on the right. For more information, call 573-634-6482.

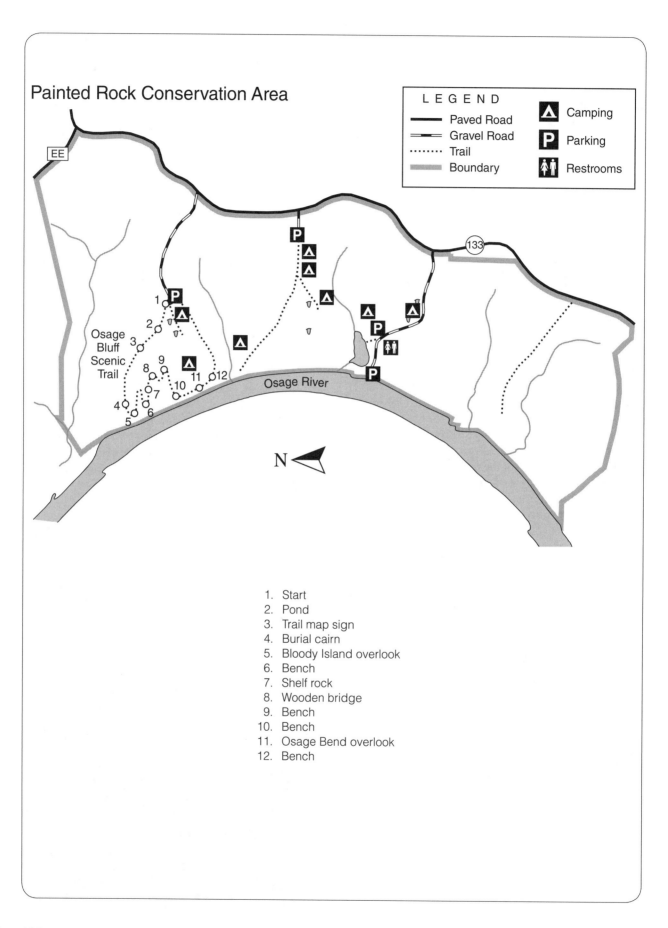

Painted Rock Conservation Area

L E G E N D

— Paved Road
Gravel Road
..... Trail
Boundary

△ Camping
P Parking
🚻 Restrooms

EE

133

Osage Bluff Scenic Trail

1
2
3
4
5
6
7
8
9
10
11
12

Osage River

N

1. Start
2. Pond
3. Trail map sign
4. Burial cairn
5. Bloody Island overlook
6. Bench
7. Shelf rock
8. Wooden bridge
9. Bench
10. Bench
11. Osage Bend overlook
12. Bench

Osage Bluff Scenic Trail

Distance Round-Trip:
1.6 miles
Estimated Hiking Time:
1.25 hours

To stand quietly next to a prehistoric blufftop burial mound, to be in the presence of trees that were living when the Ancient Ones were here, and to hear the strange call of the pileated woodpecker projects me to a different era. Old and twisted post oaks with gnarled, low-lying branches loom over gray boulders that are over 400 million years old yet are covered with vibrant green lichens and mosses. This is the land of the ancient—yet it is now, and living.

Caution: Sections of the trail lie next to 140-foot cliffs.

Trail Directions: Park in the lot for the trail, where a trail booklet may be available. Begin in the northwest corner of the lot **[1]**. In spring you may hear the high-pitched "peep, peep" of the spring peeper frog, or the call of the chorus frog, which sounds like a thumbnail run along a comb. These frogs breed in the small pond at .04 mi. **[2]** found on the left side of the trail. At .10 mi. **[3]**, you pass a trail map sign. Soon, you may get the feeling that something out of the ordinary is coming up. It was here, at the highest elevations on the bluffs, where prehistoric peoples chose to bury their dead. At .45 mi., take a moment to notice the remnants of an ancient burial cairn **[4]**. The Osage Indians, for whom the river is named, moved into the area around AD 1400, but evidence points to the probability that the cairn was here long before they came.

After a few steps, you walk out onto the Bloody Island overlook deck at .47 mi. **[5]** for a dramatic and splendid panorama of the Osage River Valley. The Osage River, which originates in Kansas and empties into the Missouri River only a few miles from here, is the state's third largest. Bloody Island is just to the north of the overlook. Legends of buried treasure on the island are numerous, and range from stories about a hidden Civil War army payroll to tales of a buried Spanish dowry.

From here, the trail narrows and becomes rocky. If you walked with people side by side on the trail before, you will probably have to walk single file now. After passing a bench at .65 mi. **[6]**, you hike downhill to find a shelf rock outcrop at .73 mi. **[7]**, where three types of rock are visible and are weathering at different rates. Notice that the softer dolomite base rock is eroding faster than the more resistant chert and sandstone layers on top of it. Eventually, dolomite undercutting causes the top two layers to collapse. Cross the wooden bridge at .78 mi. over Cove Creek **[8]**, a small, intermittent tributary to the Osage, and start hiking uphill. You pass a bench at .89 mi. **[9]**. As you hike up the next hill, notice the brushier appearance caused by the multitude of young sugar maple trees. Maples favor north-facing slopes, and can shade out oak forests unless the maples are thinned or treated by prescribed fire. At 1.09 mi. **[10]**, you are treated to a bench and more spectacular views of the Osage River Valley. At the Osage Bend overlook deck at 1.2 mi. **[11]**, look for soaring bald eagles, ospreys, and turkey vultures. Notice that the rocky cliff face offers little soil for plants and trees, yet some adapt and survive. The twisted eastern red cedar living here next to the deck on the river side, for example, has clung to cracks in the cliff face for over 600 years. Soak up your last views of the river at the bench at 1.29 mi. **[12]** before hiking back to the parking lot.

- See remnants and features that tell stories of the park's rich cultural history.

- Hike next to the natural tunnel of a 63-foot-tall rock bridge, the remnant of an ancient cave passage, now collapsed.

- See a potpourri of karst features—a natural bridge, a cave entrance, a karst window, sinkholes, a pirated stream, and a collapsed cave chasm—all on one short trail.

Area Information

People have always been attracted to remarkable geologic features like the rock bridge at Rock Bridge Memorial State Park. A small town known as Rockbridge Mills had sprung up near the bridge by the early 1800s. Over time, it included a gristmill, paper mill, blacksmith shop, general store, post office, and whiskey distillery. Although the settlement is no longer here, the geologic features continue to attract and intrigue visitors.

After your hikes, you can visit the Pierpont general store, just 1 mile south of here. Still featuring a wooden plank floor and still selling ice cream and soda, the store originally stood near the rock bridge but was moved after a fire in 1907.

Although the rock bridge is the centerpiece of the park, it is only a small remnant of something larger though much less obvious—Devil's Icebox Cave. Although perforated with sinkholes and partly destroyed by erosion, Devil's Icebox is still a living cave and, with over 6 miles of mapped passage, it is Missouri's seventh longest. The rock bridge and cave are part of a vast and ancient system of limestone, underground streams, air-filled passages, and surface

drainage—a landscape known as karst topography. Come and explore!

Directions: The park is 5 miles south of downtown Columbia on Highway 163.

Hours Open: The park is open year-round from dawn until dusk.

Facilities: Picnic areas and playgrounds are near the park office. The site also offers bicycling, horseback riding, orienteering, and fishing. Tours of Devil's Icebox Cave are given by reservation only for a fee. Connor's Cave, which shares the same entrance as Devil's Icebox Cave, is open to the public year-round. No guide or fee is required.

Permits and Rules: Bicycling is allowed on most trails, but cyclists must heed the open or closed signs along the two main entrance roads to the park. The Trail Condition Hotline (573-442-2249) informs riders when the trails are temporarily closed because of wet conditions. Bicycling is never allowed in the Gan's Creek Wild Area. Horseback riding is permitted only in the wild area from June 1 through October 31. Trail condition rules also apply to equestrians. No rock climbing, rappelling, or ATV use is permitted. Entry to Devil's Icebox Cave is prohibited except to those participating in park-led tours. All pets must be leashed. Bicyclists must wear helmets.

For Further Information: Rock Bridge Memorial State Park, 5901 South Highway 163, Columbia, MO 65203; 573-449-7402.

Park Trails

Karst Trail (🥾🥾, 1.75 miles). The dozens of sinkholes seen from this trail are visible proof that this land (called a sinkhole plain) is resting on the roof of the Devil's Icebox Cave system. The trailhead is on Fox Lane, just .5 mile east of the Pierpont store.

Deer Run Trail (🥾🥾🥾, 3 miles). This trail takes you up and down wooded hills and along the banks of the Little Bonne Femme Creek. The trailhead is at the end of the picnic loop with the playground.

High Ridge Trail (🥾🥾🥾, 1.75 miles). The trail takes you alongside Clear Creek and onto an open hilltop with rolling, grassy slopes and great views of surrounding wooded hills. The trailhead is on Rock Quarry Road, .1 mile north of the driveway to the Devil's Icebox parking lot.

Grassland Trail (🥾, 2 miles). Like the Karst and High Ridge trails, this trail goes through areas being restored to native grassland by selective cutting and burning. The trailhead is on Rock Bridge Lane, .8 mile south of the driveway to the Devil's Icebox parking lot.

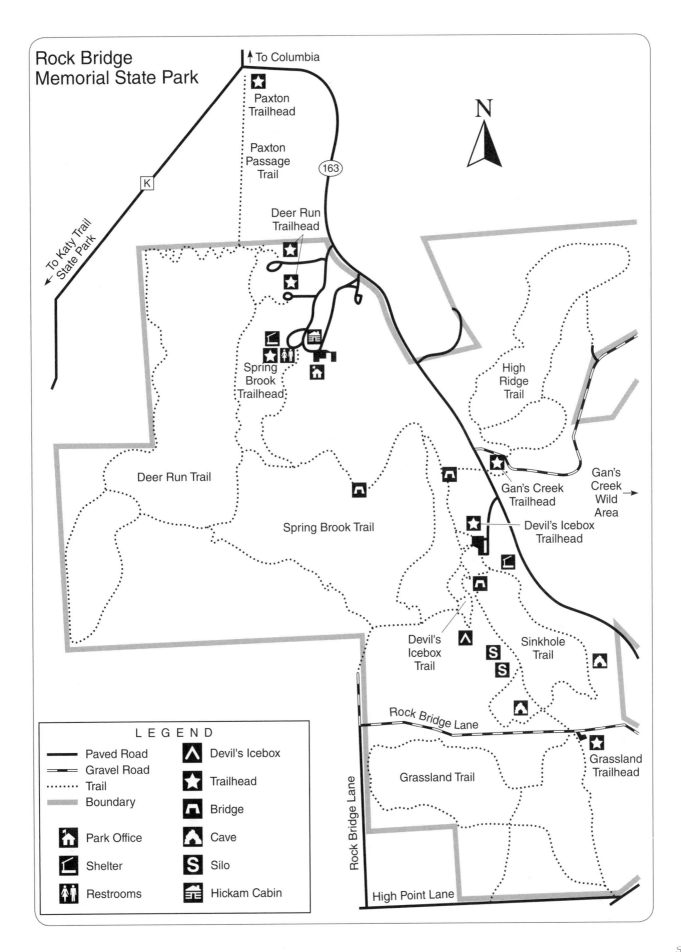

Rock Bridge Memorial State Park

↑ To Columbia

★ Paxton Trailhead

Paxton Passage Trail

(163)

K

To Katy Trail State Park

N

Deer Run Trailhead

★
★

High Ridge Trail

Spring Brook Trailhead

Deer Run Trail

Spring Brook Trail

★ Gan's Creek Trailhead

Gan's Creek Wild Area →

★ Devil's Icebox Trailhead

Devil's Icebox Trail

Sinkhole Trail

S
S

Rock Bridge Lane

★ Grassland Trailhead

Grassland Trail

Rock Bridge Lane

High Point Lane

LEGEND

— Paved Road		⋏	Devil's Icebox
Gravel Road		★	Trailhead
Trail		🌉	Bridge
Boundary		⌂	Cave
🏠 Park Office		S	Silo
Shelter			Hickam Cabin
Restrooms			

Devil's Icebox Trail

 Distance Round-Trip: .75 mile
Estimated Hiking Time: 45 minutes

As if looking down into a sinkhole to view an underground river wasn't bizarre enough, I then found that this cave stream is home to a pink planarian, a type of flatworm. Found nowhere else in the world, the pink planarian reproduces by splitting itself right down the middle!

Caution: The steps to the cave entrance may be slippery due to rain, ice, or snow.

Trail Directions: Park in the lot for the Devil's Icebox trailhead (1 mi. north of Route N on Highway 163) and begin the trail at the interpretive signs **[1]** at the west end of the lot. Near the trailhead, you cross a pair of wooden bridges over Rock Bridge Creek. Blue-eyed mary and wild sweet william color the streamside, and hackberry, box elder, and Ohio buckeye trees shade the trail. Turn left at .04 mi. **[2]** at the intersection with the Spring Brook Trail. Just after crossing a third bridge, turn left at the intersection at .06 mi. **[3]**. As you hike toward the rock bridge, notice the rock wall on your right. Rock was quarried from this site in the early 1800s and was used for foundations and for a dam under the rock bridge. Performers and politicians used this flat platform as a stage. Columbine now graces the vertical limestone walls. A sign describes the rock bridge at .10 mi. **[4]** and the gristmill and distillery that once stood on this spot. Return to **[3]** and turn left, up the steps, to continue. Turn right on

the boardwalk at .18 mi. **[5]**. Turn right at .22 mi. **[6]** to descend some wooden steps and then some stone steps. At the bottom of the stone steps, turn left at .26 mi. **[7]** for an overlook of Rock Bridge Creek. Look upstream to see the steep sides of the canyon that were once part of a cave passage. The rock bridge is the portion of the cavern's roof that did not collapse. Return to **[7]** and go straight up some wooden steps to continue.

Enjoy another overlook of the stream at .32 mi. **[8]** and turn right to continue. At .35 mi. **[9]** you see a sinkhole on the right, which drains to Connor's Cave, just below it. The Devil's Icebox overlook at .39 mi. **[10]** puts you on top of another portion of the cave roof still intact. The sinkhole to your left, lined with lush mosses and ferns, is the only known entrance to Devil's Icebox Cave. The sinkhole on your right, called a karst window, offers a glimpse of the cave stream that has already traveled 7 mi. underground. Nearby, the stream returns to the surface before flowing under the rock bridge. Descend the steps to your left. If you are here on a warm day, you will suddenly realize the reason for the name of this sinkhole. Here are two cave entrances: The Devil's Icebox Cave, on the right, requires reservations and a guide for entry. Connor's Cave, on the left, is open year-round, and no guide or fee is required. Ascend the steps and take the boardwalk on your right to continue. At .48 mi. **[11]**, go straight at the intersection with the Sinkhole Trail. After passing another overlook on your left, turn right on the boardwalk at **[6]** to return to the trailhead.

1. Start
2. Left turn
3. Left turn
4. Rock bridge
5. Right turn
6. Right turn
7. Left turn
8. Overlook
9. Sinkhole
10. Devil's Icebox overlook
11. Go straight

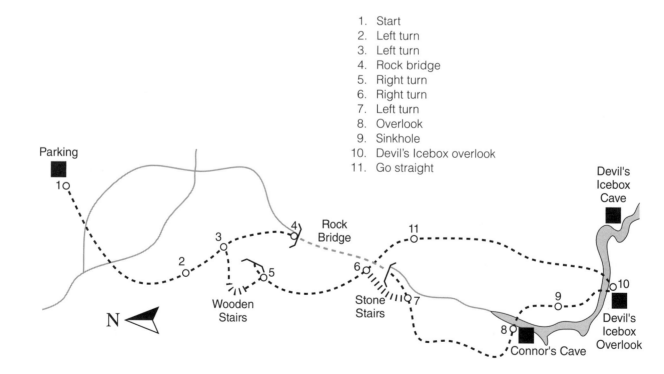

Spring Brook Trail

 Distance Round-Trip: 2.5 miles
Estimated Hiking Time: 1.5 hours

Being caught in a sudden rain shower in the woods isn't so bad. Gray tree frogs start up their musical trills, the aroma of nature's greenhouse rises to your nostrils, and wet-weather waterfalls contribute their splashing, short-lived music.

Caution: A friendly, shallow, and refreshing wade is scheduled just before the 2 mi. mark. Do not attempt this river crossing during periods of high water. Also, watch out for bicyclists.

Trail Directions: Park at the Gilbert picnic shelter near the park office and begin the trail [1] near the restrooms. Go straight at the intersection at .02 mi. [2]. Pass a frightful honey locust tree on your right and continue through a thicket of cedars and brush. Turn left at the intersection at .35 mi. [3]. Soon you descend to a flat bottomland of the Little Bonne Femme Creek, where the massive trunks of cotton-woods and sycamores erupt from the carpet of lush floodplain plants.

Enjoy a scenic view of the winding creek from the bridge at .55 mi. [4]. You pass a wet-weather waterfall at .61 mi. [5], nestled in a limestone outcrop on your right. Turn left just after you pass a bench at .80 mi. [6]. Jack-in-the-pulpit, as well as ginger, bloodroot, and wild geranium, adorns the rich slope on your right. Cross a wooden bridge at .97 mi. [7] and turn right. Cross a smaller bridge and go straight at the spur at 1.09 mi. [8]. Soon you reach the parking lot for the Devil's Icebox Trail [9].

Begin the Devil's Icebox Trail, crossing the pair of wooden bridges. Turn right on the wide, rocky path at 1.21 mi. [10]. The trail passes a variety of senior trees, some of which may have been here when this trail was a road in the 19th century. The trail travels alongside the boardwalk of the Devil's Icebox Trail for a short distance before veering off to the right. Go straight at the intersection at 1.35 mi. [11] and turn right at 1.46 mi. [12]. You pass through an old field with grassy openings. The thickets of blackberries, roses, and gooseberries indicate that this area was probably once grazed; the plants that survived were the thorny ones that the cows passed over.

At a zigzag in the trail at 1.69 mi. [13] is a grove of persimmon trees. Look for tall, thin-trunked trees with knobby bark. In fall, these trees produce a delectable fruit with such flavor that entire cookbooks have been written about them. Although it looks like poison ivy, the shrub at the base of these trees is fragrant sumac, a plant that announces autumn by turning shades of yellow, deep violet, and scarlet. Turn left at the intersection at 1.74 mi. [14]. Cross a small stream and turn right at 1.89 mi. [15], just after passing giant red oak and sycamore trees on your right. Now it's time for a little wade! Normally, the water here is only a few inches deep, and you might even find enough dry stepping-stones to cross the river [16] (1.90 mi.) without getting wet. Turn right when you get to the other side. Go straight at several spur intersections here. Turn right at 2.10 mi. [17] just after crossing a small stream and turn left when you return to [3] to finish your hike.

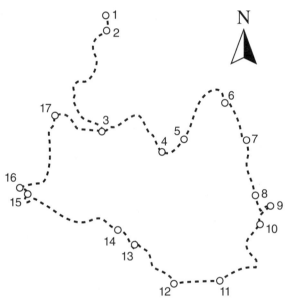

1. Start
2. Go straight
3. Left turn
4. Bridge
5. Wet-weather waterfall
6. Left turn
7. Right turn
8. Go straight
9. Devil's Icebox trailhead
10. Right turn
11. Go straight
12. Right turn
13. Persimmon grove
14. Left turn
15. Right turn
16. River crossing (wet)
17. Right turn

Sinkhole Trail

Distance Round-Trip: 1.6 miles
Estimated Hiking Time: 1 hour

A sinkhole is a depression or hole in the surface caused by the removal of rock or soil beneath it. Sinkholes may form gradually, as when water dissolves underlying bedrock, or they may form suddenly, as when the cave roof below collapses. Could a sinkhole fall into a sinkhole?

Trail Directions: Park in the lot for the Devil's Icebox and start the trail at the south end of the lot **[1]**. Go straight at the intersection at .04 mi. **[2]**. The foundation on the rock outcrop on your left is a remnant of the thriving industry of the Rockbridge Mills area, which began in 1822. Soon, you pass a picnic shelter on your left. The trail parallels an intermittent stream for a while. Just before the trail crosses the stream and goes uphill, take the small spur on your left at .45 mi. **[3]** that goes up the ravine to Polly's Pot Cave. On your way, notice the musclewood (American hornbeam) trees—small, smooth-barked trees so named for the long ridges under their bark that resemble veins or muscles under skin. At .51 mi. **[4]**, you reach the small, gated entrance to Polly's Pot Cave, which is named for one of the landowners in the area, who found the cave while gathering greens. After returning to the main trail, turn left to continue.

As you climb the hill, the trail passes over several areas of exposed bedrock. In one of these flat rocks at .68 mi. **[5]**, look for a single, long rut about 3 inches wide. This track was made by the wheels of countless wagons which traversed this trail when it was a road, hauling corn, whiskey, and supplies to and from Rockbridge Mills. At a bench at .72 mi. **[6]**, the trail swings to the right. At .76 mi. **[7]**, you hike near the first of many sinkholes along the trail.

At .93 mi. **[8]**, go straight (bear slightly to the left) at this intersection with the white connector. At .97 mi. **[9]**, take the short spur to the left to view the entrance to Hog's Graveyard Cave. To make use of the corn mash left over from whiskey production, the Rockbridge distillery owner added a major hog operation. This cave was a convenient place to dump hog waste and carcasses. Return to the main trail and turn left to continue. The sinkholes are larger and more numerous here, and the trail turns and swerves to dodge them. Soon you enter an old field. The brushier, thornier vegetation is what grew up after the area was used

as a pasture or barnyard. A silo at 1.19 mi. **[10]** and a small stock pond testify to the earlier agricultural use of the land. Turn left at the intersection with the white connector at 1.23 mi. **[11]**. A second, larger silo looms at 1.27 mi. **[12]**, looking strangely out of place in this now wooded setting. These silos are thought to have been built between the 1920s and 1940s.

Bear right at the fork in the trail at 1.51 mi. **[13]**. With the boardwalk of the Devil's Icebox Trail in view on your left, turn right at the intersection at 1.59 mi. **[14]**. Turn right again when you reach the stream at 1.70 mi. **[15]**. Turn left at the intersection **[2]** to return to the parking lot.

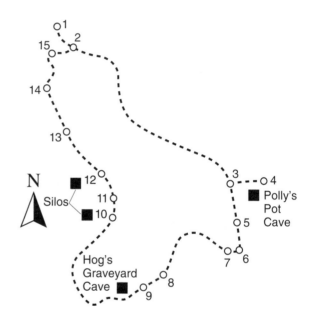

1. Start
2. Go straight
3. Spur to Polly's Pot Cave
4. Polly's Pot Cave
5. Wagon wheel track
6. Bench
7. Sinkhole
8. Go straight
9. Hog's Graveyard Cave
10. Silo
11. Left turn
12. Silo
13. Bear right
14. Right turn
15. Right turn

57. Lake of the Ozarks State Park

- Visit Missouri's largest state park, explore its 17,441 acres, and discover its stunning array of opportunities for outdoor recreation, education, exercise, and relaxation.

- With a naturalist as a guide and handheld lanterns to light the way, explore the subterranean beauty of Ozark Caverns.

- Hike the Coakley Hollow Trail, with a boardwalk over a cold, seepy fen and two swinging bridges over spring-fed streams.

Area Information

Lake of the Ozarks was formed in 1931 when the Union Electric Company of St. Louis dammed the state's third largest river, the Osage, to create a hydroelectric reservoir of 55,342 surface acres and 1,150 miles of shoreline. Two years later, as part of President Roosevelt's New Deal programs, a system of National Recreation Demonstration Areas was developed to convert poor farmland into outdoor recreation areas that could later be transferred to the states. Eighty-five miles of shoreline of the Grand Glaize Creek was identified as a park site, the land was transferred to the federal government, and Lake of the Ozarks was born.

The National Park Service originally managed Lake of the Ozarks. In the 1930s the CCC built six group camps, log cabins, and stone bridges in the park. Most of this work appears on the National Register of Historic Places. The site was turned over to the state in 1946.

Although opportunities for water-based recreation abound at Lake of the Ozarks, the natural attractions of the park include a major cave and a variety of hiking trails. In an urbanized hubbub of shopping, lodging, amusements, and entertainment that encompasses the rest of the lake area, the state's largest park is an oasis of natural beauty.

Directions: The main entrance to the park is at the north end, off Highway 54. From Osage Beach, take Highway 42 east for 3.6 miles. Turn right on Highway 134 and go .5 mile to the park office.

Hours Open: The park is open from dawn to dusk year-round. The park office is open from 8:00 a.m. to 4:00 p.m. Monday through Friday. The visitor center is open and tours of Ozark Caverns are given from mid-April through mid-October. Call ahead for hours and tour times, which are variable.

Facilities: The park offers swimming beaches with bathhouses, boat ramps, a marina with boat rentals, picnic areas, a campground, group camps, a camper's store, primitive rental cabins, tours of Ozark Caverns,

a visitor center, a trail center, stables with horses for rent, an amphitheater, and an airport. Fishing, swimming, boating, and skiing are available on the lake.

Permits and Rules: Bicycles are restricted to paved roads and to the Trail of Four Winds. Horses are restricted to the Trail of Four Winds and Squaw's Revenge Trail. Backpack camping is allowed on the Woodland Trail, but campfires are prohibited there. Pets must always be leashed. Alcoholic beverages are prohibited on swimming beaches and parking areas.

For Further Information: Lake of the Ozarks State Park, P.O. Box 170, Kaiser, MO 65047; 573-348-2694 (park office) or 573-346-2500 (Ozark Caverns).

Park Trails

Woodland Trail (🥾🥾🥾, 6 miles). This hiking and backpacking trail features the diverse habitats of Patterson Hollow Wild Area. The trail begins at the trail center, located .5 mile south of the park office.

Trail of Four Winds (🥾🥾🥾, 16.5 miles). Open to hikers, bicyclists, and horse riders, this trail features a scenic overlook of a wooded valley and unusual rock formations. The trailhead is on the west side of the main park road, 2 miles from the entrance.

Fawn's Ridge Trail (🥾🥾, 2.5 miles). This trail begins across the road from the picnic area near the stables. The first .5 mile is wheelchair accessible.

Aquatic Trail. This unique, self-guiding trail for boaters interprets 14 natural features along a lake shoreline marked by buoys. Booklets are available at the park office.

Bluestem Knoll Trail (🥾🥾, .75 mile). See tall native grasses and scattered trees on this loop trail through a savanna that is undergoing restoration. The trail begins .10 mile north of the trail information center.

Squaw's Revenge Trail (🥾🥾🥾, 2 miles). Used for regularly scheduled horseback rides, this trail begins behind the stables and winds through forested hills and onto blufftops above the lake.

Lake View Bend Trail (🥾🥾🥾, 1.5 miles). This trail begins at the campground gatehouse and connects the amphitheater, beach, and campgrounds 3 and 4.

Honey Run Trail (🥾🥾🥾, 2.5 miles). Hike along dry forested slopes and into Honey Run Valley in this more remote part of the park. The trail begins just north of the service area between Ozark Caverns and McCubbins Point.

Shady Ridge Trail (🥾🥾🥾, 1 mile). This trail winds along a secluded cove of the lake at the Grand Glaize Beach area. The trailhead is at the boat launch.

Lake Trail (🥾, 1 mile). This trail is near the Outpost camper cabins and loops between the gravel road and a lake cove shoreline.

205   South Central

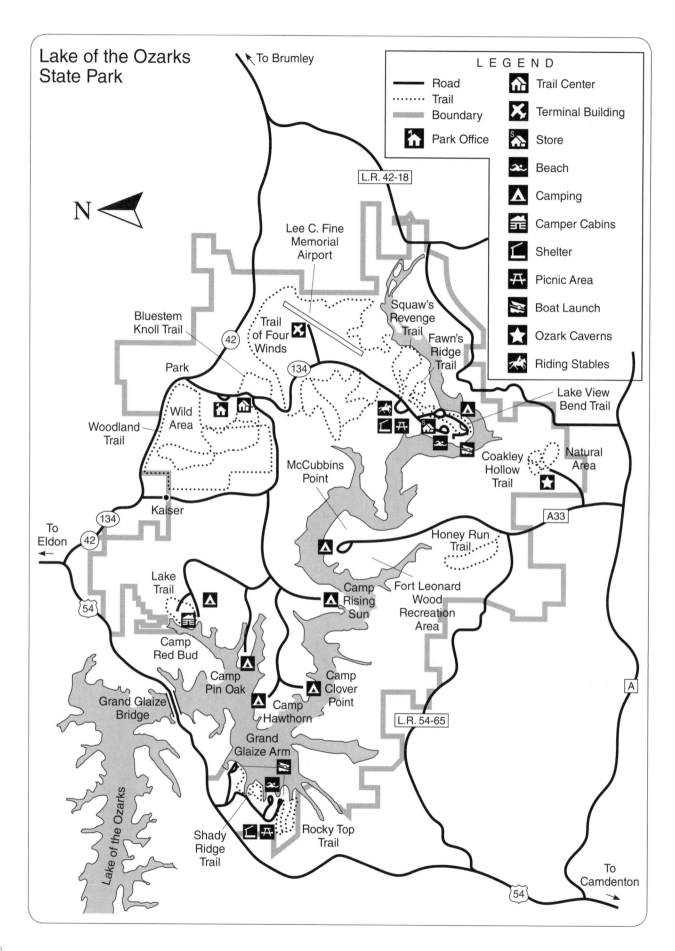

Lake of the Ozarks State Park

↑ To Brumley

LEGEND

- —— Road
- ······ Trail
- ▬▬ Boundary
- 🏠 Park Office
- 🏠 Trail Center
- ✖ Terminal Building
- Ⓢ Store
- 🏊 Beach
- ⛺ Camping
- 🏕 Camper Cabins
- 🏠 Shelter
- ⛱ Picnic Area
- 🚤 Boat Launch
- ★ Ozark Caverns
- 🏇 Riding Stables

L.R. 42-18

Lee C. Fine Memorial Airport

Bluestem Knoll Trail

Trail of Four Winds

42

134

Squaw's Revenge Trail

Fawn's Ridge Trail

Park

Wild Area

Woodland Trail

Lake View Bend Trail

Natural Area

Coakley Hollow Trail

McCubbins Point

A33

Kaiser

134

To Eldon

42

54

Honey Run Trail

Fort Leonard Wood Recreation Area

Lake Trail

Camp Red Bud

Camp Rising Sun

Camp Pin Oak

Camp Hawthorn

Camp Clover Point

Grand Glaize Bridge

Grand Glaize Arm

L.R. 54-65

A

Shady Ridge Trail

Rocky Top Trail

Lake of the Ozarks

To Camdenton

54

Rocky Top Trail

   Distance Round-Trip: 3 miles
Estimated Hiking Time: 1.5 hours

When I stepped out from beneath the stunted post oaks onto the Rocky Top Glade, I was reminded that glade comes from an Old English word meaning "bright" or "cheerful." Glades have a way of surprising you. As you walk onto them, the temperature goes up, and your spirits will, too.

Caution: Use caution at the edges of the bluff, which is a veritable cliff.

Trail Directions: This trail is at Grand Glaize Beach, on the west side of the park. From the main entrance to the park, at the north end, take Highway 42 west to return to Osage Beach. From here, take Highway 54 west 4.5 mi., turn left at the sign for Grand Glaize Beach, and follow the signs to the picnic shelter. The trail begins across the road from the picnic shelter.

Begin at the signboard **[1]**. Fill out a registration card at the trailhead before you begin. The trail ascends some craggy dolomite rocks before taking you to a small glade at .04 mi. **[2]**. Note the thick bluestem grasses, brilliant yellow coneflowers, and the lacy leaves of purple prairie clover . . . but this is only the beginning. Walk through the shade of several gnarly post oaks and emerge onto the trail's namesake—an expansive and impressive glade at .08 mi. **[3]**. Think of the sun scorching the trees right off the top of this ridge, leaving only the thin soil and ridges of dolomite rock. With the trees gone, plants that have adapted to these hot and dry conditions flourish, and Missouri glades are known for their magnificent displays of wildflowers. Step onto the glade and feel the temperature go up. Watch for six-lined racerunners and other lizards zipping in front of you as the trail takes you through this miniature, rocky "desert."

Next, you pass through a savanna landscape, a grassland with interspersed trees. Look for rattlesnake master at .48 mi. **[4]**, an erect plant with ball-shaped flower heads and bluish spear-shaped leaves with bristles along their edges. The plant was once purported to be a treatment for snakebite, and its species name, *yuccifolium*, means "with the leaves of a yucca." At .65 mi. **[5]**, turn right, following the sign for the second loop. After crossing an intermittent stream, turn right again at the intersection at .74 mi. **[6]**. You now enter a dry dolomite forest, with white oak and chinquapin oaks shading hillsides covered with flowering dogwood and dolomite fragments.

At 1.48 mi. **[7]**, a spectacular view of the lake opens before you as you step to the edge of a towering bluff. Tiny boats move as if in slow motion, leaving white Vs behind them. Countless fingers of water reach into the shady draws of the forest in all directions. Hike among the scraggly dwarf hackberry trees and nodding gray-head coneflowers of a blufftop glade as the lake views continue all around the bluff edge. After you reenter the forest, you hike midslope in a scenic, open woods. On your right, a small cove of the lake tapers to a quiet, secluded point as you hike, affording chances to glimpse fishing herons in the shallows or sunning carp just below the surface.

Turn right when you return to an intersection **[6]**. After recrossing the stream, turn right when you return to another intersection **[5]**. You enter a savanna at 2.55 mi. **[8]**, actually a lower slope of Rocky Top Glade, above you on your left. The lake cove reappears on your right, as leadplant and elephant-ear-like prairie dock grow right down to the shoreline. As the trail swings to the left, at the edge of the water, turn left, uphill, on the wide, rocky trail at 2.94 mi. **[9]**, which returns you to the picnic shelter.

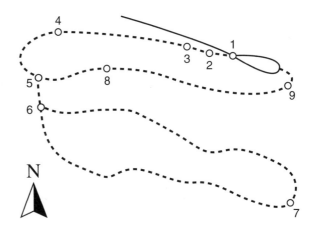

1. Start
2. Small glade
3. Big glade
4. Rattlesnake master
5. Right turn
6. Right turn
7. Lake overlook
8. Savanna
9. Left turn

Coakley Hollow Trail

 Distance Round-Trip: 1 mile
Estimated Hiking Time: 45 minutes

From spring-water streams to arid glades, from lush grasslands to a fen that hides glacial survivor species, this trail would be a winner, even without its two swinging bridges!

Caution: The gate to this part of the park is locked nightly, and closing times vary according to the season. Be sure to check the trailhead or the visitor center for the closing time before you begin the trail.

Trail Directions: The Coakley Hollow Trail begins near the Ozark Caverns visitor center, at the south end of the park. From the main entrance to the park, at the north end, take Highway 42 west to return to Osage Beach. From here, take Highway 54 west 10.8 mi. to Highway A. Turn east on Highway A, go 7.1 mi., and turn north at the sign for Ozark Caverns. Follow the signs for the caverns and find the visitor center 1.7 mi. north of Highway A. Park at the visitor center; the trailhead is just a few yards from the parking lot.

Before or after your hike, stop in at the visitor center, which is also the starting point for naturalist-led tours of Ozark Caverns. Coakley Hollow is an interpretive trail, and self-guiding trail booklets are available from the trailhead or the visitor center. Numbered stations on the trail do not correspond to numbered features in this book. Begin at the sign for the trail [1]. You'll feel the sway of the swinging bridge as you hear the trickle of the remarkably clear and picturesque stream below. Later, you can find the origin of this stream at Mill Spring, which is a short and pleasant hike off the park road, .15 mi. from the visitor center. Like the temperature of the air inside Ozark Caverns, the temperature of this water, when it emerges from the tiny cave opening at Mill Spring, is a nearly constant 55 degrees year-round.

Across the suspension bridge, the trail takes you on a side slope where lichen-covered chert boulders lie scattered between trunks of various types of oaks and hickories. Native Americans often used chert, or flint, to make arrowheads and tools because of its hardness and ability to form fine, sharp edges. Look underneath the boulders near the trail at .27 mi. [2] to discover the dens of groundhogs, skunks, or foxes. Christmas ferns and ebony spleenwort, two ferns that stay green all year long, soon line both sides of the trail.

Turn right on the wide, moss-covered path at .52 mi. [3] and turn left at .54 mi. [4], following yellow arrows. The steps at .56 mi. go over a seep [5], a wet area caused by water flowing over sheets of bedrock just under the surface of the soil. After crossing a

bridge under some pawpaw trees, you reach a second swinging bridge over a clear stream at .59 mi. [6]. After crossing the stream, you enter a savanna [7] (.60 mi.). Native grasses and wildflowers thrive here because of large openings in the forest canopy and the absence of an understory. In the middle of this savanna is a glade [8] (.64 mi.), a rocky, dry opening suitable only for plants and animals specially adapted to this sun-drenched microenvironment.

Turn left at .77 mi. [9] at the spur to the remnants of a dam. This pile of rock and earth is all that remains of a dam that channeled the stream to power a gristmill, built here in the 1870s by an Irish settler named Coakley. Turn left after returning to the main trail. At .92 mi. is a boardwalk over Coakley Hollow Fen [10]. An unusual type of wetland, fens are boglike areas kept saturated by groundwater that constantly seeps to the surface. To recognize and preserve the special natural community of plants that have adapted to these cool, saturated soils, this four-acre area was designated a state natural area in 1982. The music of a spring-fed stream accompanies you as the visitor center comes into view ahead.

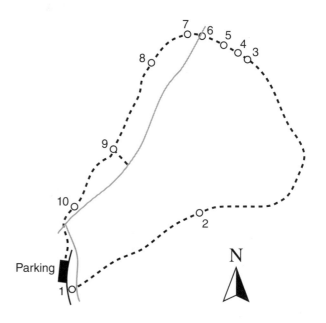

1. Start
2. Boulder shelters
3. Right turn
4. Left turn
5. Seep
6. Swinging bridge
7. Savanna
8. Glade
9. Spur to dam
10. Coakley Hollow Fen

- Bring your camera; you'll hike through seas of yellow coneflowers on one of the finest and largest glade–woodland mosaics in the state.
- Survey the world below from the castle ruins perched atop a 250-foot-high cliff.
- See Ha Ha Tonka Spring erupt from the base of a dolomite bluff and fill a surprisingly blue pool with 48 million gallons of water per day.

Area Information

Nowhere else in the state can you see so many different karst features in such a concentrated area as Ha Ha Tonka State Park. Surface streams cut their way through dolomite bedrock, intersecting and eventually collapsing an immense, ancient cavern system. This collapsed canyon includes sinkholes deep enough to trap cool air where glacial relicts, plants surviving from the last ice age, still thrive.

Ha Ha Tonka is located in a transition area between the prairie landscape farther west and the rugged forested hills to the east. The Ha Ha Tonka glade–woodland mosaic is just such a blend of rolling prairie and interspersed trees. For centuries, periodic fires shaped this landscape, and early settlers wrote about passing through these "oak orchards" with ease, their wagons and stock unencumbered by brush and thickets. Prescribed fires maintain this highly diverse community of native grasses and wildflowers, with sometimes as many as 200 species on a single acre.

Grandly situated on a bluff overlooking the spring and canyon are the ruins of a European-style stone castle. Native sandstone for the castle was quarried on site. A miniature railroad was constructed to haul the stone, worked by stonemasons from Scotland. No expenses were spared. But in 1906, one year after construction had begun, the castle's owner, Robert Snyder, was killed in an automobile accident. Although the elegant castle was eventually completed, it was gutted by a fire just 20 years later. All that remain today are the ruins, adding their intrigue to Ha Ha Tonka's already interesting landscape.

Directions: From Camdenton take Highway 54 west for 2.4 miles. Turn south on Highway D for 1.6 miles to the park's visitor center.

Hours Open: The park gates open at 8:00 a.m. from November through March, and at 7:00 a.m. from April through October. The gates are locked at sunset. The visitor center is open from 8:30 a.m. to 5:00 p.m. daily year-round.

Facilities: Many shady picnic sites are available, and the visitor center features outdoor exhibits. Two courtesy docks are in a cove of Lake of the Ozarks for visitors who arrive by boat, and fishing is available.

Permits and Rules: Cave entry in the park is allowed only by permit. Contact the park office for a permit at least one week before desired entry. Camping is allowed only on the Turkey Pen Hollow Trail by backpackers. Campfires are prohibited in the park. Swimming, fishing, or any access to the water is prohibited in the spring branch. Pets must always be leashed.

For Further Information: Ha Ha Tonka State Park, 1491 State Road D, Camdenton, MO 65020; 573-346-2986.

Park Trails

Castle Trail (🥾🥾, .5 mile). This trail leads to the castle's carriage house, some overlooks, and the castle ruins. It begins between the two parking lots for the castle ruins.

Quarry Trail (🥾🥾, 2 miles). This trail starts by the castle and leads to two old quarries.

Boulder Ridge Trail (🥾🥾, 1.5 miles). This little-used trail passes near large lichen-covered boulders and offers views of the lake. It begins at the parking lot for the lake cove.

Island Trail (🥾🥾🥾, .75 mile). See remnants of fallen caves, including a precarious block of dolomite known as Balanced Rock. The trail begins at the old mill site, on the Spring Trail.

Oak Savanna Interpretive Trail (🥾, 450 feet). This paved trail with four interpretive stops is accessible to those with disabilities. It begins at the Turkey Pen Hollow trailhead.

Devil's Kitchen Trail (🥾🥾🥾, 1 mile). Walk under a horseshoe-shaped cliff and see a cavern opening with a window in its roof. The trail begins at the Turkey Pen Hollow trailhead.

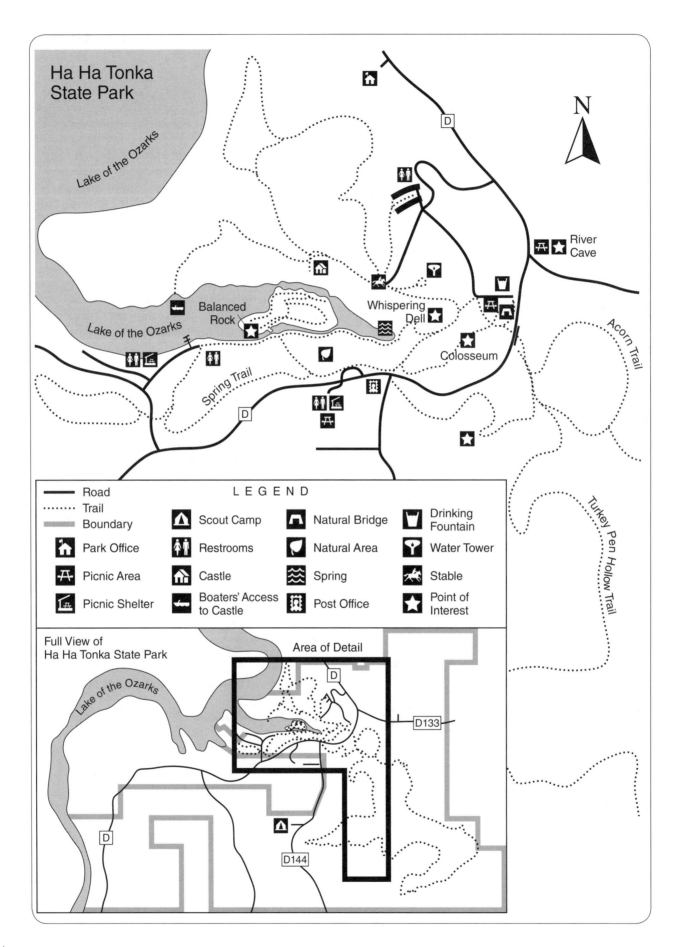

Ha Ha Tonka State Park

N

Lake of the Ozarks

River Cave

Balanced Rock

Lake of the Ozarks

Whispering Dell

Colosseum

Spring Trail

Acorn Trail

Turkey Pen Hollow Trail

D

LEGEND

—— Road			
······ Trail			
▬▬ Boundary			
Scout Camp	Natural Bridge	Drinking Fountain	
Park Office	Restrooms	Natural Area	Water Tower
Picnic Area	Castle	Spring	Stable
Picnic Shelter	Boaters' Access to Castle	Post Office	Point of Interest

Full View of Ha Ha Tonka State Park

Area of Detail

Lake of the Ozarks

D

D133

D

D144

Spring Trail

 Distance Round-Trip: 1.5 miles
Estimated Hiking Time: 1 hour

Laughter is a universal human reaction, crossing all generations and cultures. In the Osage language, Ha Ha Tonka means "laughing waters."

Caution: The boardwalk steps can be slippery when wet.

Trail Directions: Park in the lot across Highway D from the old post office. This trail offers several hiking options; you can shorten it by using a white connector trail or lengthen it by adding the .75 mi. Island Trail. The trailhead for the Island Trail is at the old mill site on the Spring Trail.

Begin at the descending steps at the north end of the lot **[1]** and turn left when you reach the bottom. Follow blue arrows on this trail. Turn left at the connector link at .07 mi. **[2]**. At .33 mi. **[3]**, the trail takes you onto an open, restored glade. Cedar stumps and fire scars are evidence of the park staff's efforts to remove thickets and restore this special community. Look for the large, lemon yellow flowers of the Missouri evening primrose, which opens in late afternoon and closes with the morning sun. Also look for coneflowers, Indian paintbrush, and snakes and lizards, scurrying away near the trail. Some scenic views soon open on your left.

Pass beneath large, tropical-looking pawpaw leaves after you return to the woods. A cove of Lake of the Ozarks will appear through the trees. You soon pass a parking lot for the lake and a dock to accommodate park visitors who arrive by boat. Turn right at .72 mi. **[4]** onto a paved trail that takes you along the lakeshore. At .87 mi. **[5]** is a picnic shelter and an old mill site where at least two gristmills stood. One mill burned in 1836, and another was destroyed in 1931 to make way for Lake of the Ozarks. A stone dam and millstone still remain. Here also is the trailhead for the Island Trail. Go straight at the connector at .88 mi. **[6]**.

Keep an eye on the shallow slack water on your left and look for aquatic turtles basking on logs, sunfish fanning out circular nests with their tails, and dragonflies hovering at intervals between their high-speed maneuvers. The unusually blue water of

the Ha Ha Tonka Spring pool soon comes into view at .98 mi. **[7]**. Look on top of the cliff on your left to see the castle ruins, which look imposing and mysterious from this angle.

Scramble through a fracture between some boulders at 1.13 mi. **[8]** that create a natural toll gate to the spring (no charge) and you'll find Ha Ha Tonka Spring, Missouri's 12th largest, at 1.16 mi. **[9]**. Until now you might have thought that the difficulty rating for this trail was in error. Alas, you now face 316 wooden steps that lift you 200 vertical feet in no time. Enjoy some breathtaking (if you have any breath left) views of the spring pool, cliff, castle ruins, and lake cove along the way. At 1.29 mi. **[10]** is an overlook over the Whispering Dell sink basin. Formed by the collapse of a cavern roof, it is so named because it contains remnants of caverns capable of transmitting slight sounds along their length. Turn right to continue. Turn right again at 1.38 mi. **[11]**, where the boardwalk ends. You come across three forks in the trail at 1.44 mi. **[12]**; bear right at each of them. Ascend the wooden steps on your left at the trailhead to finish your hike.

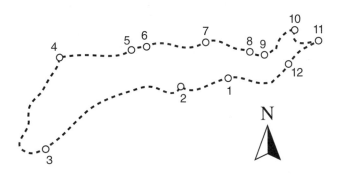

1. Start
2. Left turn
3. Restored glade
4. Right turn
5. Old mill site
6. Go straight
7. Spring pool
8. Natural toll gate
9. Ha Ha Tonka Spring
10. Whispering Dell overlook
11. Right turn
12. Three forks

Acorn Trail

 Distance Round-Trip: 1 mile
Estimated Hiking Time: 45 minutes

"The traveler in the interior is often surprised to behold at one view, cliffs and prairies, bottoms and barrens, naked hills, heavy forests, and rocks, and streams, and plains, all succeeding each other with rapidity and mingled with the most pleasing harmony." —Henry Rowe Schoolcraft, from Journal of a Tour into the Interior of Missouri and Arkansas in 1818 and 1819

Caution: Woodlands and glades are prime chigger and tick habitats. Try wearing long pants and duct-taping your pant legs around your hiking boots before spraying with insect repellent.

Trail Directions: Park in the lot east of Highway D between the parking lot for River Cave and the old post office. Begin the trail at the sign for Ha Ha Tonka Savanna Natural Area **[1]**. An interpretive brochure for this trail is available, although numbered stops in the brochure don't correspond to the numbers here. Hike this trail in May or June to see plenty of the park's signature wildflower, the yellow coneflower.

Bear right at the intersection with the Oak Savanna Interpretive Trail and turn left at .07 mi. **[2]**, where the Acorn Trail splits from the Turkey Pen Hollow Trail. Follow the green arrows for the Acorn Trail.

You are entering a beautiful landscape, though one of the most threatened ones in the state—a blend of glades and woodlands. The soil is thin and dry on the rocky glades, preventing trees from becoming large or numerous. The areas of interspersed trees surrounding the glades are called woodlands. Although the tree canopy can cover 50 percent or more in woodlands, little brush and few shrubs are present. Native grasses and wildflowers flourish in this open landscape.

At .20 mi. **[3]**, at signpost #2, notice several small oak trees with dark bark and small points at the tips of their leaves. These are blackjack oaks, one of the few trees that can withstand the hot, dry conditions of these glades and woodlands. Look on the horizon to your left for a good view of the Ha Ha Tonka water tower, built in the early 1900s to serve the castle compound. As you hike on the north-facing slope at .30 mi. **[4]**, notice that the trees are larger. North- and east-facing slopes hold more moisture because during the heat of the day the sun's angle is not as direct as it is on south- or west-facing slopes. More moisture means bigger trees, which build more soil, which holds more

moisture, and the cycle continues. The opposite cycle occurs on south- and west-facing slopes.

Go straight at the intersection with the Turkey Pen Hollow Trail at .60 mi. **[5]**. As you approach the south-facing slope, you return to a rocky glade landscape, complete with prairie clover, coneflower, prairie dock, Missouri evening primrose, and compass plant, which aligns its leaves to point north and south to reduce their direct exposure to the sun. Soon, you crest a hill, and a scenic landscape unfolds before you at .75 mi. **[6]**. This area has been actively managed since 1983 using prescribed fire. Natural community ecologists believe that these glades and woodlands closely resemble the presettlement landscape that Henry Rowe Schoolcraft and other early explorers wrote about in their journals. Interestingly, research shows that this type of open landscape with interspersed trees is the landscape most attractive to people worldwide.

Go straight at the intersection with the Turkey Pen Hollow Trail at .82 mi. **[7]** and go straight at .86 mi. **[8]** at the Devil's Kitchen Trail. Turn left at the intersection **[2]** to return to the trailhead.

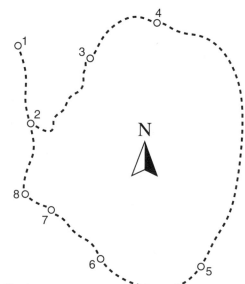

1. Start
2. Left turn
3. Blackjack oaks
4. North-facing slope
5. Go straight
6. Scenic landscape
7. Go straight
8. Go straight

Turkey Pen Hollow Trail

 Distance Round-Trip: 7 miles
Estimated Hiking Time: 4 hours

You'll enjoy the surprises on this trail—rocky glades splashed with wildflowers, sweeping vistas of woodlands and forests, and, next to a cool stream, an enchanting sandstone bluff covered with ferns.

Caution: Woodlands and glades are prime chigger and tick habitats. Try wearing long pants and duct-taping your pant legs around your hiking boots before spraying with insect repellent.

Trail Directions: Park in the lot east of Highway D between the parking lot for River Cave and the old post office. Begin the trail at the sign for Ha Ha Tonka Savanna Natural Area **[1]**. Follow the red arrows for the Turkey Pen Hollow Trail. (To shorten this trail to 5 mi., take the white connector at **[13]**.) Bear right at the trail's first fork. Go straight at .07 mi. **[2]** at the intersection with the Acorn Trail. Turn left at .12 mi. **[3]** at the intersection with the Devil's Kitchen Trail. Turn right at the intersection at .16 mi. **[4]**.

Soon, the picturesque woodland landscape opens before you. If you are here in May or June you'll walk through a sea of yellow coneflowers. Just after entering the woods, the trail skirts a sinkhole on your left at .28 mi. **[5]**. Near the 1 mi. mark, you are treated to a 180-degree panorama of scenic glades, woodlands, and distant forests **[6]**. If you feel something pulling on your sock, you may have discovered the sensitive brier, a creeping plant about ankle high that resembles a miniature mimosa tree. Touch the leaves and watch them slowly fold!

Turn left at 1.81 mi. **[7]** at the white spur. After crossing a small stream at 2.25 mi. **[8]**, you walk uphill onto a glade **[9]** (2.30 mi.). Situated on these south- and west-facing slopes, these thin, rocky soils are the hottest, driest parts of the woodland. Notice the stunted trees. Plants and animals must be specially adapted to thrive on these minideserts. After you cross another stream you come across a wet-weather spring in a jumble of rocks on your left **[10]** (2.52 mi.). After a zigzag in the trail, make left turns at both 3.08 and 3.11 mi. **[11]**. Turn left again at the intersection at 3.38 mi. **[12]**. Turn right at the intersection with the white connector at 3.49 mi. **[13]**.

Bear left at a fork in the trail at 3.66 mi. **[14]** and enter a forest. Notice the brushy subcanopy layer and the abundance of shade. After crossing a small stream twice, you find an interesting sandstone bluff at 4.69 mi. **[15]**. Go straight at the intersection with the backpack camp spur at 5.14 mi. **[16]** and go straight at the white connector at 5.66 mi. **[17]**.

Panoramic views open down the valleys on your left. Turn right at the intersection at 6.59 mi. **[18]**. Cross under a power line and meet the Acorn Trail at 6.71 mi. **[19]**, where you turn left to complete your hike.

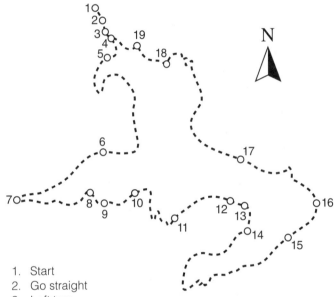

1. Start
2. Go straight
3. Left turn
4. Right turn
5. Sinkhole
6. Scenic view
7. Left turn
8. Stream crossing
9. Glade
10. Wet-weather spring
11. Two left turns
12. Left turn
13. Right turn
14. Bear left
15. Sandstone bluff
16. Go straight
17. Go straight
18. Right turn
19. Left turn

- See the big, round, blue spring that the local Native Americans referred to as the "Eye of the Sacred One."
- Hike through a 296-foot-long S-shaped tunnel, one of the state's largest and most beautiful natural tunnels.
- Bring your wildflower book—you may see as many as 45 species blooming at one time on the Savanna Ridge Trail.

Area Information

Like many other springs in Missouri in the mid-1800s, Bennett Spring was used by early settlers as a source of free power. The spring's steady 100-million-gallon-per-day output powered a series of gristmills, the most successful of which belonged to Peter Bennett, known for his generous donations of flour to needy families during the Civil War. Area farmers, waiting their turn at the mill, camped and fished in the scenic spring valley.

Built by the CCC in 1937, the triple-arched bridge near the trout hatchery isn't the only major bridge in the park. An even more spectacular bridge, or tunnel, is in the woods about four miles upstream. The Bennett Spring Natural Tunnel, a remnant of an ancient cave roof, is 100 yards long!

Mention Bennett Spring in a group of Missourians, and tales of *Salmo gairdneri*, the rainbow trout, are likely to ensue. Although trout are not native to Missouri, the state's numerous springs provide water that is cold enough for trout. Trout were stocked in the Bennett Spring Branch as early as 1900, and the first trout hatchery appeared on the site in 1924. One of the state's oldest and most popular parks, the site owes its popularity to its spring. Anglers and their families compose most of the park's visitors.

Directions: From Lebanon take Highway 64 west for 11 miles to the park entrance.

Hours Open: The site is open year-round from sunrise to 10:00 p.m. The nature center is open from 9:00 a.m. to 5:00 p.m. daily. Sirens audible along the entire spring branch announce the opening and closing of fishing hours, which change seasonally. Trout season is open from March 1 through October 31.

Facilities: The park features fishing for rainbow trout in its 1.5-mile-long spring branch. Several campgrounds are available, as well as a nature center with exhibits, a swimming pool, a dining lodge, rental cabins, an amphitheater, a camp store, a trout hatchery, picnic areas, and a boat ramp on the Niangua River.

Permits and Rules: A state fishing license and daily permit required for trout fishing are available from the park store. Fish feeding is allowed in the hatchery's rearing pools near the park store, but only food bought on site may be used. Swimming in the spring branch is not allowed, but anglers may wade. Pets must always be leashed.

For Further Information: Bennett Spring State Park, 26250 Highway 64A, Lebanon, MO 65536; www.mostateparks.com/bennett/natcenter.htm; 417-532-4338 (park office) or 417-532-4307 (cabin reservations).

Park Trails

The park's other trails (except the .30-mile loop behind the nature center) are linear. Hiked together, they total 2.45 miles (one-way.) Starting at the spring and going downstream, these are the trails:

Spring Trail (🥾, .65 mile one-way). This trail begins at the west side of the spring and follows the spring branch to the hatchery.

Bridge Trail (🥾, .75 mile one-way). Begin at the CCC-era triple-arched bridge on the east side of the stream, traverse some oak-hickory woods, and finish at the Oak-Hickory Trail loop.

Oak-Hickory Trail (🥾🥾, .30 mile). This loop trail begins at the amphitheater and winds through a forest behind the nature center. Access this trail from the nature center or the Bridge Trail.

Bluff Trail (🥾🥾🥾, .25 mile one-way). The upper section of this trail climbs a bluff, offers great views of the stream and park, and connects the Bridge and Whistle trails.

Whistle Trail (🥾, .40 mile one-way). This trail begins from the upper section of the Bluff Trail, explores a more peaceful section of the stream, and ends at the bridge near the Niangua River.

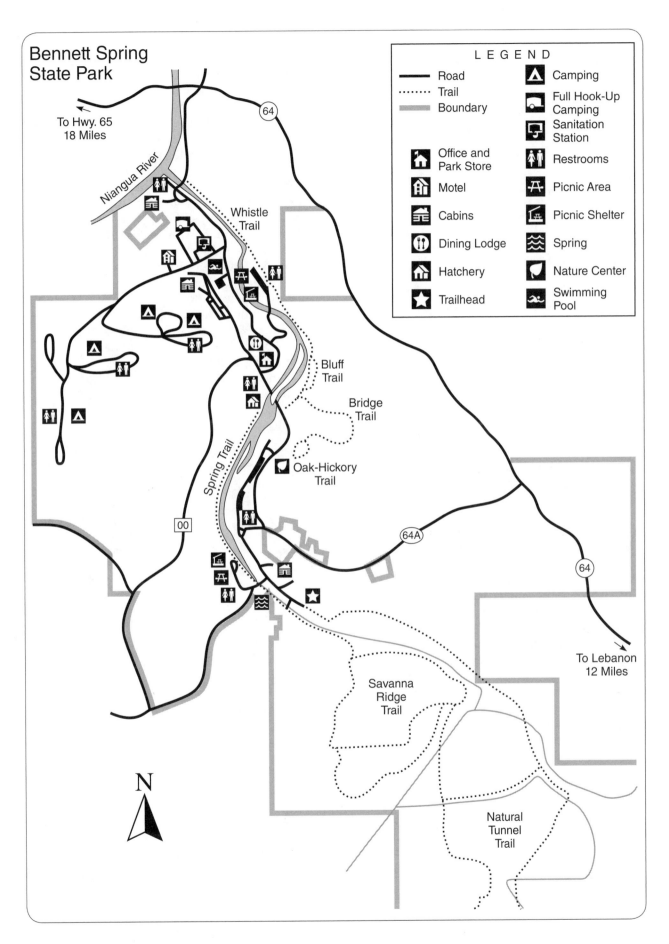

Bennett Spring
State Park

To Hwy. 65
18 Miles

Niangua River

64

Whistle
Trail

Bluff
Trail

Bridge
Trail

Oak-Hickory
Trail

Spring Trail

00

64A

64

To Lebanon
12 Miles

Savanna
Ridge
Trail

Natural
Tunnel
Trail

N

LEGEND

——	Road		Camping
····	Trail		Full Hook-Up Camping
▬▬	Boundary		Sanitation Station
	Office and Park Store		Restrooms
	Motel		Picnic Area
	Cabins		Picnic Shelter
	Dining Lodge		Spring
	Hatchery		Nature Center
	Trailhead		Swimming Pool

Natural Tunnel Trail

 Distance Round-Trip: 7.5 miles
Estimated Hiking Time: 3.75 hours

Because of its S shape, the tunnel looks like a cave until you step inside and see the glow of light coming from the other opening. From inside, the entrance looks exotic; Virginia creeper trails from the roof and tropical pawpaw leaves are reflected in the still pools of the tunnel stream.

Caution: Bring a flashlight if you want to explore inside the tunnel; it's dark and rocky in the middle part. Stinging nettles encroach on the trail in places, especially on the east loop.

Trail Directions: After you are in the park, follow the signs for the spring and the trailhead, marked by "TH" signs. Park in the lot for the trailhead, at the end of the road just southeast of the spring.

Begin the trail between the interpretive signs at the parking lot **[1]** and turn left at the first intersection. Follow blue arrows on this trail. You are now on the east loop. The trail soon takes you into a streamside forest, where the vegetation is thick and limbs of black walnut, hackberry, and basswood trees arch over the trail. Just after passing under a grand sycamore tree leaning over the trail, look for a trickle of water falling off a boulder next to the trail on your left. Two water-loving plants are here at .43 mi. **[2]**—jewelweed (a favorite of hummingbirds) and water hemlock (one of North America's deadliest plants). At .59 mi. **[3]**, a tiny spring erupts next to the trail on the left.

At .81 mi. **[4]**, cross a streambed and resume the trail slightly to your left on the other side. Climb a wooded hill with many Christmas ferns and maidenhair ferns to reach a connector link and wooden bench at 1.07 mi. **[5]**; turn left here. Turn right at the intersection with an old road at 1.17 mi. **[6]** and enter an old field, now grown up with locust trees and lots of blackberries. Purple milkweed and butterfly weed are attended by great spangled fritillaries and black swallowtails.

Just after crossing a gravel streambed, look on your left for some steep bluffs on the side of the ridge. When you see a streambed opening on your right at 1.53 mi. **[7]**, step into the bed to see some dolomite bluffs carved into fantastic shapes by the stream. These erosional features foreshadow what awaits you at the end of the trail. Turn left at the intersection with the west loop at 1.75 mi. **[8]**. An expansive old field opens on your left, filled with more locusts and blackberries. Turn right at 2.09 mi. **[9]** at a crossing with an old road. Go straight through two pipeline clearings and bear right at the fork in the trail at 2.47 mi. **[10]**. Turn right at an old road crossing at 2.62 mi. **[11]**.

The trail now parallels a small stream. Just after crossing this stream for the third time, you'll see the black mouth of the natural tunnel yawning through the trees at 3.5 mi. **[12]**. Make your way under some beautiful dolomite ledges dripping with water and wild hydrangea (another water-loving plant) and step inside the opening. Feel the breeze inside the natural wind tunnel and see the calcite deposits on the ceiling and walls. This is a good place to explore and relax.

Return to **[8]**, which you reach at 5.25 mi. Turn left, cross a small stream, and begin an uphill hike. Fern medleys cover some ravine sides. At the top at 5.8 mi. **[13]** are several views of distant wooded ridges and valleys. You pass a farm pond and cross a stream before reaching the connector link at 6.34 mi. **[14]**; go straight here. Cross another stream and turn right at the intersection at 6.83 mi. **[15]**, joining a section of the Savanna Ridge Trail. Turn right at the intersection at 7.28 mi. **[16]**. Just after passing a house, turn right on the gravel road and cross a concrete bridge. Turn right again at the end of the bridge to return to the trailhead.

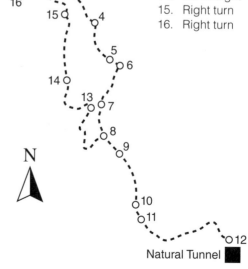

1. Start
2. Water-loving plants
3. Tiny spring
4. Stream crossing
5. Left turn
6. Right turn
7. Erosional features
8. Left turn
9. Right turn
10. Bear right
11. Right turn
12. Natural tunnel
13. Overlooks
14. Go straight
15. Right turn
16. Right turn

Savanna Ridge Trail

Distance Round-Trip:
2.35 miles
Estimated Hiking Time:
1.25 hours

I knew I risked a chigger infestation by leaving the wide, mowed path through the old field grown up in acres of blackberry briars. But the shiny, ripe blackberries squished between my teeth like little soft balloons filled with sweet juice, warmed by the June morning sun. The chigger welts would heal, I figured.

Caution: Applying repellent against chiggers and ticks in summer is a good idea.

Trail Directions: Park in the lot for the trailhead, just southeast of the spring. The Natural Tunnel Trail and Savanna Ridge Trail share a trailhead here. Start between the interpretive signs at the parking lot **[1]** and turn right at the first intersection. Follow green arrows on this trail. Turn left on a concrete bridge at .07 mi. **[2]** and watch for kingfishers perching on dead tree limbs and great blue herons stalking the shallows of this slack water. Turn left again on the trail on the other side at .13 mi. **[3]**.

Just after crossing a small stream, turn right at the intersection at .30 mi. **[4]**. Walk uphill into the woods, keeping an eye out for brown mounds of earth about 1 foot high and 2 feet wide on the left side of the trail. These hills are made by mound-building ants, which excavate extensive tunnels underground for their colony. Look for wing-stem sunflowers—yellow-flowered plants about waist high with wings that run parallel to their main stems. They join spiderwort, Christmas ferns, and black-eyed susans in an interesting jumble of colors and textures.

Prescribed fires keep underbrush in check and release nutrients back into the forest soil. Wildflowers and native grasses can flourish in areas that are periodically burned, and the diversity of species at .62 mi. **[5]** illustrates this. Among many others here are pale purple coneflowers, feverfew, and beardtongue. Rich yellows of two kinds of coreopsis bloom over purple spikes of leadplant. You soon reach the connector link at .69 mi. **[6]**, where you turn right and cross two small streams. Continue uphill and continue finding wildflowers. Here are sunny ox-eye daisies, pealike blooms of goat's rue, and fragile and slender Deptford pink.

The trail swings to the left and finally takes you downhill. You pass through a large colony of bracken ferns at 1 mi. **[7]**. Notice that each frond section looks like a separate leaf.

Some overlook views appear through the trees at 1.23 mi. **[8]**. Notice the elephant-ear-like leaves of prairie dock amidst the bluestem grasses in these forest openings. Look for the yuccalike leaves of rattlesnake master near the trail. Turn right at the intersection with the connector link at 1.38 mi. **[9]** and turn left when the trail meets the Natural Tunnel Trail at 1.54 mi. **[10]**.

At 1.95 mi. **[11]**, you enter an old field filled with thickets of brush and blackberry briars. If you're here in late June or July, you should experience blackberries for yourself—one of Missouri's tastiest wild edibles. The berries start out green before turning red. They're not ripe until they are a deep, dark purple. Turn right at an intersection that you passed earlier **[4]** to complete your wildflower hike.

1. Start
2. Left turn
3. Left turn
4. Right turn
5. Wildflower display
6. Right turn
7. Bracken fern colony
8. Overlooks
9. Right turn
10. Left turn
11. Old field

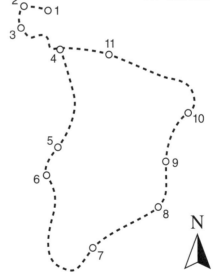

- Tarantulas, scorpions, armadillos, and road-runners? Hiking the glades of southwest Missouri can make you feel as if you've gone south of the border.

- Find the uncommon smoke tree. If you come in June or July, you can see what makes it smoke.

- Climb 133 steps to the top of a U.S. Forest Service lookout tower for clearer insight into an analogy of the landscape made in 1818.

Area Information

The White River section of the Ozarks straddles the border between Missouri and Arkansas in Missouri's southwest corner. Named for the major river that is responsible for carving its famous hilly terrain, the White River section is characterized by steep ridges, deep valleys, conical knobs, and extensive open glades. When glades occurred on knobs, they were named balds because thin, rocky soils allowed few trees to grow. Natural periodic fires and fires set by Native Americans kept cedar, sumac, and other brush from invading the balds.

The first settlers of the area were primarily old-stock Americans from Appalachia. The Civil War was particularly divisive here and produced an aftermath of vicious feuding and guerrilla fighting. One of the largest and most flagrant vigilante clans that roared through the region in the 1880s was the Bald Knobbers, a part of Ozark culture that serves as a motif for the thriving local tourism industry.

Today, much of the White River Valley's original culture and environment has been displaced. Major dams on the river have created Norfork, Bull Shoals, Taneycomo, Table Rock, and Beaver lakes. Fortunately, Hercules Glades Wilderness is one of several areas designated to preserve a portion of this unique, original Ozark landscape. Hercules Glades is one of seven wilderness areas in Missouri managed by the Mark Twain National Forest, U.S. Forest Service. The wilderness has three public trailheads and four interconnected loop trails in addition to the two featured trails.

Directions: The area is near the Arkansas border, north of Bull Shoals Lake. To reach the **Coy Bald Trailhead** (west side), take Highway 160 east from Forsyth 10.2 miles to Cross Timbers Road, where you turn left. Go 1.7 miles to the T and turn right. Take an immediate left and go 1.4 miles to the parking lot at Coy Bald. To reach the **Lookout Tower Trailhead** (east side), take Highway 160 east from Forsyth 20.8 miles to Highway 125, where you turn north. Go 7.3 miles and turn left at the sign for the area. Go .2 mile to the parking lot at the tower.

Hours Open: The wilderness is always open.

Facilities: Picnic tables, grills, and parking for horse trailers are available at both trailheads. The Lookout Tower Trailhead also has a lookout tower, restrooms, and two primitive campsites.

Permits and Rules: Horses are allowed, but ATVs are prohibited. Hunting is permitted, but not within 150 yards of the trail. Campers must observe regulations designed to protect the wilderness beauty. Choose a campsite away from the trail and avoid constructing a fire ring. Cut no standing trees (live or dead) and extinguish all campfires, scattering their evidence before leaving. Leave no litter, trail-marking ribbons, or other evidence of your presence.

For Further Information: District Ranger, U.S. Forest Service, Ava–Cassville–Willow Springs District, 1103 South Jefferson, Ava, MO 65608; 417-683-4428. For a map of the entire Mark Twain National Forest or topographic maps of all seven districts and seven wilderness areas, contact the Forest Supervisor's Office, 401 Fairgrounds Road, Rolla, MO 65401; 573-364-4621.

Other Areas of Interest

Also in the Mark Twain National Forest, just 2.8 miles south of the lookout tower, the **Glade Top Trail** is a 23-mile scenic driving trail. The Glade Top Trail, Missouri's only national scenic byway, offers vistas of the White River Hills, the Springfield Plateau, and the St. François and Boston Mountains. For more information, call 417-683-4428.

Dubbed the new Nashville, **Branson** offers a multitude of music shows, shopping villages, water parks, restaurants, and other entertainment attractions, including the theme park **Silver Dollar City**. Branson is 35 miles south of Springfield on Highway 65. For more information, call the Branson Chamber of Commerce at 417-334-4136 or visit www.bransonchamber.com.

Hercules Glades Wilderness

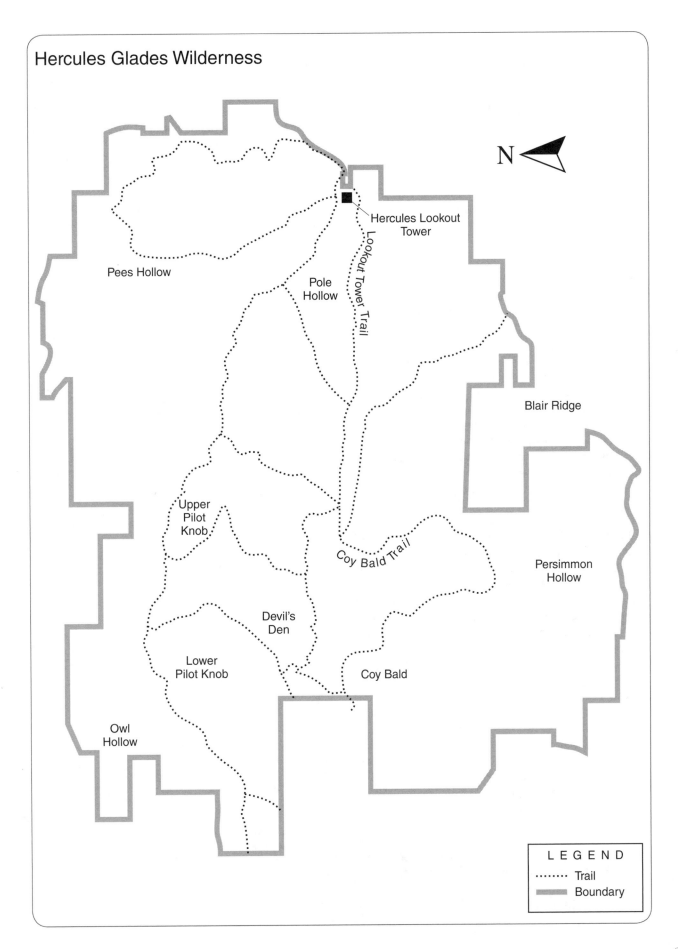

N

Hercules Lookout
Tower

Lookout Tower Trail

Pees Hollow

Pole
Hollow

Blair Ridge

Upper
Pilot
Knob

Coy Bald Trail

Persimmon
Hollow

Devil's
Den

Lower
Pilot Knob

Coy Bald

Owl
Hollow

L E G E N D

········· Trail

━━━ Boundary

Coy Bald Trail

Distance Round-Trip:
6.75 miles
Estimated Hiking Time:
3.75 hours

As I was leaving the trailhead, I spied a roadrunner, cocking its head from side to side and strolling along the road ahead. It suddenly stretched out and became all neck and tail, and all hopes of a photograph vanished in about 2.2 seconds!

Caution: Bring a compass and topo map if you plan to extend this hike or explore off the trail. Bring sun protection and extra water. Wear orange clothing during hunting seasons.

Trail Directions: Park in the lot for the Coy Bald Trailhead and begin the trail straight across the lot from where you entered **[1]**. Please register at the trail box near the trailhead. Turn left at the intersection at .09 mi. **[2]**. While descending a rocky trail shaded by post oaks, black hickories, and cedars, turn left at the fork at .25 mi. **[3]**. At .56 mi. **[4]**, you find a campsite on your left, the solid bedrock streambed of Long Creek in front of you, and a white limestone bluff, streaked black by manganese. Notice that each level of the bluff has its own little glade, complete with bluestem grass and blooming wildflowers. Desiccated trunks of ancient cedars cling from the top edge.

Follow the trail to the right and cross Long Creek. Look for Ozark witch hazel growing in the streambed and flat, gray, flaky pieces of shale among chunks of limestone and chert. Just across the stream, you find another campsite under a large white oak at .69 mi. **[5]**. Turn right and cross another streambed. From here, you hike through several glades separated by patches of forest. Some glades have cedars, whereas others are more open. Some are rocky and sloped; others are flat. All feature prairie grasses and a surprising variety of wildflowers. Go straight at the three-way intersection at 1.59 mi. **[6]**. Notice the way the bluestem grasses make the round glade at 1.99 mi. **[7]** look blue and green at the same time—just the way the water looks in a big, round spring.

Turn right at the intersection at 2.48 mi. **[8]** and cross Long Creek again, which may be dry. Just across the stream, you find a campsite on your left. Turn right here. At 2.64 mi. **[9]** is the trail to the Blair Ridge Road trailhead; go straight. After crossing another dry, rocky streambed, go straight at the four-way intersection at 2.75 mi. **[10]**. Climb a steep, rocky hill to a glade where sunshine yellow black-eyed susans contrast with craggy, nearly black dolomite rocks. The small pond on your right at 3.20 mi. **[11]** illustrates the ability of cattails to collect soil and eventually fill

in shallow ponds. The terrific glade-top views that soon open on your left and right are only a preview of what is to come.

Notice the small, bushy trees with oval, wavy leaves at 3.69 mi. **[12]**. These are smoke trees, which are restricted in Missouri to glades and bluffs of a few southwestern counties. The appearance of smoke is from the profusion of hairy stalks that remains on the tree after the flowers have fallen away in June and July. At 3.76 mi. **[13]**, you step onto a ridgetop glade over a third of a mile long that offers spectacular vistas every step of the way. On both the left and right, beyond plunging valleys, are distant knobs and balds, some showing horizontal stripes of exposed limestone layers. The foreground is lit up with blazing star, prairie dock, and gum plant. In early summer, look for the saucer-sized, lemon yellow blossoms of Missouri evening primrose. After passing another cattail pond, you reach another overlook at 5.03 mi. **[14]** that offers uninterrupted views of dozens of outlying ridges and deep valleys. On your way back to the trailhead, you hike on a side slope of Coy Bald at 6.28 mi. **[15]**. Turn left at an intersection **[2]** to finish your glade hike.

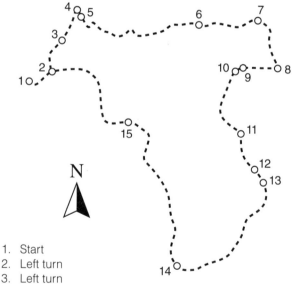

1. Start
2. Left turn
3. Left turn
4. Long Creek and bluff
5. Campsite
6. Go straight
7. Round glade
8. Right turn
9. Go straight
10. Go straight
11. Cattail pond
12. Smoke trees
13. Glade overlook
14. Glade overlook
15. Coy Bald

Lookout Tower Trail

Distance Round-Trip:
4.5 miles
Estimated Hiking Time:
2.25 hours

"Sometimes we crossed patches of ground of considerable extent, without trees or brush of any kind. . . . Frequently these prairies occupied the tops of conical hills, or extended ridges . . . and resembling, when viewed on perspective, enormous sand-hills promiscuously piled up by the winds."
—*Henry Rowe Schoolcraft, 1818*

Caution: Bring a compass and topo map if you plan to extend this hike or explore off the trail. Wear orange clothing during hunting seasons. Vegetation may encroach on the trail near Long Creek.

Trail Directions: Park in the lot for the Hercules Lookout Tower. Climb the tower, which offers superb views of the White River Hills in a 360-degree sweep and provides an appreciation for Schoolcraft's analogy. The trailhead is at the far end of the lot (west end), behind a picnic area. Please register at the trailhead before you begin.

Start your hike on a wide, rocky trail on a ridgetop [1] in a forest of oak, hickory, black walnut, and cedar. All the nut trees attract squirrels, and you are apt to see plenty of them here, thrashing in the upper limbs and chasing each other around trunks. Carolina buckthorn (Indian cherry) fruits will be tinged red, and wild grapes will fall onto the trail in clusters by late summer. After you start descending the ridge on a trail of chert gravel and slabs of dolomite bedrock, take the spur on your left at 1.12 mi. [2] to a curious, human-made collection of stones. Was it a homestead cabin foundation? A Native American burial cairn? Before the young trees crowded in, this site offered a splendid view across a deep valley. After thinking about who, what, or why, turn left on the main trail to continue.

At 1.22 mi. [3], you enter a glade that continues for a half mile downhill, over limestone gravel and bedrock. Unless you are here in winter, you'll find a festival of wildflowers. Among the conspicuous prairie dock, gum plant, and aster, tiny flowers grow on rock beds with no apparent soil. Between smoke trees and cedars, the tallest peak in the area, Pilot Knob, is visible to the northwest. After the glade tapers off into the bottoms of Long Creek, cross an intermittent stream at 1.94 mi. [4] and pass through an old field of tall lespedeza and sumac. Just before reaching Long Creek, turn right at the intersection at 2.20 mi. [5]. In a few steps you find another streambed, where you turn right [6] (2.23 mi.). Hike in the streambed, looking for softball-sized green Osage oranges. Turn right at 2.26 mi. [7] onto a steep, rocky trail up into the forest.

On your way uphill, look for the blue, lip-shaped blossoms of skullcap, and scratched and burrowed places on the ground made by armadillos. Along with roadrunners (and black bears, to a lesser extent), armadillos are moving into Missouri from their more typical southern range. After passing through another old field with winged elm and persimmon trees, you enter a series of glades, interspersed with patches of dry woods. Near the top of the ridge, chinquapin oaks surround a large glade at 3 mi. [8], where views of distant ridges and knobs extend from both sides. Blooming onions look like lavender fireworks explosions in the bluestem grass, and flying parades of butterflies attend fields of coneflowers, blazing star, and goldenrod.

Turn right at the three-way intersection at 3.40 mi. [9]. You then hike on a narrow, dry ridge with blackjack oaks and a shortleaf pine grove. Go straight at the intersection at 4.35 mi. [10] to return to the lookout tower.

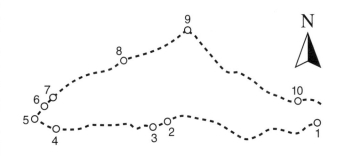

1. Start
2. Spur to rock collection
3. Half-mile glade
4. Stream crossing
5. Right turn
6. Streambed
7. Right turn
8. Scenic glade
9. Right turn
10. Go straight

61. Ruth and Paul Henning Conservation Area

- Hike in the White River Balds, the largest concentration of dolomite glades in the United States.

- Watch prairie racerunner lizards zip by. Try to catch a glimpse of one of their predators, the roadrunner.

- See a glade exploding with wildflowers—Missouri evening primrose, indigo, Indian paintbrush, and coneflower.

- Find hand-dug wells, rock foundations, and other remnants of homesteads built in the late 1800s.

Area Information

Crowning some of the tops and side slopes of the White River Hills, just west of Branson, are some of Missouri's most special and threatened habitats—glades. Glades are rocky, sunny, dry openings that often occur on steep slopes that face the hot afternoon sun. Life on these glades is rich with plants and animals that are specialized to cope with these harsh conditions.

Area homesteaders, too, had to be sturdy, adaptable, and resourceful, and the glades have long influenced the history and culture of the region. Because of their treeless, barren appearance, glades are locally referred to as balds. Post–Civil War vigilante groups and guerillas often met on the balds and became known as baldknobbers. Harold Bell Wright's 1907 book, *Shepherd of the Hills*, referred to several balds and other natural features of the area, and some of the book's characters were based on local homesteaders. Ozark culture became further publicized when Paul Henning, a native Missourian, produced and directed the popular television series *The Beverly Hillbillies*, *Pet-*

ticoat Junction, and *Green Acres*. Today, Ozark culture is the dominant theme of nearby Branson's thriving entertainment and tourism industry.

Most of the area's 1,534 acres was donated by or purchased from Ruth and Paul Henning, and is now owned by the Missouri Department of Conservation. A portion of the site, the White River Balds Natural Area, is composed of the scenic glades and surrounding woodlands.

Directions: To reach the main trailhead parking lot at the south end of the area, take Highway 465 (Ozark Mountain High Road) west for 7 miles from the intersection of Highways 465 and 65. At Highway 76, go east for 2 miles to the parking lot on the left.

Hours Open: The site is open year-round. At the parking lot at the south end, at White Cedar Bald, the gates open at dawn and close at dusk. At the north end, the area is open from 4:00 a.m. to 10:00 p.m.

Facilities: At the trailhead at the south end of the area are interpretive signs, restrooms, and an overlook.

Permits and Rules: Hunting, camping, and fires are not permitted. Destroying or collecting plants or animals is prohibited. Horses and bicycles are not permitted on hiking trails. Pets must always be leashed.

For Further Information: Missouri Department of Conservation, Branson Forestry Office, 226 Claremont Drive, Branson, MO 65616; 417-334-3324; www.mdc. mo.gov.

Other Areas of Interest

The **Shepherd of the Hills Fish Hatchery and Conservation Center**, on Highway 165 just below Table Rock Dam, offers tours of the hatchery, exhibits, aquariums, hiking trails, and a picnic area. For more information, call 417-334-4865. **Table Rock State Park**, on Highway 165 just south of Table Rock Dam, offers a marina, a dive shop, boat rentals, camping, and picnic areas. For more information, call 417-334-4704. The **Table Rock Lakeshore Trail** is a 2.2-mile hiking and biking path that connects Table Rock State Park with the **Dewey Short Visitor Center**, which offers exhibits on the area and is operated by the U.S. Army Corps of Engineers. For more information, call 417-334-4101.

Area Trails

Dewey Bald Trail (🥾, .5 mile). This trail begins at the south end of the main trailhead parking lot, close to Highway 76. Hike on a pleasant, shady, paved path in the woods to reach a 40-foot tower that you can climb for great views of the White River Hills.

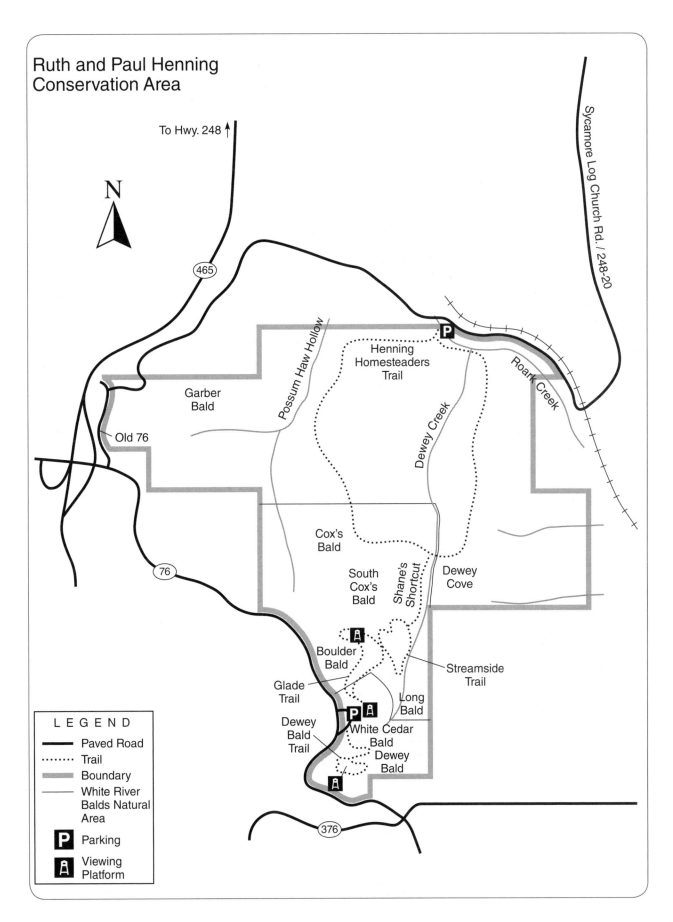

Ruth and Paul Henning Conservation Area

To Hwy. 248 ↑

N

465

Sycamore Log Church Rd. / 248-20

Possum Haw Hollow

Henning Homesteaders Trail

Garber Bald

Old 76

Dewey Creek

Roark Creek

P

76

Cox's Bald

South Cox's Bald

Shane's Shortcut

Dewey Cove

Streamside Trail

Boulder Bald

Glade Trail

Long Bald

Dewey Bald Trail

White Cedar Bald

Dewey Bald

P

376

LEGEND

— Paved Road
····· Trail
▬ Boundary
— White River Balds Natural Area
P Parking
Ã Viewing Platform

Glade and Streamside Trails

 Distance Round-Trip: 1.75 miles
Estimated Hiking Time: 1 hour

Summer comes early on the glade. Insects and reptiles begin to stir sooner in spring on sun-drenched south- and west-facing slopes. Few trees block the sun, and rocks hold and radiate heat all afternoon and into the evening.

Caution: The trail is extremely rocky in sections, and many of the rocks are loose.

Trail Directions: Park in the lot for the trailheads on White Cedar Bald at the south end of the area. Interpretive signs in the parking lot explain the geology and the unusual plants and animals that live on the glades. The Glade Trail begins **[1]** from a covered overlook deck at the north end of the parking lot.

Ignore the intersection with a service road at .12 mi. and turn left at the main intersection marked by a sign at .13 mi. **[2]**. Views of the open glades begin to open on your right. It may seem that little could live in this rocky, hot, and dry landscape, but many plants and animals are adapted to the desertlike conditions. Prickly pear cactus, as well as the rare smoke tree and Ashe juniper, also known as the white cedar, live here. Other glade residents here include scorpions, tarantulas, armadillos, roadrunners, eastern collared lizards, and a variety of other reptiles.

Step onto the overlook deck at .41 mi. **[3]** for splendid views of this unusual natural community. On the glade in front of you, notice the long lines of layered dolomite, exposed in the thin soil. From the air, these concentric rings of rock look like targets. After the trail swings sharply to the right, exposed rock lies on both sides of you and rock layers sometimes form natural stone steps.

At the intersection at .76 mi. **[4]**, turn left to start the Streamside Trail. Notice the difference the sun makes as you step into the shade. As you go downhill, the accumulation of soil and moisture allows trees to grow bigger. Larger trees mean more leaves, which make more soil, which holds more moisture, and the cycle continues. On the treeless steep slopes of the glade, the opposite cycle occurs.

Soon, the trail parallels an intermittent stream. Take advantage of the bench at .91 mi. **[5]** to sit and listen to a little water music. At .94 mi. **[6]** is the intersection with Shane's Shortcut, which connects to the Henning Homesteaders Trail. Turn right here to continue the Streamside Trail. Soon, you hike next to another stream, Dewey Creek. If you are here in spring, you'll find a variety of woodland wildflowers—trillium, violets, toothwort, anemone, and trout lily.

After the trail swings to the right, turn left at 1.20 mi. **[7]** at the intersection with the Glade Trail. Back you go to the sunny and rocky slope of the glade. Pass a bench at 1.28 mi. **[8]**. You may see evidence of fire on the glade—dead cedar trees or pieces of charred wood. Prescribed fire is the most important management tool used to maintain healthy glades. Fire releases nutrients back into the soil and invigorates glade grasses and wildflowers. Fire also keeps cedars and other aggressive shrubs and trees from taking over the glades. Pass another bench at 1.40 mi. **[9]**. At 1.55 mi. **[10]**, bear right at two forks in the trail. Turn left at the intersection at **[2]** to return to the trailhead.

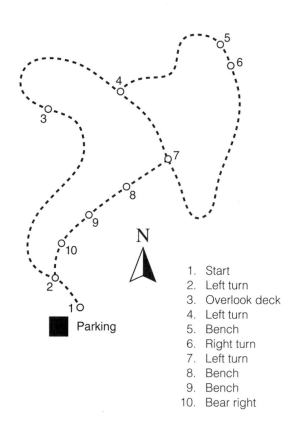

1. Start
2. Left turn
3. Overlook deck
4. Left turn
5. Bench
6. Right turn
7. Left turn
8. Bench
9. Bench
10. Bear right

Henning Homesteaders Trail

Distance Round-Trip: 3.7 miles
Estimated Hiking Time: 3 hours

Just a few miles from the glitz and neon of one of the entertainment meccas of the United States, you can hike on this trail and contemplate life of 130 years ago. See the post oaks and cedars that once grew in early settlers' yards, and marvel at their precious hand-dug wells. Transportation was by horse, mule, or foot, and entertainment was walking to the neighbor's place on the next bald to join in some conversation or fiddle playing on the front porch.

Caution: The trail is extremely rocky in sections, and many of the rocks are loose.

Trail Directions: The Henning Homesteaders Trail can be accessed from the Streamside Trail via a connector link known as Shane's Shortcut, which is .3 mi. one-way. Otherwise, the trailhead is at the northeast end of the area. To reach the trailhead for the Homesteaders Trail from the trailheads on White Cedar Bald at the south end of the area, travel south on Highway 76 and turn left (east) on Shepherd of the Hills Expressway. Turn left (north) on Highway 248 and go 3.6 mi. Turn left (southwest) on Sycamore Log Church Road and go 3.3 mi. You pass the log church, go under a railroad trestle, and find the trailhead parking lot on the left.

From the parking lot, walk back to the road, turn left, and cross the low-water bridge over Roark Creek. The trail begins [1] just across the creek on the left side of the road. After hiking along Roark Creek for a while, you find a long, concrete wall near the intersection with Dewey Creek at .28 mi. [2]. This wall was built around 1920 to protect a store that once stood here from creek floods. Swing to the right in front of the wall and cross Dewey Creek. Just across the creek at .32 mi. [3], take the short spur to the right to see the remains of the homestead of James Cox, who was listed in the 1840 census of this area. Look for fence remnants and a hand-dug well, now covered with a metal grate. Return to [3] and turn left. At the trail intersection at .40 mi. [4], take a few steps to your left and look in the woods to see the remains of a pole barn that was built in the 1920s to store hay grown in the Roark Creek bottom. Return to [4] and turn right. Look on both sides of the trail at .68 mi. [5] for cedar tree stumps. During the Depression, cedar posts brought one penny each. Later, the American Eagle Pencil Company cut cedar here from 1945 to 1948.

After passing beneath a power line, you find the remains of the Jones homestead at 1.29 mi. [6], where Willard Jones's father was born in 1872. A pile of rocks is all that remains of a fireplace. A yucca, which probably grew in the yard, still survives. A giant cedar tree marks the remains of another homestead at 1.42 mi. [7]. This was the home of Reuben Isaacs, who was

appointed Taney County sheriff after Sheriff Galba Branson was shot to death by baldknobbers during a picnic on July 4, 1889. The clay pipe marks a well that was added after the turn of the century. The spur on your left at 1.51 mi. [8] is .10 mi. long and will take you beneath some shortleaf pine trees, Missouri's only native pine. Many pines were harvested in the early 1900s for lumber and railroad ties. Return to the main trail and turn left. Turn right at the intersection at 1.71 mi. [9], and you soon find another hand-dug well, probably from the late 1800s, next to the trail. Imagine digging a well with a shovel in this rocky soil!

After crossing a small stream with a wet-weather waterfall, you cross scenic Dewey Creek at 2 mi. [10]. Take off your hiking boots and soak your hot feet! Go straight at the intersection with Shane's Shortcut at 2.02 mi. [11] and find a picturesque waterfall at 2.32 mi. [12]. Cross the stream just beyond the waterfall and continue on the other side. You experience the open glade at 2.53 mi. [13] briefly before reentering the woods. After passing beneath another power line, you find the remains of the Newt Cox homestead at 2.75 mi. [14], built around the turn of the century. You can still see some of the post oaks, which lined the home's drive, and some of the cut rock used in the foundation. Pass beneath another power line, and find some barbed wire deeply embedded in trees at 3.09 mi. [15].

You find the remains of the last homestead site at 3.57 mi. [16], where you can see another hand-dug well, a spring, and a retaining wall, which may have been used to hold back some of the spring water. Hike between two large red oaks at 3.79 mi. [17], which are about 130 years old, before you return to the trailhead.

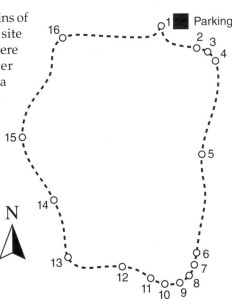

1. Start	10. Dewey Creek
2. Dewey Creek	11. Go straight
3. Spur to James Cox homestead	12. Waterfall
4. Intersection	13. Glade
5. Cedar stumps	14. Newt Cox homestead
6. Jones homestead	15. Barbed wire in trees
7. Isaacs homestead	16. Homestead remains
8. Spur to pine plantation	17. Twin red oaks
9. Right turn	

Southwest

The southwest region of Missouri is the area south of Highway 70 and west of Highway 65.

Topography

Approximately 10 percent of this region, a narrow band south of the Missouri River, has geologic characteristics like those of north Missouri—an area often referred to as the glaciated plains. Deep soils are formed from loess, glacial till, or alluvium, and the area has gentle terrain.

Farther south, another 40 percent of the region is occupied by the Osage Plains, a distinctive area along the Kansas border that contains remnants of Missouri's once-vast prairies. Soils are composed of sedimentary residuum or shallow loess. Though unglaciated, Osage Plains topography is characterized by gently rolling hills and plains, blending gradually into other areas of Missouri around it.

The southern 50 percent of the region is composed of two distinct sections of the Ozarks. The Springfield Plateau, like the Osage Plains, is unglaciated yet relatively flat. Drainages have not dissected the land deeply, and the terrain is mostly gently rolling hills. The White River section, on the Arkansas border, is more typical of the rest of the Ozarks. The White River and its tributaries have carved deeply into the limestone bedrock, creating a rugged landscape. Long, steep-sided ridges and conical hills, or knobs, characterize the area.

Major Rivers and Lakes

The Missouri River flows across the north boundary of this region and, as in the other regions, the river strongly influences the soils, terrain, and plant and animal communities surrounding it. Other rivers of the region include the Blackwater, Osage, Little Osage, Spring, and James rivers. The White River, for which

the lower Ozarks section of this region is named, once meandered back and forth between Missouri and Arkansas but has been dammed to create five reservoirs. Not a single mile of the river flows freely in Missouri. Table Rock Lake is the only White River impoundment in this region.

Truman Lake, Missouri's second largest, is a twin of Lake of the Ozarks. Like its twin, it was created by damming the Osage River. With 55,000 surface acres of water, Truman is one of the largest hydroelectric reservoirs in the Midwest and only a few hundred acres smaller than Lake of the Ozarks. The U.S. Army Corps of Engineers designed the reservoir to provide power and recreation opportunities for the public. The dam began generating power in 1979. Other lakes in the region include Pomme de Terre, which offers fishing for northern muskies. A steady southwest wind from the Springfield Plateau seems always to be blowing across 25,000-acre Stockton Lake, making it popular with sailing enthusiasts.

Common Plant Life

From top to bottom, the majority of the region differs greatly from presettlement times. Agriculture has replaced most of the area's original communities. About 45 percent of the glaciated plains was prairie, but the deep soils and gentle terrain made ideal farming conditions. Only fragments of forest and savanna remain in the northern part of this region. Prairie covered about 75 percent of the Osage Plains before settlement. Streams have shallow valleys and broad floodplains with many sloughs and marshes. Although deeper soils have been plowed for crops and areas of thinner soil have been converted to pasture, most of the state's remaining prairie is here. The

Springfield Plateau is characterized by fragmented forests, pastures, and early successional shrubby habitats, but a few savanna remnants persist. The White River section has deciduous forest mixed with some pine, as well as major glade landscapes.

Prairie grasses like little bluestem, Indian grass, and big bluestem, which may reach 6 to 8 feet tall, dominate the prairies of the Osage Plains. Wildflower types often depend on the bedrock present and amount of moisture, and include tickseed coreopsis, downy sunflower, false dragonhead, gay feather, pencil flower, cream wild indigo, purple prairie clover, Venus's looking glass, birdsfoot violet, and prairie rose gentian.

Savannas are often thought of as transition zones between prairies and forest, where prairie plants grow beneath open canopies of widely spaced trees. Chinquapin oak, red cedar, and white ash trees, and little bluestem, sideoats grama, and Indian grasses dominate the limestone and dolomite savannas of the Springfield Plateau. Other plants include rattlesnake master, various sunflowers, adder's tongue fern, Seneca snakeroot, white prairie clover, rose gentian, and black-eyed susan.

When glades occurred on the conical knobs of the White River area, they were often called balds because of their relative lack of trees. Dolomite glades of the White River section are dominated by little bluestem, sideoats grama, and prairie dropseed grasses, dotted with stunted, often gnarled trees and shrubs. The smoke tree may be present. Wildflowers include silky aster, blue heart, Missouri evening primrose, yellow coneflower, pale purple coneflower, compass plant, rattlesnake master, and prairie dock.

Common Birds and Animals

The upland prairies of the Osage Plains are home to numerous birds including the prairie chicken, horned lark, northern harrier, dickcissel, upland sandpiper, meadowlark, Henslow's sparrow, grasshopper sparrow, and scissor-tailed flycatcher. Other animals include the coyote, badger, ornate box turtle, glass lizard, bullsnake, prairie kingsnake, and crayfish frog, and legions of butterflies. Prairie State Park also maintains a herd of American bison to roam freely in its native habitat of presettlement times.

Birds often living in savannas include the red-tailed hawk, kestrel, indigo bunting, bluebird, redheaded woodpecker, great crested flycatcher, prairie warbler, blue-winged warbler, and goldfinch. Other animals include the coyote, red fox, wild turkey, white-tailed deer, gray squirrel, ornate box turtle, rough green snake, prairie ringneck snake, and fence lizard.

The Bachman's sparrow and roadrunner are two birds largely restricted to dolomite glades in southwestern Missouri. Besides the roadrunner, the glades here are home to several other species of animals like the collared lizard, tarantula, and scorpion, which are typically associated with habitats of the southwestern United States. Other reptiles include the six-lined racerunner, coachwhip snake, western worm snake, copperhead, and western pygmy rattlesnake. The armadillo, another animal associated with the Southwest, is also increasing its range in southern and central Missouri.

Climate

The southwest region's temperatures average 57 degrees F in spring, 78 degrees F in summer, 58 degrees F in fall, and 30 degrees F in winter. Mean annual precipitation varies from 39 inches at the top of this region to 43 inches at the bottom.

Best Features

- Missouri's largest tallgrass prairie at Prairie State Park, complete with fields of wildflowers and roaming bison
- Peaceful, parklike oak savannas, with qualities of prairies of the west and forests of the east
- Exceptional and diverse plant communities on the White River balds
- Animal communities with a southwestern twist in the White River Hills
- Osage Village—the site of 200 lodges where the Osage were living when first encountered by Europeans
- Beautiful spring and the Devil's Kitchen at Roaring River State Park
- The tristate Spooklight

62. Knob Noster State Park

- Hike through a beautiful, open savanna while searching for striking redheaded woodpeckers, showy prairie wildflowers, and a kaleidoscope of butterflies.

- Learn why savannas are considered food factories for wildlife.

- Discover an oxbow of Clearfork Creek—a small but important wetland in the forest.

- Meet a green dragon, face to face, next to the trail.

Area Information

The town of Knob Noster was named in the 1850s for two hills, or knobs, northeast of town. Somebody added *noster*, the Latin word for *our*, and "our knobs" (Knob Noster) stuck. Knob Noster State Park, like Cuivre River and Lake of the Ozarks state parks, began as a National Recreation Demonstration Area (RDA). The federal government created RDAs in the 1930s by buying poor farmland, restoring it, and developing it for recreation near population centers. From 1936 to 1946, the park was named Montserrat and was administered by the National Park Service. Workers from CCC and WPA programs built two group camps in the park, as well as small lakes, bridges, and several buildings. The National Park Service transferred the 3,567-acre park to the state in 1946.

Although the park's land has greatly healed from its history of poor farming practices, overgrazing, and coal mining, management continues today to restore parts of the area to its presettlement condition. One hundred and fifty years ago, much of the area was a savanna landscape, a prairie grassland with interspersed trees. Savannas provided food for a diversity of wildlife species. Wide-crowned oaks produced valuable acorns for turkey, deer, and rodents, and provided nest homes for woodpeckers, owls, and small mammals. Tall prairie grasses and forbs provided food for large grazing mammals and grassland birds, as well as legions of insects. Displays in the park's visitor center explain the role that savannas played in Missouri's history and describe the park's progress in restoring some of these valuable natural communities.

Directions: From Knob Noster, on Highway 50, take Highway 23 south for 1.2 miles. Turn right at the sign for the park.

Hours Open: The site is open year-round from dawn to dusk. The visitor center is open from 9:00 a.m. to 4:30 p.m. daily.

Facilities: The park features a visitor center with exhibits and environmental activities for kids downstairs. A campground is available, as well as an equestrian trail and camp, two group camps, an amphitheater, and picnic areas. Fishing and boating are available on several small lakes. Park users may, for a fee, use the Royal Oaks Golf Course, managed by Whiteman Air Force Base. Entry is off Highway 23.

Permits and Rules: Horses are restricted to the McAdoo Equestrian Trail. Bicycles are restricted to paved roads and the McAdoo Equestrian Trail. Boats are allowed on the lakes but must be carried on; motors are restricted to trolling motors. Swimming is not allowed. Pets must be leashed.

For Further Information: Knob Noster State Park, 873 SE 10, Knob Noster, MO 65336; 660-563-2463.

Park Trails

Buteo Trail (👣👣, 1 mile). This trail follows the entire shoreline of Lake Buteo, offering scenic views of the lake and opportunities to see a variety of wildlife. The trail shares a trailhead with the Hawk Nest Trail, at the lake's spillway.

McAdoo Equestrian Trail (👣👣, 5 miles). Open to hikers, equestrians, and bicyclists, this trail traverses a variety of habitats in hilly and dissected terrain. The eastern section of the trail approaches Clearfork Creek in several places. The trail begins 1.6 miles southwest of the visitor center, on Highway DD.

Opossum Hollow Trail (👣👣👣, 1.5 miles). This trail passes three small lakes and many wolf trees in a crowded forest that was once a savanna. The trail begins at the end of the park road that leads to Morel Lake, 3 miles west of the visitor center, off Highway DD. A renovation of this trail includes a 7-mile hiking and biking trail, scheduled to be completed in 2009.

Knob Noster State Park

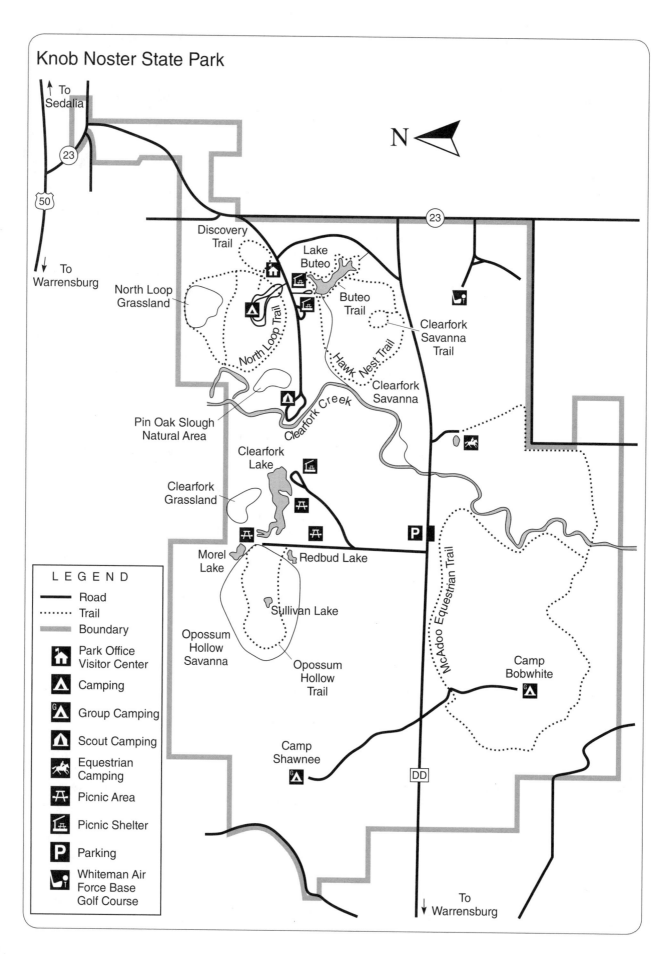

To Sedalia

To Warrensburg

Discovery Trail

North Loop Grassland

North Loop Trail

Lake Buteo

Buteo Trail

Clearfork Savanna Trail

Hawk Nest Trail

Clearfork Savanna

Pin Oak Slough Natural Area

Clearfork Creek

Clearfork Lake

Clearfork Grassland

Morel Lake

Redbud Lake

Sullivan Lake

Opossum Hollow Savanna

Opossum Hollow Trail

McAdoo Equestrian Trail

Camp Bobwhite

Camp Shawnee

To Warrensburg

LEGEND

— Road
...... Trail
━━ Boundary

Park Office Visitor Center

Camping

Group Camping

Scout Camping

Equestrian Camping

Picnic Area

Picnic Shelter

P Parking

Whiteman Air Force Base Golf Course

Hawk Nest and Clearfork Savanna Trails

 Distance Round-Trip: 2.5 miles
Estimated Hiking Time: 1.5 hours

"The view opens upon boundless and beautiful prairies, dotted with clumps of trees. . . . Clumps of trees, away from any stream or water, is another peculiar feature of this region." —Ephraim M. Anderson, a Missouri Confederate soldier, describing the Knob Noster vicinity in 1861

Caution: Be careful on the lake spillway; algae can make it slippery.

Trail Directions: Follow the signs for Lake Buteo, which is just south of the campground, and park in the lot for the lake. This trail shares a trailhead with the Buteo Trail and is marked with a signboard **[1]** at the edge of the lake. Cross an intermittent stream over some large rocks near the spillway. Pass a picnic shelter on your right and continue straight. Just after passing a limestone restroom building on your right, built in the 1930s by a WPA work-relief program, take the far left trail at .21 mi. **[2]** at the intersection with some old roads. Take every available left turn on a wide, mowed path. Pass a large, open field on your right and continue on your left. Cross the small, wooden bridge at .41 mi. **[3]** and enter Clearfork Savanna.

As the trail parallels a small tributary to Clearfork Creek, it skirts the savanna and clearly illustrates its characteristics. Notice that the trees on the left are large and widely spaced. A lack of understory allows prairie plants to grow and lends an open appearance. Contrast the savanna with the habitat on your right, which is a creek bottom that has a dense understory of small redbud, ash, and Ohio buckeye trees. Most of the interspersed savanna trees here are white oaks, with an occasional shagbark hickory or black walnut. At .62 mi. **[4]**, you cross two small streams. Just after climbing out of the last bottom, look on your left for green dragon, an unusual, larger relative of jack-in-the-pulpit. Its central cluster of shiny, green fruit turns bright red in fall.

As you continue, listen for the song of the field sparrow, the tempo of which increases at the end like the sound of a Ping-Pong ball dropped on a table. The dickcissel lives here, too. Look for the male, which has a yellow breast with a black bib. Go over two small, wooden bridges at .96 mi. **[5]**. At 1.3 mi. **[6]**, turn left to begin the Clearfork Savanna Trail, a small loop trail that takes you into the heart of the savanna. Turn right

at 1.32 mi. **[7]**. Deeply cut drainages create a rolling grassland; several hill starts and stops face you at once. The post oak canopy is wide open in places, allowing prairie plants like blazing star and purple prairie clover to thrive among the bluestem grasses. The leaves of the rough-leaved sunflower feel exactly like sandpaper. Turn right when you return to **[7]** and turn left at **[6]**.

Pick at blackberries as you continue and go straight at the spur on your right at 1.86 mi. **[8]**. Pass through a patch of spanglegrass and ignore the old road on your left at 2.12 mi. **[9]**, marked with an orange-painted post. You reach Lake Buteo at 2.19 mi. **[10]**, where you turn left on a small, wooden bridge. Splendid views of the lake are interrupted only by bullfrogs hurtling into the water, bluegills sucking hapless grasshoppers from the surface, and dragonflies whirring about. Follow the lakeshore until you reach the dam at 2.35 mi. **[11]**, where you turn right. After making your way across the spillway, turn right to complete your savanna hike.

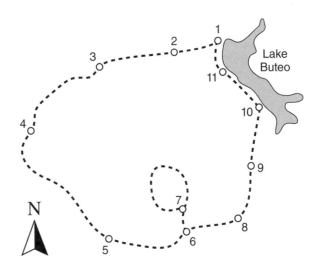

1. Start
2. Left turn
3. Wooden bridge
4. Two stream crossings
5. Two wooden bridges
6. Left turn
7. Right turn
8. Go straight
9. Go straight
10. Lake Buteo
11. Right turn

Discovery and North Loop Trails

Distance Round-Trip: 2.75 miles
Estimated Hiking Time: 1.75 hours

Several prairie plants join the vigorous bluestem grasses in the grassland restoration area. Along with blazing star and sunflowers is sensitive briar, a trailside sock-puller.

Caution: Small, loose rocks make footing unsure on several inclines.

Trail Directions: Begin the Discovery Trail on the east side of the visitor center, at the edge of the forest **[1]**. You soon cross a small, wooden bridge. At .14 mi. **[2]**, No-Name Creek meanders below you and passes beneath a WPA-built stone bridge on your far right. Several small trees have sprouted from the top of a limestone boulder that has tumbled near the creek bed. As you make your way between the creek on your right and a slope on your left, covered with a variety of oak and hickory trees, notice the trail work—occasional limestone stepping-stones and steps installed by work-relief laborers in the 1930s.

Take the small spur on your right at .24 mi. **[3]** down to the creek. Look for the Louisiana waterthrush, a small, dark brown bird with a streaked breast that spends most of its time on or near streambeds and bobs its tail up and down almost constantly. You're likely to see aquatic insects and snails scuttling on the bottom of pools, with a sampling of minnows darting above them. Notice the flat, gray rocks here that crumble in thin sheets. This is shale, a sedimentary rock similar to slate, but softer. Turn right after returning to the main trail.

Keep an eye out for a variety of birds in the canopy and understory. The small trees next to the trail with puffy, yellow-green "lanterns" are American bladdernut. Turn right at .60 mi. **[4]**. Turn right again at .64 mi. **[5]** immediately after crossing a small, wooden bridge. You are now beginning the North Loop Trail. If you see bright orange-yellow, earlike growths on the forest floor, you have probably discovered the chanterelle mushroom, a common summer fungus, especially after a shower. Ignore the connector link at .73 mi. **[6]** and go straight.

No-Name Creek soon appears again on your right, and the trail traverses small ridges dissected by drainage streams. At 1.34 mi. **[7]** is an open grassland restoration area, being managed to return to its presettlement condition. As much as a third of Missouri was once covered in prairie, and extensive savannas occurred at transition areas where prairie and forest met. Many trees bordering the grassland here are

shingle oaks, with narrowly oval leaves. Settlers split these oaks for siding and roofing shingles.

Turn right at the intersection with a fire road at 1.52 mi. **[8]** and go straight where the connector link joins the trail at 1.75 mi. **[9]**. Bear right, just after crossing a small bridge over an intermittent stream. An abandoned channel of Clearfork Creek appears on your right at 1.81 mi. **[10]**. When streams are allowed to meander, naturally and unchannelized, they provide valuable wetlands, such as this oxbow. Many kinds of amphibians, aquatic plants, and insects need habitat like this to reproduce. Look for the arrow-shaped leaves of arrowhead and the tall, branchy blooms of water plantain.

The trail passes moist limestone bluffs on the left. After passing beneath a power line, you cross several small streams as you continue through the mixed oak-hickory forest. At 2.57 mi. **[11]**, you enter the campground. Hike straight across the campground loop and reenter the forest at the trail sign at the edge of the woods. Turn right when you return to an intersection **[5]** and cross the small, wooden bridge. Keep going straight on this section to return to the visitor center.

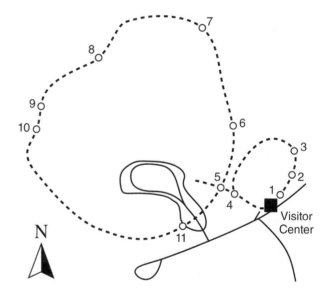

1. Start
2. No-Name Creek
3. Spur to creek
4. Right turn
5. Right turn
6. Go straight
7. Grassland
8. Right turn
9. Go straight
10. Creek oxbow
11. Campground

63. Harry S Truman State Park

- Hike along the top of a limestone bluff with a magnificent overlook of Truman Lake, one of the largest hydroelectric reservoirs in the Midwest.

- Keep your nose open on your glade–savanna hike; the diverse plants in this sun-baked landscape produce a potpourri of aromas as they warm.

- Spy the showy and smelly western wallflower, a plant typical of the southwestern Great Plains found in no other state park in Missouri.

- Find a patch of prickly pear cactus, which produces large, yellow blossoms in early summer and is the only cactus that grows wild in Missouri.

Area Information

At birth, Harry Truman, the nation's only president to hail from Missouri, was given the middle initial S (but no name) for his grandfathers, both of whose names began with an S. Similarly, the state park named for the president serves double duty. Situated near the eastern edge of an area of the state known as the Osage Plains, Harry S Truman State Park contains characteristics of both the prairies to the west and the Ozark forests to the east. The prairie elements of the park are visible among its savannas and glades on south- and west-facing slopes, and its Ozark flavor is exhibited in its rugged, dissected hills.

Located on a 1,440-acre tip of a peninsula, the park is surrounded on three sides by Truman Lake, a 55,000-acre reservoir formed by damming the Osage River. The U.S. Army Corps of Engineers designed the reservoir to provide hydroelectric power and recreation opportunities for the public, and the dam began generating power in 1979. The park's peninsula is divided into two sections. The western section contains the park office and campground, and the eastern section is designed as a day-use area for the public. Both sections cater to the water-recreation enthusiast.

Directions: From Warsaw, take State Route 7 north (toward Tightwad) for 6.4 miles. Turn north on Highway UU and go 2.6 miles into the park. The visitor center (at Kaysinger Bluff Park, at the east end of the dam) is 1.4 miles west of Highway 65.

Hours Open: The park is open during daylight hours year-round. The park office is open from 8:00 a.m. to 4:30 p.m. Monday through Friday from November through March and from 7:00 a.m. to 3:30 p.m. Monday through Friday from April through October.

Facilities: The state park offers an extensive campground, a full-service marina (including boat rentals), boat ramps, sandy swimming beaches, an amphitheater, and picnic areas. Boating, fishing, and skiing are available on Truman Lake. The U.S. Army Corps of Engineers operates a visitor center with a panoramic view of the lake, interpretive displays, an audiovisual room, a restored homestead site, and a short hiking trail. The visitor center facilities are free to the public.

Permits and Rules: Alcoholic beverages are prohibited on all state park beaches and parking areas. Pets must always be leashed.

For Further Information: Harry S Truman State Park, 28761 State Park Road, Warsaw, MO 65355; 660-438-7711 (park office); 660-438-2423 (marina); 660-438-2416 (visitor center).

Other Areas of Interest

The **U.S. Army Corps of Engineers** operates a number of recreation facilities that primarily feature water recreation and camping along all arms of the Harry S Truman Reservoir. For more information, call 660-438-2416.

Harry S Truman State Park

LEGEND

——	Road
·······	Trail
▬▬	Boundary
🏠	Park Office
⛱	Picnic Area
🏕	Shelter
🚻	Restrooms
⛺	Camping
⚓	Marina
🚤	Boat Launch
🏠	Shower House
🏊	Beach
⛰	Amphitheater
🌲	Wood Lot
♻	Sanitation Station
⋀	Fee Collection
P	Parking

Harry S Truman Reservoir

N

Bluff Ridge Trail

Western Wallflower Savanna Trail

UU

To 7

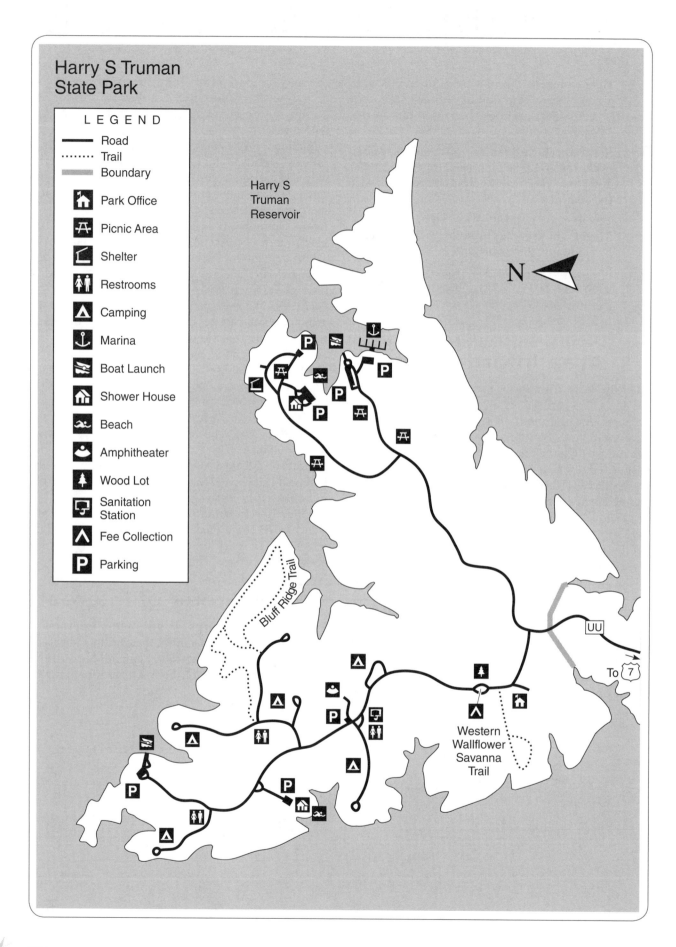

Western Wallflower Savanna Trail

Distance Round-Trip: .75 mile
Estimated Hiking Time: 30 minutes

Come in May, June, or early July to catch the trail's name-sake in bloom. It occurs in no other state park in Missouri. The western wallflower is hard to miss—it's a tall, bright orange, perfumed show-off.

Caution: Consider sun protection if you are here in summer; the trail takes you through the savanna and onto a cheerful (but shadeless) glade.

Trail Directions: Park in the lot for the trailhead, between the park office and the fee-collection booth for the campground. Begin at the interpretive kiosk **[1]**, which describes savannas and illustrates several savanna and glade plants that you are likely to see along the trail. The trail begins on a descending path and introduces you to the savanna right away. Notice the widely spaced oak trees, the lack of understory, and the prairie grasses and plants flourishing between the trees. Natural fires maintained expansive savannas in presettlement times. Because of effective fire suppression in the last century and a half, nearly all savanna landscapes have grown up in successional forests. Prescribed fires are used today to maintain a few remnants of this unique, once-extensive landscape.

At .13 mi. **[2]**, the savanna eases into a glade, which is rockier, drier, and more open. Notice that most of the white oaks are replaced by chinquapin oaks, which are shorter, farther apart, and more tolerant of drier conditions. Turn left at .14 mi. **[3]**. Big bluestem grass sometimes turns purple at its ends. The stems of little bluestem are flat at their base. Look for the dark green, frilly leaves of purple prairie clover and the bright yellow blooms of sunflowers. Some splendid views of the lake open at .18 mi. **[4]**. Notice that the trees are more numerous at the lower end of the hill (back to savanna).

Sniff the air as you hike to smell the aromas of several sun-warmed mints, grasses, and other plants. If you are here in summer, you will need no reminder that you are on a glade, sometimes known as a minidesert. Nevertheless, several patches of prickly pear cactus appear at .39 mi. **[5]**. The large, oval part of the cactus is really a thickened stem; its real leaves are only about a quarter of an inch long and fall off soon after the plant's last growth spurt. Look for the indigo bunting here, a small, brilliant, almost iridescent blue bird that is sometimes mistaken for Missouri's state bird, the bluebird. At .41 mi. **[6]**, just as the trail bends to the right, notice the stand of leadplant, with its hairy, gray leaves.

As you reenter the partial shade of the savanna at .50 mi. **[7]**, you are in a good spot to appreciate the gradation of three types of communities. Notice the dense, shady forest on your left, with its developed understory and lack of ground plants. As you look to the right, the tree canopy opens up and a savanna develops. Look farther to the right to see a glade in the rockiest, most open spot of the savanna. Notice, too, that the communities shift almost imperceptibly. Transition areas like this are often considered savanna–glade mosaics, or complexes. After stepping out into the sunny glade again, you return to **[3]**, where you turn left to return to the trailhead.

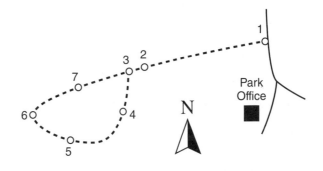

1. Start
2. Glade
3. Left turn
4. Lake overlook
5. Prickly pear cactus
6. Leadplant
7. Community mosaic

Bluff Ridge Trail

 **Distance Round-Trip:** 2 miles
Estimated Hiking Time: 1 hour

As I was near the blufftop lake overlook, the ominous rumblings in the sky took on a whole new meaning for me. I had just passed a huge oak next to the trail that had literally exploded from a lightning strike only a few days before.

Caution: Watch your step; the trail is home to an assortment of different-sized rocks.

Trail Directions: This trail begins in the middle of the camping area, on the west side of the park. Park at shower house #3; the trailhead is just across the street. Begin at the interpretive kiosk **[1]**, which explains the importance of fire as a tool to maintain habitats like forests, glades, and savannas. An oak forest, for example, can evolve into a maple forest if fire is suppressed. Maples are beautiful in fall but provide little food for wildlife and shade out more beneficial trees. Once thought destructive, periodic fire strengthens natural communities by maintaining their diversity.

Descend a rocky hill beneath a variety of oaks, hickories, ashes, and basswoods. As the trail bends to the left at .23 mi. **[2]**, notice the abundance of rock and the absence of almost all trees and plants but cedar. Cedars can flourish in the thinnest and driest of soils, and will quickly take over any rocky area where fire is suppressed, crowding out almost everything else. The huge knots on the chinquapin oak trunk at .31 mi. **[3]** are burls, which are abnormal growths caused by disease or some other injury. Makers of fine furniture cherish burls for their interesting, twisted grain patterns.

After crossing a deep ravine that drains into the lake on your left, you climb a rocky hill with fern-like leaves of lousewort on both sides of the trail. Lousewort produces light yellow flower clusters in April and May and was once thought to be a remedy for lice. The trail swings to the right at the top of the bluff. Views appear through the trees of the lake's blue water and, opposite, white limestone bluffs. Go straight at the intersection with the connecting link at .50 mi. **[4]**. As you hike along this blufftop, you may notice charred stumps and logs from prescribed fires,

which park managers use to achieve the same effects that periodic, natural fires produced in presettlement times. Notice that many of the older trees have broken tops, missing limbs, and lightning scars—evidence of their high exposure here to violent weather.

At .98 mi. **[5]**, step out onto the open limestone ledge for a magnificent overlook of the lake. Tributaries to these flooded riverbeds have created scores of quiet coves, pocketed by woods. Some of the coves are still filled with the skeletons of standing timber. If you are here in winter, scan the trees near the lake and the skies overhead for bald and golden eagles. After passing through another cedar-covered glade, the trail takes you through an open glade at 1.18 mi. **[6]**, where the cedars have been removed and prairie grasses and wildflowers thrive.

At 1.54 mi. **[7]**, you enter a savanna with widely spaced mature trees. You may notice a little charcoal at the base of their trunks, but these oaks, unlike cedars, are resistant to fires. Go straight at the connecting link intersection at 1.65 mi. **[8]** to reach the pavement of the campground loop at 1.72 mi. **[9]**. Turn right here to return to the trailhead.

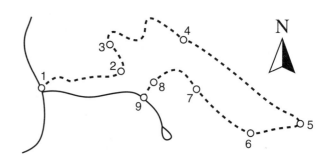

1. Start
2. Cedar-covered glade
3. Chinquapin burls
4. Go straight
5. Lake overlook
6. Open glade
7. Savanna
8. Go straight
9. Right turn

- Hike through a restored savanna with interspersed limestone outcrops and glade openings, resplendent with spring and summer wildflowers.

- Visit the ancient chinquapin and post oaks of the savanna—many are over 200 years old and have thick, spiraled trunks and craggy limbs.

- For a dramatic view of the lake during any season, hike to the end of a long peninsula to the rocky promontory known as Indian Point.

- Find the remnants of a Native American cairn at the end of a ridged, rocky peninsula.

- Try to fool a muskellunge.

Area Information

For thousands of years, American Indians lived along Missouri's rivers, where game, shelter, water, and fertile soil were plentiful. French trappers and traders explored the state's rivers in the late 1600s, finding an abundance of beaver, otter, and other valuable furbearers. When the French came to southwest Missouri, they named one of its rivers Pomme de Terre ("apple of the earth") for some plants resembling potatoes that grew on its banks. Now thought to be potato beans or prairie turnips, these "apples" were used by American Indians for food.

The 1800s brought to the area white settlers, who cleared or grazed much of the prairielike savanna. In the early 1960s the U.S. Army Corps of Engineers dammed Pomme de Terre River for flood control, forming 7,800-acre Pomme de Terre Lake. Today, the 734-acre Pomme de Terre State Park is leased from the corps. The park is divided into two units, the Hermitage and Pittsburg areas, each of which has a full set of facilities. In total, the park has more campsites than any other Missouri state park. Although the emphasis is water-based recreation, the park is also successfully restoring a savanna landscape to its presettlement conditions.

Northern muskies stocked in Pomme de Terre Lake offer anglers an unusual challenge. These large, toothy game fish add to the lake's more common inhabitants—bass, bluegill, catfish, and crappie.

Directions: Hermitage Area—From Hermitage, on Highway 54, take Highway 254 west for 3 miles to Carson's Corner. Turn south on Highway 64 and go .7 mile. Turn right at the sign for the park. **Pittsburg Area**—From Nemo, take Highway 64 east toward Pittsburg for 2.5 miles. Turn west on Highway 64B and travel 1.7 miles into the park. (Use Highways 64 and 64B to travel between park units.)

Hours Open: The park is open during daylight hours year-round. The park office (Pittsburg area) is open from 8:00 a.m. to 4:30 p.m. Monday through Friday year-round.

Facilities: The park offers a large campground, a marina (with boat rentals), swimming beaches, boat ramps, picnic areas, and an amphitheater. Fishing, boating, and skiing are available on the lake.

Permits and Rules: Strict federal and state laws prohibit the disturbance of archaeological sites and artifacts. Refrain from climbing on the rock cairns or disturbing them in any way. Alcohol is prohibited on the beaches. Pets must always be leashed.

For Further Information: Pomme de Terre State Park, HC 77 Box 890, Pittsburg, MO 65724; 417-852-4291.

Other Areas of Interest

The **U.S. Army Corps of Engineers** operates a number of recreation facilities along the lake that primarily feature water recreation and camping. The corps also operates a small visitor center at the east end of the dam. For more information, call 417-745-6411.

An interesting .5-mile walking tour interprets an American Indian village on top of a hill at **Osage Village State Historic Site**. Bedrock outcrops still bear the signs of use by the Osage for cracking nuts, pounding flour, and sharpening tools. The site marks the location where 2,000 to 3,000 Osage lived when they first encountered Europeans, around 1700. The site, west of Pomme de Terre, is 2.1 miles west of Fair Haven, off Highway C. For more information, call 417-682-2279 (Harry S Truman Birthplace State Historic Site).

Schell-Osage Conservation Area, just east of Osage Village, is a wetland wildlife area that includes marshes, bottomland, and upland timber. The area has major concentrations of waterfowl in fall, winter, and spring, and offers hunting, fishing, limited camping, and a 1.5-mile linear hiking trail. The area is owned by the Missouri Department of Conservation. For more information, call 417-876-5226.

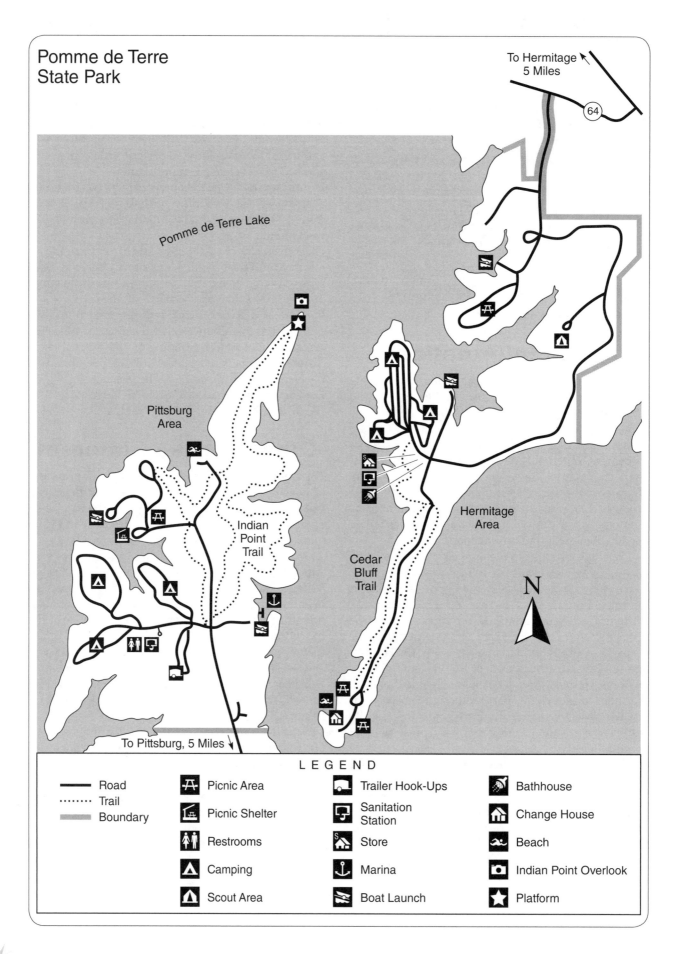

Pomme de Terre State Park

To Hermitage
5 Miles

64

Pomme de Terre Lake

Pittsburg
Area

Indian
Point
Trail

Hermitage
Area

Cedar
Bluff
Trail

N

To Pittsburg, 5 Miles

LEGEND

—— Road	Picnic Area	Trailer Hook-Ups	Bathhouse
······ Trail	Picnic Shelter	Sanitation Station	Change House
—— Boundary	Restrooms	Store	Beach
	Camping	Marina	Indian Point Overlook
	Scout Area	Boat Launch	Platform

Indian Point Trail

Distance Round-Trip: 3 miles
Estimated Hiking Time: 1.5 hours

Settlers wrote in their journals about riding their wagons easily through "oak openings" or open "oak orchards." Natural fires had eliminated most of the understory, leaving widely spaced oak trees above oceans of prairie grasses and herbs.

Caution: This property is owned by the U.S. Army Corps of Engineers and leased to the state park system. Strict federal and state laws prohibit the disturbance of archaeological sites and artifacts. Refrain from climbing on the rock cairns or disturbing them in any way. Also, the trail can be difficult to follow in places because of the open nature of the savanna. Try to follow numbered features closely.

Trail Directions: This trail is at the southern, or Pittsburg, area of the park. Park in the lot for the trailhead, which is across the road from the campground entrance. Begin at the sign for the trail [1], next to the amphitheater, and go straight, into the savanna [2].

Savannas, which are transition areas between prairies and forests, were once common in Missouri. Today, because of logging, grazing, and conversion to forests, savannas are an uncommon and threatened natural community. The soil is thin here, and sometimes limestone and dolomite bedrock protrudes from the surface. Just after passing through a large patch of spanglegrass (with extremely flattened seed heads), you cross the main park road at .34 mi. [3]. The savanna is so open that you can see coves of the lake through the trees. Turn right at the trail marker at .60 mi. [4], just before you reach the road. Go straight at the wide, old road intersection at .72 mi. [5].

Notice the barbed-wire fence remnants deeply embedded in an old chinquapin oak, just as the trail bends left at .89 mi. [6]. Big grazers like elk and bison fed on rich savanna grasses in presettlement Missouri. Later, settlers fenced savannas for their cattle. Cross the park road at .92 mi. [7] and go straight at the connector link at .97 mi. [8]. Red cedars join the chinquapin oaks. Fire, which maintains the savanna, often burns off the lower limbs of cedars that are large enough to survive. You soon see water on both sides as this ridged peninsula becomes narrower.

At 1.38 mi. [9] are the remnants of a Native American cairn. Bluffs or ridgetops like this were often chosen as sites for cairns, which were used for monuments, burials, and landmarks. Archaeological excavations have dated the cairn to the Mississippian cultural period. Go straight at 1.48 mi. [10] to take the spur to the overlook. The breeze starts to kick up as you make your way to Indian Point overlook, which you reach at 1.56 mi. [11]. Sunsets are magnificent here, but the view of the lake arms and the island are great anytime. To continue, return to [10] and turn left.

As more views of the lake open on your left, you hike through a glade at 1.69 mi. [12]. Purple prairie clover, rose verbena, and coneflower add their splashes of color. The trail continues through the savanna and follows the shoreline. After crossing two intermittent drainages at 2.09 mi. [13], stay as close to the water as is convenient until you reach a second cairn remnant at 2.39 mi. [14]. Buttonbush and several other aquatic plants are nearby. Hike around the cairn and pass a large sign on the shore that reads "L2." Soon, you pass some ancient, twisted, craggy oaks at 2.61 mi. [15] and see the marina on your left. You pass some wing-stem sunflowers and rattlesnake master before arriving at the connector link at 2.94 mi. [16], where you go straight. Return to the trailhead just across the park road.

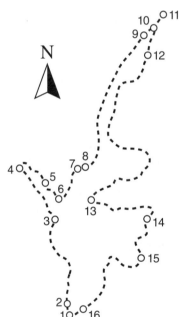

1. Start
2. Savanna
3. Road crossing
4. Right turn
5. Go straight
6. Fence remnants
7. Road crossing
8. Go straight
9. Cairn remnants
10. Go straight
11. Indian Point overlook
12. Glade
13. Two drainages
14. Cairn remnant
15. Ancient oaks
16. Go straight

Cedar Bluff Trail

 Distance Round-Trip: 2 miles
Estimated Hiking Time: 1 hour

Keep alert—you'll be amazed at the wildlife that you can see and hear on this skinny, ridged, wooded peninsula.

Caution: Watch for traffic on the park road; you cross it twice.

Trail Directions: This trail is at the northern, or Hermitage, area of the park. Park in the lot for visitors, next to the bath house. The trail begins **[1]** at the signboard, across the road from the campground entrance.

Begin on a rocky trail that leads down a shaded hill. As a small cove of the lake appears on your right, scan the edges for the largest North American heron, the great blue heron, which stands a full 3 feet tall. Startled great blues emit three or four loud, hoarse squawks. The green heron, about a third the size of the great blue, feeds along the lake here, too. At .07 mi. **[2]**, near a stand of yellow false foxglove wildflowers, a spur to your right takes you down to a courtesy dock for the park store. Stand on the dock and watch bluegills and green sunfish patrol the water under the dock and near the shore, waiting for unfortunate terrestrial insects to fall in.

Turn right after returning to the trail. You wind around some tall lespedeza and buttonbush near the water before emerging onto an open, rocky point at .14 mi. **[3]**. Turn right, toward the lake, for a magnificent overlook. Overhanging dolomite bluffs make up the shoreline on your left, and gentle, wooded hills of the Springfield Plateau line the horizon over the water. Turn away from the lake and hike into the woods to continue.

In a mixed forest of white oak, post oak, cedar, and sugar maple, you reach a trail intersection at .30 mi. **[4]**. Bear right here. The trail takes you about midslope, between the top of the ridge on your left and the lakeshore on your right. Listen for the pileated woodpecker, a crow-sized, shy bird usually heard more often than seen. Its drumming on resonant logs is loud, slow, and softer at the end, and its loud, repetitive call is reminiscent of a monkey's chatter. Notice the twisted trunks of the old chinquapin oaks near the ridgetop. Their wide-sprawling limbs indicate that they grew in a more open setting in the past, having no need to grow tall to compete for sunlight.

At .61 mi. **[5]**, go straight at the connecting link. Watch for groundhogs; park staff have noticed that they've taken a liking to this peninsula and its surroundings. Another animal that you may meet along

the trail is the box turtle. If you find one, count the rings on any of the large scales of its shell to find its age—box turtles can live up to 80 years! Males usually have red eyes, whereas females have yellow or brown eyes. You hike beneath some shagbark hickories and cedars before emerging into the clearing of the picnic and beach area. Turn left here and cross the park road at .93 mi. **[6]**.

Where the trail is sunny, look closely for the sparkling crystals of quartz in the sandstone. Where the trail becomes sandy and dusty, look for small, bowl-shaped depressions made by ant lions. These small, predatory insect larvae lie at the bottom of each "lion pit," waiting for crawling insects to tumble in. Several clear views of the lake open on your right. If you are here during winter, look for bald eagles soaring over the lake or perching on nearby trees. Just after passing a glade remnant, occupied by gray-head coneflowers, black-eyed susans, and lots of bluestem grass, go straight at the connecting link at 1.42 mi. **[7]**. A groundhog burrow is on your left at 1.59 mi. **[8]**; approach quietly and you may spy its inhabitant. After crossing the park road at 1.71 mi. **[9]**, return to an intersection **[4]**, where you turn right to finish your hike.

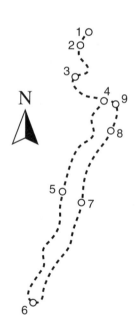

1. Start
2. Spur to dock
3. Spur to overlook
4. Bear right
5. Go straight
6. Road crossing
7. Go straight
8. Groundhog burrow
9. Road crossing

- Come to Wilson's Creek and learn about the battle that marked the beginning of the Civil War in Missouri.

- Tour the battlefield where 15,000 soldiers from both sides gathered and more than 2,500 men were killed or wounded.

- See postmaster John Ray's home, one of only two surviving structures on the site from the battle, which was used as a Confederate field hospital during and after the battle.

Area Information

With civil war imminent, most Missourians favored neutrality, but radical Secessionists and Unionists divided the state, and Missouri's sons quickly filled the ranks of military units that formed everywhere.

The battle of Wilson's Creek was the second major engagement of the Civil War, after Manassas, and marked the beginning of the war in Missouri. The battle here involved 15,000 Confederate and Union soldiers. More than 2,500 men were killed or wounded during the bloody six-hour struggle. The National Park Service manages Wilson's Creek National Battlefield to interpret this important battle, preserve its site, and commemorate the soldiers on both sides who died and are buried here.

Directions: From Springfield, take Highway 60 west. Just outside town, take Highway M east for .7 mile. Turn south on Highway ZZ for 1.5 miles and turn left at the sign for the battlefield.

Hours Open: The battlefield is open from 8:00 a.m. to 9:00 p.m. during summer, until 7:00 p.m. in spring and fall, and until 5:00 p.m. during winter. The entire site is closed on Thanksgiving, Christmas Day, and New Year's Day.

Facilities: The site features a visitor center with a museum. Living-history demonstrations and guided tours are also scheduled. A 5-mile auto tour route takes visitors to all the major points on the battlefield. Abundant interpretive signs are located along the way. A biking and jogging route, a picnic area, and horseback trails are also provided.

Permits and Rules: A small entrance fee is required. Bikes are restricted to the auto tour route, and horses are restricted to authorized horse trails. Using firearms or metal detectors, collecting artifacts, and disturbing buildings, plants, or animals are prohibited. Skates and skateboards are not allowed. Pets must always be leashed. Please acknowledge the memorial qualities of the site and refrain from any activities that might be deemed disrespectful.

For Further Information: Wilson's Creek National Battlefield, 6424 West Farm Road 182, Republic, MO 65738; 417-732-2662, ext. 227.

Other Areas of Interest

Bass Pro Shops Outdoor World is the world's largest sporting goods store. Featuring aquariums, a wildlife museum and displays, waterfalls, and restaurants, the store is one of Missouri's biggest attractions. The store is northeast of Wilson's Creek, in Springfield, at the corner of Highway 60 and Campbell Street. For more information, call 417-887-7334.

Springfield Conservation Nature Center is one of five nature centers operated by the Missouri Department of Conservation, and features exhibits, an auditorium, nature programs, and hiking trails. The center is .5 mile from the intersection of Highways 65 and 60, and admission is free. For more information, call 417-888-4237.

Hundreds of animals from around the world live at **Dickerson Park Zoo**. The zoo is at the north end of Springfield, at the junction of I-44 and Highway 13. For more information, call 417-833-1570.

Site Trails

Nature Trail (🐾🐾, .5 mile). This trail traverses a mixed forest and crosses an intermittent creek. It includes several loops that begin and end at the picnic area, behind the visitor center.

Ray House and Springhouse Trails (🐾🐾, .5 mile). These short trails connect the only two surviving structures from the battle. The trails begin at stop #2 on the auto tour route, 1.5 miles from the visitor center.

East Overlook and Pulaski Arkansas Battery Trails (🐾🐾, .5 mile). These short trails connect the east battlefield overlook with the Pulaski Arkansas Battery. The trails begin at stop #3 on the auto tour route, 2.1 miles from the visitor center.

Wilson's Creek National Battlefield

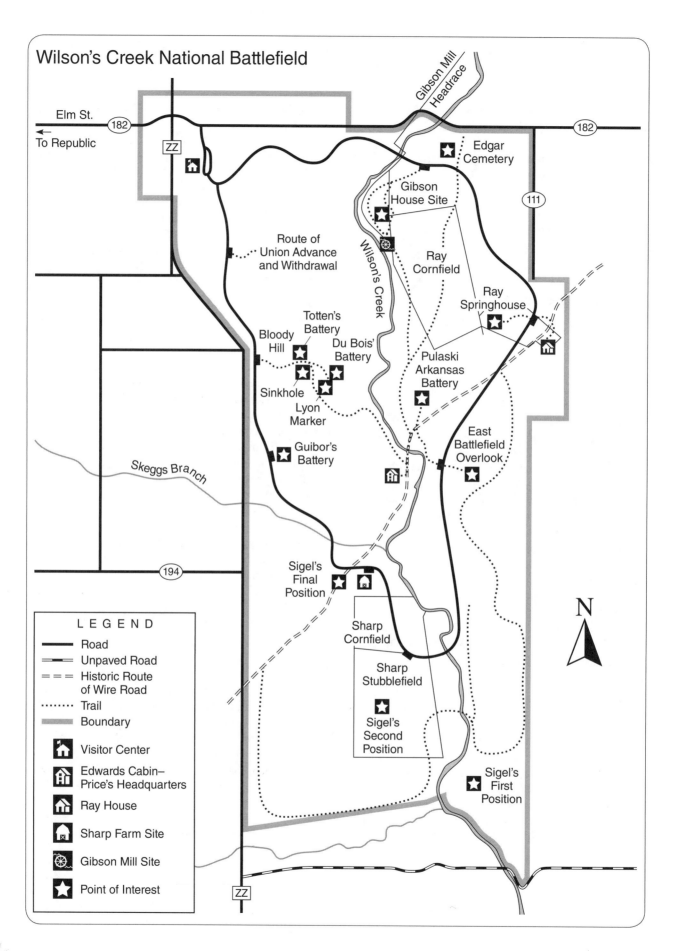

Elm St.
To Republic

Gibson Mill Headrace

Edgar Cemetery

Gibson House Site

Route of Union Advance and Withdrawal

Ray Cornfield

Wilson's Creek

Ray Springhouse

Totten's Battery

Bloody Hill

Du Bois' Battery

Pulaski Arkansas Battery

Sinkhole

Lyon Marker

East Battlefield Overlook

Guibor's Battery

Skeggs Branch

Sigel's Final Position

Sharp Cornfield

Sharp Stubblefield

Sigel's Second Position

Sigel's First Position

N

LEGEND

- Road
- Unpaved Road
- Historic Route of Wire Road
- Trail
- Boundary

- Visitor Center
- Edwards Cabin– Price's Headquarters
- Ray House
- Sharp Farm Site
- Gibson Mill Site
- Point of Interest

Gibson Mill Site and Ray Cornfield

Distance Round-Trip: 1.75 miles
Estimated Hiking Time: 1 hour

The trail reveals an old mill and home site, where the Gibson family crouched in the cellar on August 10, 1861, seeking refuge from the thunderous cannons that shattered the morning air.

Caution: The last half of this trail is in the sun; you may want to bring some protection. Horses are allowed on this section. Stay on the 6-foot-wide section of the auto tour route when you hike back to the trailhead. Watch out for bicyclists there.

Trail Directions: Park in the turnoff for stop #1 of the auto tour route, .8 mi. from the visitor center. The trail begins in a prairielike field that was John Gibson's oat field at the time of the battle [1]. The Gibsons lived in a cabin near the creek, just ahead, and on the day before the great battle, they found themselves surrounded by 12,000 Confederate soldiers. This spot marks the northern end of the Confederate camps, which extended 2 mi. south along the creek.

The trail quickly descends to the wooded corridor of Wilson's Creek. After passing an interpretive sign about Gibson's mill and a wooden bridge, turn right at the intersection at .10 mi. [2]. Look for the flaky, peeling bark of black cherry and the lined, orange-tinged bark of Osage orange next to the trail. Osage orange wood was prized by Native Americans for making bows, and, before barbed wire became available, settlers planted the trees as living fences because they grew in impenetrable thickets.

The Gibsons made their living by grinding grain and processing wool with the mill that stood just ahead. To provide a constant supply of water falling on the tall waterwheel that powered the millworks, John Gibson performed an amazing engineering feat; with a shovel and perhaps a neighbor and a mule, Gibson constructed a narrow earthen canal .75 mi. long! The millrace channeled water from a small dam upstream and crossed the creek on a raised trestle. The canal gained elevation over the creek, and when it spilled onto the waterwheel, it was 9 feet above the creek. At .30 mi. [3], at an interpretive sign, you can see remnants of this earthen invention.

After crossing a small, wooden bridge, turn right at .35 mi. [4] to find the Gibson mill site at .37 mi. [5]. In 1966 archaeologists discovered the mill's foundation, waterwheel, gearing, and millstones, as well as evidence that the mill burned sometime after the war. Return to [4] and turn right. At .49 mi. [6] is the Gibson house site, where a sign explains the 1966 archaeo-

logical excavations here. You can still see parts of the limestone foundation of the house. Return to the mill site and continue the trail on your left.

As the trail follows Wilson's Creek, look for great blue and little green herons, standing in the water or perching nearby. Watch the trail ahead for rabbits and deer—both animals are plentiful in the recovering savannas and prairies of the battlefield. Just after crossing a small bridge, you arrive at a three-way intersection where an Osage orange tree and a walnut tree are growing together [7] (.98 mi.). Turn left here to begin the Ray Cornfield Trail. The only major fighting on this side of Wilson's Creek occurred here. On the morning of the battle, John Ray watched from his front porch as his cornfield became a battlefield and Union forces were driven back across the stream. At 1.07 mi. [8], just after passing a split-rail fence, ignore the spur on your left. As some expansive views open, look on the horizon on your left to see Bloody Hill, scene of the most intense and savage fighting of the battle. As you pass through a thicket of wild plum trees at 1.37 mi. [9], notice the animal paths that cross the trail. Turn left on the pavement of the auto tour route at 1.60 mi. [10] to return to the trailhead.

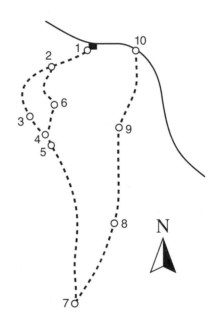

1. Start
2. Right turn
3. Millrace remnants
4. Right turn
5. Mill site
6. House site
7. Left turn
8. Go straight
9. Wild plum thicket
10. Left turn

.oody Hill and Wire Road

Distance Round-Trip: 2 miles
Estimated Hiking Time: 1 hour

For more than six hours, the armies pounded each other in steady and fierce combat, often at close range. In all, over 80 percent of casualties of the battle fell on Bloody Hill, making it one of the bloodiest fights in the war. Survivors of the battle described the day's relentless heat, blinding clouds of gunpowder smoke, and great heaps of the dead and wounded.

Caution: The last half of this trail is in the sun; you may want to bring some protection. Horses are allowed on this section. Stay on the 6-foot-wide section of the auto tour route when you hike back to the trailhead. Watch out for bicyclists there.

Trail Directions: Park at the turnoff for Bloody Hill, which is auto tour route stop #7, 4.2 mi. from the visitor center. Part of this trail is a self-guiding route, and numbered stations along the trail correspond to numbers in a tour booklet, available from the visitor center for 50¢. Numbered stations do not correspond to numbered features in this book.

Near some interpretive signs, begin on a wide, gravel path **[1]**. The cannon at .15 mi. **[2]** is in the position that the 2nd U.S. Battery maintained during most of the battle. This battery was led by Captain James "Bottle-Nose" Totten, so nicknamed for his fondness for brandy. Cannon projectiles included solid shot, shot designed to explode, and canister shot, which were like giant shotgun cartridges. Although his army was outnumbered more than two to one, the Union leader, General Nathaniel Lyon, planned a surprise attack on the Confederates, camped along Wilson's Creek. The intersection at .22 mi. **[3]** marks the spot that Lyon's army of 4,200 men had reached by 6:00 a.m., advancing from the northwest. From across the creek, to the east, four cannons of the Pulaski Arkansas Battery opened fire on Lyon's army, slowing their advance. Turn left here.

Fierce charges and countercharges came in waves, as the Union desperately tried to hold its hilltop position. After you hike through a glade of exposed limestone bedrock and prickly pear cactus, you reach a stone monument at .31 mi. **[4]** that marks the approximate spot where General Lyon fell at about 9:30 a.m. while leading the 2nd Kansas Infantry against the Missouri State Guard. "I am killed!" Lyon exclaimed, as he collapsed into the arms of his orderly after a musket ball passed through his chest. At the three-way intersection at .37 mi. **[5]**, turn left. Note the thick forest here. One Iowa private wrote, "The few trees were rather large . . . and everything could be distinctly seen under them." The National Park Service has begun a program of prescribed fires to restore the battlefield to its 1861 landscape of prairie and savanna.

At .55 mi. **[6]**, where the trail turns left, you see the slope that Southerners attempted to crest three times during the battle, each time suffering heavy casualties. The small cabin at the bottom of the slope marks the site of the headquarters of Confederate General Sterling Price. Price was well liked by his troops, who nicknamed him Old Pap. Turn right at .58 mi. **[7]** and descend to the creek valley. At .85 mi. **[8]**, at an iron bridge, turn right. You are now on historic Wire Road, which connected Springfield, Missouri, with Fort Smith, Arkansas, at the time of the battle. You soon pass an interpretive sign at the Edwards cabin, where Price was eating his breakfast of cornbread and beef at the time of Lyon's attack.

After Wire Road dips into the welcome shade at the Skegg's Branch crossing, you climb a hill. Turn right at 1.31 mi. **[9]** on the pavement of the auto tour route and take the spur on your right at 1.82 mi. **[10]** that leads to Guibor's battery. Captain Guibor assisted the Confederate infantry in their final charge up Bloody Hill by firing four cannons from this spot into the Federal line. Turn right after returning to the auto tour route to finish your battlefield hike.

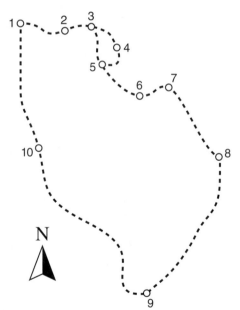

1. Start
2. Cannon
3. Left turn
4. Lyon monument
5. Left turn
6. Left turn
7. Right turn
8. Iron bridge
9. Right turn
10. Spur to battery

67. Roaring River State Park

- Visit one of the state's oldest parks, where clear streams have carved deep, narrow valleys between steep, forested knobs and ridges.
- View one of Missouri's most picturesque springs, which emerges from a peaceful cave at the base of a dramatic rock bluff, lined with lush ferns.
- Explore the Roaring River Hills Wild Area, a 2,075-acre undeveloped wilderness that is home to 26 rare or endangered plants and animals.

Area Information

Roaring River begins quietly. From a shaded cave beneath a high cliff, a deep, blue pool issues about 20 million gallons of water every day without much of a sound. Only after the river hurries around the boulders of its narrow valley does it begins to roar.

The mountainous terrain of Roaring River State Park is part of the White River section of the Ozarks. Weathered bluffs and sheltered forest coves hide caves, seeps, and springs. Clear streams cut through six different rock formations. Many of the park's plants, including yellowwood, Ozark spiderwort, and Ashe juniper, cannot be found in any other region of the state. Several southwestern species inhabit the park, including armadillos, roadrunners, and the colorful collared lizard. Winter visitors usually see bald eagles perching near the river.

Kansas City and St. Louis residents find the river's rugged and scenic setting the ideal place for fishing retreats. The Missouri Department of Conservation operates a trout hatchery near the spring and stocks the river daily during the fishing season.

Directions: Roaring River is in the state's southwest corner. From Cassville, take Highway 112 south 7 miles into the park.

Hours Open: The park is open year-round. The nature center is open from 9:00 a.m. to 5:00 p.m. daily during the fishing season. Opening and closing sirens announce daily fishing hours, which change seasonally.

Facilities: The site offers a nature center, a fish hatchery, a tackle shop and camp store, a restaurant, a motel, a gift shop, three campgrounds, a swimming pool, an amphitheater, rental cabins, a group camp, and picnic areas.

Permits and Rules: A state fishing license and a daily permit, available from the tackle shop at the CCC Lodge, are required for trout fishing. Swimming or wading in the river is restricted to certain areas. Fish feeding is allowed in the hatchery's rearing pools, but only food bought on site may be used. Pets must always be leashed. Motel and cabin reservations are recommended.

For Further Information: Roaring River State Park, Route 4, Box 4100, Cassville, MO 65625; 417-847-2539 (park office), 417-847-2330 (concessionaire), or 800-334-6946 (Department of Natural Resources, Division of State Parks).

Other Areas of Interest

Sugar Camp Scenic Drive is an 8-mile-long gravel road that leads to Eagle Rock and features splendid overlooks of the forested White River Hills, Onyx Cave picnic area, limestone glades, and a view of the White River. The drive is in the Mark Twain National Forest, just south of Roaring River. To begin, take Highway 112 south of the park for 3.4 miles and turn left on FR 197.

Piney Creek Wilderness, in the national forest northeast of Roaring River, is 8,000 acres of oak-hickory forest and features five equestrian–hiking trails. The wilderness is about 20 miles east of Cassville on Lake Road 76-6. For more information on either site, call 417-847-2144.

Park Trails

Deer Leap Trail (👣👣👣👣, 4 miles). Beginning on the walkway between the hatchery pools and the spring, this trail climbs limestone bluffs on natural rock and stone steps.

Fire Tower Trail (👣👣👣👣👣, 4.5 miles). This trail explores the Roaring River Hills Wild Area and accesses a state natural area that preserves a remnant of old-growth oak-hickory forest. The trail can be accessed from the Deer Leap Trail, the nature center, or from the parking area on Highway F.

Eagle's Nest Trail (👣👣👣👣👣, 3.3 miles). This trail follows the river for over a half mile, passes rock bluffs and a patch of sensitive ferns, and ascends to a high, chert ridgetop, clad in shortleaf pines. Middle and lower sections might be seasonally overgrown. The trail begins from the east end of campground #2.

River Trail (👣👣, .7 mile). Built in the 1930s by the CCC, this trail takes you alongside Roaring River and connects the CCC Lodge and campground #3.

Springhouse Trail (👣👣👣, .5 mile). See remnants of an old homestead site and springhouse. The trailhead is in the southwest corner of the Emory Melton Inn and Conference Center parking lot.

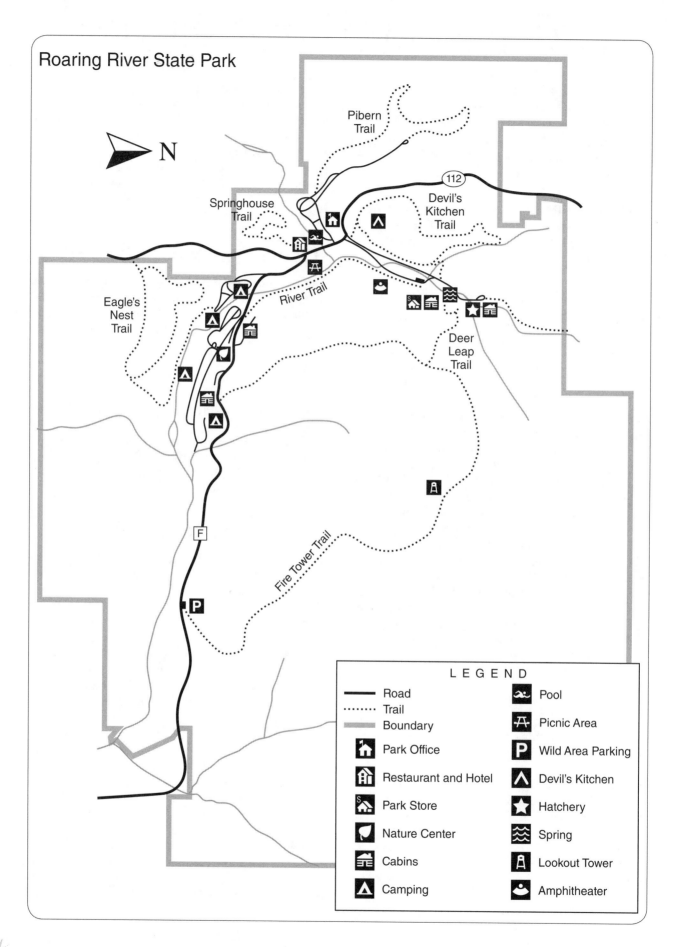

Roaring River State Park

N

Pibern Trail

Springhouse Trail

Devil's Kitchen Trail

112

Eagle's Nest Trail

River Trail

Deer Leap Trail

Fire Tower Trail

F

P

LEGEND

——	Road		Pool
····	Trail		Picnic Area
▬▬	Boundary	**P**	Wild Area Parking
	Park Office		Devil's Kitchen
	Restaurant and Hotel	★	Hatchery
S	Park Store		Spring
	Nature Center		Lookout Tower
	Cabins		Amphitheater
	Camping		

Devil's Kitchen Trail

Distance Round-Trip:
1.75 miles
Estimated Hiking Time:
1.25 hours

The Devil's Den, the Devil's Backbone, the Devil's Sugar Bowl . . . in all, over 80 natural features in Missouri are named after old Beelzebub.

Caution: Small, loose rocks cover several steep hills.
Trail Directions: Park in the lot for the CCC Lodge, near the hatchery; the trailhead is just across the river. An interpretive brochure for this self-guiding trail is available at the nature center. Numbered stations along the trail do not correspond to numbered features here.

Begin at the sign for the trail **[1]** and hike along a rocky, intermittent stream. On your way to the top of this ridge, you come across four types of sedimentary rock—dolomite, shale, limestone, and chert—each at its own level. You reach the first level at a three-way intersection at .10 mi. **[2]**, where you turn right on a big slab of dolomite bedrock. As you continue, you see geology in action. The bluff on your left is limestone, whereas the part of the hill you are walking on is dolomite. Because limestone is less resistant than dolomite, the bluff is eroding faster than the trail, creating what is called a bench.

Take the spur on your left at .25 mi. **[3]** to a small cave in the limestone, created when rainwater trickled through cracks in the rock. Many animals in the park, including bats, mice, cave crickets, and even bobcats use shelter caves. Turn left after returning to the main trail and cross the intersection of two intermittent streams. Ignore the spur on your left at the blocky boulders that have broken off the bluff at .45 mi. **[4]**.

At .51 **[5]** is a spur on your right that leads to another small cave across the creek. After heavy rainfall, a small stream flows from the mouth of this cave. Turn right after returning to the main trail. As the trail swings left, it takes you to a higher layer of rock. Notice the crunchy, jingling sounds under your feet. This is chert, a hard rock that collects on trails and in streambeds because it does not break down chemically as dolomite and limestone do. Several overlooks of the surrounding steep ridges appear through the trees. At the top, at .86 mi. **[6]**, you have climbed 325 feet from the trailhead and are standing beneath native shortleaf pine trees, some of which are 200 years old.

If you didn't see the little spring cave at 1.26 mi. **[7]** or hear its trickling stream, you would probably still find it because of the cloud of frigid air that rolls out of it and hits you in the shins as you hike by. Take a close look at the entrance to the cave and you'll see a layer of shale between layers of limestone above and dolomite below. Gray, flaky shale isn't much more than compressed clay, and, as a rock, it is extremely soft. At 1.36 mi. **[8]** is an odd and interesting array of rocks—the Devil's Kitchen. After several massive limestone blocks broke off the bluff, a layer of shale within the rocks failed to support their weight and caused further sliding. Rocks shifting above were caught by rocks below, forming the kitchen's roof. After exploring the kitchen, turn left on the main trail and turn left at the spur at 1.45 mi. **[9]**. The music of Roaring River accompanies you back to the three-way intersection **[2]**, where you go straight to return to the trailhead.

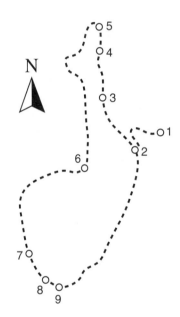

1. Start
2. Right turn
3. Spur to cave
4. Go straight
5. Spur to cave
6. Ridgetop
7. Spring cave
8. Devil's Kitchen
9. Left turn

Pibern Trail

Distance Round-Trip:
1.75 miles
Estimated Hiking Time:
1 hour

In 1847 the first land surveyors described the Roaring River Hills as "the steepest description of stony mountains entirely unfit for cultivation." Thanks to lack of development, this rugged landscape is still home to the striking painted bunting, bobcat, and an occasional black bear.

Caution: Small, loose rocks cover several steep hills.
Trail Directions: Park at the turnaround loop at the north end of campground #1 and begin at the sign for the trail **[1]**. After crossing a wide, rocky streambed at the trailhead, you hike into a lush grove of spicebush and pawpaw on the other side. In September and October, shiny, bright red berries decorate the limbs of the aromatic spicebush, and green peanut-shaped fruits hang from pawpaw trees. Enormous sycamore and black walnut trees are further indicators of the moist, rich soil here. Just across the stream, gray and white limestone bluffs loom through the trees like cloaked giants, moving in and out of forest shadows.

At .17 mi. **[2]**, turn left into the streambed. Wingstem sunflowers on the banks are 7 feet tall by late summer, and blooming jewelweed splashes green and bright orange on the mostly white rocks. As you hike in the streambed, layers of overhanging limestone ledges climb the bluff next to the river, evidence of the stone-carving work that the water has completed over eons. Just past the ledges, find the trail into the woods on your left. The trail takes you alongside more rock shelves on your left. Blocky boulders, tumbled down from higher bluffs, fill another stream valley on your right. Although the boulders wear the dark green mosses of time, they look as if they've been suddenly frozen in their violent and rumbling trip from above.

After taking you uphill and passing some moist, shaded slopes covered with wild ginger and liverleaf, the trail turns left at .24 mi. **[3]**, away from the rocky ravine. Now the ravine on the left is so deep that you can't see the bottom—only the tops of trees. The ridge on your right is so steep you can't see the top—only the fractured, weathered, rocky shelves just above you. Some of the shelves hide small shelter caves, used by chipmunks and mice for homes and food-caching dens. As you continue on this side slope, you find gravelly areas of chert pebbles on the trail. In Missouri,

Native Americans made weapons and tools almost exclusively of chert because it is as hard as glass and fractures with fine, sharp edges.

At .68 mi. **[4]**, just before the trail swings to the left, you hike beneath grand, towering bluffs, many with shelter caves, overhanging ledges, and interesting eroded shapes. You soon descend into another streambed, with many boulders that have broken off from these bluffs. At .85 mi. **[5]**, some of the bluffs on your right have weathered into chimneylike pinnacles with flat tops. Look for bloodroot, wild hydrangea, and Christmas ferns crowding around the moisture of small seeps next to the trail.

At .97 mi. **[6]**, you cross a small, wooden bridge over an intermittent spring emerging from the bluff on your right. From here, you descend the hill on a trail full of rocks and tree roots. Ignore the spur to the stream at 1.27 mi. **[7]**. At the intersection at 1.35 mi. **[8]**, where a small building is on your right, turn left. After crossing the limestone bedrock of the streambed, you emerge into the campground behind site #55. Turn left on the pavement at 1.37 mi. **[9]** to finish your hike.

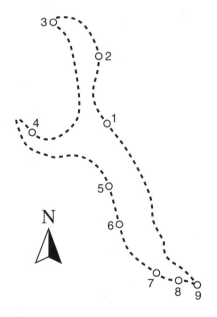

1. Start
2. Left turn into streambed
3. Left turn
4. Overhanging bluffs
5. Pinnacles
6. Intermittent spring
7. Go straight
8. Left turn
9. Left turn

- Even if you don't plan on hiking, drive to the trailhead. The 6.3 miles from Pineville to the trailhead is one of the most scenic drives that you'll find anywhere in the state.

- Find the rare Ozark chinquapin in one of its few remaining habitats.

- Depending on where you live, Big Sugar Creek may be a little out of the way. Go anyway. You'll be glad that you did!

- Wow!

Area Information

Big Sugar Creek, Missouri's only state park within the Elk River section of the Ozarks, features plants and animals that are less common or absent elsewhere in the state. Characterized by oak-pine woodlands, deeply dissected hills, intermittent streams, and countless rock ledges, the park is home to 345 different kinds of plants and 134 kinds of birds. Although most Ozark streams drain north and east, Big Sugar Creek and its tributaries drain south into the Arkansas River basin and contain several species that live nowhere else in Missouri, including the Neosho orangethroat darter and northern crayfish.

Big Sugar Creek State Park is also one of the few places where you can still find the Ozark chinquapin tree, which survives in Missouri in only a few counties that border Arkansas. Not to be confused with the chinquapin oak, a common tree on glades and woodlands, the Ozark chinquapin is rare. Formerly common, the Ozark chinquapin has been nearly eliminated by the same blight that decimated the American chestnut tree. Because of the diversity and distinctive natural features of the park, most of its 2,048 acres have been designated as the Elk River Breaks Natural Area.

Big Sugar Creek State Park is still in the development stage. Plans include a picnic area, a group camp area for organized youth groups, and a canoe launch on Big Sugar Creek. But don't wait for more facilities before you visit. Come and see why this park, even though it may be a little out of your way, is well worth the drive.

Directions: Follow Route W through the town of Pineville until you reach 8th Street. Turn east on 8th Street (which turns into Big Sugar Creek Road) and travel 6.3 miles to the parking lot for the trailhead on the left.

Hours Open: The site is open year-round.

Facilities: The Ozark Chinquapin Trail is currently the only facility open at the park. Restrooms and an informational kiosk are located at the trailhead parking lot.

Permits and Rules: Horses and ATVs are not permitted on the hiking trail.

For Further Information: Big Sugar Creek State Park, c/o Roaring River State Park, Route 4, Box 4100, Cassville, MO 65625; 417-847-2539; www.mostateparks. com/bigsugar.htm. For more information on the Ozark chinquapin, visit www.ozarkchinquapin. com.

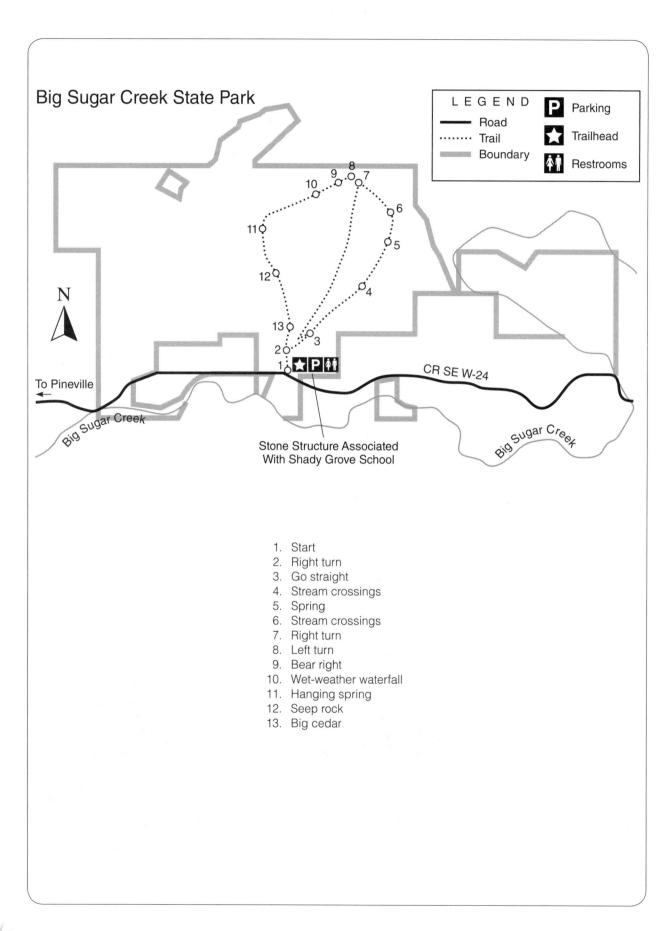

Big Sugar Creek State Park

8

9 7

10

6

11

5

12

4

13

3

2

1 ★ **P** 🚻

CR SE W-24

To Pineville
←

Big Sugar Creek

Big Sugar Creek

Stone Structure Associated
With Shady Grove School

N

1. Start
2. Right turn
3. Go straight
4. Stream crossings
5. Spring
6. Stream crossings
7. Right turn
8. Left turn
9. Bear right
10. Wet-weather waterfall
11. Hanging spring
12. Seep rock
13. Big cedar

Ozark Chinquapin Trail

 Distance Round-Trip: 3.75 miles
Estimated Hiking Time: 2 hours

Intriguing rock outcrops, interesting terrain, charming wildflowers, scenic woods—they all made their unique contributions. By themselves, in fact, they would make a great trail. But it was the stream, always there yet constantly surprising me with its changes, that made this a memorable trail.

Caution: There are many stream crossings on this trail.

Trail Directions: Follow Route W through the town of Pineville until you reach 8th Street. Turn east on 8th Street (which turns into Big Sugar Creek Road) and travel 6.3 mi. to the parking lot for the trailhead on the left. The trail begins **[1]** at an informational kiosk at the north end of the parking lot.

Introduce yourself to the creek and get acquainted as you cross it at .15 mi. First this creek, and then another, will accompany you for nearly the entire trail. Just past the creek crossing, turn right at the intersection at .17 mi. **[2]** and bear right at a fork in the trail just a few steps later. Soon, you find yourself in the middle of a pleasant scene. Rugged, scenic rock outcrops adorn the slope on your left, and a crystal-clear stream splashes over layers of limestone bedrock on your right. You'll be in this same pleasant scene with a hundred variations before you finish your hike.

As you hike, look for the Ozark chinquapin tree, the trail's namesake, a small tree with spear-shaped leaves 6 to 10 inches long and with toothed edges, like a saw blade. Its fruit, a sweet nut, grows inside a spiny bur. Go straight at the intersection with the connector at .36 mi. **[3]**. The trail meanders back and forth across the stream several times as you hike in a flat little pocket between two towering ridges. The ridges

look as though they are made of giant piles of gravel, and you can hear the chert rocks clink and jingle as you hike over them. After the trail crosses a couple of small tributaries at .80 mi. **[4]**, the stream undercuts thin layers of rock, which creep right down into the streambed. If you are here after a rain, a small spring may be flowing on your left at 1.14 mi. **[5]**. Cross the stream at 1.33 mi. **[6]** over some brown chert bedrock. After crossing again twice more you wind your way slowly uphill. Turn right at the intersection with the connector link at 1.78 mi. **[7]**. Reach the peak of the ridge, marked by some giant trees, at 1.85 mi. **[8]**, where you turn left. Bear right at the fork in the trail at 1.91 mi. **[9]**.

As you reach the bottom of the valley, another stream will soon escort you on your right. You find a picturesque wet-weather waterfall at 2.27 mi. **[10]**, where the stream has carved bedrock into an amphitheater shape and water cascades down layers of undercut rock. You encounter several stream crossings, wet-weather waterfalls, and more stream scenes—each as beautiful as the one before—as you continue. At 2.65 mi. **[11]**, look on your left for a hanging spring, where water erupts from the side of the slope and flows downhill for about 30 feet before disappearing again in the gravelly hill. Similarly, you may notice sections of the stream that flow, disappear, and reemerge farther downstream. At 2.97 mi. **[12]**, you find a seep rock, a vertical wall of limestone kept wet by a seep above it. Near its base, you hike on a natural sidewalk.

At 3.51 mi. **[13]**, you find a cedar so big that it looks like a pine tree. Give it a hug. Unless you have apelike arms, your hands won't be able to touch on the other side! You hike among a wonderland of moss-covered boulders and cross the creek a couple more times before you reach **[2]**, where you go straight to return to the trailhead.

69. George Washington Carver National Monument

- Hike through the forest and next to the streams where George Washington Carver spent his boyhood and shaped his interest in botany.
- Walk through a restored house built by Moses Carver in 1881.
- Learn how to make lye soap.
- Saunter on the banks of a serene spring pond flowing with life, from muskrats, turtles, and bass to dragonflies, minnows, and whirligig beetles.

Area Information

George Washington Carver was born into slavery in a 14-foot-by-14-foot one-room cabin sometime in the early 1860s on the Moses Carver farm in Diamond, Missouri. Kidnapped by bushwhackers, orphaned as an infant, and plagued by sickness, Carver believed nevertheless that he could achieve whatever he set out to do. On his way to national prominence as one of the foremost scientists of his era, Carver influenced many young people to advance their education or move in a new direction.

Receiving national attention by discovering hundreds of uses for the peanut, sweet potato, and soybean, Carver left a career as a research botanist at Iowa Agricultural College to work with Booker T. Washington at Tuskegee Institute in Alabama, where he taught botany and agriculture. Director of agricultural research at Tuskegee for 47 years, Carver devoted his life to devising better farming methods for poor farmers of the South, who were trying to eke a living from land exhausted by cotton. Carver coaxed farmers away from cotton to soil-enhancing, protein-rich crops such as peanuts and soybeans. By teaching crop diversification and conservation, Carver helped many Southern farmers rise from the enslavement of subsistence farming.

George Washington Carver National Monument, at Carver's birthplace, was dedicated in 1953 to commemorate Carver's life, his work, and his humane philosophy. Carver did his work with its potential benefit to people in mind and was always modest about his success. Concerning success, Carver had this to say: "It is not the style of clothes one wears, neither the kind of automobile one drives, nor the amount of money one has in the bank, that counts. These mean nothing. It is simply service that measures success."

Directions: The site is just southeast of Joplin. From Diamond, turn west on Highway V and go 2 miles. Turn left on Carver Road. Go .7 mile and turn right at the entrance.

Hours Open: The visitor center and grounds are open daily from 9:00 a.m. to 5:00 p.m. year-round. The site is closed Thanksgiving, Christmas Day, and New Year's Day.

Facilities: The site features a visitor center with exhibits and a 30-minute documentary on Carver. A self-guiding trail interprets the area where Carver spent his boyhood. The Carver Discovery Center has interactive exhibits about nature and science. A picnic area is also available. Call about special events, programs, and activities.

Permits and Rules: Picking wildflowers is prohibited. Fishing, wading, or swimming in the streams or spring pond is not allowed. Pets must be leashed at all times.

For Further Information: George Washington Carver National Monument, 5646 Carver Road, Diamond, MO 64840; 417-325-4151; www.nps.gov/gwca.

Other Areas of Interest

What would a trip to the southwest corner of Missouri be without visiting the **Spooklight**? Whether a soft white glow in the distance, a necklace of shimmering lights, or an orange ball of fire that silently glides up and down country roads, the Spooklight of the Missouri-Oklahoma line has delighted, intrigued, and mystified residents, visitors, and scientists for over a hundred years.

To find the Spooklight, take I-44 west of Joplin. At exit 4, take Highway 43 south to Highway C, where you turn southwest to the little town of Hornet. From Hornet, turn west on West Hymer Road until it ends at State Line Road. From here, go .2 mile to the north or .8 mile to the south; the east–west roads (Oklahoma's E40 and E50 roads) are prime Spooklight viewing spots. For more information, look for *Tri-State Spooklight*, a booklet published in the mid-1950s by Juanita Kay, and *Earth Lights Revelation* by researcher Paul Devereux.

Carver Trail

Distance Round-Trip: .75 mile
Estimated Hiking Time: 45 minutes

"My work, my life, must be in the spirit of a little child seeking only to know the truth and follow it." —George Washington Carver

Caution: Gates to the park are locked at 5:00 p.m. daily.

Trail Directions: An interpretive guide for this self-guiding trail is available from the visitor center for 50¢. Lettered stations along the trail do not correspond to numbered features here.

Begin the trail at the bust of George Washington Carver, just outside the visitor center **[1]**. Carver overcame slavery, becoming an orphan, sickness, violence, and racism to become a world-renowned scientist, educator, and humanitarian. When asked to speak at the commencement at Selma University in Selma, Alabama, on May 27, 1942, Carver read a poem titled "Equipment." Push the button below the bust to hear Carver read the poem in his own voice. Go straight, toward the small log cabin, to continue.

The log cabin at .05 mi. **[2]** marks the site where George was born into slavery sometime in the early 1860s. George lived in a tiny one-room cabin like this one with his mother, Mary, and his brother, Jim, until Confederate bushwhackers kidnapped him and his mother. George was returned, but his mother was never seen or heard from again. After the kidnapping, George and Jim moved into the nearby cabin of their owners, Moses and Susan Carver, who raised them as their own.

George was a sickly child and was relieved of many farm duties, freeing him to spend many hours in the forest, painting pictures of plants on rocks with homemade paints and brushes, and collecting wildflowers for his garden, hidden in the brush. The statue at .13 mi. **[3]** commemorates Carver's boyhood spent here and his intense curiosity about nature, which continued throughout his life. Take the spur on your left to the small spring, where George collected drinking water for the household. Return to the statue and cross the arched bridge to continue.

Turn right at the spring pond at .28 mi. **[4]** to walk around its banks. Williams Spring, which emerges beneath the far end of the pond, is named for Moses Carver's niece and her husband, who lived just north of the spring. Walk around the pond until you return to **[4]**, where you turn right. The house at .48 mi. **[5]** was built by Moses Carver in 1881 after a tornado destroyed his cabin and George's birthplace cabin. George never lived in the house but returned during his travels to visit the Carvers. The restored house contains interpretive material and is open to visitors. Continue the trail beneath a sprawling oak tree.

After crossing two small streams, you reach a sign marking the site where Moses Carver planted persimmons at .58 mi. **[6]**. Next to the sign, a persimmon trunk remains, with knobby, alligator-hide bark. As you leave the woods, you enter a prairie in the process of being restored. At .69 mi. **[7]** is the Carver cemetery, where Moses and Susan Carver are buried, along with many of George's childhood acquaintances. George is buried at Tuskegee Institute. Continue through the restoring prairie to return to the visitor center.

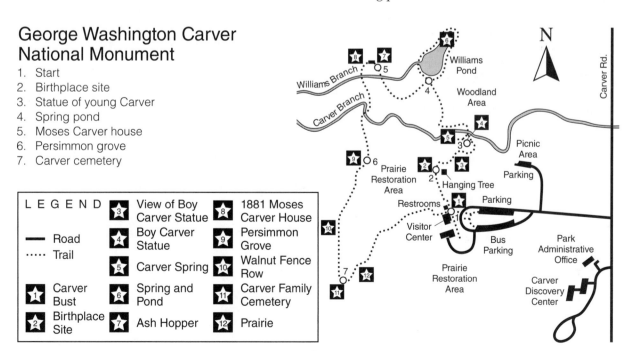

George Washington Carver National Monument

1. Start
2. Birthplace site
3. Statue of young Carver
4. Spring pond
5. Moses Carver house
6. Persimmon grove
7. Carver cemetery

LEGEND

— Road
···· Trail

1 Carver Bust
2 Birthplace Site
3 View of Boy Carver Statue
4 Boy Carver Statue
5 Carver Spring
6 Spring and Pond
7 Ash Hopper
8 1881 Moses Carver House
9 Persimmon Grove
10 Walnut Fence Row
11 Carver Family Cemetery
12 Prairie

Southwest

70. Prairie State Park

- See American bison roaming freely on Missouri's largest remaining tallgrass prairie.

- Hike in a prairie so undisturbed that it contains four state natural areas, each recognized for its exceptional natural qualities.

- Bring your camera. Over 400 species of native wildflowers and grasses are found here, as well as 150 species of birds, 25 mammals, and 88 butterflies and moths!

Area Information

On a hiking trail at Prairie State Park, with infinite waves of grasses and wildflowers and views of grazing bison on gentle hills that roll to the horizon in all directions, you may not believe that you are in a remnant of a landscape. But of the 13 million acres of tallgrass prairie that once covered more than a third of the state, over 99 percent is gone.

Luckily, the state's largest remaining tallgrass prairie is preserved today at Prairie State Park. Because glaciers never reached the Osage Plains region of southwest Missouri, the prairies here are older and more diverse than the prairies of the northern glaciated plains. Fortunately, too, 65 to 70 percent of the park has never been plowed, leaving intact the all-important prairie root system, which has taken centuries to develop.

Although bison and elk were eliminated in Missouri in the 19th century, they have been returned to Prairie State Park to live in their natural habitat. Prairie chickens still gather at their booming grounds in April and perform their famous mating rituals. At least 24 other rare or endangered species live here as well.

Directions: The park is in southwest Missouri, next to the Kansas border. From Lamar, take Highway 160 west 10.4 miles to Highway 43, where you turn north and travel 4.9 miles to Highway K. Turn west on Highway K and go 4.1 miles to Highway P. Turn south on Highway P and go 2.2 miles. Turn left on a gravel road at the sign for the park and go 1.8 miles to the visitor center.

Hours Open: The park is open year-round. The visitor center is open from 10:00 a.m. to 4:00 p.m. Tuesday through Saturday and from 1:00 p.m. to 4:00 p.m. on Sunday. The visitor center is closed on Monday. From November through March, the visitor center is closed on Sunday and Monday.

Facilities: The park offers a visitor center with interpretive exhibits and a picnic area. Limited primitive camping can be arranged by contacting staff at the visitor center.

Permits and Rules: Before hiking, visitors should stop in the visitor center for information on the location of the bison, which are allowed to roam freely in the park. Fires are restricted in the park, and smoking is not allowed on the trails. Pets are prohibited on the trails and must be leashed elsewhere in the park. Bikes and horses are not allowed on the trails.

For Further Information: Prairie State Park, 128 NW 150th Lane, Mindenmines, MO 64769; 417-843-6711.

Other Areas of Interest

The only Missourian ever elected U.S. president was born in Lamar, 15 miles east of Prairie State Park. **Harry S Truman Birthplace State Historic Site** offers free tours of the Truman home, built between 1880 and 1882. For more information, call 417-682-2279.

Battle of Carthage State Historic Site, south of Lamar in Carthage, is the site of a Civil War battle in which 6,000 Southern troops forced 1,000 Union soldiers to retreat down the stagecoach road to Sarcoxie. For more information, call 417-682-2279.

In Dadeville, east of Lamar, **Stockton State Park** features water recreation on 25,000-acre Stockton Lake, a popular spot for sailing. The park offers camping, a marina, a motel, cabins, a restaurant, boat ramps, fishing, boating, swimming, and picnic areas. For more information, call 417-276-4259.

Park Trails

Coyote Trail (🐾🐾, 3 miles). This rolling prairie trail may be partially closed because of a fence for the elk. Check with park staff for the status of the trail. The trail may be accessed from the picnic area or from a connector link from the Gay Feather Trail.

Gay Feather Trail (🐾🐾, 1.5 miles). Named for the tall, spiked, purple wildflower that blooms here all summer, this trail features a diversity of wildflowers and traverses Regal Prairie Natural Area. The trailhead is .9 mile south of the visitor center. The trail is linked to the Coyote and Drover's trails.

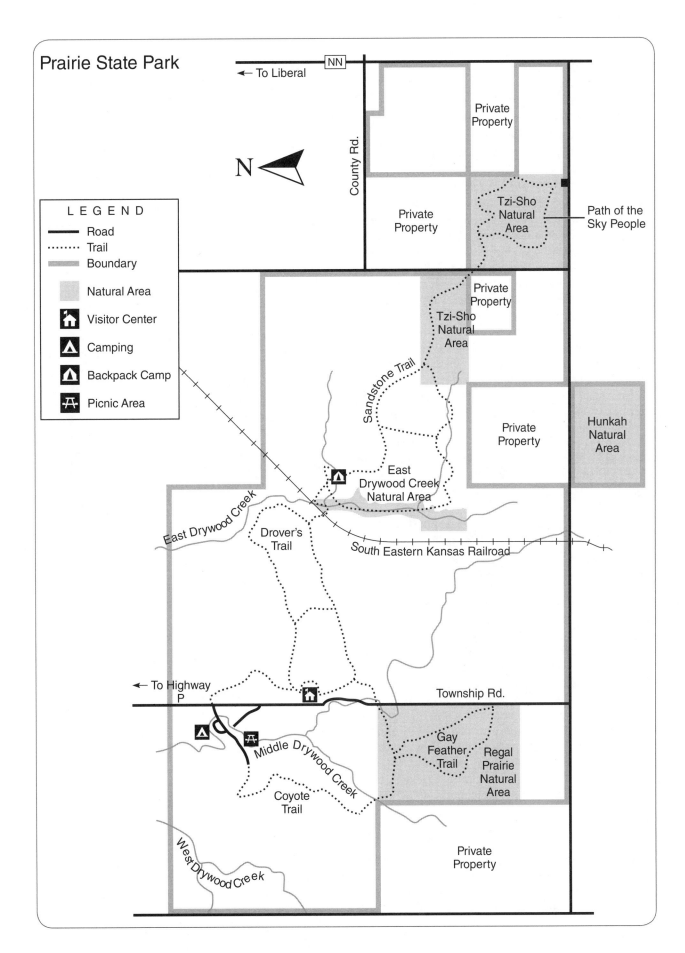

Prairie State Park

NN
← To Liberal

N

County Rd.

Private Property

Tzi-Sho Natural Area

Path of the Sky People

LEGEND
— Road
····· Trail
▬ Boundary
░ Natural Area
🏠 Visitor Center
▲ Camping
▲ Backpack Camp
🏕 Picnic Area

Private Property

Private Property

Tzi-Sho Natural Area

Private Property

Hunkah Natural Area

Sandstone Trail

East Drywood Creek Natural Area

East Drywood Creek

Drover's Trail

South Eastern Kansas Railroad

← To Highway P

Township Rd.

Middle Drywood Creek

Gay Feather Trail

Regal Prairie Natural Area

Coyote Trail

West Drywood Creek

Private Property

Drover's Trail

Distance Round-Trip: 2.5 miles
Estimated Hiking Time: 1.5 hours

Something about the prairie pulls your gaze outward and upward, and it's hard to decide which is bigger—the sky or the prairie. You get a feeling of freedom in this unusual vastness, and you realize that you are in a special place.

Caution: Before hiking any trail in the park, stop at the visitor center for information about the location of the bison, which are allowed to roam freely in the park. For your safety, do not leave your vehicle until you have this information. Do not touch the 8-foot-tall electric fence. To use the spur to the backpack camp, go under the fence only where the electric wires are insulated. Also, unless you are here in winter, a repellent against ticks and chiggers is recommended.

Trail Directions: Park in the lot for the visitor center. Begin at the sign for the trail **[1]**, which is next to the front of the building. At the trailhead, take the left fork of the trail. This trail is named for a type of prairie shepherd, who grazed sheep and cattle on the prairie. Although domestic animals have been absent from the prairie for some time, you may see recent evidence of the resident bison. As the trail leads you into an ocean of prairie grasses and wildflowers, keep your senses alert. You'll find that this native prairie is an incredibly diverse and thriving landscape.

The prairie grasses have a way of responding to the wind as if they are part of it. Breezes tease and bend their tops, just as puffs lightly ripple the surface of water. Indian grass, slough grass, and little bluestem grass grow here. By midsummer, look for the "turkey feet" seed heads of big bluestem. Early settlers wrote about prairie grasses growing as tall as a person on horseback, and by fall, several kinds of grasses here will be 8 feet tall, with roots just as long. Turn right at the intersection at .08 mi. **[2]**. Look for dozens of dragonflies, skimming the tops of the grass for mosquitoes and reflecting the sun off cellophane wings. The northern harrier, an endangered bird of prey commonly found here, hunts in a similar fashion, gliding slowly and watching, just over the top of the grass. You may be startled at any time by the explosion of northern bobwhites or greater prairie chickens, their wings thumping like tiny helicopters. Watch them glide away and melt into the horizon.

Turn left at the intersection at .31 mi. **[3]** and go straight at the connector link at .35 mi. **[4]**. Notice how much taller the plants grow where the trail dips into shallow draws. As you hike, you pass entire fields of wildflowers, in a kaleidoscope of colors and shapes. Look for the gray, heart-shaped leaves of ashy

sunflowers, the pealike pods and white blossoms of wild indigo, and the tall, purple, upright spikes of blazing star, shining like beacons in the emerald sea of grass.

Go straight at the four-way intersection at .94 mi. **[5]**. The broad, shallow valley in front of you, lined with shrubs and small trees, is that of East Drywood Creek, the state's most outstanding prairie stream. Look for red-winged blackbirds, perched on top of shrubs, and cliff swallows, swooping and diving overhead. Just after passing through a patch of coneflower and leadplant, go straight at 1.15 mi. **[6]** at the spur on your left. If you find a bare, bowl-shaped depression in the prairie, you have discovered a bison wallow—a spot where bison, especially bulls, roll on the ground for dust baths when it's dry and mud baths when it's wet.

Turn right at 1.40 mi. **[7]**, just before reaching a tall electric fence. Turn right again at the intersection at 1.46 mi. **[8]**, turning away from the fence. Go straight at a four-way intersection and go straight at the connector link at 1.85 mi. **[9]**. As the waves of wildflower colors wash on each side of you, watch for large, green katydids and razzing, rattling cicadas that start up from the grass, flutter downwind, and land, rather awkwardly, on plant stalks. At the spur on your left at 2.26 mi. **[10]**, turn right, toward the visitor center. Turn right at the fork in the trail at 2.31 mi. **[11]** to finish your prairie hike.

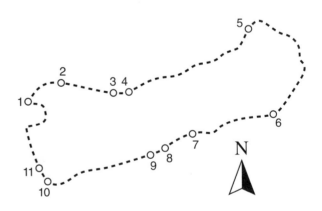

1. Start
2. Right turn
3. Left turn
4. Go straight
5. Go straight
6. Go straight
7. Right turn
8. Right turn
9. Go straight
10. Right turn
11. Right turn

Path of the Sky People and Sandstone Trails

 Distance Round-Trip: 6.5 miles
Estimated Hiking Time: 4 hours

The prairie is a barrage of entertainment. Between sweeping vistas, animated cloud formations, and resplendent seas of wildflowers are endless streams of displays, interactions, and interruptions from a multiplicity of prairie creatures.

Caution: Cross the electric fence only at the trail crossing, where the wires are insulated. Do not trespass on private property, which borders the Tzi-Sho Natural Area on three sides. Unless you are here in winter, a repellent against ticks and chiggers is recommended.

Trail Directions: From the visitor center, turn south on Township Road and go 1.3 mi. Turn east on Central Road, go 2.6 mi., and park in the lot for the Tzi-Sho Natural Area, on your left. Tzi-Sho (pronounced "tissue") is the Native American word for "Sky People," one of the grand divisions of the Osage nation. This trail takes you through two of the four natural areas in the park, the Tzi-Sho Natural Area and the East Drywood Creek Natural Area, both distinguished natural tallgrass prairies. This hike is a combination of two trails that present many options for shorter (or longer) hikes.

Begin at the sign for the trail [1], in the corner of the parking lot, and bear left at the trailhead. If you are here in the morning, you'll see and hear a tremendous variety of wildlife. Watch for scissor-tailed flycatchers, perched on power lines or on the open prairie. Their long, streaming tails help them maneuver in flight. Upland sandpipers are summer residents, and the rare prairie chicken lives here all year long. As vast prairie vistas open in front of you, scan the skies for northern harriers and other hawks, and watch for the heads of deer, foxes, and coyotes bounding through the prairie grasses.

Turn left at .80 mi. [2] to begin the Sandstone Trail. Notice the islands of sumac, often with singing birds perched at their tops. In the right proportion, these islands are important shelter and nesting areas for many animals. Park managers use prescribed fire to keep sumac and other shrubs from taking over the prairie. The musical songs of meadowlarks often accompany you as you hike, and the squeaky trills of tiny sedge wrens sometimes come in stereo, on both sides of the trail. Watch for the olive-headed Henslow's sparrow, and listen for the "tick, tick, bzzzzzzz" of the grasshopper sparrow.

At 1.01 mi. [3], turn right on the gravel road for a few steps and crawl under the insulated electric fence on your left to continue the trail. Here, American feverfew, wild indigo, and flowering spurge, whose five-lobed white flowers are just over a quarter of an inch long, paint entire fields white. Other fields are yellow with goldenrod and splashed purple with ironweed and blazing star. Turn right at the three-way intersection at 1.57 mi. [4]. After passing some large sandstone slabs, go straight at the connector link at 2.21 mi. [5]. Soon you see some persimmon groves and the small sandstone ledges that border East Drywood Creek. Look around on the trail for the burrows or the dried shells and pincers of prairie crayfish. In spring or fall, look for striking yellow-headed blackbirds.

Turn left at 2.84 mi. [6], at the spur to the backpack camp, and turn left at 2.91 mi. [7], at the connector link to the Drover's Trail. The trail soon approaches East Drywood Creek Natural Area, recognized for its healthy prairie stream and its diverse life. After descending into a small, rocky draw, the trail swings to the left. After crisscrossing the creek several times, go straight at the connector link at 4.35 mi. [8]. Here you find two ponds on your right, left from the days when cattle grazed this part of the prairie. Watch here in the ponds for ducks and other wildlife. Turn right after returning to [4] and turn left at [2]. Hike the other half of the Path of the Sky People to finish your prairie hike.

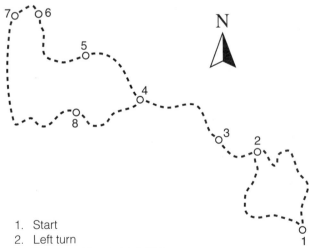

1. Start
2. Left turn
3. Road and fence crossing
4. Right turn
5. Go straight
6. Left turn
7. Left turn
8. Go straight

- Escape the traffic and computer and walk in the tranquil gardens of the 22-acre Kansas City Sculpture Park.

- Hike, feast, and frolic in Country Club Plaza, where you can view Italian and American sculptures, shop till you drop, listen to outdoor jazz for free, and indulge in an extraordinary cornucopia of culinary choices.

- Witness Community Christian Church's 1.2-billion-candlepower Steeple of Light, a vision of Frank Lloyd Wright's not realized until 1994.

Area Information

Like many other cities, Kansas City owes its beginnings to a confluence of two rivers. Fur trappers along the Kansas and Missouri rivers brought their pelts to the trading post that François Chouteau established in 1821 where the two rivers join. At this transfer point, settlers outfitted their wagons for the journey to the Far West. Later, the city grew with industries involving wheat, cattle, corn, and one of the largest railway terminals in the country.

In 1922 city planners designed Country Club Plaza as the nation's first suburban shopping district. This outdoor museum of Romantic Spanish architecture and European art has continuously added to its collection since then. Free outdoor concerts are scheduled during summer and the famous Plaza Lights burn nightly from Thanksgiving through mid-January.

The Nelson-Atkins Museum of Art has extensive collections representing all areas and periods of artistic expression. The Kansas City Sculpture Park, on the museum grounds, is home to the nation's largest collection of works by Henry Moore, considered one of the greatest sculptors of the 20th century.

Directions: The Country Club Plaza hike begins at Mill Creek Park, between J.C. Nichols Parkway, 47th Street, and Main Street in Kansas City. The Nelson-Atkins Museum of Art is bordered by Brush Creek Boulevard (47th Street), Oak Street, and 45th Street, three blocks east of the Country Club Plaza shopping district.

Hours Open: Both areas are open year-round. Most of the Plaza stores are open from 10:00 a.m. to 9:00 p.m.

Monday through Saturday and from noon to 5:00 p.m. on Sunday. Jazz clubs and many restaurants are open later. The sculpture park is open seven days a week during daylight hours. The Nelson-Atkins Museum building is open from 10:00 a.m. to 4:00 p.m. Tuesday and Wednesday, 10:00 a.m. to 9:00 p.m. Thursday and Friday, 10:00 a.m. to 5:00 p.m. on Saturday, and noon to 5:00 p.m. on Sunday. The museum is closed on Mondays and several holidays. Admission is free every day for the museum and the sculpture park.

Facilities: Facilities abound in the Plaza. The art museum has restrooms, a restaurant, and a bookstore. Both the museum building and the sculpture park are wheelchair accessible.

Permits and Rules: Do not touch or climb on sculptures or wade in the fountains.

For Further Information: Kansas City Convention and Visitors Association, 800-767-7700; Nelson-Atkins Museum of Art, 4525 Oak Street, Kansas City, MO 64111; 816-751-1278; www.nelson-atkins.org.

Other Areas of Interest

Almost all the personal possessions remain the way the Bentons left them at **Thomas Hart Benton Home and Studio State Historic Site**. Painter of large, dynamic murals, Benton was Missouri's most noted 20th-century artist. Guided tours are available for a fee. For more information, call 816-931-5722.

Area Trails

Gillham Park Trail (🐾, 1 mile). This loop trail is made of recycled roofing shingles. The trail traverses the borders of the park, between West Gillham Road, 47th Street, and Harrison Street. The park is only .18 mile east of the art museum.

Mill Creek Park Trail (🐾, 1 mile). This double-loop trail has a rubberized surface and several fitness stations along the way. Next to the Plaza, the trail offers views of several Spanish-inspired towers.

Loose Park Trail (🐾, 1.2 miles). Travel .9 mile south on Broadway from the Plaza to find the park at the corner of 51st Street and Wornall Road. The trail takes you next to a fountain lake, a Civil War battle site, spacious meadows, and a splendid rose garden.

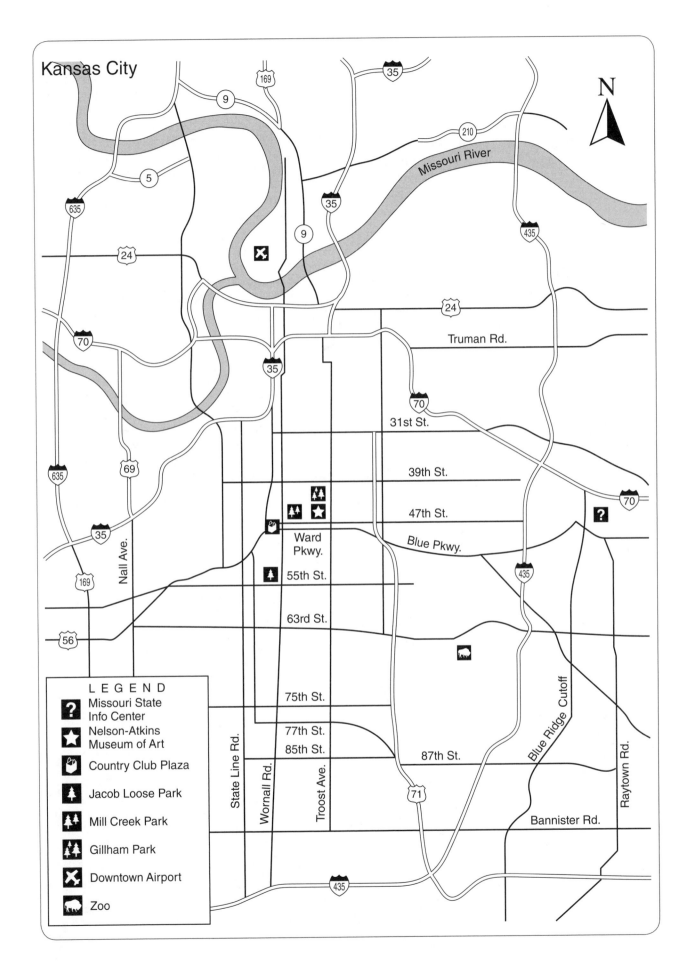

Kansas City

Missouri River

Truman Rd.

31st St.

39th St.

47th St.

Blue Pkwy.

Ward
Pkwy.

55th St.

63rd St.

75th St.

77th St.

85th St.

87th St.

Bannister Rd.

Nall Ave.

State Line Rd.

Wornall Rd.

Troost Ave.

Blue Ridge Cutoff

Raytown Rd.

LEGEND

? Missouri State
Info Center

★ Nelson-Atkins
Museum of Art

Country Club Plaza

Jacob Loose Park

Mill Creek Park

Gillham Park

✕ Downtown Airport

Zoo

Country Club Plaza

  Distance Round-Trip: 1 mile
  Estimated Hiking Time: 1 hour

Wear your finest Italian suit when you come to the Plaza, or your shorts, or your overalls—you'll fit in no matter what you wear. And this is one of the only museums of fine art where you can view the exhibits, talk as loudly as you want, and eat pretzels dripping with mustard at the same time.

Caution: Be careful crossing streets; there are many distractions for pedestrian and driver alike.

Trail Directions: Begin the hike at the south end of Mill Creek Park [1], .5 mi. southwest of the Nelson-Atkins Museum of Art. Free parking is plentiful on the streets and in lots and garages in and around the Plaza. Notice the white Community Christian Church just to the east of the park, on Main Street. Steepleless by day, this church has a perforated dome that beams the 1.2-billion-candlepower Steeple of Light by night, which reaches several miles into the stratosphere. Originally designed by Frank Lloyd Wright in 1940, the steeple was lit for the first time on December 10, 1994.

Also known as the City of Fountains, Kansas City boasts a variety of monumental fountain sculptures all over town. The J.C. Nichols Memorial Fountain here [2], dedicated to the developer of the Plaza, is probably the city's best known. The four dramatic horsemen, sculpted in Paris in 1910, represent the world's rivers.

Cross 47th Street and J.C. Nichols Parkway. Seville Light [3] (in this intersection) and Giralda Bell Tower [4] (.07 mi.) are replicas of the original structures in Seville, Spain, and set the theme for the Plaza as an open-air public art gallery of Romantic Spanish architecture and European art. Fountains, sculptures, and murals of bronze, marble, and ceramic tile adorn the entire district.

At .09 mi. is Chandler Court [5], one of five courtyards in the Plaza and a great place to meet and relax. Some courtyards are stopping places for the trolley and horse-drawn carriages. Continue west on 47th Street. After passing the Fountain of Neptune [6] (.19 mi.), originally from Worcestershire, England, cross Central Street and continue west. You pass various sidewalk cafés, all with accompanying tempting aromas, while crossing Broadway and Pennsylvania Street.

Turn left on Jefferson Street at .39 mi. [7] and again on 48th Street at .50 mi. [8]. After passing a smorgasbord of specialty shops, including an Irish pub designed and built in Ireland, turn left on Pennsylvania Street. Turn right at .61 mi. [9] and continue east on Nichols Road. You pass several fountains, some of which were bought in Italy in the 1920s, before turning left on Wyandotte Street at .90 mi. [10]. Turn right at Chandler Court [5], where you might want to stop for a cheesecake at the Cheesecake Factory (they have over 40 kinds) before finishing the hike at Mill Creek Park.

1. Start
2. J.C. Nichols Memorial Fountain
3. Seville Light
4. Giralda Bell Tower
5. Chandler Court
6. Fountain of Neptune
7. Left turn
8. Left turn
9. Right turn
10. Left turn

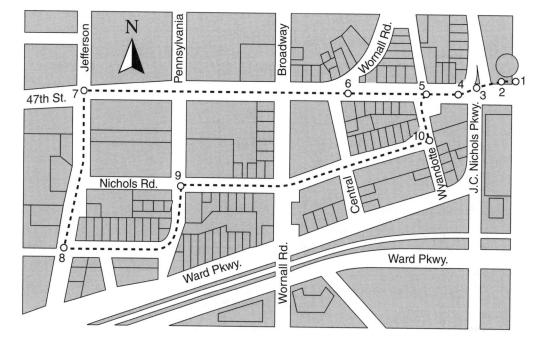

Kansas City Sculpture Park

 Distance Round-Trip: 1 mile
 Estimated Hiking Time: 45 minutes

"Seraphs share with thee knowledge but art o man is thine alone." —Inscription on the northeast end of the Nelson-Atkins Museum of Art

Caution: Please do not touch or climb on the sculptures or allow children to do so.

Trail Directions: The park is located on the grounds of the Nelson-Atkins Museum of Art. The hike begins **[1]** at the 17-foot-high badminton shuttlecock at the northwest corner of the museum.

Probably no other single object is a better signature for the art museum, or even for Kansas City, than this four-part sculpture named *Shuttlecocks*. Installed in 1994, this was the first outdoor sculpture commissioned for the park. Walk eastward, toward *Rush Hour* at .04 mi. **[2]**, the cluster of bronze people frozen in their walking hurry. Continue behind *Rush Hour* and descend the steps next to the building. Continue down the ramp and more steps until you reach a wide, brown walkway at .12 mi. **[3]**, where you go straight.

On your right, the expanse of the 22-acre manicured landscape opens before you. Overall, the exhibits and clusters of trees contrast with the large openness of the south plaza, which imparts its own feeling of peacefulness. Two more shuttlecocks look as if they fell from the sky here, adding their touch of humor and playfulness.

Take the grassy spur on your right at .17 mi. **[4]** to view the first piece by British sculptor Henry Moore, the park's featured artist. Moore wanted his sculptures to be seen in nature against rocks, trees, and sky. His works, set in landscapes in more than 20 countries, explore five basic themes: mother and child, the reclining figure, internal and external forms, animal forms, and nonrepresentational forms. After viewing the reclining figure entitled *Hand*, return to the main path and turn right. Turn left on a gray brick sidewalk at .24 mi. **[5]** and turn right at the first intersection. Turn right again onto a red brick sidewalk. At *Sheep Piece* at .36 mi. **[6]**, follow the path as it curves left and takes you to *Reclining Connected Forms* at .43 mi. **[7]** in a private garden. Continue to reach *Large*

Totem Head and *Large Torso: Arch* at .42 mi. **[8]**. Turn left as you return to *Sheep Piece* and turn right at the intersection at **[6]**.

Soon you reach the big, green, south plaza, a good place to rest, read, or join the shuttlecocks and just sprawl. Continuing the path will take you to Moore's *Seated Woman* at .65 mi. **[9]**, where you turn right. Turn right again at *Three-Way Piece No. 1: Points* at .74 mi. **[10]** and ascend some steps. Walk toward the main museum entrance and go up the steps toward a circle garden. Turn right and ascend the steps next to another shuttlecock. In this patio courtyard at .91 mi. **[11]** are two more works by Moore. After viewing these, descend the steps, skirt the west end of the building, and return to **[1]**.

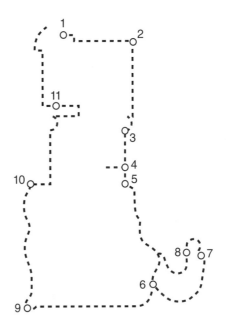

1. Start
2. *Rush Hour*
3. Go straight
4. Right turn
5. Left turn
6. *Sheep Piece*
7. *Reclining Connected Forms*
8. *Large Totem Head* and *Large Torso: Arch*
9. *Seated Woman*
10. Right turn
11. Courtyard

About the Author

Kevin M. Lohraff has been helping people learn about, enjoy, and appreciate nature since 1987. He has worked for the National Park Service, the Missouri Department of Natural Resources, and the Missouri Department of Conservation in the positions of Park Ranger, Park Naturalist, Ecological Stewardship Crew Member, Natural History Biologist, Aquatic Education Assistant, Interpretive Programs Supervisor, and Assistant Nature Center Manager. Currently, Lohraff is the Outdoor Skills Education Coordinator for the Missouri Department of Conservation, where he helps people learn skills that help them enjoy and connect with the outdoors.

Lohraff holds a bachelor's degree in biology from Missouri State University. A resident of Centertown, MO, he enjoys canoeing, fishing, and gravel-bar camping on Ozark streams.